P9-CQW-485

MYTHOLOGY AND YOU

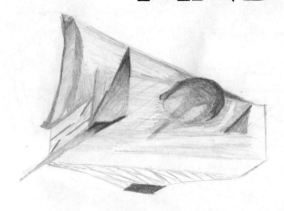

Classical Mythology and Its Relevance to Today's World

DONNA ROSENBERG

SORELLE BAKER

NATIONAL TEXTBOOK COMPANY • Lincolnwood, Illinois U.S.A.

Photo Credits:

Richard M. Rosenberg
David M. Rosenberg

1988 Printing

Copyright © 1984, 1981 by National Textbook Company
4255 West Touhy Avenue
Lincolnwood (Chicago). Illinois 60646-1975 U.S.A.
All rights reserved. No part of this book
may be reproduced, stored in a retrieval system, or
transmitted in any form or by any means, electronic,
mechanical, photocopying, recording or otherwise,
without the prior permission of National Textbook Company.
Manufactured in the United States of America.
Library of Congress Catalog Number: 80-80569

890RD 987654

The Greek myths have appealed to people of all ages for more than two thousand years. They have enriched all forms of literature, from poetry and novels to newspapers and advertising. They have become an integral part of our cultural heritage.

These myths have remained vital because they are exciting tales of action that reveal universal psychological truths about human behavior. They address the fundamental questions each human being asks: Who am I? How much power over my life do I have? What is the nature of the forces beyond my control? Given the existence of evil and death and the nature of my own limitations, what can I hope to achieve in the course of my life?

The Greek myths speak to the human condition. They depict hope and fear, aspiration and frustration, success and failure. The characters in these myths, whether gods or heroes or ordinary human beings, are magnifications of ourselves. As they face the challenges in their lives, some of them struggle intelligently against each obstacle, while others succumb to blind impulse. We learn from these alternative models that, to a great extent, each of us is responsible for our own fate. Now, as then, a person may have money, power, and talent, but if he is not sensitive to the needs of others, he is a failure as a human being. Now, as then, we cannot escape our ultimate fate, death. However, we can choose to face the challenges in our daily lives with determination, courage and thoughtfulness. Then we will emerge richer in self-knowledge, self-respect, and experience, and we will have earned the admiration of others as well.

The universal appeal of Greek myths lies in their ability to tell us about human nature and ourselves. When these stories are modified, they lose their power. Modern writers, particularly those who write for a student audience, continue to retell the Greek myths with significant omissions and destructive additions. *Mythology and You* redresses this problem. The study of multiple translations of the major Greek and Roman sources of Greek myth has restored the acccuracy, interest, and impact that are present in the original versions. Introductory background material, provocative thought questions, and creative activities supplement each myth. Like the ancient Greeks, our objectives are to entertain, to instruct, and to inspire.

THE GREEK WORLD

2600 B.C.

MACEDONIA

Mt. Olympus

Dodona

Larissa

THESSALY

Achelous River

Iolcus

Mt. Pelion

Mt. Oeta

Mt. Parnassus

Calydon

ITHACA

Delphi

Thebes

Peneius River

BOEOTIA

ELIS

Sicyon

Mt. Cyllene

Megara

Mt. Cithaeron

ARCADIA

Corinth

Mycenae

ATTICA

Alpheius River

Argos

Athens

Lerna

Epidaurus

Mt. Lycaeüs

Troezen

PELOPONNESUS

Pylos

Taenarum

CYTHERA

THRACE

BLACK

Sea of Marmara

LEMNOS

Hellespont

Troy

ASIA MINOR

MYSIA

AEGEAN SEA

SCYRUS

LYDIA

CHIOS

Mt. Sipylus

Mt. Tmolus

Icarian Sea

ICARIA

DELOS

SERIPHUS

CYCLADES

NAXOS

CRETE

Mt. Ida

Cnossus

Mt. Dicte

N

0   100 kil.

0   100 m.

It is an interesting, though idle, speculation, what would be the effect on us if all our reformers, revolutionaries, planners, politicians, and life-arrangers in general were soaked in Homer from their youth up, like the Greeks. They might realize that on the happy day when there is a refrigerator in every home, and two in none, when we all have the opportunity of working for the common good (whatever that is), when Common Man (whoever he is) is triumphant, though not improved—that men will still come and go like the generations of leaves in the forest; that he will still be weak, and the gods strong and incalculable; that the quality of a man matters more than his achievement; that violence and recklessness will still lead to disaster, and that this will fall on the innocent as well as on the guilty.

H.D.F. Kitto, *The Greeks* (1951)

CONTENTS

The Parthenon, upon the Acropolis of Athens, was dedicated to the goddess Athena and was considered her dwelling upon the earth. An earlier temple to Athena preceded this one.

The Value of Myths

Originally the Greek myths were stories passed orally from one generation to the next. What is the power of these stories that they remain vital after three thousand years? Why do children clamor to hear them? Why do poets, writers, and even advertisers allude to them? Why do anthropologists, sociologists, clergymen, psychiatrists, historians, and teachers of literature, study them?

The answer to these questions can be found in an analysis of the nature of myth. However, for scholars of various disciplines to agree upon a definition of myth would be as difficult as finding a needle in a haystack. Each has viewed myth from a particular perspective and has placed a different significance on it. Thus, to some scholars, myths are simply the imaginative product of a primitive mind. To others, they are sacred tales that were believed only by those who belonged to a particular tribe or religion; or, they were pure fantasy masquerading as reality, simply an early form of science fiction. Until recently, few scholars in any discipline considered myths to be either literal or symbolic representations of reality, past or present.

Yet, it has been the ways in which myths are real that has kept them meaningful to humankind for thousands of years. If they were merely fantasy or the secret language of a closed society, human beings would have discarded them as irrelevant or trivial. One has only to be aware of the Minoan civilization evident on the island of Crete during the period 2500–1400 B.C. to realize that the mind that created myths was sophisticated enough to create four-story buildings with indoor plumbing and skylights, written records, a system of weights and measures, a calendar based upon astronomical data, and the game of chess.

Far from being merely fantastic or cultish, myths are a treasure of realities—a kaleidoscope which, depending upon the age and experience of the reader, reflects and illuminates his experiences, fantasies, hopes, and fears. Myths have continued to capture the imagination and the soul of man for thousands of years because they depict and reveal behavior and problems common to all human beings. They deal with people who could be alive today, reminding us that human nature has not changed throughout the long course of history. Thus, the ancient myths speak clearly to modern man. They focus directly upon the nature of man, as he was in the past, as he is in the present, and as he will continue to be in the future. They examine how man copes with his physical, social, religious, and political environment.

With little interest in scenic detail or historical background, the myths immediately plunge into a human situation. They use a specific event, such as the entrance of a wild animal, a cataclysmic event, or a human challenge, to examine how man reacts to the problems of living. Through the actions of individuals, who are always portrayed in human terms even when they are divinities, the myths reveal the nature of man. Because we share that nature, we can identify with these individuals and respond to them. Some we admire, others we reject. However, it is a tribute to the wisdom of the minds that created these myths that we must always take the characters seriously, for in them we confront many of our own potentialities, for good and for evil.

Myths originally served two purposes: to explain and to teach. The Greek myths explained man's origins to the ancient Greeks. They described how the world and man were created and what kind of order existed in the universe. They explained the existence of natural phenomena for which modern man may or may not have acquired scientific explanations. Invariably, the mythic explanation of the natural world was in terms of religious beliefs that provided man's earliest answers to universal questions. Given a multitude of natural phenomena which he could neither understand nor control, man populated the invisible world with a multitude of immortal deities, created in his own image, each of whom controlled one aspect of the natural environment. Such a religion is called polytheistic; such gods are called anthropomorphic. Humankind could relate through prayer, sacrifice, and other rituals, to these gods. Although they were more powerful than humans, they possessed human form and human personalities. They created order out of chaos, providing a rational scheme of life in place of confusion and question.

In addition to explaining natural and religious origins, myths also explained political origins, related how kingdoms became established, and provided men with a history of their people and with that of their neighbors. Thus, their myths told the Greeks how their lives had become what they were.

The Greek myths also taught man how to behave in society.

Although the Greek gods did not give man an authoritative moral code by which to live, the Greek myths conveyed a moral directive. They examined the extent to which man is a victim of circumstances and the extent to which he brings his destiny upon himself. By examining the decisions human beings made and the consequences which resulted, the Greek myths supplied humankind with a gallery of models, both positive and negative. By learning from the mythical characters, who usually were so realistically presented that such people, in fact, could have existed, man imposed a meaningful pattern upon his life and upon his world.

Although the principle purpose of the myths was to explain and to teach, in order to be effective, they had to be entertaining, for they were the product of an oral culture. If they were dull, no one would have listened to them; no one would have made the major effort to memorize them for transmission to succeeding generations. Therefore, the expert storytellers endowed them with a spectacular quality. The stories invariably would start in a quiet, routine manner and would gradually build up to an unforgettable conclusion. The listener who became familiar with this technique would find himself waiting expectantly for the action he knew would occur, smiling to himself as he recognized the human responses that would lead to destruction. There is little question that blood, gore, and personal tragedy have done their share in perpetuating the popularity of myths. Today, these aspects of life still sell newspapers and glue listeners to their television sets. Now, as then, violence and personal tragedy are an integral part of human life.

For modern man, the Greek myths reflect the attitudes and priorities of the ancient cultures which produced them. Yet, they are relevant today because many of these ancient social, ethical, and religious attitudes continue to be important. Those who treat others with arrogance and disrespect still bring personal disaster upon themselves. Man still must conquer his fears and accept challenges which appear to be insurmountable, in order to achieve a sense of self-satisfaction and accomplishment. The kind of person a man is, remains today as then, more important than what he accomplishes; it lingers behind the event like an after-taste, either sweet or bitter. Man continues to be violent. He continues to covet his neighbor's (or neighboring country's) possessions, and he will still go to war in order to gain more territory and power. Man has continued to impose his patriarchal, or male, attitudes upon the fabric of society, determining the role of women as well as his own role. The concepts behind the ancient matriarchal or female-dominated Mediterranean religions become more meaningful, and the ancient Greek conflict between these opposing sociological and religious schemes becomes more relevant in modern society where the roles and opportunities of men and women are changing rapidly.

Thus, the myths reveal eternal truths about the nature of man and his quests in life. They reflect attitudes and feelings that are common to all men, in any time. Artists and writers constantly allude to them and recreate them as they explore the relationships between man and man, man and society, and man and God.

Historical Background

About 2600 B.C., Greek-speaking warrior tribes marched from central Europe and southwestern Russia and invaded Macedonia, to the northeast of Greece. They were herders of cattle and excellent horsemen. They used bronze and copper in their tools and weapons. Along with their horses and their bronze tools, they brought a new, male-dominated religion, which, in time, became the religion modern man associates with the ancient Greeks. Their myths were dominated by heroic male gods, such as Zeus, Poseidon, and Hades. Their lives were dominated by a heroic weapon, the spear.

About 1900 B.C., these warriors began to move southwest into Greece. They encountered natives whose descendants came from Asia Minor, across the Aegean Sea. The natives were peaceful, agrarian peoples, who lived in scattered, independent villages and followed a female-dominated religion. The chief deity was a great mother-earth goddess, called the Mother Goddess or the Great Goddess.

By about 1600 B.C., the invading warriors had conquered all of Greece. They made themselves at home in their new land, learning the farming and craft skills of the native population. To these they added the horse, a new-style house (rectangular, supported in the front by two columns, the prototype of the Greek temple), and a new religion. These ancient Greeks are usually called the Mycenaeans, after their most powerful community (Mycenae).

From approximately 1600 B.C. to approximately 1150 B.C., the Mycenaeans prospered in Greece. They developed several thriving political and economic centers in the Peloponnesus peninsula and the nearby mainland: Pylos, Tiryns, Mycenae, Athens, and Thebes. Ancient sections of some of these cities have been excavated in modern times; other possible sites of Mycenaean culture have not been excavated due to the location of modern cities or the presence of later ruins. The Mycenaeans were an aggressive people. They built well-fortified palaces that were the center of the community, and became wealthy by raiding or trading with foreign cities. The Mycenaean society valued leadership and heroism. An individual, with excellence in the skills of war, could quickly become a leader of the community.

The Mycenaeans eventually confronted the Minoans. The center of the Minoan civilization was the large island of Crete to the southeast of Greece. Much older and more highly developed than the Mycenaean civilization, the Minoans had lived in peace and in splendor for hundreds of years. Their navy controlled the Mediterranean Sea and provided them with an extensive market for their products (pottery, wine, metalwork, and olive oil). They were an agricultural people, who, like the natives of Greece, worshipped the Mother Goddess or the Great Goddess. The structure of their society reflected matriarchal principles, particularly the superiority of women, respect and appreciation for the beauty of all life, and an emphasis upon gracious, peaceful living. From about 1750 B.C. until about 1450 B.C., their civilization produced its greatest achievements, including written records and many-storied splendid palaces such as Cnossus, which contained a multitude of rooms and indoor plumbing.

The Mycenaean Greeks conquered Minoan Crete in about 1450 B.C. The conquest possibly followed cataclysmic earthquakes or volcanic eruptions in the Mediterranean, which destroyed the palaces on Crete, including King Minos's Cnossus, and covered their once fertile farmland with a thick layer of ash. The Mycenaeans brought a new written language called *Linear B* to Crete. It is an archaic form of Greek and has been found on the Greek Peloponnesus at Pylos. Under Greek rule, Crete continued to thrive. Each civilization influenced the other.

After the conquest of Crete, the palaces of the Mycenaeans became more elaborate and better fortified. Ownership of land determined social rank, and the aristocrats spent their time managing their palace-states, hunting, and pirating other, non-Greek communities. Each Mycenaean center was a kingdom. Kingship was prized, and the king who left his palace unattended in order to raid a foreign kingdom often returned to find a new king upon his throne and exile or death awaiting him.

There are few reliable sources which describe life in Mycenaean and Minoan times. Although the Minoans left written records, called *Linear A*, the script is sufficiently different from *Linear B* so that, as yet, no one has been able to translate it. Therefore, scholars must combine their expertise in a variety of fields and try to deduce what the people in these ancient cultures believed and did, based upon the artifacts which have survived a time span of approximately 3,500 years. They study numerous decorated objects, such as weapons, jewelry, pottery, and goblets. These were often inscribed with scenes from daily life and from mythology. They study painted wall murals, grave decorations, carved ivory plaques, the numerous tablets found at Pylos written in *Linear B*, and the works attributed to the great Greek poet Homer.[1]

The Mycenaean *Linear B* tablets discovered at Pylos were found in a palace that burned in about 1200 B.C. (approximately the date of the fall of Troy). These tablets list the names of many gods, such as Hera, Artemis, Poseidon, Zeus, Hermes, and Dionysus. One tablet includes the names of ten human sacrifices. There appear to have been male and female priests. Although religion must have been important, the existing tablets do not contain religious texts, myths, or prayers. Moreover, there are no written laws, penalties, or taxes to be paid to priests or to divinities.

Archaeologists have found no remains of temples used for public worship. In addition, there is no physical evidence as yet of public worship in caves or on mountain tops, as there is in Crete. With the exception of portable altars, there do not appear to be religious shrines in the palaces that have been excavated. The pictorial representations of gods simply reflect the feminine goddess that is so common on Minoan artifacts. Therefore, scholars theorize that religion was an individual affair, in which a man worshipped alone or in small groups at home, and that there were no public occasions that called for the construction of specific buildings and specific ceremonial objects.

Later, when the Greeks built temples, they tended to construct them on the sites of palaces from the Mycenaean Age. Whether this reflects some religious purpose of the older palace or simply a convenient location is open to speculation. Scholars must be careful not to deduce too much from very little evidence. One of our few sources for information on the religious beliefs and practices of the Mycenaeans is the myths, which were based on the ancient oral tradition. These were written down many years later, first by Homer in the eighth century B.C., and then by Hesiod in about 700 B.C.

Homer related myths that had been memorized and passed along verbally from one generation to another. When he reshaped part of this oral tradition into *The Iliad* and *The Odyssey*, he included aspects of the Mycenaean civilization at the time of the Trojan War (approximately 1200 B.C.),[2] which were no longer evident in his own time. He described palace-states that no longer existed, as well as figure-eight, body-length shields and chariots that were not used in his time and seemed fictional to his listeners. Nevertheless, he repeated the myths exactly as he had learned them, and modern archaeology has shown that he was generally correct in his descriptions. He introduced the Greeks of his age, and all succeeding ages, to their cultural history.

1. *The Iliad, The Odyssey,* and *The Homeric Hymns* are attributed to Homer, although several different poets may have created these works. Scholars place Homer's epics between the approximate dates of 850 B.C. and 700 B.C.
2. Archaeology has shown that Troy fell on more than one occasion. Heracles burned it in about 1300 B.C. (See Section IV, The Heroes, Heracles.) It fell to the Greeks in the Trojan War, probably just before 1200 B.C. Scholars have traditionally compromised on the date as being 1184 B.C.

Religious Background

As we have learned, in about 2600 B.C., Greek-speaking tribes left their northern homes and reached Macedonia, the area to the northeast of Greece. They remained there for approximately seven hundred years. In about 1900 B.C., many tribes left Macedonia, journeying southwest into Greece. It was three hundred years later, about 1600 B.C., before their descendants occupied southern Greece, a region called the Peloponnesus—a large peninsula directly south of the Greek mainland.

As they traveled into the new territory, these tribes encountered an agrarian population which was scattered in small pockets along the rugged seacoast. Mountain ranges made much of the land inaccessible and ill-suited for farming. The native inhabitants were a hardy people, who through hard work, lived off the sturdy fruits of the soil—corn, barley, and wheat providing the basic elements of their daily diet.

Each community was small and sufficiently isolated from its neighbors so that it had developed a strong sense of independence. Although each self-contained village worshipped a local divinity under a local name, these communities shared similar religious beliefs and practices which, in turn, affected the social organization and the ethical and moral values of their daily lives.

Being farmers, it was natural for these people to revere and to worship the earth. It was Mother Earth who supplied them with the food they needed in order to survive. It was Mother Earth who received those who had died, both plant and human. It was also Mother Earth who brought forth new life from land that had looked lifeless for months, and who nourished it so that it reached maturity. These people felt a kinship with all of nature. They, too, were born, matured, and died, just as the plants and animals around them. Therefore, Mother Earth was as responsible for their own fertility as she was for that of the plant and animal kingdoms, and they, too, like the plants and, presumably, the animals, must be reborn in some way after death. Their religion was centered upon the belief in the endlessly recurring cycle of birth, maturity, death, and rebirth. Their economic security and the continuation of their race was dependent upon the continuous operation of this cycle. As long as they worshipped Mother Earth properly, they expected that the cycle would continue without interruption.

Consequently, each self-contained community worshipped a local mother earth goddess who was a goddess of fertility, and who was their supreme divinity. This Great Goddess or Mother Goddess lived within the earth and was the mother of both the living and the dead. She received prayers and sacrificial offerings from her worshippers, and, in return, showered them with blessings: fertility of plant, beast and man, good health, and economic prosperity.

Religious life throughout the Mediterranean was dominated by the belief in this great Mother Goddess. As an Egyptian Great Goddess explained in a book written in about 150 A.D.:

"I am the natural mother of all life, the ruler of the elements, the first being, the chief of all gods, the queen of the world below, the first of those in the world above. I govern the light in the sky, the winds of the ocean, and the silences of the underworld. My single, divine nature is worshipped throughout the earth in many forms with various ceremonies and under various names. Thus, the early races of Attica call me Athena, the Cypriots, Aphrodite; the Cretans, Artemis; the Sicilians, Persephone; the Eleusinians, Demeter; and others, Hera."[1]

The agrarian society reflected these religious attitudes in its structure and in its values. The community was ruled by a queen who was the major priestess of the great Mother Goddess. She probably received this position of authority because she was the youngest daughter of the last ruling priestess-queen. (Choosing the youngest daughter would insure the longest rule in each succession, for the last born would be the last to die.) All mortal women were considered daughters of the Mother Goddess. Their position in their society reflected the matriarchal community's attitude toward the Great Goddess. Thus, women dominated the existing social and religious rituals and institutions.

The family was of principal importance in the matriarchal society. Status and inheritance and name came from the mother, who, with the help of her brother, ruled the family. The father was an unimportant figure, for there was complete sexual freedom. A woman could love whomever and as many men as she chose. In fact, in early times, people did not realize that a male was necessary for procreation. Motherhood was a mysterious, miraculous event, possibly aided by wind or water. Daughters and sisters were honored above sons and brothers, and the youngest daughter was most favored since she would preserve the family line the longest.

Moreover, in this society, the primary moral and ethical obligation of an individual was to his own family group, especially to his sisters and mother. This involved protection and, when necessary, revenge. The greatest crime in the matriarchal society was the crime of child against mother. It was considered so heinous that society provided no way for the child to atone for it.[2] In the case of crimes between different families, retribution was the accepted procedure. Each family was obligated to avenge a crime with a crime in kind against the perpetrator. The ensuing chain reaction had no set limits. Neither court, nor judge, nor jury existed. Retributive justice also did not distinguish between intentional and accidental crimes.

Despite retributive justice and human sacrifice, the matriarchal society tended to be a peaceful society, one turned in upon itself, rather than one that looked out toward its neighbors. The life of the family centered upon the mother, the hearth, and the home. Mother love was a humane and pacifying influence, creating an aura of honor, trust, hospitality, generosity, concern, and reverence for all life.

Life in matriarchal communities was also earth-centered. Life arose from the depths of the earth, and the dead returned to the earth from which they had sprung. The earth was a dark mother, a region the sun never penetrated. Consequently, man approached the Great Goddess in darkness. Time was measured from one night to the next. Religious rites, meetings, and important religious, social, and political occasions were held at night. The moon was more important than the sun. The months were calculated by the cycles of the moon, producing uniform weeks of seven days, uniform months of twenty-eight days, and a lunar year of thirteen months plus one day.

Once humankind realized the role of the male in procreation, the ruling priestess-queen took a young male consort, who was called the sacred king. The sacred king earned this great honor by winning a number of special contests that required both extraordinary courage and remarkable skill. He might have substituted for the priestess-queen on particular sacred occasions, dressing in her royal robes, wearing false breasts, and borrowing her symbols. However, his prime function was to insure fertility. The sacred king's powers were so important that any illness or the possibility of his death was viewed as a catastrophe. Therefore, in order to preserve the vitality and thus the fertility of the sacred king, the matriarchal society devised a system whereby it killed the sacred king while he was still in the prime of life and enthroned his young successor.

At first, the sacred king was killed on the last day of each year (the odd day on the annual calendar). Priestesses tore apart his body and consumed his raw flesh in order to acquire his powers of fertility. Meanwhile, his blood was sprinkled upon the earth and farm animals in order to fertilize them. It was the custom in Thrace for the sacred king to be sacrificed at the end of his reign by means of horses. The king's body would be tied to horses' tails. As the horses ran free, the king's body would be torn apart, fertilizing the soil with his blood. In a similar Thracean ceremony, priestesses wearing horse masks, would chase the king, kill him, and then eat his flesh.

The sacred king, in time, devised ingenious ways to delay his death. First, he adopted a second sacred king who substituted for him as the priestess-queen's consort for a given period of time, often one to three days. Upon the expiration of his term, the substitute sacred king would be sacrified. His flesh would be eaten, and his blood would be sprinkled upon crops and animals. Meanwhile, during the time that he was not the sacred king, the original king might remain in a burial chamber as if he were dead or simply remain apart from his customary duties. Then, upon the death of his substitute, the original sacred king would resume his position.

Later, the matriarchal society agreed to extend the sacred king's reign from one thirteen-month year to one "great" year of one hundred lunar months (approximately eight years). Since the fields and animals still needed to be fertilized annually, in the interim, the king would pretend to die for one day each year while a boy-surrogate took over the throne. At the end of the day, the boy would be killed, his blood would be sprinkled upon fields and animals, and the sacred king would resume the throne. Finally, society was willing to use animals instead of young boys as sacrifices, and a sacred king was able to reign for a second term.

1. Lucius Apuleius, *The Golden Ass* (150 A.D.).
2 . This idea creates the central issue in the great *Oresteia* trilogy by the fifth-century B.C. playwright Aeschylus, in which Orestes is told that he must murder his mother because she has murdered his father.

This idea also creates the central issue in *Antigone*, the tragedy by the fifth-century B.C. playwright Sophocles. Antigone buries the brother who has been a traitor, thereby placing her obligation to her family before her obligation to the laws of her country.

I

IN THE BEGINNING
Creation

The head of Poseidon, awesome Lord of the Sea, is part of a large sculpture in which the god stands poised to hurl his trident (which has been lost) against an enemy.

The arrival of the Greek-speaking tribes in Greece gradually eliminated the matriarchal system. One by one, the aggressors conquered the independent villages and took over their religious shrines. They adopted aspects of the culture they encountered, but they transformed the local religion into one that would accommodate their own male-dominated point of view. Patriarchal gods married the local earth goddesses. Under the Greek invaders, the principal deity became male (Zeus). The principal oracle, that of Themis at Pytho, also became male (Apollo at Delphi). With the support of his Olympian religion, the king established himself as the principal ruler of the community, and inheritance usually fell upon the oldest male son. Daughters became the property of their fathers, bestowed in marriage as their father chose. Wives became subject to the wills of their husbands. By approximately 1300 b.c., the king could reign for his entire life, and by about 1200 b.c., the eldest son had become the legal heir to the throne. When a man married, his wife now came to live with him. Society's values became more goal-oriented and acquisitive. People became more aggressive, glorying in heroic courage, death in battle, and in the riches of conquest.

1 The Rule of Uranus

INTRODUCTION

The myth of Uranus's rule represents the attempt of the ancient Greeks—the Mycenaeans—to explain the origin of the universe. Because they had inherited a patriarchal, male-dominated religion, their creation myth reflects those values. However, it clearly has been superimposed upon a matriarchal creation myth, just as the invading Greeks imposed themselves upon the native agrarian people. Thus, Gaea, the Great Goddess or the Mother Goddess, created and nourished Uranus, Pontus, the Hundred-handed giants, the Cyclopes, and the Titans. Uranus became the king and ruled by brute force, and yet he wasn't at peace because his wife was not completely subject to his domination.

Gaea lulled Uranus into a false sense of security. Then, Uranus was dismembered as a sacred king would have been, and his blood fertilized the sea and the soil, producing "crops" as the sacred king's blood would have done. However, Uranus wielded much more power than a sacred king would have had, and the "crops" became the three Furies and the race of Giants. Furthermore, the sacred king of the matriarchy was replaced by a new king who chose a wife. The world became dominated by men.

ANTICIPATIONS

1. Are there things that people say they have seen today, which, so far, have not been proven? What are the existing arguments or documentation for
   a. UFO's (Unidentified Flying Objects)?
   b. The Lochness Monster?
   c. Big Foot?
   d. The Bermuda Triangle?

2. In your opinion, which theory of the creation of our universe do you
   believe and why?
   a. God created the world in six days.
   b. The "Big Bang" theory.
   c. Life grew and evolved from small cells.

THE MYTH

In the beginning there was only emptiness, and the emptiness was called
Chaos. From Chaos emerged the first three immortal beings: Gaea, the
earth mother; Tartarus, the deathless being who ruled the darkest depths
of the earth called the Underworld; and Eros, the handsome god of love
and desire, whose presence enabled much of creation to occur.

Without any partner, Gaea gave birth to the starry sky called Uranus.
By herself, Gaea also brought forth the mountains and Pontus, the sea.

Then Gaea married her son, Uranus, and together, they became the
parents of three monstrous children called the Hundred-handed giants.[1]
These were the largest, strongest, and most frightening of all the children
Gaea would bear Uranus. Each giant had fifty heads and one hundred incredibly strong arms. From the moment of their birth, Uranus feared
their potential power. Therefore, he confined them to the Underworld,
decreeing that they live forever in darkness. Consequently, the Hundred-
handed giants hated their father Uranus with a passionate, implacable
hatred.

Next Gaea bore Uranus the three Cyclopes.[2] Their appearance was
also unique in that each Cyclops had only one huge wheel-shaped eye set
in the middle of his forehead.[3] The Cyclopes were skillful as well as
strong, so that they became the first immortal craftsmen. Uranus became
jealous of their strength and beauty and afraid of their potential power.
Therefore, he bound them with the strongest chains and hurled them
deep within their mother, Gaea's, body. They fell for nine days and nine
nights, finally reaching, on the tenth day, the dismal Underworld, which
was as far beneath the surface of the earth as the sky was above it. There
they remained imprisoned with their three brothers, the Hundred-
handed giants. Thus, the Cyclopes also detested Uranus, their tyrannical
father.

Gaea then bore Uranus the first generation of immortal gods. Later,
Uranus named them Titans ("Stretchers") because they had stretched
their power and had overthrown his rule. With the exception of Crius,
whose role was insignificant, these thirteen Titans either controlled the
major functions in the universe, or they became the parents of powerful
children who did. Oceanus became the god of the Oceanus River, which
encircled the earth. He married his sister Tethys and, together, they

became the parents of all the river gods and sea goddesses. The Titan Coeüs married his sister Phoebe, and they became the parents of Leto, later the mother of Artemis and Apollo.[4] Hyperion became the god of the sun. After he married his sister Theia, he became the father of Eos (Dawn), Helius (Sun), and Selene (Moon). The Titan, Iapetus, married a sea goddess and became the father of Atlas, Prometheus, and Epimetheus.[5]

Themis, an earth goddess and prophet like her mother Gaea, taught mortal men to obey laws, to live in peace, and to sacrifice to their deathless gods. Mnemosyne originated the use of reason and memory and applied names to all existing objects and ideas. Themis, Mnemosyne, Rhea, and Dione all became the mothers of famous children.[6] The youngest and shrewdest of Gaea's thirteen Titan children was Cronus. Although he helped mortals become more civilized by introducing the concept of justice, his personal ambition terrified the deathless gods. Cronus hated his father, Uranus. He coveted Uranus's tremendous power, but was clever enough to hide his true emotions.

Uranus ruled his Titan children without fear of rebellion. He was convinced that he had permanently secured his position of power by banishing the Hundred-handed giants and the Cyclopes to the Underworld. He did not care that the fate of the Hundred-handed and the Cyclopes caused his wife great pain and anguish. He did not care that many of his children hated him. He was all-powerful, and that was all that mattered.

Gaea, however, was not as docile as she appeared. Beneath her loving exterior, she seethed with rage and resolved to free her children in the Underworld. When she felt that her Titan children would support her, she planned a devious retaliation for Uranus's cruelty. First she created the great tool-making stone, flint, which she shaped into a huge sickle. Then, when it was finished, she approached the Titans and encouraged their revenge.

"My children," she began. "You know that your father is an evil being. If you have the necessary courage, at last we have the means to avenge his wicked deeds."

Gaea's suggestion met with silence. Her children were too terrified of their father to reply. Finally, Cronus, her most cunning child, summoned enough courage to respond.

"Mother," he announced, "I will promise to help you punish cruel Uranus, because, indeed, he alone is to blame for his evil deeds, and I have no love for him in my heart."

Gaea's eyes sparkled and her spirits lifted as she listened to her fearless son. His self-confidence also inspired a willingness to help among his brothers and sisters, making Gaea jubilant.

As daylight faded into dusk, Gaea concealed Cronus in a secret place by the sea. There she presented him with the flint weapon she had made, warning him to respect its curved edge of sharp teeth. Then she confided to him her violent plan.

Before long, Uranus arrived, bringing with him the blanket of night. Desiring Gaea's comfort and love, he lay down upon the shore and embraced his wife, unaware that he lay within an arm's reach of treachery and doom. The gathering darkness concealed the long black arm that reached out and grabbed Uranus in its hand. The reclining god could not see the huge, black, sickle-shaped shadow waving menacingly above his body. Quicker than thought, Cronos mutilated his father and threw the severed parts into the sea. Uranus screamed in agony, for immortality provides no shield against pain and suffering. The excruciating pain wiped out every thought except the most significant realization. With all of his children and his wife against him, Uranus recognized that his rule had come to an abrupt end.

The sea carried the pieces of Uranus's body away, and Gaea's body absorbed the blood he had shed. From this blood, Gaea, in time, gave birth to more monstrous beings: the three Furies[7] and a new group of powerful Giants.[8] The Furies were fierce and intimidating, but just. Disgusting in their appearance, these female creatures were wingless, black, creatures whose eyes dripped poisonous tears and whose fiery breath scorched their victims with a bloody venom. They would destroy any mortal child who killed a parent or blood relative because they would pursue the murderer until he became insane.

1. The Hundred-handed giants were named Briareüs (strong), Gyes (earthborn), and Cottus.
2. The Cyclopes were early bronze-working metalsmiths named Arges (brightness), Steropes (lightning), and Brontes (thunder).
3. Ancient metalsmiths covered one of their eyes with a patch for protection against flying sparks, leaving only one eye visible.
4. The myths of Artemis and Apollo are told in Section II, The Olympian Family, and in Section III, The World of Man (in Niobe, and in The Calydonian Boar Hunt).
5. The myths of Prometheus and Epimetheus are told in Section III, The World of Man.
6. The myths of the children of Themis, Rhea, Mnemosyne, and Dione are told in Section II, The Olympian Family.
7. Meleager's mother calls upon the Furies in The Calydonian Boar Hunt (Section III, The World of Man).
   Orestes is pursued by the Furies in the *Oresteia* trilogy by Aeschylus.
8. Heracles and the gods fight these Giants in the myth of Heracles (Section IV, The Heroes).

2 The Rule of Cronus

Among mortal men, it was inevitable that each generation would be replaced by the succeeding one. When Cronus attempted to remain in power permanently and failed, his failure corresponded to the cycle of life and death in the world of mortal man. Thus, the rule of Cronus repeated the general pattern of the rule of Uranus. Rhea, the Mother Goddess, bore Cronus six children, and Cronus ruled the universe by force.

However, Cronus was more clever than his father. Instead of burying his children in the earth, he incorporated them into his own body. Primitive man believed that a person could acquire the characteristics of what he ate. One who ate a god became divine, or one who ate a courageous animal gained courage. Therefore, it was a great honor for an enemy to be eaten by his foe. In the matriarchal religion, priestesses of the Great Goddess or the Mother Goddess consumed the flesh of the sacred king in order to acquire his powers of fertility.

Cronus believed he was safe because he had consumed his children. However, he had not reckoned with Rhea, who had hidden two male off-spring from him. These two would destroy their father's power and one would assume the throne.

The late Greeks gave Cronus the title of *Father Time*. With his famous sickle, Cronus would harvest the grains of time. Words such as "chronology" and "chronicle" are derived from this concept.

THE MYTH

As soon as they were in control of the universe, the Titans rescued their six brothers from Tartarus and made Cronus their king. Cronus, however, immediately imprisoned the Hundred-handed giants and the

Cyclopes in Tartarus once again, thus indicating that he would be as cruel a tyrant as his father Uranus had been.

Cronus was doomed to rule with suspicion and doubt continually gnawing upon his sense of security. Gaea, who as an earth goddess had the gift of prophecy, informed Cronus, in his father's presence, that one day he, too, would be overthrown by his son. When Cronus protested that his great strength would protect him, his parents reminded him that no one can escape his or her fate.[1]

Cronus, however, determined to try. He married his fair-haired sister, Rhea, whom he loved. Unfortunately, in the course of time, she bore him the children he feared. Their first child was a lovely daughter, Hestia. When Rhea dutifully brought the baby to her husband, his parents' prophecy burned within his head, obliterating any other thoughts. While Cronus appeared calm and loving as he reached out for his child, as soon as he held her in his arms, his eyes gleamed with a wild fire. A malicious grin of victory darkened his face. He quickly opened his gigantic mouth and swallowed his infant daughter whole: head, arms, legs, and all. Rhea could not believe her eyes. Then, without a word, Cronus turned his back on his wife and left the room.

In the next three years, Rhea bore her husband three more children: the beautiful daughters, Demeter and Hera, and a mighty son, Hades. Each time Rhea presented her husband with his newborn child, she hoped that he would share her joy. However, each time he beheld one of his children, the fearful prophecy roared through his mind, making his head throb and his flesh cold. Would this child grow up to threaten his power? Cronus could not take that risk. Calmly and lovingly, he would reach out for his child, but as soon as he felt its life in his arms, his eyes would display that wild gleam of fire, and the malicious grin of victory again would darken his face. He quickly would open his gigantic mouth and swallow the infant whole. Then, without a word, he would turn his back on his despondent wife and leave the room.

Rhea's sorrow and anger became intolerable. She decided that, from this time forth, she would protect her newborn children from their mad father. Then, when they were fully grown, they would help her avenge their father's crimes against their sisters and brother.

Consequently, Rhea was well-prepared for the birth of her fifth child the following year. She was determined to pit all of her cunning skills against her husband's crazed mind. As soon as this child was born, she rejoiced to find that she had a healthy, strong son. Naming the infant Poseidon, she secretly stole away from the palace and hid the baby among the lambs in the sheepfold. When she returned, she told Cronus that she had given birth to a horse and showed him a newborn foal. Calmly and lovingly Cronus accepted the foal as he had welcomed his other children. With the old prophecy raging through his mind, the gleam of wild fire shone from his eyes, and the malicious grin darkened his face. He opened his gigantic mouth and swallowed the foal whole. Then, without a word, he turned his back upon his wife and left the room. Meanwhile, Poseidon was reared by immortal sea deities on the island of Rhodes. Here he grew to maturity in safety.[2]

The following year, when Rhea discovered that she would give birth to her sixth child, she became frantic with fear. Could she deceive her husband successfully a second time? She ran to her parents, Gaea and Uranus, and asked them to help her think of a new plan whereby she could secretly give birth to this baby. When Gaea remembered that Cronus had imprisoned her other children, the Hundred-handed giants and the Cyclopes, and when Uranus remembered Cronus's attack upon him, they willingly helped their daughter conspire against their son. They revealed to Rhea the prophecy that Cronus was destined to be overthrown by his son, and they sent her to the fertile island of Crete for her next childbirth.

When Rhea's sixth and last child was born, an awesome radiance emanated from the powerful infant's body. Rhea named the newborn child Zeus (the shining one), and put Gaea in charge of his care. Gaea first hid the infant Zeus in a deep cave beneath the earth on Mount Dicte,[3] on the island of Crete, where immortal nymphs nourished and reared him. The goat, Amaltheia, provided him with milk, nectar, and ambrosia. His nurses hung his cradle from a tree branch so that Cronus would not be able to find him on land, on the sea, or in the heavens. Cretan youths called Curetes[4] guarded him by marching around the tree from which his cradle hung. They banged their spears against their small brass shields so that their clatter would shield his cries from Cronus's ears.

Meanwhile, Rhea had returned to her husband's palace. There, she took a great stone, about the size and weight of a newborn child and tightly encased it in long, narrow bands of cloth just as she would have wrapped the infant Zeus himself. When Cronus asked to hold his newborn child, Rhea obediently put this bundle into her husband's arms. Again, upon holding what he thought was his infant son, the frightening thought that this might be the child who would cause his death plunged Cronus into madness. Calmly and lovingly, Cronus rocked the well-wrapped bundle, while his lowered head concealed the gleam of wild torment in his eyes. With the familiar malicious grin of victory, Cronus suddenly opened his gigantic mouth and swallowed the rock just as he had swallowed his other children. Then, without a word, he turned his back upon his relieved wife and left the room.

Rhea kept her secret, but the prophecy made Cronus wonder whether his wife had deceived him. However, no matter where he searched, he could not find any child of his. Therefore, he did not realize that, on the island of Crete, the son he had so feared was actually alive and growing to manhood.

When Zeus had reached maturity, Gaea and Rhea knew that the time had come to avenge their children. They confided the prophecy about Cronus's destiny to Zeus, who prepared to become the instrument of his father's fate. Zeus went to Metis, a daughter of the Titans, Oceanus and Tethys, for help because she was reputed to be the wisest of all the immortals. Metis tricked Cronus into swallowing a tasty, drugged drink, which gave him excruciating stomach pains. While Rhea looked on with long-awaited satisfaction, Cronus's stomach became so upset that it disgorged its contents, one after the other. First Cronus vomited up the rock which he had swallowed last. Then, one by one, he spewed up his four children, each of whom emerged from Cronus's belly alive and filled with implacable hatred for Cronus. Before Cronus had recovered, Poseidon and Zeus had joined their brother and sisters.

Together, the children of Cronus confronted their father and asked him if he would relinquish his power peacefully. The prophecy that he would be overthrown by his son thundered through Cronus's head, obliterating their words. "Never!" he roared. Then Cronus turned his back on his enemies and proudly stalked out of the room.

1. One definition of fate: the inevitable replacement of one generation by the succeeding generation.
2. Some writers say that Cronus swallowed Poseidon as he had swallowed his first four children.
3. Other writers say Mount Ida, on Crete.
4. On Crete, the Curetes were companions of the sacred king. They clashed their weapons during religious rituals in order to frighten off evil spirits.

HUMAN EXPERIENCE

Power and Influence from Others

Feeling that power lay outside of itself, humankind wished to assimilate the characteristics and gain the powers of others. Priestesses of the Mother Goddess ate the flesh of the sacred king in order to incorporate his fertility. Zeus and Cronus consumed their enemies to increase their power.

Today, instead of incorporating people's strength or character physically, we "take on" their characteristics. Through imitation, we make the traits of others our own by identifying with them. When we admire the qualities or character of other persons, they become *role-models* for us. They are living examples by which we can guide ourselves in becoming like them in the ways we desire. Therefore, our own development is based, in part, on characteristics, values, and beliefs we identify with and admire in other people.

3 War Between the Titans and the Gods

INTRODUCTION

The pattern of creation reached its climax with the war between the new order and the old order. Zeus showed more intelligence than Cronus. He acquired the help of the wisest immortal Metis and used her to help him overthrow his father. It was a testimony to the strength of the matriarchal system that the wisest divinity was still a female. Zeus also acquired other political allies. He was the first male ruler to work with other immortals in order to accomplish an important goal.

The idea of rewarding allies and punishing enemies was a mortal custom transferred to the immortal kingdom. It was one more way in which the divine world of the myths reflected the human world. The myths gave the gods human appearance, human personalities, and human goals. Their conflicts followed the pattern established by human society and their emerging government did, also. We call such gods anthropomorphic.

THE MYTH

For ten long years the children of Cronus, called the "gods," fought Cronus and many of the other immortal Titans for control of the universe, without success for either side. The gods and Titans were so evenly matched that the gods feared the war might never end. Fortunately for the children of Cronus, Gaea decided to help them. Concerned as always about her many children, Gaea wanted her Hundred-handed giants and her Cyclopes to enjoy the freedom the other immortals had. Since Cronus had imprisoned them, she asked Zeus and his brothers to set them free. To motivate her grandchildren to obey her request, she explained that they would be able to win their war against the Titans if these six immortals fought on their side. Zeus, Poseidon, and Hades were delighted to help her since they would be helping themselves at the same time.

The three gods descended into the kingdom of Tartarus where they killed the guard and released their uncles from their chains. The Cyclopes were so grateful for their freedom that they rewarded their three liberators with spectacular gifts. To Zeus they gave the thunderbolt and lightning, which they had created secretly and which Gaea had kept hidden from the other immortals. Since these were invincible weapons, they would enable Zeus to rule immortals and mortals with absolute authority. To Hades they gave the helmet of invisibility, which would make him invisible whenever he chose to wear it. To Poseidon they gave the three-pronged fishing spear called the trident. With it, Poseidon would be able to cause storms at sea and earthquakes upon land.

In order to renew their strength, Zeus gave the Cyclopes and the Hundred-handed giants nectar to drink and ambrosia to eat. When they were ready to return to the world of sunlight, Zeus addressed them with great seriousness:

"Children of Gaea and Uranus," he began. "We children of Cronus have been fighting the Titans for many years without prospect of victory for either side. We ask you to join your strength with ours in order to help us achieve victory and power."

To this, the Hundred-handed Cottus replied: "Immortal Zeus, son of Cronus and Rhea, because you have freed us from eternal bondage in this sunless land, we certainly shall help you defeat the Titans."

Thus, with their new weapons and their strong allies, the children of Cronus resumed their battle against the Titans. The Hundred-handed giants took the offensive against the Titans, bombarding them with immense rocks that they broke off the cliffs with their multitudinous hands. The Titans, however, were not intimidated by their monstrous brothers. As they met the latest challenge to their power, their counterattack shook the earth, the mountains, and even the land of Tartarus.

The titanic rampage provoked Zeus to exercise his full power. Becoming violent in his rage, Zeus left his stronghold on Mount Olympus, gathered the clouds, and repeatedly hurled his thunderbolts and lightning upon his enemies. His weapons transformed the earth's surface into a sheet of flames which consumed forests, rivers, and seas. Meanwhile, the Hundred-handed giants hurled thousands of rocks upon the Titans, who, being immortal, could not die but felt the agony of injury. Between the onslaught of fire and the deluge of rocks, the Titans could not summon sufficient power to retaliate. Overpowered at last, they retreated into the depths of the earth, where, in the land of Tartarus, the victors bound them in heavy chains for eternity.

The gods then transformed the region of Tartarus into an inescapable prison. Poseidon placed bronze gates in a bronze wall surrounding the dark land, and Zeus gave the Hundred-handed giants the honor of guarding their great enemies. So consuming was their hatred of the Titans that they were willing to obey Zeus's wishes and dwell eternally in this dark land, isolated from the other immortals.

Zeus selected a special, eternal punishment for the strongest Titan, Atlas, who had been Cronus's principal ally. He condemned his enemy to stand erect with his feet firmly planted at the earth's edge and hold the sky upon his raised hands and head forever in order to keep it from falling upon the earth.

With the imprisonment of the Titans, the first war was over, and a new age began.

4   The Rule of Zeus

With the emergence of Zeus as the lord of the Olympian gods, the progression from the confusion of Chaos to an ordered universe was complete. Zeus became the great protector among the gods. He established a council, composed of the twelve major Olympian gods. Including himself, there were Poseidon, Hera, Demeter, Apollo, Artemis, Hermes, Ares, Athena, Aphrodite, Hephaestus, and Dionysus. Important, but not included, were Hades, Hestia, Persephone, and Eros. Zeus enforced justice by listening to both sides of an argument, just as a mortal king on earth would do. He guaranteed that those who took oaths would keep their word by devising a just and awful punishment for those who did not.

In the myths, Zeus and Poseidon were similar in that they ruled their different kingdoms with responsibility and justice. Both carried a trident-shaped weapon, which originally symbolized rain, thunder, and lightning. Zeus struck the clouds with it, as Poseidon struck the earth and the sea. It is believed that Zeus was born on the island of Crete and was reared there. Poseidon was worshipped on Crete as the major deity. *Linear B* tablets found on Crete mention Poseidon's name more than that of any other god.

There are conflicting views in ancient Greek literature about the location of the Underworld. Some writers place it upon the surface of the earth, at the far western end of the known world. Others locate it beneath the earth.

THE MYTH

Once they gained control of the universe, the gods forced their Titan prisoners to relinquish their titles. Obeying Gaea's advice, the children of

Cronus chose Zeus as their king. The three brothers, Zeus, Poseidon, and Hades, determined their dominions by drawing lots. Zeus drew the sky, Poseidon drew the sea, and Hades the Underworld, including the land of Tartarus. Zeus then made his sister Hestia goddess of the hearth and home; his sister, Demeter, goddess of grain harvests and the fertility of the earth. His sister, Hera, became the goddess of marriage and childbirth and the queen of Mount Olympus, where most of the children of Cronus intended to live. After these decisions had been made, Zeus summoned all of the immortals to an assembly on the summit of Mount Olympus. There he announced that anyone who had fought on his side against Cronus would be able to retain the powerful role he had held under Cronus's rule or gain a new position of equal power.

The river goddess, Styx, a child of the Titans Oceanus and Tethys, had taken her children and had been the first of the uncommitted immortals to volunteer to help Zeus in the war against the Titans. In return for her courage and loyalty, Zeus rewarded Styx with a special gift.

"From this time forth," the Lord of Olympus commanded, "any god who swears a sacred oath must solemnly declare it upon Styx's eternal waters.

"Styx's river forms the boundary of the Underworld. Thus, whenever a god must defend his word as the truth or whenever he makes a sacred promise, I shall send the messenger goddess, Iris of the golden wings, down to the dark land of Hades with a golden pitcher. There she will collect the icy waters of the River Styx as they fall down a steep, tall cliff and return with her filled pitcher to Mount Olympus. Upon her arrival, Iris will give the pitcher to the god who is making the oath, and he will proclaim his oath by pouring out the sacred water and swearing on it as he pours.

"Furthermore," the Lord of Olympus continued, "I have determined a fixed, intimidating punishment for any immortal who breaks his sacred word. He will be forced to lie upon a bed in a deep coma for one full year. In this state of deep sleep, he will neither eat ambrosia, nor drink nectar; he will neither speak nor even breathe. Moreover, he must face a milder, although still difficult, punishment for nine additional years. During this time, the offending god will be completely ostracized by all other immortals and unable to communicate with any of them in any way. In the tenth year, however, his punishment will cease, and, once again, I will permit him to rejoin the immortals in our celebrations and conferences."

From then on, as the Lord of Olympus had intended, all of the deathless gods considered an oath sworn upon the River Styx to be unbreakable. Many swore upon its waters, but no one ever broke his word.

Upon taking command of the dismal kingdom beneath the earth, Hades, the Lord of the Underworld, placed Charon, an aged, grim slave, in a rowboat upon the River Styx. Hades ordered him to spend eternity ferrying the shades[1] of properly buried dead mortals across this river into the kingdom of death. Charon charged each passenger the fare of one obol[2] for the ride. Consequently, a person was buried with this fee in his mouth

A shade whose body had not been properly buried could not cross the River Styx and enter the Underworld. Instead it was condemned to experience an eternity of shame and dishonor as it futilely wandered along the far shore of the River Styx.

Once a shade had crossed the River Styx, in order to pass through the gates into grim Hades' dismal kingdom, it had to be inspected by Hades' giant watchdog, the pitiless, savage monster, Cerberus. Cerberus had three dogs' heads, a serpent's tail, and a row of snakes' heads running down his back. Although he welcomed all entering shades by wagging his tail in a friendly manner, he would watchfully wait for any who would dare to attempt escape. These he would consume, delighting in the taste of the shades. The few mortals who had to enter the Underworld while they were alive carried honeyed wheat cakes with them in order to appease the monster's dreadful disposition and appetite.[3] Usually, Hermes the Wayfarer guided them safely past this dreadful hound.

Under the leadership of far-seeing Zeus, the Olympian gods helped mortal man learn to lead a better life. The Lord of Olympus became a wise and just ruler. He taught humankind to be fair with one another, to avoid violence, and to solve arguments in a lawful manner. He punished those mortals who acted impiously or unjustly.

Poseidon, the Lord of the Sea, taught mankind how to build ships and how to tame horses for transportation and for labor in the fields.

Dark Hades, Lord of the Underworld, taught mortal men to treat the dead with respect. He established funeral ceremonies and proper burial rites.

Zeus's three sisters also brought benefits to mortal men. Golden-throned Hera protected marriages and helped women with childbirth. Lovely Hestia taught mortals how to build houses and then safeguarded them. Demeter, mother of wealth, taught mortals how to gather wild corn, how to prepare it for nourishment and planting, and how to preserve it.

In the years that followed, other monstrous children of Gaea tried to overpower Zeus and the Olympian gods, but without success. Their tremendous power was no match for the collective intelligence of the Olympians. In addition, Zeus's reign established order in the universe, which so pleased most of the immortal gods that they were willing to defend Zeus against any threat to his authority.

1. The shades are spirits of dead mortals. Shades appeared the same to the eye as they had

when they were alive, but they had no physical substance. (One could not touch them, although they were visible.)
2. An obol is an ancient Greek coin.
3. See the story of Psyche and Eros (Section IV, The Heroes).

REFLECTIONS

1. The myth of Atlantis suggests that a piece of land once may have extended all the way across the Atlantic Ocean on which there was a great civilization. An earthquake, it is thought by some, sank Atlantis to the bottom of the sea, abolishing this culture.

   Using any current research, such as Jacques Cousteau's searches on the ocean floor, debate as to whether Atlantis existed.
2. Is there any acceptance of the belief that gods from outer space came to earth? Debate.
3. Write an original creation myth that explains some natural phenomenon, such as:
   a. the earth
   b. man
   c. seasons
   d. sun and moon
4. In pantomime, present a skit of any of the myths in this section. Keep your choice secret and let the class guess and relate the story you have wordlessly dramatized. The person who guesses is the next to perform.
5. How is Uranus's rule different from what Gaea's would have been?
6. How are their personalities different?
7. What qualities does Uranus have that keep him in power?
8. How is Cronus able to conquer him and why?
   a. Why does Cronus rebel against Uranus?
   b. Why is he successful?
   c. Why is Zeus able to conquer him?
   d. Why can't Cronus, who is powerful and immortal, avoid his fate?
9. What qualities does Cronus have that keep him in power?
10. Compare and contrast Cronus and Uranus. Is the son better than the father? Explain.
11. What qualities does Rhea possess?
12. What qualities does Zeus possess? Why is he so successful?
13. Compare and contrast Zeus and Cronus. Is the son better than the father? Explain.
14. What changes does Zeus bring about in the organization of the universe?

5 Typhon

The myth of Typhon serves three purposes. First, it illustrates the ability of Zeus to maintain order in the universe, even against a formidable foe. Again Zeus used his qualities of leadership. He guided the gods to safety, was willing to accept wise advice from a minor god, and fought Typhon single-handedly. He was able to defeat the enemy and to return to power because he had the support of the other gods. His rule provided a good model for a mortal king.

The myth of Typhon also explains a natural phenomenon; the volcano of Mount Aetna in Sicily. Erupting volcanoes have destroyed a whole society's productivity. They have even buried entire cities such as Pompeii and Herculaneum in Italy. Therefore, their unpredictable force is and was greatly feared.

This myth also explained why Egyptians worshipped gods in animal forms. According to this myth, the gods of the Egyptians were the Olympian gods, but represented in the forms they had assumed when they had been pursued by Typhon.

ANTICIPATIONS

1. Give examples of events in nature that can cause harm to man.
2. Discuss to what extent science can predict and control these events.
3. Do any of these events occur in your area? Is it a source of fear? Of excitement? How do you cope with it?
4. Why are hurricanes given the names of people?

THE MYTH

The monster Typhon[1] presented the first major challenge to the authority of Zeus. After Zeus and the Olympian gods had removed the Titans from power and had imprisoned them in Tartarus, Gaea grieved for her Titan children and sought revenge against the Olympian gods. Therefore, with Tartarus as the father, Gaea gave birth to Typhon, a gigantic monster who was larger, stronger, and more terrifying than any of her other children. Typhon's appearance was grotesque. Fifty dragons' heads emerged from each shoulder. In each head, reptile-like tongues flicked in and out, spewing forth fire and smoke. Moreover, each head spoke with strange voices. Sometimes the immortals could understand Typhon's words. However, at other times, Typhon bellowed like a bull, roared like a lion, or barked like a dog. His body was winged, yet he had god-like legs around which hissing snakes coiled. He stood taller than the mountains, and his heads often touched the stars. One of his hands reached far to the East, the other far to the West.

At his mother's direction, Typhon challenged the right of Zeus to rule the Olympian gods and the universe. With terrible roars and hisses, and spewing streams of fire from his one-hundred mouths, Typhon set forth to conquer his enemies. As he approached Mount Olympus, he hurled fiery rocks at the fortress. Far-seeing Zeus thundered an urgent warning to the other Olympians, which shook the heavens above and the world below, as well as the earth's surface and the ocean. The monster belched flaming storm winds which Zeus met with searing lightning bolts. The incredible heat charred the earth, scorched the sky, and boiled the seas. Hades, grim Lord of the Underworld, and the imprisoned Titans trembled with fear.

The Olympians were so frightened at the sight of Typhon that they abandoned Mount Olympus and fled to the parched land of Egypt, where they sought refuge from the invading monster. There, the shepherd god, Pan, cunningly counseled the Olympians to transform themselves into animal forms in order to deceive their pursuer. Accepting Pan's advice, loud-thundering Zeus became a ram. Far-shooting Apollo became a crow; Hermes the Wayfinder became a stork; and ivy-wreathed Dionysus became a goat. Arrow-raining Artemis became a cat; golden-throned Hera became a snowy-white cow; and silver-footed Aphrodite became a fish. Pan threw himself into a river, transforming the lower part of his body into a fish and the rest of himself into a goat.[2]

When Typhon reached Egypt, he could not find the Olympians. Seeing only various kinds of animal life, Typhon turned north toward the Mediterranean Sea. As soon as Typhon had turned his back upon the animals, Olympian Zeus resumed his shape, gathered his thunderbolts and, keeping a safe distance from his monstrous enemy, struck Typhon from behind, stunning him. Then the Loud-Thunderer[3] was able to approach Typhon and wound him with a stone sickle.

Typhon quickly recovered his senses, realized his peril, and tried to flee. However, Olympian Zeus seized him, and the two immortal beings struggled hand-to-hand for ultimate power.

Typhon fought fiercely. He twisted his body around Zeus like a giant snake, thereby immobilizing the Olympian. Then Typhon wrenched the stone sickle out of Zeus's hands and used it to remove the tendons from the Olympian's hands and feet.

Unable to use these muscles, loud-thundering Zeus was now powerless. He could offer no resistance when Typhon picked him up and carried him on his shoulders to the island of Sicily. There, Typhon hid him in a well-concealed cave, along with the severed tendons that the monster had wrapped in a bearskin. Typhon then left a creature that was half-dragon and half-maiden, to guard his prisoner and disappeared into the Sicilian countryside.

Time passed. Zeus had given up all hope of rescue when Hermes the Wayfinder and Pan, god of shepherds, arrived at the secluded cave. Since Typhon had not seen any Olympian but Zeus in Egypt, he had made no effort to disguise the path he took as he transported his prisoner north to Sicily. Fortunately for his pursuers, the smoke from his fiery dragons' heads guided them reliably across the Mediterranean Sea. Therefore, upon reaching Sicily, the Wayfinder and the Shepherd God found the scorched trail apparent. They followed it, but very slowly and very carefully, for fear of meeting Typhon. Meanwhile, the dragon-maiden, knowing the prisoner to be helpless and the cave's location to be concealed, slept.

Upon reaching the hidden cave, Hermes and Pan soon found an opportunity to steal into its darkness. There, upon becoming accustomed to the dim light, they spied Olympian Zeus, lying helpless upon the damp, earthen floor. The Loud-Thunderer directed them to the bearskin, where they located his severed tendons. Quietly, Hermes and Pan replaced the injured tendons in Zeus' hands and feet. Then, the three gods stealthily stepped out of the cave into the fresh, sweet air of freedom. Careful to leave no trail behind them, they returned to Mount Olympus.

The Lord of Black Clouds[4] quickly regained his strength and resumed the battle. Setting out in his chariot, pulled by winged horses, he searched the Mediterranean area for Typhon. As soon as he saw the revealing dragon-smoke, Zeus, who delighted in thunder, rained thunderbolts down upon Typhon.

Typhon fled north to Thrace in the hope of escaping, but without success. When he realized that he could not evade far-seeing Zeus, he picked up entire mountains and hurled them at the great Olympian. However, Zeus's thunderbolts carried such force that they forced the mountains back upon Typhon.

With blood gushing from his huge body, Typhon headed southwest across Greece, closely tracked by Zeus. Try as he could, the wounded giant could not evade his pursuer's terrible lightning bolts. By the time the monster reached Sicily, all of his dragon heads had burst into flames. Typhon was blind, bleeding, and burning. He could no longer withstand the furious onslaught. Crippled, he collapsed upon the Sicilian soil. There his body heat ignited the forests and melted the land beneath him. Since loud-thundering Zeus knew that he could not kill his immortal enemy, he picked up Mount Aetna and threw it down upon Typhon's body, burying him eternally beneath this massive mountain.

Typhon still groans today as the mountain presses relentlessly upon his chest. Lying on his back, he spews forth thick clouds of dust and vomits fiery ashes. Any shift in his body causes storm winds, which choke men with dust and scatter ships at sea. Periodically, Typhon struggles mightily to dislodge the mountain which imprisons him. Then the earth quakes from his exertions, and he engulfs the surrounding area in a torrential flood of fire.

1. Also called Typhöeus or Typhaon.
2. These animal forms explain the Egyptian worship of the animal form of these gods.
3. Zeus.
4. Zeus.

REFLECTIONS

1. Assume that Mount Aetna has recently erupted. Write a newspaper account of the disaster as if Typhon, himself, had caused the eruption. Be sure to give Typhon interesting motivation.
2. Write a myth attributing another type of natural phenomenon to one of Gaea's giant children.
3. Write a character sketch of Typhon.

HUMAN EXPERIENCE

Fantasies and Magic

Human fantasies created the gods of Olympus, despite the fact that people believed that it was the gods who created men and women. They endowed their gods with powers and privileges that mortals were denied. Simultaneously, they attributed to the gods the savagery and violence of their own emotional drives. The gods were exempt from the laws of humankind.

The gods used violence and savagery in war to wreak devastation far beyond what man was capable of doing. They could enlist fire, floods, storms, thunderbolts, pestilence, deceits and tricks that were limited only by the fantasies of the authors who created them.

The fantasy of an Underworld where our spirits go after death is a notion found in all ancient cultures. No one wanted to feel that once dead, that was the end. Humankind's yearning for a place to go after death existed in Egyptian, Babylonian, Hindu, and Greek cultures. It continues to exist in Christianity and other modern religions, as well. Men and women would die, but their shadows, or shades, would exist in some form in the universe. The persistence of that belief as well as the idea that the gods dwelled on high, on Mount Olympus, gave a location—the Underworld, Hades—to what could have been only thought and yearning.

Today, most terrifying of all is the potential of the weapons with which modern science has armed us. For sheer destruction, devastation, and the power of annihilation, hydrogen bombs and intercontinental ballistic missiles have made modern human beings more terrifying in their capacity to destroy than the whole panoply of the Greek gods. In every case, the ability to create and use fantasies that take us beyond the present, makes more tolerable the most frightening situations.

Children use fantasies to give themselves hope that they can modify situations which cause them despair and anger. They seek relief from the frustrations of the world by resolving their troubles through fantasy and dreams. Fantasies are useful because they give hope for the future.

The ability to fantasize gave rise to another important aspect of people's increasing ability to cope with their environment and their natural wish to understand it better. Before the days of science, anxiety resulted from their inability to understand powerful natural phenomena, and their own drives and instincts. They felt that external and internal realities were separated, somehow, from their own control. If they felt evil or destructive impulses, they saw them as emanating from other people, from beasts, or from nature. So they lived with the sense of being surrounded by terrifying dangers that could pounce at any time.

Human beings also believed formerly in the omnipotence of their own thoughts. If they wished the death of a person, they felt they might cause that death merely by having the wish. Therefore they feared the thoughts of others, and warded off those evil thoughts by rites, rituals, and magic. Humankind used magic to insure its survival and to protect the environment from the dread of supernatural forces. Through magic, it was felt that nature could be made subject to human will, that enemies could be punished, and wishes be fulfilled.

While modern science leads to the abolition of superstition and reliance upon magic, it in no way should abolish fantasy. Fantasy as a creative force can point toward future scientific endeavors. When we fantasize something, that fantasy can help us see a way to make it come true. Mankind has always wanted to fly, as did Daedalus in the myth, but it took technology thousands of years between the wish for flight and the advent of the Wright brothers' primitive airplane. Once the flight fantasy became a reality, however, it was not more than seventy years more before a man landed on the moon.

Today, for many people the scientist has replaced the magic rite and ritual which was originally intended to curry favor with the gods. The scientist is using the tools of research and technology to help him tame the forces of nature, including weather, crops, and illness. Nevertheless, injustice, war, and death continue to exist in modern society. Each culture confronts and explains these problems in different ways.

II

THE OLYMPIAN FAMILY
The New Religion

The Great Goddess Demeter (on the left) is giving the gift of grain to Triptolemus, who is the eldest son of Metaneira. Her daughter, the goddess Persephone, stands behind the youth, blessing him with her hand upon his head.

W hen the first Greek-speaking, Bronze Age tribes invaded Greece during the period 1900 B.C.–1600 B.C., they brought with them a new, male-dominated religion. They persuaded the native inhabitants to accept and adopt this new religion. Their religious revolution was successful because they permitted each community to worship its old gods in the old way, as long as it worshipped Olympian Zeus and his mighty brothers as well.

They also permitted their major god, Zeus, to marry the Mother Goddess or Great Goddess of each local community. Each town, isolated from other communities because of the mountainous terrain, worshipped the same earth goddess, but under a different name. Therefore, as the invading tribes slowly made their way through Greece, Zeus acquired an extraordinary number of wives. In fact, by the time the Mycenaean Greeks had conquered the entire peninsula, Olympian Zeus had become the world's best-known lover.

Greeks in later, more civilized times, became embarrassed by such a promiscuous divinity. Yet, the great Olympian's unbridled passions had united a land and its multitude of neighboring island communities under one religion. The conquerors had won the land by force, using their bronze weapons to overpower the local farming communities. However, they had won the hearts of the people with the strategy of religious tolerance and the intermarriage of Zeus with the local earth goddesses.

ANTICIPATIONS

1. Greek gods were anthropomorphic, and were, therefore, similar to human beings. Why were all Greek gods related?
2. Who makes the decisions in your home—mother, father, children, or grandparents?

3. What kind of behavior is rewarded in your home?
   a. kindness
   b. achievement
   c. independence
   d. dependence
   e. neatness
   f. honesty
   g. other
4. What rewards do you receive from your parents when your behavior pleases them?
   a. money
   b. special food
   c. gifts
   d. embrace
   e. general feeling of approval and love
   f. other
5. Make a chart of your family tree, going back as far as possible. Include great-grandparents, grandparents, aunts, uncles, cousins, and second cousins.
6. List each member of your family and his or her relationship to you. Then, write three adjectives that describe each person's personality.
7. How have the nature and the importance of arts and crafts changed in the course of history? Discuss the role of mechanization.

6 Metis and Athena

Originally, in the matriarchal society, Athena was a local Mother Goddess or Great Goddess like Gaea and Rhea. In that role, her blessings helped the people of pre-Mycenaean Athens produce offspring and food, the two things they needed for the survival of their community.

However, according to the patriarchal Olympian religion, Athena was the daughter of Zeus and Metis. Zeus acquired the quality of wisdom by marrying and then swallowing the Titan Metis, whose name meant practical wisdom or counsel. Then Zeus, although a male divinity, took over the female function of giving birth. With the help of another male divinity, he delivered Metis's child, the goddess Athena.

Thereafter, Athena remained her father's favorite daughter, for, being Zeus's brainchild, she represented the qualities that Zeus himself possessed and prized. She lost the motherly qualities she had possessed in the earlier religion and instead became an athletic-looking virgin goddess. She was fond of mortals, helping women by training them in various practical handicrafts[1] and inspiring courageous young men by advising them in the art of defensive warfare and in the pursuit of heroic adventure.[2] She appreciated in others the characteristics she herself possessed: dignity, sound judgment, and an alert, intelligent mind. She despised passion untempered by reason. Athena became one of the three major Olympian divinities, the other two being Zeus and Apollo.

1. See the myth of Arachne (Section III, The World of Man).
2. See the myths of Perseus, Bellerophon, Heracles, and Jason (Section IV, The Heroes).

THE MYTH

Olympian Zeus had a passion for beautiful women and became known for his amorous pursuits. For his first wife, he chose Metis, the daughter of the Titans, Oceanus and Tethys, who had helped him by giving Cronus the drugged drink. It was a superb choice, for Metis, whose name means "wisdom" or "cunning," was the wisest of all the immortal gods. However, when Metis was expecting her first child, Uranus and Gaea, who wanted Zeus to remain in complete authority over the universe, visited their grandson and told him of Metis's destiny. She would give birth to two children. The first, a daughter, would equal her father in strength and in wisdom; the second, a son, would overpower his father and become the supreme ruler of the universe.

To offset the second part of the prophecy, Zeus conceived a plan which equalled the talents of his clever wife. He remembered that Metis possessed the ability to change her shape at will, because she had performed a number of transformations in the attempt to avoid his amorous advances. Therefore, when Metis was about to give birth to her daughter, Zeus flattered her with honeyed, conniving questions. For his personal enjoyment, would she display her marvelous talent of transforming herself? She would? How wonderful! Could she change herself into a fire? Running water? A lion? A boar? A snake? Zeus's enthusiasm for each transformation was infectious. Therefore, when he asked Metis to become something very small, without any hesitation, she complied. He immediately caught her in his hands and swallowed her.

When the time came for the birth of his daughter, Olympian Zeus developed an excruciating headache. Unable to tolerate the pain, he persuaded Prometheus[1] to split open his head with an axe. Out leaped the grey-eyed goddess Athena, fully grown and clothed in armor of shimmering gold. Metis had made the armor in which her daughter was born, and this war gear always terrorized the armies who fought against her. Battle-stirring Athena became the equal of her father, Zeus, as the prophecy indicated she would, and she was also his favorite child. She became the patron goddess of arts and crafts and of mortals who displayed heroic or resourceful behavior. Metis, meanwhile, continued to give her husband advice from within his body. She was never able to bear Zeus a second child, and thus, Zeus's plan was successful!

1. Some writers say Hephaestus.

REFLECTIONS

1. If Athena was Zeus's favorite daughter, what does this reveal about his values? What does it reveal about the values of the Greeks?
2. Pretend that you are Zeus or Athena visiting the United States today. Keep a journal of your impressions of modern life.
3. Make a family tree of Zeus's family. Add to this tree as you read.
4. Why was Athena born from the head of Zeus?

7 Themis and the Fates Mnemosyne and the Muses Eurynome and the Graces

INTRODUCTION

Like all the immortal loves and offspring of Zeus, Themis, Mnemosyne, Eurynome, and Dione are presented in these two chapters in the chronological order in which Zeus loved them. They are grouped together because they have no major myths of their own that reveal their personalities, although they and their children play important roles in many of the Greek myths. Therefore, their stories are much less dramatic than those of the Titans (Cronus, Prometheus, and Leto) and those of the gods (Athena, Hera, Apollo, Artemis, Hermes, Demeter, and Dionysus).

ANTICIPATIONS

1. How does one acquire beauty and charm today?
2. Discuss ways in which people today can support the arts.
   a. financial aid
   b. training
   c. sponsorship
   d. contests and exhibitions
3. What is the role of fate in your life? To what extent do you determine what happens to you?

THE MYTHS

Themis and the Fates

Zeus took the Titan Themis, a daughter of Uranus and Gaea, as his second wife after Metis. Like her mother, Themis was a prophet, whose knowledge of future events earned her special reverence among the immortals. As Zeus's wife, she appropriately became the mother of the three Fates or Moerae, meaning "parts," or "portions." The Fates distributed each mortal's destiny and bowed only to Zeus's will. The first of the three, named Clotho (spinner), spun the thread of each mortal's life. The second Fate, Lachesis (distributor of fortunes), measured the thread of each mortal's life, thus determining its length. The third Fate, Atropos (inflexible), was the most feared by mortal man, because she used her dreaded shears to cut the thread of each mortal's life, thus determining his death.[1]

Originally, the three Fates were pre-Olympian goddesses. They were powers beyond the control of Zeus, and the power of the gods, too, was subject to their will. In time, they became part of the Olympian family, their chief role being to determine the destiny of mortal man. As the Olympian religion developed and male gods became more important, Zeus gained some degree of control over the Fates, which made them less awesome to both gods and men.

1. The Fates appear in The Calydonian Boar Hunt (Section III, The World of Man).

Mnemosyne and the Muses

Zeus next loved the Titan Mnemosyne (memory), a sister of Themis, and through her became the father of the nine Muses. The immortal Muses created the alphabet and poetry. Consequently, poets prayed to them for artistic inspiration.

Although poets often invoked the Muses, they seldom used their names. Originally, there were three Muses, called Melete (practice or attention), Aoede (song) and Mneme (memory). Later their number increased to nine, and their names changed: Calliope (beautiful voice), who became the mother of Orpheus[1]; Cleio (celebrate); Melpomene (singer and dancer); Euterpe (happy delight); Erato (lovely); Terpsichore (enjoyment of dancing); Urania (heavenly); Thaleia (good cheer); and Polyhymnia (many songs). Although the Muses were involved in the particular sphere that they were named for, they each crossed over into other areas, and classical writers were never agreed as to what particular responsibility each had.

1. The myth of Orpheus appears in Section III, The World of Man.

Eurynome and the Graces

Then, Metis's sister, Eurynome, bore Zeus the three beautiful Graces, who gave beauty and other gracious gifts to mortal women. They were called: Aglaea (radiance), Euphrosyne (merriment), and Thalia (good cheer). However, the Graces, like the Muses, varied in number and in name, depending upon the writer. They have been painted by artists more frequently than they have appeared in Greek myths.

8 Dione, Aphrodite, and Eros

Aphrodite, like Athena, was incorporated into the Olympian religion from the earlier matriarchal religion. Originally, the worship of Aphrodite may have reached Greece with people from Asia Minor. In pre-Mycenaean times, she was a goddess of fertility and love, representing nature and love in bloom. Her love was passionate and knew no bounds. Marriage and other responsibilities did not deter her. Aphrodite was always closely connected with the sea, and some people still believe that eating seafood increases one's ability to love.

When Zeus took control of Dione's oracle at Dodona, he claimed Aphrodite as his daughter.[1] Again, like Athena's mother, under the male-dominated Olympian religion, Aphrodite's mother was not considered important. Aphrodite became known only as her father's daughter. Moreover, given the masculine emphasis of the religion of Zeus, Aphrodite, as the love goddess, became less significant than she had been in the previous matriarchal society when a woman loved as many men as she chose.

THE MYTH

According to one of the writers of the myths, Zeus loved the Titan Dione, sister of Mnemosyne and Themis, and fathered with Dione the gold-wreathed Aphrodite, the goddess of love. However, another writer stated that Uranus's severed parts produced a white foam in the sea, from which Aphrodite emerged fully mature.[1] First she floated over the waves of the dark sea to the island of Cythera, off the southern coast of Greece. Then she floated east to the island of Cyprus, where she stepped ashore. Wherever she stepped, grass immediately began to grow. From the time of Aphrodite's birth, Eros was her companion, and Desire was her servant. Together they joined the Olympian gods, where they created the sweetness and delight of love for birds and beasts, mortals and immortals. Thus, gold-wreathed Aphrodite supervised young love and weddings.[2]

Eros represented uncontrollable passion. As they did with many other aspects of the human personality, the Greeks turned an internal process into an external force. Therefore, when a mortal "fell in love at first sight," the Greeks said that he had become the victim of one of the love-inspiring arrows of Eros. The gods, too, were subject to the power of Eros. Consequently, the immortal Olympians feared Eros more than any other god except Zeus, for he was unpredictable and capricious and could make them feel ashamed of their feelings and behavior.[3]

The tribes who brought the religion of Zeus to Greece created Eros as part of the divine order of the universe. Early classic writers called Eros one of the primeval forces, without which creation, immortal or mortal, could not have occurred. Later writers made Eros a more youthful god and gave him Aphrodite for a mother. Eros never became a part of the council of the twelve ruling gods on Mount Olympus.[4]

1. Although Homer claims that Zeus is the father of Aphrodite, Hesiod claims that Uranus is her father and that she was born from the foam which surrounded his severed parts in the sea.
2. Aphrodite takes an important role in the myths of Pygmalion and Atalanta (Section III, The World of Man) and in Jason and the Golden Fleece (Section IV, The Heroes).
3. See the story of Eros and Psyche (Section IV, The Heroes).
4. For the twelve Olympian gods on the Council, see Section I, In the Beginning—The Rule of Zeus.
    Eros may have been omitted because he represented uncontrolled (sexual) passion. This caused conflict in society, and the Mycenaean Greeks valued marriage as a sacred bond between a man and a woman.

REFLECTIONS

1. What function did the Fates serve and what did their tasks explain about the Greek view of death?
2. What did the existence of the Muses, the Graces, and Eros explain about the Greeks who created them?
3. Compare Aphrodite with Athena. Why were both goddesses necessary?
4. Choose one of the gods in this chapter and prepare an interview with one of them. Provide both questions and responses.

9 Hera, Hephaestus, and Ares

INTRODUCTION

Like Athena, Hera was a local Great Goddess who was incorporated into the religion of Zeus. She was worshipped in pre-Mycenaean Argos by the local people who grazed herds of cattle and flocks of sheep upon their fertile plains. Given the extensive power Hera originally wielded as the Great Goddess, her reluctance to marry Zeus and to become merely one more of his conquests was understandable. Yet, his power was too strong for her, and she had to submit to his authority. Her rebellious nature indicated her strength and independence. Her attitude toward the Titan Leto indicated a rivalry between two great Mother Goddesses.

Hera's claim that she conceived Hephaestus without Zeus's aid may have had its origins in the matriarchal religion that preceded Zeus. At that early time, the role of the male in conception was not understood. To them, all creation centered completely within the female. In addition, the idea that Hera would throw Hephaestus out of her home took its meaning from the matriarchal society where inheritance occurred from mother to daughter. Children were reared by their mother's brother while their father was irrelevant to their lives. (Father was helping rear his sister's children.) When a male married, he usually went to live in the home of his wife. The matriarchal society permitted its goddesses and women to love as many males as they chose.

Ironically, upon her marriage to Zeus, Hera became the protector of marriages. Among the Mycenaean Greeks, the marriage bond was sacred. Hera, however, continued her previous role as the helper of women. Like her daughter Eileithyia, she helped women with childbirth. Although her supremacy had been usurped by her husband, Hera's power was evident in the fear she inspired among mortals when she caused the lovely Titan Leto to search the earth and heavens for a place to give birth to her children.

There was a famous sacred statue of golden-throned Hera in Argos which depicted her seated upon a throne of gold and ivory. It was the custom in ancient Greece for the townspeople to chain the statues of their earth goddesses to the thrones they sat upon in order to prevent the divine spirit within the statue from escaping. The people feared that if the spirit left its stone body, the community would lose the protection of its patron goddess.

Hephaestus originally was worshipped as a god of fire in Lycia, in Asia Minor. Then this worship spread to the islands of the Aegean, particularly the volcanic island of Lemnos. Finally it reached the Greek mainland. According to the version of the myth in which Hera conceived and bore Hephaestus without Zeus's help, the worship of Zeus was probably established on the Greek mainland before the worship of Hephaestus arrived there. Yet, Hephaestus became one of the twelve major Olympians. The metalsmith was an artist, and the people of the time respected his unusual ability and rewarded it. Men of the Bronze Age believed that tools and weapons contained magical attributes, which they enriched by such practices as dipping their weapons into a brave enemy's blood in order to incorporate his strength and courage into their weapons. Therefore, it is not surprising that Hephaestus shared a sacred shrine with Athena, his sister craftsman, in Athens. On Mount Olympus, the gods were equally appreciative of their fellow immortal. Their fascination with his metalwork and other artistic achievements reflects this attitude of ancient Greeks toward the skilled craftsman.

Although Ares, the acknowledged son of Zeus and Hera, was one of the twelve ruling Olympians, he was unpopular both among the immortals and among the Greeks because he represented what the Greeks believed to be the worst aspects of war: rashness, brutality, and barbarism. Although the Greeks often engaged in warfare and therefore appreciated the need for courage and excellence upon the battlefield, they disliked Ares's rash spirit of destruction. As a warrior, Ares was the opposite of Athena: undisciplined, irrational, complaining, and cowardly. Ares was worshipped in Thebes, but his other famous shrines were not located in Greece. He was also worshipped in areas near the Black Sea, such as Colchis. Thrace may have been his original homeland.

ANTICIPATIONS

1. Is there a relationship between creativity and physical disability?
2. When you choose a friend, on what basis do you make that choice:
   a. personality?
   b. appearance?

Hera married Zeus unwillingly because she was aware of his fascination with other beautiful women. He had already had six other loves when he tricked Hera into seeking him by transforming himself into a cuckoo. She caught the bird as a pet, but Zeus then resumed his real form and forced her to marry him.

Gaea attended her grandchildren's wedding and brought Hera a spectacular gift, a tree on which apples of gold were growing. Hera was delighted and had it planted in her gardens far in the West, near Mount Atlas. When Atlas's daughters, the Hesperides, kept picking the apples, Hera placed the huge dragon, Ladon, in the garden to guard the tree. He had one hundred heads and as many different voices, and he was a diligent watchman.

Hera bore Zeus four children: Hebe, the cupbearer of the gods; golden-helmeted Ares, the god of war; Eileithyia, goddess of pregnancy and childbirth; and lame Hephaestus of the strong arms, the renowned metalsmith. Hera claimed that she had conceived Hephaestus without any act of love, to show that she was as independent of Zeus as he had been of her when he gave birth to Athena. Hera angrily complained:

"Notice how cloud-gathering Zeus shames me. Apart from me, he has given birth to grey-eyed Athena, a daughter who excels among all the deathless gods."

Hera felt even more embarrassed when Hephaestus, the child she had hoped would compete with Athena's excellence, turned out to be lame. The distraught mother could not bear his deformities, so she cast him out. "With my own hands," she admitted, "I took him and threw him into the deep sea."

Thus, the newborn infant, screaming hysterically with fear, fell from the summit of Mount Olympus to the dark waters below. However, just as the waves were about to engulf his body, silver-footed Thetis, daughter of the ancient sea god, Nereus, raised her arms out of the sea and caught him. She took the trembling infant beneath the dark sea to the hidden cave which she shared with Eurynome, and there the two goddesses secretly reared the little, lame god. For nine years, Hephaestus lived and played in the underwater cave. With these substitute mothers, he experienced only gentleness and love, and he became a reflection of the treatment he received. Thus Hephaestus developed into a kind, loving god, who was as beautiful within as he was misshapen without.

The lame god learned that he could receive great satisfaction and joy from expressing the love he felt and the beauty he observed in his underwater home. First, using shells, pebbles, coral, and other jewels of the sea, and later working with the gold and silver the sea-goddesses brought him, he began to create magnificent jewelry. While the ocean roared outside his cave, in the secure peace of his sheltered home, he fashioned necklaces, bracelets, and brooches, and each was a unique work of art. No one else, whether god or man, could create such beauty.

When Thetis and Eurynome realized Hephaestus's brilliant talent as a goldsmith, they encouraged him to make golden sandals for all the Olympians. He agreed to their request and, when they next attended an assembly of the deathless gods, Thetis and Eurynome arrived bearing Hephaestus's gifts. They brought golden sandals for Zeus and all the other Olympian gods, all, that is, except for Hera. For his mother, Hera, the lame god had designed a golden throne. The immortals were captivated by the beauty of their sandals, and especially by the incomparable beauty of Hera's throne. They pleaded with Thetis and Eurynome to bring the young artist up to Mount Olympus so that he could join his family and live in splendor.

Hera was proud that Hephaestus had remembered his mother. She was especially pleased that the other gods were envious of her gift. Why, what were golden sandals, compared to a magnificent throne! Without making an excessive display, Hera sat down upon her golden throne. She conversed in royal comfort until the assembly began to disperse. Then, when she tried to rise, she found that she could not move. Although she could not see them, she could feel that she was bound to her chair with invisible cords. She tried gentle pressure; she tried sudden force; she wriggled in one direction; she strained in the opposite direction. However, she could not break loose. She was inextricably bound to her golden throne. None of the immortals could free her, because no one could see her fetters.

There golden-throned Hera sat, while Eurynome and Thetis returned to their cave beneath the sea and to the brilliant craftsman. Would he free Hera? Most certainly not! After all, she had thrown him away! In fact, he said that he did not have a mother. So there Hera sat, while the gods did their best to persuade Hephaestus to come to Mount Olympus and to forgive and free his mother. But Hephaestus remained adamant.

Finally, loud-roaring Dionysus, whom the lame god trusted as his friend, made Hephaestus drunk and persuaded him to join the gods on Mount Olympus. There Hephaestus confronted his mother, Hera, at long last. The queen of Olympus swore an oath on the River Styx that he, indeed, was her child. Because she had publicly acknowledged him as her son, the lame smith forgave her and freed her.

Olympian Zeus then gave his royal son Hephaestus his choice of what he wanted. The renowned smith chose the grey-eyed goddess, Athena, as his gift, but she refused to take any husband. Therefore, he selected golden Aphrodite, and they were married.

Gold-wreathed Aphrodite, however, preferred handsome men, especially Hephaestus's brother, golden-helmeted Ares. When shining Helius saw Ares dishonoring Hephaestus's marriage, he told the lame god. Hephaestus knew that he was no match physically for the golden-helmeted god of war. However, Hephaestus's weapons were his imagination and his clever hands. Going to his forge, the lame craftsman made an invisible chain which could not be bent or broken. He wove it into a fine net, which he carried to his bedroom. There he hung it from the roof beams and fastened it around the bedposts. When he was satisfied with the arrangement of his trap, he pretended to travel to the island of Lemnos.

Golden-helmeted Ares secretly watched with delight as the lame smith left. Then he and Aphrodite hastened to a reunion in that specially prepared bed. As they lay down, a cobweb of chains descended upon them, confining them as if they were in a cage, naked and embarrassed.

When shining Helius informed the metalsmith of his success, Hephaestus felt partially avenged. He then summoned his father, loud-thundering Zeus, to witness the shameful scene. Poseidon, the Earth-shaker, far-shooting Apollo, and Hermes, the Wayfinder, could not resist the unusual entertainment, but the goddesses kept a modest distance.

Hephaestus remained on Mount Olympus until he sided with his mother, Hera, in a dispute with loud-thundering Zeus. This so angered the Lord of Olympus that, in his fury, he grabbed his son's foot and threw him off Mount Olympus, the second time Hephaestus had been thrown from there. The lame god soared through the sky for an entire day and then fell upon the island of Lemnos, becoming more lame than ever.

Later, Hephaestus returned to Mount Olympus, where he was forgiven by Zeus. Thereafter he designed magnificent armor for Thetis's great mortal son, Achilles, in the war against Troy. He also made golden arrows for Artemis, the archer-goddess, and silver ones for her far-shooting brother, Apollo. He created Pandora for his father, far-seeing Zeus, and he built grand palaces for all the Olympian gods. Thus, although he was in many ways the least fortunate of all the immortals, lame Hephaestus was the most talented.

His mother, golden-throned Hera, on the other hand, spent most of her time exacting cruel vengeance upon the many loves and children of her unfaithful Olympian husband. She never could be very proud of her other son, golden-helmeted Ares. Although he was the first to create armor and to arm mortal soldiers, he lacked courage and self-discipline. The immortals despised him for his emotional outbursts and his destructive nature.

1. Compare and contrast Hephaestus and Ares with regard to
   a. physical appearance.
   b. personality.
   c. contribution to society.
2. What do you most admire in Hephaestus? What do you admire in Ares?
3. Create a dialogue between Hephaestus and Ares in which they discuss the war between the Titans and the gods.
4. The gods favored Hephaestus over Ares, yet Hephaestus was thrown off Mount Olympus twice. As the goddess Athena, explain to Hera and Zeus why Hephaestus should live on Mount Olympus.

10 Leto and Apollo

Apollo, like Athena, became one of the three major Olympian deities. Yet, like Athena, he existed in his own right before the patriarchal religion of Zeus incorporated him. Scholars believe that Apollo, like his mother Leto and his sister Artemis, probably originated in Asia Minor, in the area of Lycia or possibly Troy. Since many communities claimed his birth, his birthplace was described as the moving island of Delos. Even as an Olympian deity, Apollo remained the protector of his mother and was known as "Leto's son."

One of Apollo's titles in Asia Minor was god of mice. As a mouse god, Apollo, like mice, would have been born where the sun never shone, beneath the earth's surface. He also would have been a prophetic god, since those who worshipped mice considered these rodents to be oracular animals. Mice were also feared as the bringers of plague. Apollo, in this early form would have been a god who brought both death and healing: by controlling the population and activities of mice, he had it within his power to bring plague upon mortals or to remove it.

Once he became an Olympian god, Apollo kept his ability to heal and to bring sudden death. The mighty archer with his silver bow was thought to cause all deaths from illness, accident, and natural causes such as old age. Apollo had the power to bring an easy death upon a mortal by shooting him gently with one of his silver arrows. Thus, whenever a mortal died, the Greeks attributed his death to specific external causes. The three Fates determined how long a mortal would live, but his death would be caused by other men, or by Apollo, or, in the case of suicide, by the person himself.

With incorporation into the Olympian family, Apollo retained his oracular power. He acquired local oracles, throughout Greece and established himself at Delphi, by killing the serpent, Python, which guarded the sacred shrine of the Titan Themis at Pytho.

The new patriarchal religion thereby scored a major victory: the reigning prophetic Great Goddesses, first Gaea and then Themis, had been replaced by a male divinity who would henceforth perform their role. The role of mother earth as prophet was so important to humankind that Apollo's power was assured among the deathless Olympians. For hundreds of years, people of high and low estate continued to seek the oracle's advice about the conduct of their lives. The oracle remained reliable, possibly because the answers given by the oracle Pythia were so cryptic and ambiguous that numerous interpretations were possible.

Apollo advocated the principal ideal of the Greek people, *know thyself*. In order to know what they were, men and women also needed to remember what they were not. They were not immortal gods. The deathless gods would endure eternally, whereas humankind, in spite of its resemblance to the gods in form and in attributes, would perish at a time which would be beyond its knowledge and beyond its control. On the other hand, human beings were also not animals. They possessed the ability to reason and were capable of responding to situations with premeditated behavior. Therefore, they should reject excess emotionalism and let discipline, restraint, and thought dictate their approach to life. Then they would achieve the *golden mean*.

Like the music of his lyre, Apollo himself embodied the moderate behavior he espoused. He became the most intellectual and spiritual of the Olympian gods, second in esteem only to Zeus, his father. His thoughtful restraint set him apart from many of the other Olympian gods, who were impetuous and volatile. Gods and men stood in awe of Apollo, respecting and envying his ability to control his emotions and determine his responses.

ANTICIPATIONS

1. People have always wanted to know their future. Today, astrologers allegedly reveal our destinies. Find the sign under which you were born. Using the horoscope section of your local newspaper, bring to class the prophecy that applies to you. Discuss the prophecies for each month.
   a. To what extent does your prophecy apply specifically to you?
   b. To what extent does this prophecy apply to everyone else in the room as well?
   c. How do you determine the validity of such prophecies?

THE MYTH

Leto, daughter of the Titans Coeus and Phoebe, was another love of Olympian Zeus. Golden-throned Hera hated Leto because she knew that the lovely Titan was destined to bear a son who would be dearer to Zeus than Hera's own royal sons, Hephaestus and Ares. Therefore, she imposed an irrevocable punishment upon the gentle Titan. Leto, she announced, must give birth in a location where the sun never shone. Furthermore, Hera threatened divine vengeance upon any city which helped Leto.

Python, the huge dragon that guarded the oracle of Themis at Pytho, on Mount Parnassus, was another enemy of Leto. Python knew that it was destined to be killed by a child of Leto's. Therefore, when the monster learned that Leto was pregnant, it chased her from place to place over the known earth in the attempt to prevent her from giving birth. No community would give Leto refuge because each city feared great Hera's wrath.

However, the Lord of Olympus, who protected those he loved, ordered the wind to carry Leto safely away from Python to Zeus's great brother, Poseidon. Although no immortal could retract another immortal's decree, he could take action that would affect its impact. Thus, the Lord of the Sea took lovely Leto to the rocky island of Delos and flooded the island so that Python would not be able to find her there. The ruse worked, and Python returned to the oracle at Pytho.

Until Leto arrived, Delos was a floating island, buffeted by wind-tossed waves. However, once Leto arrived, four tall pillars rose from the depths of the sea and permanently fixed the island's location. Then, while strong winds swept huge waves upon the island's shores blocking out the rays of the sun, Leto knelt and clung to a palm tree. There she gave birth to twins, the god Apollo and the goddess Artemis.

Leto's aunts, Rhea, Dione, and Themis, were present at the birth of the twins. They bathed the newborn infants with fresh water, wrapped them in new, white sheets and tied the sheets with golden bands. Then Themis fed the babies with nectar and ambrosia.

As soon as long-haired Apollo had consumed the food and drink of the immortals, he kicked so vigorously that he broke the bands and removed his confining infant sheet. While his attending relatives gasped in amazement, he matured before their staring eyes. Then, the young golden-clad god announced, "I want to carry the curved silver bow and the lyre and reveal to mortal men the will of my father Zeus."[1] With these words, far-shooting Apollo left the goddesses and set out to find a location for his oracle.

Four days after his birth, he came upon the site of Pytho on the slopes of Mount Parnassus. There, Python, remembering the prophecy that he would be killed by Leto's child, tried to prevent the god's entrance. However, Apollo immediately killed him with his invincible silver bow and arrow for attempting to kill his mother Leto.[2] He then took over the oracle from the Mother Goddess, Themis,[3] and announced, "I shall build a beautiful temple here and, through prophecies, I shall give mortals reliable advice."

As far-shooting Apollo stood thinking about what kind of mortals should serve his temple in Pytho, he spied a swift, black Cretan ship sailing west in the direction of Pylos. The men on board looked so brave and able that the Far-Shooter[4] decided to investigate them further. Quickly changing himself into a dolphin swimming in the dark sea, he leaped boldly upward, out of the water, and, with a high, graceful arch of his shining body, he landed upon the deck of the ship.

There the great animal thrashed about, rattling the wooden beams and frightening the sailor-merchants. The mortals learned that part of their fears were justified. Although no harm came either to themselves or to their ship, they found themselves embarked upon a most peculiar voyage. Their ship sailed on and on, no matter how or where they tried to guide it. They were unable to land upon the sandy shores of Pylos, which had been their original destination. Instead, they found themselves heading north toward Ithaca and then east again toward the dawn. Finally, the ship sailed into the community of Crisa, which was the closest seaport to Pytho. There, the dolphin leaped back into the sea, flashing fire like the midday sun.

A short time later, the Lord of the Silver Bow[4] again boarded the Cretan ship with a flying leap, this time in the disguise of a vigorous young man. He then inquired of the seamen:

"Who are you, strangers? Are you traders from King Minos of Cnossus, or are you wandering pirates who court danger and bring death and destruction to your victims? Why aren't you busily preparing to go ashore for fresh food? You are resting here on board as if you were afraid of something."

The Cretan captain responded courageously, "Stranger, you look more like one of the deathless gods than a mortal youth, so welcome and good luck to you. Please tell us, where are we? Some immortal determined our direction and forced us away from our original destination. Now we simply would like to return home to Crete."

To this, the young man explained: "You will never return to your families and your homes for I am Apollo, the son of Zeus, and I have brought you to these shores to take charge of my temple. You will know the wishes of the Olympian gods, and mortal men will honor you always. Therefore, prepare an altar upon the shore, and pray to me as Delphinius,[5] since it was in the shape of a dolphin that I first appeared to you. Call my altar Delphinian, and my temple and sanctuary high above us in Pytho, Delphi.[6] When you have poured libations to the other deathless gods who live on Mount Olympus, and after you have eaten, then follow me up Mount Parnassus to my sacred location."

The Cretan seamen obeyed the divine commands. However, when

they reached Delphi, they were disturbed by the rocky landscape. The captain asked anxiously: "How can we live up here, on land which will not support vineyards or meadows?"[7]

Apollo smiled upon him. "You are foolish to prefer the hard life of farmers to a life of ease. Mortal worshippers will bring you a multitude of sheep. As my priests, you will live very well as long as you keep my temple, reveal my will to mortal men, and live honorably."

And so they did.

1. Apollo became the god of archery, music, and prophecy.
2. For this, Apollo is often called Pythian Apollo, and the prophetess who delivered his oracles is called the Pythia.
3. All oracles were originally female.
4. Apollo.
5. Delphinius derives from the Greek word *delphis*, which means "dolphin." Thus, Delphinius is a flower that means "he of the dolphin."
6. *Delphys* means womb in Greek. The ancient Greeks considered Delphi to be the navel or the exact center of the earth.
7. Today olive orchards surround the site of Delphi.

REFLECTIONS

1. Why did Apollo appear before the sailors in the form of a dolphin?
2. Choose people with whom you want to work, and dramatize Apollo's choice of his priests.
3. Choosing one of the following, write a report on an early aspect of medical treatment. Include the reason for the procedure.
   a. blood-letting
   b. surgery
   c. use of herbs
   d. dentistry
   e. charms and potions

11 Leto and Artemis

Artemis probably originated in Asia Minor like her mother, Leto, and her twin brother, Apollo. However, she was worshipped in Greece as the Great Goddess or the Mother Goddess before the Greek-speaking tribes from the North brought the worship of Zeus into ancient Greece. Those who worshipped her in the early times did not have the male-dominated Olympian concept of marriage. As we have seen, a woman was permitted to love freely as long as the men were not members of her group or clan. Originally, Artemis wielded tremendous power, including the supervision of such life giving processes as the birth and nurturing of children. Ironically, sacrifices to her apparently included human beings, both male and female.

When the religion of Zeus incorporated Artemis, the external appearance and habits of this goddess changed drastically. Artemis became a maiden goddess who defended her virginity with her golden bow. She left the farmer's fields for the solitude and natural beauty of the forests and mountain meadows. There she roamed freely among the wild animals, hunting some while protecting others, or else she joined maiden goddesses in collecting wildflowers. Those gods and mortals who, upon occasion, were permitted to accompany Artemis, always shared her dedication to celibacy.

However, Artemis did not resign all of her former powers. On the island of Crete she was called the Mistress of Wild Things. She continued to help women with childbirth along with Hera and Eileithyia,[1] and to direct them in the care of their young children. She was considered to be the cause of sudden death if a woman had not been ill before she died. Like her brother Apollo, Artemis's golden arrows could bring a gentle death when she chose.

Artemis continued to demand human sacrifices even after she had become one of the twelve major Olympian deities. This was how she traditionally avenged any slight to her honor, such as a neglected altar or harm to one of her sacred animals. It is possible that her demands for sacrifice were so savage that mortals were tempted to evade them.[2] However, death invariably was the punishment for such neglect.

1. The existence of three goddesses who help mortal women with childbirth suggests that giving birth was a very hazardous situation for women and for infants.
2. See the myth of the Calydonian Boar Hunt (Section III: The World of Man).

THE MYTH

When Artemis became three years old, the Lord of Olympus commanded lovely Leto to bring their young daughter to Mount Olympus so that the little goddess could receive special gifts from her great father. When they arrived, Olympian Zeus placed his child upon his knee and asked her what presents she would like to have.

The lovely little goddess replied:

"I would like you to give me a golden bow and golden arrows, made for me by the giant Cyclopes who make your lightning bolts. Next, I would like you to dress me in a knee-length tunic so that I can move easily as I hunt wild animals. I also would like you to command the sixty maiden daughters of Oceanus to become my personal attendants. Finally, I would like you to give me all the mountains on earth to be my sacred locations, for I intend to live there. Cities do not interest me. Since the Fates have decreed that I shall help women in childbirth and then teach them how to nourish their young children, I shall visit the cities only when women need my aid."

Zeus hugged his little daughter and replied:

"It is worth facing jealous Hera's anger to have you as my child. I will grant all your requests and more besides. The mortals in thirty cities will honor you above all other immortals, and many other mortals will worship you. Moreover, you shall become the protector of streets and harbors."

Then Olympian Zeus summoned his renowned lame smith, Hephaestus, and told him to take Artemis to Brontes, one of the three giant Cyclopes who helped Hephaestus. Hephaestus carried the little goddess into his workshop, where she sat bravely upon the Cyclops's lap. Then she commanded:

"Great Cyclopes, make for me a golden bow with golden arrows and a golden quiver to hold them. In return for your gifts, I shall feed you the wild animals which I shall kill with these weapons." Brontes agreed, and Hephaestus, the lame smith, gave the Archer-Goddess a golden chariot and golden bridles for the two deer which would transport it.

Artemis of the Raining Arrows became a great huntress. She always guarded her maidenhood with her well-strung golden bow and her golden arrows and punished with demands for human sacrifice those who violated her sacred shrines.

REFLECTIONS

1. What did Artemis's association with hunting reveal about the Greeks who worshipped her?
2. What qualities must such a goddess possess?

12 Maia and Hermes

The Titan Maia originally was a local Great Goddess whose sacred shrine was a cave on Mount Cyllene in Arcadia. When the invading Greek-speaking people moved into Arcadia, Olympian Zeus added Maia to his group of female conquests.

Their child, Hermes, was one of the most appealing Greek divinities, possibly because he exhibited personality traits that a broad segment of people can appreciate. He was the most "human" of the Greek gods, combining a lively intelligence with imagination, goodness, and a sense of humor. It was difficult to resist his irrepressible, fun-loving personality, because his mischievous deeds did no serious harm and, in fact, were not intended to hurt anyone.

Like Cronus and Prometheus, Hermes was crafty and cunning. These qualities were more necessary and were more appreciated in certain societies and in certain stages of civilization than they were in others. They accompanied a society in transition from the pastoral to the urban. They reflected independent, self-centered, acquisitive values as opposed to group-dominated values that emphasized conformity and equality. Thus, when Zeus made Hermes the patron god of liars and thieves, he also made him the patron of merchants, whom the ancient Greeks believed were also cunning and crafty. The myth gave Hermes credit for establishing a uniform system of weights and measures. Consequently, Hermes can be viewed as the father of commerce.

Of all the Olympians, Hermes was the friendliest to mortals. Because his personality enabled him to sympathize with their plight, Hermes was at their side whenever they needed a guide. As his father Zeus's messenger, Hermes helped the hero Perseus.[1]

He was the God of Roads, guiding travelers while Zeus protected them.[2] As part of this function, Hermes was the god who, upon a mortal's death, guided his or her shade down to the land of grim Hades. Thus, the son of Maia accompanied mortals on all their journeys, those made in daylight and those taken in the dark of night. When they were most afraid, Hermes was there, compassionately, to understand and to direct, to reassure and to protect.

1. Hermes also helps the hero, Odysseus, in *The Odyssey*. In *The Iliad*, Hermes compassionately leads King Priam of Troy through the camp of the Greek warriors to the tent of Achilles to plead for Hector's body.
2. Scholars have seen a connection between Hermes' name and the Greek word *herma* or *hermaion*, which mean "stone heap." For years, Hermes had been called the God of the Stone Heap, since from the days before Zeus, travelers would leave a stone upon an existing pile at a crossroads in thanks for their successful journey. However, some modern scholars of ancient Greek script (*Linear B*) feel that others have read too much meaning into too little evidence.

ANTICIPATIONS

1. Is it an asset or a handicap to be clever? Discuss.
2. In what ways do people lie to themselves and to others?
   a. excuses
   b. denial
   c. rationalization
   d. blaming others
   e. silence
   f. half-truths

THE MYTH

While married to Hera, Zeus also loved Maia, who was the daughter of his great Titan enemy, Atlas. Maia shyly lived inside a dark cave, on the wooded and rocky slopes of Mount Cyllene, in Arcadia, away from all the immortal gods. There Zeus loved her secretly at night, while the unsuspecting queen of Olympus slept, and, there, their child, Hermes, was born. Even as an infant, glad-hearted Hermes was a calculating schemer, an expert musician, and a robber of cattle.

Hermes was born as dawn with rosy fingers made the day light. Shortly thereafter, he became hungry for adventure and, therefore, left his cradle in order to search for the cattle of Apollo. However, as he left his cave, he came upon a tortoise. "Oh, what good luck!" he exclaimed. "Alive you may be a spell against witchcraft, but dead you shall make beautiful music." He proceeded to pick up the creature and carry it back inside the cave, where he cut off its legs and scooped out its organs with an iron chisel. Then he cut reed stalks of proper size, pierced the tortoise shell, and fastened the stalks to the shell. Next, he stretched oxhide over the shell, added two arms and a bridge, and stretched seven sheep-gut strings along the bridge.

Shining Helius's chariot had pulled the sun high in the heavens by the time clever Hermes had completed his instrument. The infant then plucked each string with a plectrum, creating lovely music, and in a beautiful voice, he sang of Olympian Zeus and of Maia, and of his own glorious birth.

Soon, however, he tired of his new toy. Placing it in his cradle, he remembered that he had intended to search for the cattle of far-shooting Apollo. Now he left the cave in search of meat, for, by this time, he was very hungry.

The horses of Helius were pulling the chariot of the sun into the ocean when Hermes came upon the immortal cattle of the gods grazing in their meadows. Since their cowherd, the Far-Shooter, was nowhere in sight, Hermes craftily led fifty cattle backward over the sandy shores of the loud-roaring sea so that all their tracks led toward the meadow. To disguise his own footprints, the clever infant wove a pair of wicker sandals from leafy myrtle twigs. Then, as he drove the small herd of cows, the infant shepherd noticed an old man working in his vineyard.

"Pretend that you have seen nothing and heard nothing," the young god called out to the old man, "because no one is harming anything which is yours." Then, Hermes drove the cattle through the countryside toward Pylos until dawn with rosy fingers would soon remove the sheltering cover of night.

Shining Selene, Goddess of the Moon, was watching from the heavens while cunning Hermes watered, fed, and penned the stolen cattle in a cave. Next, he created a way of making fire by rubbing sticks together. Upon this fire, he sacrificed two cows, roasting their meat and dividing it into twelve portions for the Olympian gods (including himself), while he stretched their skins on a hard, dry rock. Although the sweet smell of the meat sorely tempted him, he could not permit himself to eat the sacred sacrificial flesh.

When Hermes had finished his work, he threw his sandals into the river and extinguished his fire with sand. He returned to his dim cave as dawn with rosy fingers made the day light. He had met no living creature on his return. However, he quickly climbed into his cradle to the right of his lyre, wrapped himself in his infant sheet, and innocently lay there playing with his wrappings.

Maia, however, was not deceived by her infant son's pretext of innocence. "What is going on here, little schemer?" she asked. "What have you been doing outside in the middle of the night? If Leto's son doesn't tie you up and drag you away, you'll become a cattle thief! I'm afraid you're going to be nothing but a mischief-maker!"

Cunning Hermes replied, "Why, Mother, how can you accuse me, a mere infant, who is most afraid of displeasing his mother? However, I shall do my best to provide for the two of us. I have no intention of giving up gifts and honor by living isolated from the other immortals in this dismal cave. We should live in friendship with the immortal gods, and be wealthy as they are. If my father will not make me an honored god, I shall become a great robber, and if the Far-Shooter tries to find me, I shall steal from his rich temple in Delphi."[1]

Dawn was making the day light when Apollo found the old man grazing his flock and spoke to him: "Old man, I am searching for my curved-horn cattle, which wandered away from the meadow at sunset last evening. Have you seen anyone pass by with them?"

The old man replied, "It is hard to remember all that happens because one sees so many things, some good, others evil. However, as I was working in my vineyard, I think I saw a child, actually an infant holding a staff, who drove some curved-horn cattle backwards so that their heads faced him."

Apollo of the Silver Bow quickly continued on his way. He saw a huge bird with wings widespread and recognized, by this omen of Zeus's eagle, that the culprit was another of his father's sons. Soon he discovered the strange backward-turning tracks of cattle, plus even stranger tracks which he could not interpret.

"What wonders do my eyes behold!" he exclaimed. "These are cattle tracks, but they are heading toward the meadow. And here are other tracks which cannot belong to mortal men or to wolves, or bears, or lions, or even Centaurs."[2]

Far-shooting Apollo hurried on his way, and he soon arrived at the hidden cave on Mount Cyllene. There, he angrily entered the dark cavern. When cunning Hermes saw that Apollo was furious about his cattle, he rubbed his eyes with his little hands and snuggled into his infant sheet as if he were a sleepy, newborn baby. However, he really was very much awake.

The Lord of the Silver Bow noticed lovely Maia and her little son. Then he inspected their cave closely for signs of the theft. Finally, he spoke to the clever infant. "Oh, child, you had better tell me quickly what you have done with my cattle, or I shall hurl you down into dark Tartarus where you will remain imprisoned forever."

To this threat, crafty Hermes replied:

"Son of Leto, do I deserve such harsh words from you? What would I know about your cattle? Do I look like a shepherd? I have cared only for warmth, for my mother's milk, for a warm bath, and for a good nap. How could I, a newborn child, drive cattle? This would indeed be a wonder, even among the deathless gods. After all, I was only born yesterday, and my feet are not tough enough to trod the rough ground. However, if you wish, I will swear by my father's head that I have not heard anyone speak of your cattle, nor have I seen anyone steal them."

Meanwhile, the wily infant turned away from Apollo and whistled casually, pretending that Apollo's story had nothing to do with him. The

Far-Shooter laughed appreciatively at his step-brother's skill in deception. He picked up the precocious infant and replied: "I think you are a mischievous rascal! Your innocent words do not fool me! You probably have robbed many a house tonight. Surely you deserve the title of master thief. I shall find my cattle, and you will direct my search."

As Apollo carried Hermes out of the cave, the cunning child cried out, "Where are you taking me, mighty son of Leto? Let our father, Zeus, decide which of us is right."

Apollo agreed, and the two stepbrothers climbed to the top of Mount Olympus. There the scales of judgment were set before them, and the assembly of immortals gathered to hear their arguments.

When Hermes the Shepherd and Apollo of the Silver Bow stood before Olympian Zeus, their loud-thundering father turned to Leto's great son and asked him: "Apollo, why have you brought this infant child to Mount Olympus?"

The Lord of the Silver Bow told his great father about the theft of his cattle including the backward tracks of the animals and the second set of tracks which looked as if someone were walking upon oak branches strapped to his feet. He also reported the words of the farmer and the declaration of the wily infant as he lay snuggled in his cradle in the depths of the dark cave.

Once Apollo had finished, the infant shepherd defended himself before the council of deathless Olympians. Using the same approach he had devised earlier for the benefit of his great step-brother, the wily infant again pleaded honesty, infancy, ignorance, and innocence. He concluded his defense with a declaration of his love for his majestic father. Meanwhile he innocently looked all about him and held his infant sheet prominently over his arm, so that the great council would consider his young age and believe in his innocence.

Olympian Zeus laughed aloud at his clever child's skillful denial. However, he was not deceived. He commanded the wily young shepherd to show far-shooting Apollo where he had hidden the cattle, and the infant god did not hesitate to obey his great father's decree.

As soon as the two sons of Zeus reached sandy Pylos and the cave in the cliff, Apollo spied the two cowhides drying upon the rock. When he realized that the newborn infant had actually slaughtered two cows, he was filled with amazement and admiration for the strength and talent of Maia's son.

Hermes, meanwhile, was uncertain of the Far-Shooter's reaction to his deed, now that all the evidence was before him. Consequently, the clever infant decided to soothe his brother's anger by introducing his lyre, which he proceeded to play with great musicianship.

The Lord of the Silver Bow laughed with delight as he listened to

Hermes' songs, and he wished that that instrument were his own. Therefore, he announced to Maia's son:

"Cunning thief of cattle, your music is worth fifty cows. So, I think we can settle our argument peacefully. But, tell me, how did you ever learn to make such marvelous music? I have never heard anyone play so well. Now, you and your mother will receive great respect from the Olympians. In fact, I will make you an honored leader among the deathless gods. I will present you with glorious gifts, and I will never deceive you."

Glad-hearted Hermes replied artfully: "I do not object if you wish to learn my skill, for you are among the most powerful and illustrious of the immortal gods, and I would like to be your friend. Therefore, take my lyre. Play it with a gentle touch, and it will reward you with melodious sound. Receive this gift from me, and, in return, give me glory. Meanwhile, I will herd your cattle. You are a good bargainer, so you no longer have any need to be angry with me."

The Lord of the Silver Bow accepted the lyre and gave Maia's son a shining whip for the cattle, which delighted the new cowherd. Together, they drove the cows to the sacred meadow, then returned to the snow-covered summit of Mount Olympus, accompanied by Apollo's beautiful music. Clever Hermes, also, was busily creating lovely sound, for he was playing his latest musical invention, a pipe made from reeds.

Then far-shooting Apollo said: "Son of Maia, since our great father has commanded you to teach mortal men the skills of commerce, I fear that you may cleverly steal my lyre and even my curved bow. I would be relieved if you would take the great oath of the gods, upon the waters of the River Styx, that you will never make me one of your victims."

After Hermes agreed and had taken this oath, Apollo took a sacred oath in return. He promised that Hermes would always be his best friend among both the immortal gods and mortal men. This oath Olympian Zeus confirmed by sending forth his eagle. The Far-Shooter then promised to give Maia's son a splendid, triple-branched, golden staff which would prevent harm and would accomplish every good task.

The one gift Maia's son asked of great Apollo which could not be granted was the skill of divine revelation. To this request, Apollo replied: "It is not Olympian Zeus's will for you or for any other immortal to learn his mysterious mind. I have sworn a sacred oath that I alone of the deathless gods shall know great Zeus's wise counsel."

"However, there are three winged sisters who also dwell on Mount Parnassus. When I was a young cowherd, they taught me to prophesy by using pebbles. I give these teachers to you for your knowledge and pleasure. Then, when you instruct a mortal, if he is fortunate, he will listen to you."

Then, from Mount Olympus, far-seeing Zeus confirmed Apollo's promises. The Loud-Thunderer also commanded Maia's clever son to become lord over boars and lions, domesticated herds, dogs, and all birds of omen. In addition, the Lord of Olympus made his cunning son the sole messenger to dark Hades, Lord of the Underworld, and the herald of truces and peaceful negotiations.

Thus, Hermes the Wayfinder became established among the deathless gods.

1. Great wealth was dedicated to Apollo and was stored in beautiful, small buildings called treasuries. Built between 657 B.C. (Corinth) and 371 B.C. (Thebes) only the ruins remain today. The major exception is the Treasury of Athens, built in 490 B.C., which was restored in 1903–1906.
2. Centaur: a creature with the head, chest, and arms of a man, plus the body and legs of a horse.

REFLECTIONS

1. Why was Hermes appealing even though he lied?
2. Why did Apollo choose Hermes to be his best friend?
3. Why did Zeus make Hermes god of merchants?
4. You are a traveling salesperson. Pick any household product and sell it to the class.
5. Role-play the appearance of Apollo and Hermes before Zeus, when they discuss the theft of Apollo's cattle.
6. Take the side of either Hermes or Apollo and present a written argument defending your position regarding the theft of the cattle.
7. Compare Hermes and Hephaestus.

13 Demeter and Persephone

Originally Demeter was a local Mother Goddess, like Rhea and Athena. She may have originated in Crete, but she was worshipped in Greece before the Greek-speaking tribes from the North brought Zeus into the area of Eleusis, near Thebes. Demeter taught mortal men how to sow and cultivate corn, which became a major source of food. Given the importance of grain and fertility to these agrarian people, the worship of Demeter was a solemn procedure which gave rise to famous religious rites.

The farming peoples needed assurance that they would survive. Their physical well-being was so dependent upon their grain crops that the Great Goddess who watched over their wheat, barley, and corn was particularly dear to their hearts. They needed divine help in order to have enough rain for their semi-arid soil throughout the spring and summer, and yet not too much rain as it would mold the seeds before they sprouted, or wreck the crops before they were harvested. Given their dependence upon their grain crops, the question of whether the seeds they had sown would sprout was literally a matter of life or death.

The long, unproductive winter gave the agrarian peoples months to worry about their next year's crop. Without a good crop, food would be very scarce during the following winter, and a poor harvest meant starvation and death. Some farmers buried a female corn doll through the winter and dug it up in the spring to see whether it had begun to sprout. A sprouting corn doll was a miracle of nature, the portent of a productive spring. The earth had lived and had died, but now it had returned to life.

The myth of Demeter, Persephone, and Hades confirmed the idea of life, death, and rebirth. It symbolized the cycles the agrarian peoples witnessed in nature each year. As long as the cycle continued unbroken, they could hope to survive. They developed an agricultural and religious ritual that became famous throughout the ancient world. Called the Eleusinian mysteries, it was based upon the myth of Demeter and Persephone.

Demeter was called "Mother of Wealth,"[1] and another name for Hades was Pluto or Plouton (the Greek word *ploutos* means wealth). Both immortals were necessary for a wealth of crops to emerge from the barren earth and mature to harvest. Persephone[2] became the vital link between the two life-giving forces, for she would alternate between the land of life and the land of death and rebirth, personally supervising the continuous operation of the life-supporting cycle of fertility.

The idea that it was possible to produce a particular result by dramatizing it founded the Eleusinian ritual. Thus, in order to assure the fertility of the grain crops, each year in Eleusis and in other locations sacred to Demeter, specially chosen people would be permitted to take the parts of Persephone, Hades, Demeter, and several minor characters, to perform the myth as a sacred play. To act in the ritual was, of course, a great honor, for the person who played the part of an immortal became that powerful being for the duration of the performance.

The myth of Demeter also emphasized the concept of hospitality. The agrarian people were a generally peaceful and non-aggressive society, treating others with humanity and generosity. The religion of Olympian Zeus continued to stress these principles, even when Mycenaean palaces had become defensive fortresses with outer walls twenty to thirty feet thick. Given the propensity of the immortals to arrive upon some mortal's doorstep disguised as a weary stranger, the host took his obligations to guests seriously. His behavior could determine his fate.

1. Metalsmiths also worshipped Demeter as the mother of their wealth, which also came from the earth.
2. The name Persephone became a sacred, secret name. Mortals always referred to her as Kore unless religious rites were involved.

ANTICIPATIONS

1. What effects do seasonal changes have upon our lives?
2. What effects did seasonal changes have upon the lives of ancient Greeks?
3. Explain in what way a person who manipulates another person is to blame for his or her actions. Explain the role of the person who is manipulated.

THE MYTH

After each volcanic eruption on the island of Sicily, grim Hades, who ruled the dead, would leave his dark land beneath the earth in order to inspect the damage. He feared that cracks in the earth would permit daylight to penetrate his kingdom. This would terrify his subjects, who had become accustomed to perpetual darkness.

The Lord of the Dead was driving his golden coach on one of these occasions when gold-wreathed Aphrodite saw him as she was resting on her flower-strewn hill. She hugged her son, Eros, who was beside her, and said, "Take your powerful weapons and shoot one of your winged arrows into the dark lord's heart, now, while he is away from his misty land. Shall grim Hades remain free of our power, when we have persuaded the Lord of Olympus[1] and the Earthshaker[2] to our cause? Also it will increase our power to make fair-haired Demeter's daughter, Persephone, our subject. She, like her childhood companions, grey-eyed Athena and Artemis of the Golden Arrows, openly scoffs at the idea of love."

Love-inspiring Eros obediently chose the sharpest arrow in his quiver, bent his bow, and directed his arrow swiftly and accurately into the dark lord's heart, where it lodged. Immediately, the Lord of the Underworld[3] noticed fair Persephone, who was radiant with joy as she played among the flowers of Sicily. His heart warmed with love for the beautiful goddess. He realized how much he and his gloomy kingdom needed her gaiety and her love. Therefore, he drove his golden chariot up to the summit of Mount Olympus where he asked Loud-Thundering Zeus—his brother and Persephone's father—for her hand in marriage.

The Lord of Olympus replied: "Our sister, fair-wreathed Demeter will never agree to this marriage. The Mother of Wealth and her daughter are devoted to the radiant beauty of the earth. Neither will agree to exchange the beauty of sunlight sparkling upon leaves and flowers for the cold, damp mists which shroud the shades of the dead. Therefore, if you want the fair Persephone you will have to abduct her. You can always find her gathering the flowers she loves in the fragrant meadows near Mount Aetna, in Sicily."

The Lord of the Underworld accepted his brother's advice as permission for the abduction. Then he returned to his dark land to make the necessary preparations for the arrival of his bride.

Shortly thereafter, the Maiden Goddess was gathering her favorite flowers: lilies, violets, hyacinths, irises, and roses, into her lap when she noticed a beautiful flower that she had never seen before. She left grey-eyed Athena and Artemis of the Golden Arrows behind with the many daughters of Oceanus in order to take a closer look. It never occurred to her that her father, Zeus of the Wise Counsels, had persuaded Gaea to create a profusion of these delightful, fragrant blossoms in order to assist her grim uncle with his plan; and that the flowers were a trap.

The fair Persephone had just reached out with both hands to gather the lovely flowers when the earth in front of her suddenly collapsed. Before the young goddess could react, a golden chariot drawn by four deathless horses emerged from the chasm. The driver, a tall, dark, handsome god, gathered her up and dashed off with her, as she struggled beneath the grip of his strong arm.

Fair Persephone tried to free herself from grim Hades' grip, but her strength was no match for his. Terrified and weeping, she cried out for help, but there was no response. Frantically, the lovely young goddess searched the fertile earth, the dark sea, and the starry heavens, hoping to see her powerful father or her loving mother hurrying to her aid, but all was still. It was as if all life had frozen, and only she and the golden chariot were moving.

The dark lord transported his captive over mountains and through valleys as he sped toward his underworld palace. The immortal horses, responding to their master's excitement and sense of urgency, sped relentlessly onward.

They were driving through a lake when a water nymph, who recognized fair-haired Demeter's daughter, cried out to Hades, "Go no further, dark lord! Fair-wreathed Demeter will never permit this. The fair Persephone does not deserve such inconsiderate treatment. What you are accomplishing by force, you should win by gentle persuasion."

With outstretched arms, the nymph desperately tried to stop the chariot, but Hades, impatient with her unsolicited advice, restrained his wrath no longer. Giving his terrible horses the rein, he took his iron scepter and plunged it into the bottom of the lake. Upon contact, it created an unobstructed passage down into the depths of the earth. Into this dark chasm the chariot descended, its rich golden glow now extinguished by the blackness of eternal night.

Meanwhile, lovely-haired Demeter suddenly heard the Sicilian mountain peaks echoing with her daughter's cries. A dreadful pain constricted her heart as she felt the terror in her child's voice. Frantically the fair-wreathed goddess rushed to the slopes of Mount Aetna, but all that remained to show that Persephone had been there was a pile of wilting flowers.

Lovely-haired Demeter searched the entire earth for her beloved daughter. To light her way, the distraught mother ignited two pitch-filled pine trees in the volcanic fires of Mount Aetna. She carried these bright torches day and night, and neither rosy-fingered dawn, nor grey dusk ever found her asleep. Neither the blazing sun, nor icy snows, nor freezing winds distracted her from her relentless pursuit. Ceaselessly she wandered over the surface of the earth, through meadows, woods, and streams, through cities and towns, across deserts and seas. However, no matter where the frantic goddess searched, no one had seen her lovely daughter. The Archer-Goddess,[4] carrying her golden bow and arrows, helped in the hunt, and golden-helmeted Athena also searched, her grey eyes now grim, as, spear in hand, she prepared to fight for her friend. However, their efforts were in vain.

One day, thirsty and exhausted from her journey, great Demeter came upon a straw-thatched cottage and decided to beg for a drink of water from whomever lived there. An old housewife responded to her knock upon the door. She gave Demeter sweet barley water to drink, even though the goddess appeared to be a common beggar with her long tangled hair and her muddy, torn clothing.

While the disheveled guest leaned against the doorway quenching her thirst, a boy named Abas approached her and examined her closely with belligerent eyes. He had overheard her humble request and was anxious to learn who was accepting his family's hospitality. Now that he had investigated the stranger, he was definitely unimpressed. A scornful grin lighted his face as he watched the beggar woman drink from the cup. "You aren't thirsty, you filthy creature! You are greedy!" he announced.

Demeter burned with rage at his insolence. She lowered the cup from her lips and stared down at him. Now that Abas noticed her eyes, he was impressed with their brightness. In fact, as her anger brought color to her haggard face, he could see that once she might have been a handsome woman. Now, however, she was simply a dirty beggar. He made no effort to conceal the sneer that his examination had produced.

Finding it easy to read his thoughts, and having had her fill of his arrogance, Demeter flung the remainder of her drink in Abas's face. To his amazement, the liquid burned wherever the drops splashed. As he stared in surprise at the strange guest, he noticed that she was much taller than she had at first appeared.

Then, he began to feel so strange that he thought only about himself. His back hurt too much to stand upright. Now he was comfortable only when he was lying down. He was shocked to realize that his arms had become much shorter and were functioning as legs. Try as he might, he could no longer stand. He could only move with a scampering motion, and then he seemed to be dragging something behind him.

By this time, the beggar woman had become a terrifying giant. Fearing that she would step on him, Abas scuttled off to the closest hiding place he could find, a crevice between two rocks in the garden.

When the old housewife returned to her guest, she looked for her grandson, whom she thought she had heard talking to the visitor, but he was nowhere to be seen. As she watched, a tiny lizard scampered off into the garden as if it were being chased by a predator. Something about its frightened movement recalled her grandson's insolent voice. Questioningly, the old woman glanced at her guest. The brilliant glow in the visitor's eyes confirmed the old housewife's fears. She wept for the youth who could not sense divinity in disguise.

The goddess continued her search. People in every land and upon every sea noticed a tall, haggard woman with a torch burning in each hand, frantically seeking something she could not find.

Finally, fair-wreathed Demeter returned to Persephone's favorite land,

Sicily. When the flowered fields still withheld the secret of her daughter's whereabouts, the Great Goddess went up to Mount Olympus and questioned shining Helius, Lord of the Sun, as he stood near his chariot. "Helius, you who observe gods and mortals," the bereft mother began, "I heard my daughter's cries as if she were being forced away against her will, but I could not see what happened to her. Since you keep watch over earth and sea, can you tell me which deathless god or mortal man carried her off?"

To this plea, the shining son of Hyperion replied, "Great Demeter, daughter of lovely Rhea, I will tell you the truth, for I pity your grief over the loss of your lovely child. Your great brother Zeus, the Cloud-Gatherer, is the only one to blame for your sorrow, for he gave lovely Persephone to your dark brother Hades to be his wife. So, with her father's approval, Persephone was seized by her grim uncle, who transported her down to his dismal kingdom. However, this should not cause you such grief. After all, the ruler of the dead is a mighty lord and one who is honored by gods and men." Having given this information and advice, shining Helius climbed into his chariot and drove off with the morning sun into the heavens above.

Fair-haired Demeter now seethed with savage rage against her great brother, Zeus, Lord of Black Clouds. She renounced the companionship of the deathless gods on Mount Olympus, resolving to dwell in the land of mortals. She transformed herself into an older woman so that no one who looked upon her could recognize her, and in this disguise she wandered through many fields and towns.

Upon reaching the city of Eleusis, northwest of Athens, she sat down at the side of the road near a shaded well. Here she would be able to quench her thirst and rest awhile, somewhat sheltered from the heat of the midday sun. When the daughters of the lord of Eleusis came to the well to fill their bronze pitchers, they saw Demeter sitting nearby and spoke to her.

"Old mother," they asked, "who are you, and where are you from? If you need employment, many women in our town would hire you as a nurse or as a housekeeper and would treat you well."

To this, the mighty goddess replied, "Dear children, whoever you are, I shall answer your questions truthfully. I was living on the island of Crete when some pirates seized me and carried me off with them. They hoped to collect gold by selling me as a slave, but I escaped from them while their thoughts were on their evening meal. I have no idea where I am, or who lives here, so if you could advise me where to seek employment as a nurse or as a housekeeper, I would be grateful to you."

The most beautiful daughter then responded: "Good woman, we mortals must accept whatever the gods give us since they are more powerful than we are. Many honorable people of noble rank will welcome you, for you also appear to be of noble birth and have the stature and bearing of an immortal. However, if you agree, wait here while we return home and see whether our own mother will employ you, for we have a young brother who needs a nurse."

The goddess agreed to wait by the well while the maidens carried their water pitchers home and discussed the matter. Their mother, Metaneira, was delighted with their news. Consequently, they returned to the well and brought the stranger back to their father's palace.

"Welcome, lady," Metaneira greeted the strange woman, "for your dignified bearing indicates one of noble birth. Yet we mortals must patiently accept whatever the gods give us. However, now that you are with us, I will share whatever I have with you. If you will agree to nurse my young son and rear him until he reaches manhood, other women will envy the rewards I shall give you."

Hoping that Metaneira's son would help ease the painful loss of her own daughter, the fair-haired goddess accepted this employment and proceeded to rear the young child as if he were truly her own son. She gave him neither food nor milk. Instead, she covered his entire body with ambrosia, and each night she placed him in the blazing fire as if he were one of the flaming logs.[5]

Being completely unaware of their employee's child-rearing techniques, Metaneira and her husband were delighted to see how quickly their son was growing and how much he was beginning to look like a young god. In fact, the Great Goddess would have made the child immortal and ageless if his mother had not spied upon her one night. As Metaneira quietly opened the door to the nursery she saw the strange woman she had hired singing to the flames in the hearth. When she discovered that her young son lay buried among the blazing logs, she shrieked with terror.

At this interruption, fair-wreathed Demeter burned with rage. She removed the child from the flames and placed him on the floor by the hearth. Then she glared at his distraught mother and declared:

"You mortals are too foolish to know what good and evil the future will bring you. I swear upon the eternal waters of the River Styx that I would have made your beloved son eternally young and alive, and I would have granted him enduring honor. Now, however, he can no longer escape that death which is every mortal's fate. However, because I nursed him and cared for him, I still will grant him enduring honor."

"Furthermore, I will give your oldest son a chariot which is drawn by winged dragons. Let him ride this chariot through the heavens and throw down upon the earth the grains of wheat I will give him so that mortals will have more food to eat. For I am the honored goddess, Demeter, who brings aid and joy to immortals and mortals. As for you, I want you to tell the people to build me a temple and an altar, and I shall instruct you in my sacred rites so that you may please me."

With these final words, Demeter assumed her divine form. She became younger, taller, and infinitely more beautiful, filling the palace with her brilliant light. Then she left.

All night long the fearful family prayed to Demeter, hoping that she would forgive their distrust. The people hastened to build the temple with its altar, and fair-wreathed Demeter was appeased.

However, the Great Goddess still longed for her own child. Her rage against Zeus had not abated. In fact, the joy she had experienced nursing the young boy now intensified her agony as a mother. Her second loss reopened her first bitter wound before it had had an opportunity to heal. The results were devastating to mortals and immortals alike.

The great Goddess of Wealth now removed herself from mortals as well from the gods. She threw herself down upon the snows of the highest mountains and ignored the needs of humankind. Originally she had made the soil fertile for the growth of nourishing plants and had taught mortals how to plow the earth, sow the corn seeds she had provided, and prepare the corn for food. Now, however, Demeter hid the seeds within the soil. The oxen plowed in vain, and man sowed his seeds in vain. Even her sacred land of Sicily, whose fertile soil produced wild wheat and barley as well as corn, suffered from her implacable anger. Without her help, the weather became the enemy of mortals.

Day after day, the blazing sun scorched the young corn plants, browning their husks and burning their tender kernels. Farmers searched the heavens for rainclouds, but in vain. The sown seeds shriveled up and rotted before they could sprout. Starving birds ravenously devoured any kernels of grain they could find, and the once fertile farmland became a barren sea of dust. Beasts of the field and forest starved to death as streams evaporated and all plant growth withered. Man, weak and sick from hunger, no longer could spare a morsel to sacrifice to the immortal gods. It seemed as if the entire human race would perish because of great Demeter's bitter anguish.

Zeus, the Lord of Olympus, observed the devastation upon the earth and felt deprived of the sacrificial honors which he and the other deathless gods enjoyed. He sent Iris of the Golden Wings to summon his fair-wreathed sister to Mount Olympus.

Demeter obeyed great Zeus's command and appeared before the Lord of Olympus. There, she knelt before him and passionately appealed to his fatherly love. "I am pleading for our child, dear brother," she began. "Even if you no longer care for me, be honorable and prove that you still love your daughter. Persephone deserves a more appropriate husband than our dark brother. What joy can she find in that dismal land of death, with a husband who abducted her? Yet, only you can return her to the world of sunlight and flowers. If you will do this for her and for me, my joy will be so great that I will forgive you for agreeing to the marriage and to the crime."

To this, far-seeing Zeus replied, "I feel the same love and responsibility for our child that you do, fair sister. Yet, is our brother's love for our daughter a crime? Does he deserve less than I do because the lot he drew gave him title to the dismal Underworld? He is, after all, our brother and a great lord."

"However, if nothing less than our daughter's return will appease your anger, I will command our brother to release her. This he will do unless she has eaten any food in his kingdom, for the Fates have decreed that any living being who eats the food of that dark land must continue to live there."

Demeter rejoined, "I will not permit the earth to yield its sweet fruits until Persephone has been returned to me." Therefore, loud-thundering Zeus sent his messenger, Hermes of the Golden Wand, down into the dismal kingdom of the dead to persuade its lord to let him bring Persephone out of that gloomy land and up to her anxious mother.

Hermes quickly descended into the depths of the earth and found fair Persephone seated beside her dark-haired husband in their palace. The son of Zeus approached his gloomy uncle and said:

"Dark-haired Hades, my father, Olympian Zeus, has commanded me to bring the lovely Persephone up to Mount Olympus to her mother, for fair-wreathed Demeter is filled with wrath and bitter anguish over the loss of her beloved daughter. The Great Goddess has removed herself from the society of immortals and mortals and has caused devastation to spread upon the earth like a plague, consuming all sources of nourishment. Therefore, mortals have become weak and sick from hunger and cannot spare a morsel to sacrifice to their deathless gods."

The Lord of All beneath the Earth smiled grimly upon his nephew as if he possessed some secret knowledge and, turning to his wife, he spoke the words she had long despaired of hearing from his lips:

"You may go to your dark-robed mother, Persephone, but remember me with kindness. As your father's brother, I am an appropriate husband for you. As my queen you rule all our subjects, and you always will receive the greatest respect, for those who offend your honor with scanty sacrifice will have to endure my eternal vengeance."

Grim Hades was still speaking to her as fair Persephone, her face alight with excitement and joy, left her husband's side to join the smiling Wayfinder.

The Ruler of All beneath the Earth then harnessed his four immortal horses to his golden chariot. As Hermes climbed into the driver's place, the dark Lord of the Dead put the reins and the whip into his hands. The lovely young goddess was mounting beside Hermes when the gardener, Ascalaphus, the son of an underworld river god, came running up to the chariot.

"Where is the fair queen going?" he shrieked. "Haven't you told her that she cannot leave?" he asked, staring at the Lord of the Dead with amazement. "Doesn't fair Persephone remember that as she wandered in the garden with you, she pulled a ripe pomegranate from one of our trees and, at your suggestion, she tasted its sweet seeds? Doesn't she realize that now she truly belongs to our kingdom?"

Persephone stopped by the chariot, her face pale, her eyes large and bleak. Not a trace of excitement or joy remained. She stared first at Ascalaphus, then at her husband, then back at Ascalaphus. The gardener was smiling expectantly, but Hades, her dark-haired lord, remained silent.

Then, with rage painting her cheeks a fiery red, the fair daughter of great Demeter suddenly turned her back on the group and proudly left them. She went to the Phlegethon River, which forms one of the boundaries of her dark lord's kingdom, and collected a pitcher of water from its flaming waves. Upon her return, she was pleased to find Ascalaphus waiting expectantly where she had left him. Her agony seemed to fascinate him.

Dipping her hand into the blazing water, the irate queen avenged herself upon the bearer of evil tidings. As she sprinkled Ascalaphus's head and face with the burning drops, his nose grew longer and curled into a crooked beak. His head became rounder, and his eyes grew larger. His arms lengthened and then sprouted yellow feathers, while his toenails developed into long, curved talons. He opened his mouth to speak, but the only sound he could emit was that of the repulsive screech-owl. Now he would proclaim evil tidings eternally.

The Lord of All beneath the Earth smiled at his lovely wife's revenge. Persephone was, indeed, a suitable queen for his dark, dismal kingdom.

Satisfied with her revenge, fair Persephone climbed into the golden chariot. Under Hermes's guidance, the four deathless horses dashed out of the palace and up through the yielding earth. Neither sea, nor meadows, nor mountains obstructed their passage, and they soon reached the summit of Mount Olympus.

There, the young goddess jumped from the chariot and ran to her mother's jubilant embrace. Their love for one another illuminated Mount Olympus as the sun brightens the earth after a thunderstorm. However, as fair-wreathed Demeter held her beloved daughter in her arms, a cloud of fear drifted across her mind, threatening her great joy.

"Did you, by chance," the anxious mother asked, "eat any food while you lived in dark Hades's dismal kingdom? This I must know, for if you abstained from your hateful husband's nourishment, then you may leave him forever to his dark land and remain in the sunlight with your father and me."

Beautiful Persephone replied, "I shall not mislead you, mother. I will tell you everything. When Hermes of the Golden Wand arrived to rescue me, I had no idea I had committed a dreadful error. Hideous Ascalaphus, son of an Underworld god, informed me that when my dark husband encouraged me to taste the sweet pomegranate seeds, he was forging our marriage bonds for eternity."

Tears flooded great Demeter's eyes as her daughter confirmed her worst fears. Theirs would be a brief reunion. Would either mother or daughter ever experience love and joy again? Fair-wreathed Demeter stood engulfed in despair.

Suddenly her own mother, the great Titan Rhea, approached her.

"Come, dear daughter," the older mother pleaded. "You can face your sorrow. I, too, suffered the loss of my children when my husband swallowed them.[7] However, I gained the strength to survive, as you, too must do. Your brother, the far-seeing Lord of Olympus, wants you to rejoin the deathless gods. In return, he offers you whatever honors you choose. He has given his word that fair Persephone will spend two of the three seasons of the year with you, either here on Mount Olympus or among the flowering meadows of the earth. The third season, only, she must spend with her dark-haired husband in his dismal kingdom."

"So, obey me, dear child. Forget your stubborn anger. Forgive your brother, and cause the life-giving seeds to nourish the mortals."

Fair-wreathed Demeter relented. Her great brother's decisions appeased her anger, and therefore she obeyed his command.

Thereafter, each year, fair Persephone would descend to her dark-haired husband's palace in his dismal kingdom, and while she was in the Underworld, great Demeter's sorrow would make the earth leafless and barren. However, in time, spring would return. Then Persephone would leave her dark lord and rejoin her loving mother, and the earth again would bloom with fragrant flowers and nourishing grains. Together, Demeter, Bringer of Seasons, and her beloved daughter would wander among the sweet meadows, collecting blossoms. Long ears of corn would provide mortals with abundant harvests, so that once again, they would be able to offer pleasing sacrifices to the deathless gods.

1. Zeus
2. Poseidon
3. Hades
4. Artemis
5. In ancient Greece, it was customary to protect infants against evil spirits which might attempt to kill them by placing them over a fire or over a heated pan; by carrying them around a central hearth or by carrying sacred fire around them.
6. Hermes
7. See the myth of Cronus (Section I, In the Beginning).

1. Write a myth in which you account for the changing seasons in another way. Set the scene in ancient Greece.
2. Take the part of Hades. Write a letter to Demeter explaining why you want Persephone to be your wife. What will she do for you and for your kingdom?
3. Role-play the following situations:
   a. Demeter and Hades come before Zeus and plead to have Persephone remain with them.
   b. Persephone discusses her preference with Zeus.
   c. Abas watches the thirsty Demeter drink the water.
   d. Metaneira watches Demeter bathe her child in the fire.
   e. Ascalaphus tells Persephone she cannot leave the Underworld.

14 Semele and Dionysus

Semele was probably a priestess of the Mother Goddess, whose worship originated in Asia Minor. However, in the religion of Zeus, she was a mortal who was loved by Zeus and thereby conceived Dionysus. Zeus eventually rewarded Semele and Dionysus with the gift of immortality.

In the traditional Greek version of the birth of Dionysus (that given in this book), Semele was killed while pregnant with Dionysus. Placing this version in matriarchal times, it is possible that her destruction represented the revolt of the sacred king against the great reigning priestess queen, who would have caused his death at the end of his term.[1] Zeus, as chief god of the patriarchal religion, can be seen as the defender and preserver of the sacred king, the male, against the power and authority of the ruling female.

When Zeus took the fetus of the infant and kept it within his own body until it was ready to be born, once again[2] the great Greek patriarchal divinity appropriated the ultimate matriarchal prerogative of giving birth. A great sexual revolution had taken place, from the supremacy of the female in a matriarchy to the supremacy of the male in a patriarchy. The males who gave Zeus the power of incubating the fetus were symbolically stripping women of their unique function of childbirth.

A second version of Dionysus' birth originated on the island of Crete and is more of a fertility myth. It reflects the agrarian worship of the Mother Goddess and the emphasis upon the life cycle of birth, death, and rebirth, which existed as a part of the Minoan civilization. Although the major Greek and Roman writers did not record this version of Dionysus' birth, it may have been accepted by a number of communities outside of Greece, and possibly by Thebes within Greece. Those communities which accepted the Minoan version appear to have dramatized it on solemn religious occasions just as communities dramatized the sister fertility myth of Demeter and Persephone.[3] Thus, in these matriarchal societies, the myth reflected current religious practices, either as a model or as a symbolic representation.

In this second version of Dionysus' birth, Zeus, in the form of a serpent, loved Persephone, who gave birth to their child, Dionysus. While the young god sat upon his father's throne, the Titans, instigated by Hera's jealousy, attacked Dionysus with knives, cut his body into pieces, boiled the pieces, and then ate them. Athena, however, rescued Dionysus' heart and gave it to Zeus. Zeus gave the heart to Semele, who became pregnant and, in time, gave Dionysus his second birth.

This version of the myth is particularly interesting because, in matriarchal societies, the sacred king was often represented as a serpent. The snake was thought to represent rebirth and immortality since it could shed its skin and emerge youthfully renewed. Consequently, the Great Goddess or her priestess is usually shown holding snakes, which represent the sacred king. Moreover, as the sacred king made an effort to prolong the term of his reign, some communities accepted the practice of permitting the sacred king to place his son upon the throne for a specified period of time. At the appropriate time, the religious community would then sacrifice the son as the sacred king, after which the original sacred king could resume the throne for another term.

Thus, when the Minoan version of the Dionysus myth was dramatized in all its bloody detail, as it was on the island of Crete and very possibly in Thrace and in Thebes as well, the sacred king (whichever king was to be sacrificed) would take the role of Dionysus and would be dismembered in the course of the performance. These sacred kings accepted their destiny either because their religion and the fervor of the people left them no alternative or because the promise of resurrection sustained them. Considered in this way, the stories of the Thracian king, Lycurgus, and the Theban king, Pentheus, which are part of the myth of Dionysus, acquire a deeper and more significant meaning.

Dionysus introduced the cultivation of grapes and the production of wine to parts of Europe, Asia, and Africa. He was also a god of trees and corn, teaching mankind farming, as did the goddess Demeter. Although Dionysus was once considered a late arrival upon Mount Olympus, the Linear B tablets found in Pylos support the idea that he was accepted in Greece at least as early as 1200 B.C.

The worship of Dionysus appears to have originated in Thrace, where he became a fertility god associated with local agriculture. His religious rites were so appealing to mortals that his worship quickly spread throughout the Mediterranean area including Minoan Crete and part of Mycenaean Greece.

The values inherent in the worship of Dionysus were the opposite of those involved in the worship of any of the other Olympian gods and particularly in opposition to the values represented in the worship of

Apollo. Whereas the Far-Shooter represented intellectual thought, self-awareness, and self-control, Dionysus personified the principles of passion, mindless madness, and self-indulgence. Dionysus encouraged mankind to forget its responsibilities and its troubles and, instead, join with him in celebrating the pure joy of being alive.

Men and women found the appeal of escapism irresistible. By joining with Dionysus in his ecstatic revels, they felt united with their god and divine themselves. By letting their emotions rule them, they gained a feeling of unity and equality with the other worshippers, because, during the rites, differences in occupation, social status, sex, and wealth no longer mattered. By abdicating their responsibilities as human beings, they experienced the total freedom of being able to do whatever they wished. Furthermore, since they were worshiping a divinity, they felt pure and righteous.

The results of these revels were devastating. Dionysus often dressed as a bull or a goat, and his participants, maenads[4], satyrs[5], and local residents, also would dress in animal skins. Emotionally involved in the frenzy of the celebration, the worshippers would become more savage than the beasts they imitated. Unconscious of their behavior, they would mutilate and destroy life solely for the thrill of violence. Such orgies filled outsiders with revulsion and terror. Many may have joined the frenzied group thinking that it was safer to join the worshippers than it would be to avoid and appear to condemn them.

Between about 800 B.C. and about 500 B.C., the Greeks formally accepted the worship of Dionysus. However, along with this acceptance came modifications of certain spontaneous religious practices. Showing great insight into human nature, the Greeks merged the worship of Dionysus with the worship of Apollo at Delphi, and scheduled periodic organized ritual observances in place of the spontaneous, frenzied, orgiastic rites.

The fusion of the god of the intellect with the god of the senses brought Apollo closer to the common people by making him a more accessible, humane god, and it raised Dionysus above the level of savage madness. According to many scholars, it also led to the birth of Greek tragic drama.[6]

Once Dionysus was worshipped at Delphi, and once religious rites in his honor were performed at specified occasions and locations, the nature of these rites changed considerably. In the seventh century B.C., the sacred performances were frenzied, improvisational choral performances involving music, dancing, and singing. By the sixth century B.C., they had evolved into a more orderly, planned ritual in which the birth, death, and rebirth of the god were performed by a chorus in order to recreate the emotional content of the original experience. Gradually, the choral dramatization of the life cycle of Dionysus was replaced by shorter choral narratives of other Greek myths, particularly those involving heroic values. These performances were still associated with Dionysus in that they served a religious purpose and were performed on religious occasions at a sacred location. However, the early, spontaneous, group improvisation of material had evolved into the creation of a narrative presentation by a particular individual. This brought the Greeks to the threshold of tragic drama, one of their major legacies to humankind.

1. Periodic ritual murder of the sacred king is discussed in Section I, In the Beginning.
2. Compare the birth of Athena in this section.
3. See introduction to myth of Demeter and Persephone in this section.
4. Female worshippers of Dionysus, who dressed in animal skins and carried *thyrsi* (poles twined with ivy or grapevines and topped with a pine cone).
5. Followers of Dionysus, who were vigorous young men with goats' legs, horses' tails, and small horns or pointed ears, and who were woodland creatures.
6. However, many scholars writing today disagree with the traditional view presented here. Instead, they think it is more likely that two great men of Ancient Greece created the tragic drama: Thespis, whom tradition considers the first actor, and Aeschylus, who first wrote tragic dramas which provided roles for individual actors. Until Thespis and Aeschylus, dramas were written for and were performed by a chorus.

ANTICIPATIONS

1. What do you choose to do when you have free time?
   a. go to the movies
   b. watch television
   c. read a book
   d. play table tennis or billiards
   e. go shopping
   f. participate in athletics
   g. join your friends at a neighborhood location
2. Under what conditions are you likely to be cruel to other people?
   a. when someone criticizes you
   b. when someone is angry with you
   c. when someone punishes you
   d. when you can't get your own way
   e. when you're in a bad mood
   f. when you lose to competition
   g. when you're not happy with yourself
   h. none of the above
3. What was Prohibition?
4. Our rules, laws, customs, and attitudes have undergone many changes. How did the Puritans view
   a. relationships between the sexes?
   b. giving parties?
   c. dressing in colorful clothes?

Zeus, who delights in thunder, fell in love with the beautiful mortal maiden, Semele. However, he loved her in disguise and in silence. When Hera found out about her husband's latest love, she was jealous as always. She decided to retaliate for the affront to her honor by destroying Semele. Disguising herself as a mortal woman, Hera became one of Semele's handmaidens and became particularly friendly with her. When Hera learned that Zeus had rashly promised to do whatever Semele asked of him, she immediately realized that this was her opportunity for revenge. She cunningly persuaded Semele to ask her lover to appear before her with the same magnificence and grandeur that he had appeared before Hera when he was courting her. Because the Lord of Olympus had given Semele his sacred word, he could not refuse her request. He presented himself before her in his chariot with his blazing lightning and thunderbolts. When he embraced her, Semele screamed in terror and burned to death in the flames.

Since far-seeing Zeus knew that she was six months pregnant with his child, Dionysus, he quickly snatched the infant from his mother's womb (Dionysus' first birth) and sewed him into his thigh in order to hide him from Hera. When Dionysus was ready to be born, Zeus removed the stitches in his thigh and delivered his infant son (Dionysus' second birth). He then commanded Hermes the Wayfinder to take the twice-born infant away from Mount Olympus and golden Hera's evil eye to Semele's sister, Ino, to be reared in the disguise of a girl.

In time, Hera discovered where Dionysus was and retaliated once again, this time by causing Ino and her husband to become temporarily insane. Then loud-thundering Zeus tried to protect his twice-born son from his wife's rage by changing him into a goat. He commanded Hermes to deliver the goat into the hands of Asian nymphs, who reared him. However, eventually Hera located Dionysus and drove him insane.

Dionysus wandered in madness through Egypt and Syria, finally entering the country of Phrygia,[1] where the Great Goddess Rhea cured him and purified him of the crimes he had committed while insane. She initiated the twice-born son of Zeus into her religious cult and gave him the Oriental costume and the wreath of ivy, which he wore thereafter.

From then on Dionysus traveled from community to community with the intention of establishing religious cults which would be devoted to his worship. Wherever he was welcomed, he taught the people how to make wine from grapes and how to harvest and store the fruits from various kinds of trees. He also taught farmers how to ease the burden of farming by yoking oxen to their plows. This permitted them to extend their areas of cultivated land and to become wealthy. He hoped that by helping mankind, mortals in return would worship him with the fervor they worshipped the other immortals. However, wherever the ivy-wreathed god was not welcomed, castastrophe occurred.

Such disaster came to King Lycurgus in Thrace when the king refused to welcome the twice-born god and his train of followers.[2] Lycurgus disliked the wild and drunken rites which accompanied Dionysian worship, so he expelled the god from Thrace and imprisoned his followers.

Dionysus took vengeance upon King Lycurgus by driving him insane. In his mad state, the king, thinking that his son was a grapevine that needed pruning, murdered him by chopping off his arms and legs with an axe. Once the damage had been done, the king's sanity returned.

As a final act of vengeance, ivy-wreathed Dionysus caused the land to remain barren for so long that the Thracians asked an oracle what they should do in order to make the land regain fertility. When the oracle responded that the death of Lycurgus would make the land bear fruit, the people murdered their king.

Next, loud-roaring Dionysus went southwest to Thebes. There, the blind Theban prophet, Teiresias,[3] warned King Pentheus of Thebes that he must honor Dionysus with proper religious rites. "If you refuse," he said, "the ivy-wreathed god will drive Theban mothers into insanity and, in that state, they will mutilate their own children and decorate the forest with their limbs. Moreover, King Pentheus, your own mother will kill you in this way."

Unfortunately, Pentheus did not follow Teiresias' advice. Therefore, when the ivy-wreathed god arrived and the Thebans flocked to join his frantic rites, King Pentheus became enraged.

"What madness has infested Thebes?" he asked. "What appeals to Thebans about this lazy foreign boy who perfumes his hair and clothes himself in luxurious robes that are decorated with gold and jewels? Has our army lost the courage to defend our city from this vagabond? I would hope that, if Thebes were to fall, it would be conquered nobly in a war."

"Enough of my own complaints," he declared. "Guards, find this vagabond, tie him up, and bring him to me. I will soon see whether he is the god he proclaims he is!"

The counselors of Pentheus tried to change his course of action, but the more they cautioned him, the more stubborn he became. Finally there was no course other than to let the guards obey his commands.

However, the guards could not find the loud-roaring god among the wild throng, so, rather than face their king empty-handed, they brought back one of Dionysus' priests as their captive, who possibly was Dionysus in disguise. When King Pentheus ridiculed the ivy-wreathed god's divinity to the captive, the priest proceeded to relate to the king the incredible story of his own introduction to Dionysus.

"I was the helmsman on a pirate ship," he began, "when the winds blew us to the island of Chios. There we moored our ship and spent the night. While I was out the next day looking for fresh water, the crew noticed a dark-haired young man in a purple cape sitting on the shore. Because he looked like a prince, they thought he would bring a good price in the slave market. Therefore, a few of the seamen headed for shore, where they seized him and brought him on board our ship. He was either half asleep, or drunk, or both, for he could not stand without support. They had intended to chain him, but no matter what method they tried, the chains always fell off his hands and feet.

"He was sitting on deck smiling with his dark eyes when I returned with the water. To me the young man clearly resembled a god, and the episode of the chains apparently confirmed my evaluation. So I asked the crew, 'Why in the world did you have to capture a mighty god? Can you not see that he does not look mortal? For all you know, you have tried to enslave Olympian Zeus, or the Earthshaker,[4] or the Far-Shooter.[5] We cannot possibly take him with us, or we will anger him! Then we will be punished for our foolishness! So, return him to the mainland."

However, no one would listen.

"The captain said, 'You are crazy! Your job is to pay attention to the direction of the wind and to the sails. You do that and leave the rest to us. We will force the boy to tell us about his wealth and his family. He is no god, but the immortals surely sent him among us to make us rich!'

"This argument brought the young man to life. 'What is all this noise about?' he asked. 'How did I get here? Where are you taking me?'

"'Tell us where you want to go, young man,' replied the captain, 'and we will take you there.' 'Take me to the island of Naxos, then,' the young man directed. 'That is where I live.'"

The helmsman-priest continued. "The captain promised, but I could tell from the signals he gave me that he was lying. I had already hoisted the sails, but I refused to disobey a god. When the captain saw that he could not force me, he told another seaman to steer the ship.

"Thus we set off. The young man stood upon the deck observing the sea. Suddenly he cried, 'We are going the wrong way! You said that you would take me to Naxos! What have I done to deserve such inconsiderate treatment?'

"Then the strangest things happened. Our ship became stuck right there, in the middle of the sea, as if it were beached upon a shore. The men tried vigorously to row it, but it would not move. They readjusted the sails, but in vain. There we sat, stranded.

"As we sat upon the sea, one of the crew pointed in silent astonishment to the topmost sail. A grapevine with clusters of ripe grapes hanging from it was growing there. Then we noticed dark vines of ivy blossoming with flowers and with ripe berries twining up the mast, concealing the ropes. These plants crept across the sails as we watched, and then they started to cover the oars too.

"There was now the sound of flutes on board, and our ship smelled strangely sweet. Wine was streaming across the deck! Struck with terror, the crew pleaded with the helmsman to head for land, but of course our ship would not move.

"Everyone then turned toward the young man. There he stood, right where we had last seen him, but now he was angry. His head was crowned with a wreath of ivy and grapes, and he was shaking a pole twined with grapevines and ivy, the *thyrsi*. Lynxes, tigers, and a spotted panther were lying on deck by his feet. A shaggy bear suddenly appeared and roared angrily. With that, the young man transformed himself into a fearsome lion, leaped toward the captain, and gripped him in his claws.

"The members of the crew, who had watched all this in spellbound disbelief, now reacted with the hysteria of terror. Their one thought was to escape, in any way, anywhere. Some of them frantically tried to make the ship move. Those working the oars, of course, were tugging at objects which would not move. They soon stopped in fear and amazement, watching their hands being transformed into long fins which could no longer grip the oars. The seaman working with the ropes also lost control when his arms became fins. He fell into the dark sea and sprouted a forked tail where his legs had been.

"Meanwhile, many of the crew were wildly leaping overboard. But even that proved to be no way of escape. As their bodies touched the water, they developed wider mouths and curved noses. Their skin became black and covered with scales, their arms became fins, and their legs grew into forked tails. Nineteen seamen had become nineteen dolphins.

"The young man, who had returned to his former self, smiled with satisfaction as he looked down upon them. They were spouting sea water as they leaped over the waves, chasing one another. Only I had been saved.

"'Do not be afraid,' said the young man, aware of my look of fear and amazement. 'I have spared you because I care about you. I am loud-roaring Dionysus, the twice-born son of Semele and Olympian Zeus.'

"And that is the end of my tale," the narrator explained. "Since that time, I have accompanied my ivy-wreathed immortal lord, and mortals have learned to honor him as one of the deathless gods."

"Take him away!" screamed King Pentheus. "Whip him! Burn him! Torture him for his child's tale; then kill him," he commanded. The guards obeyed their king's orders and imprisoned the Dionysian priest. A short time later, they suddenly burst into the king's chamber, their eyes wide with terror.

"What in the world has happened?" asked Pentheus.

"We have let the priest go!" the first guard excitedly exclaimed.

"Yes," agreed the second guard. "We were preparing his tortures when, suddenly, the gate of his prison cell unlocked itself and swung open. Before our very eyes, the chains which bound him loosened and fell to the ground. Smiling, he stood before us, a free man."

"We left him standing there and ran here," admitted the first guard. He felt a little foolish about this behavior now that they were safely in the presence of their king.

Pentheus sighed, exasperated. "All right," he said, "I see that I will have to take care of this matter myself."

Pentheus decided to go unaccompanied to the sacred summit of Mount Cithaeron and observe the wild Dionysian rites firsthand. He was seething with rage. "This vagabond boy has cunningly escaped my authority until now," Pentheus thought to himself. "This will give me the opportunity to observe him in action when he least suspects my presence. Once I have seen how he captivates his followers, I will be able to fight him more effectively."

As Pentheus approached the mountain top, shrieking voices and hysterical songs greeted his ears. He became even more determined to investigate his enemy's source of magnetism and power.

Upon reaching the top, Pentheus found a tree growing out of a cleft in the rocks. It would make a perfect shelter. From there he could observe the sacred rites without being seen by any of the participants. It was with a feeling of triumph that Pentheus climbed the tree.

His elation was short lived, however. His mother, who was a follower of Dionysus, observed him as he hid in the branches of the tree. She could not believe that her son was spying on their sacred rites. The thought was so abhorrent to her, and her shock was so great that, as King Lycurgus before her, she became temporarily insane.

Madly she ran toward her son, shrieking hysterically. "Sisters, come!" she screamed. "There is the boar which has been destroying our land. We must kill him!" Pentheus fled, and, gathering up their skirts, the maenads chased him.

Pentheus could not run fast enough to avoid his fate. He wept and begged for mercy when the crazed women caught him, but they had no mercy. Frantically, he called to his mother, trying to get her to recognize him as her son as they chopped off his hands. However, his mad mother simply shouted with enthusiasm, grabbed her son by his hair, and proclaimed, "This trophy of the hunt is mine!"

Those were the last words poor Pentheus ever heard his mother say. The maenads tore him limb from limb, distributing his body over the mountainside. His mother stuck his head upon her thyrsus and displayed it with pride. Eventually her sanity returned, and only then did she realize what she had done.

The Thebans were terror-struck upon learning how their king had died. The twice-born god had conquered their kingdom. The people sang his praises, brought incense to his altars, and celebrated his wild rites.

Golden Hera was furious that this loud-roaring child of her husband's was powerful enough to change mortals into dolphins and to make mothers kill their own children. She took vengeance wherever she could, but never again did she attempt to punish Dionysus himself.

Dionysus continued to wander from country to country establishing his religious cult. In the course of his travels, some writers say that he found Ariadne[6] on the island of Naxos and married her. Finally the ivy-wreathed god descended into the kingdom of Hades to rescue his mother Semele. He renamed her Thyone and took her up to Mount Olympus with him, where they lived ever after.

1. A country east of Greece, across the Aegean Sea in Asia Minor.
2. maenads and satyrs
3. Teiresias also played a role in the myth of Narcissus (Section III, The World of Man, and in the myth of Heracles, Section IV, The Heroes).
   His daughter, who was also a prophet, played a role in The myth of Niobe (Section III, The World of Man).
4. Poseidon
5. Apollo
6. See the myth of Theseus (Section IV, The Heroes).

REFLECTIONS

1. Why was the worship of Dionysus so controversial?
2. What did his worship reveal about the needs and values of the ancient Greeks?
3. How would Dionysus be received in our country today? Discuss.
4. Make a chart comparing Dionysus and Apollo. Under each god's name, list the ways in which he helped society.
5. What behavior did Dionysus expect from mortals?

15 Nemesis

Nemesis represented retributive justice. She was called upon by men and gods to avenge injustice and excessive pride.

In societies where the Mother Goddess was the primary deity and the framework of society was matriarchal, retributive justice was the major form of justice. A mortal's primary allegiance was to his or her own family. If a member of a family was killed or insulted by a person outside the family, the family was obligated to avenge the crime or insult. The other family in turn was then obligated to avenge that vengeance, thereby continuing the blood feud. This pattern could continue indefinitely. By making the family its own judge and jury, and by providing no other rules than "an eye for an eye," many innocent men and women were killed, and there was great social unrest and bitterness.

This pattern of justice continued under the early rule of Zeus. Yet by the time of Theseus and Daedalus (about 1450 B.C.), those mortals who committed murder were tried on the Areopagus[1] in Athens by a council of respected aristocrats who decided the questions of their guilt and punishment. Those who were found guilty were exiled from the community for eight years, or for the period of the term of the sacred king. This eliminated the repetitive pattern of retributive justice by having an impartial authority determine and enforce social behavior.

1. Daedalus and Orestes were both tried on the Areopagus. Daedalus' story was included in his myth (Section III, The World of Man). Orestes was declared innocent after a long punishment by the Furies.

   Areopagus means "Hill of Ares" or "Hill of Curses." It is actually a rocky hill near the Acropolis in Athens.

1. What does the word "nemesis" mean today?

2 . Nemesis was originally the goddess of retribution. To what extent does the principle "an eye for an eye" exist in modern society?
3. Do you feel that the ways in which punishment and crime are handled today work for the welfare of society? If so, why? If not, why not?

THE MYTH

A later love of Zeus was Nemesis, immortal daughter of Nyx (night). Nemesis was the goddess who brought retribution to those who committed crimes. She bore Zeus the famous Helen of Troy. When Zeus could not persuade Nemesis to accept his amorous advances, the Lord of Olympus transformed himself into a swan. He then asked golden Aphrodite to transform herself into an eagle and to pursue the swan.

As Nemesis sat by the shore, the eagle pursued the swan according to plan, and the swan took refuge in Nemesis's lap. Nemesis cuddled the beautiful swan and then fell into a deep sleep. While she slept, the swan embraced her and then flew away.

Within the year Nemesis gave birth to a large egg. Hermes the Wayfinder collected the egg, carried it to Sparta, and gave it to the mortal queen, Leda. Leda placed the egg in a chest and kept it until it hatched. When it did, out came Helen and Polydeuces. Leda raised these children with her own mortal children of the same age, Clytemnestra and Castor. Castor and Polydeuces became inseparable friends, while Helen and Clytemnestra married the great kings of Greece of that time, Menelaüs and Agamemnon.

REFLECTIONS

1. Have a debate on whether or not there should be capital punishment.
2. What does the existence of Nemesis, the goddess of revenge, reveal about human relationships?
3. Volunteer to report on one of the following aspects of our system of justice.
    a. the Supreme Court
    b. the appellate courts
    c. trial by jury
    d. police stations

THE WORLD OF MAN

Racing the chariot in competition was a common practice among aristocratic youths in ancient Greece. Homer describes Trojan War heroes using chariots in order to enter and leave the scene of battle.

Because the Greek myths were the product of a highly developed ancient civilization, most of them were concerned with the nature of man, his function in society, and his relationship to the gods.

The ancient Greeks realized that man was not an omnipotent being. He was always subject to events that he could not control, such as weather, illness, war, famine, and death. He attributed many of these problems to immortal beings, whom he endowed with human attributes and human shapes (anthropomorphism). Although these gods were far more powerful than man, they were not omnipotent. After all, there were many gods, each having a different personality and a different role in the universal order. Each god demanded a different attitude from man, as well as a different kind of sacrifice. Pleasing one god could often anger another. Man could make every effort to satisfy the gods through prayers of praise, proper sacrifice, and other ritual, and then he could only hope for the best.

Unlike the ancient Hebrews, the ancient Greeks never received any authoritative commandments from their gods, setting forth guiding principles by which they should live. Instead, the ancient Greeks lived by a moral and ethical code that they themselves established. They did not establish a moral code for their gods for they were very much aware of the separation between themselves and their gods. The gods were not under the jurisdiction of mortal laws, but were free and independent beings who could be cruel and capricious, or kind and just.

The ancient Greeks did not expect perfection either from human beings or from their gods. They accepted their world and their gods as they were, and concentrated upon making the best of the situation.

In most respects, the attitudes and actions of the gods corresponded to their own and were a reflection of the predominant moral and ethical values of the time. The major difference between the two existed in the realm of marriage. The Mycenaean Greeks lived in a monogamous society in which marriage between a man and a woman was a sacred bond. The promiscuity of the immortals in their myths reflected the religious conflicts of the past, where the values of an invading patriarchal society combined with or replaced the differing values of the earlier, native, matriarchal society. The Mycenaean Greeks accepted the overlay of one tradition on another, and they ignored the inconsistencies. However, Greeks of the fifth century B.C., such as Plato and Aristotle, were extremely bothered by the immoral behavior of the gods in the Greek myths. They disregarded any positive values the myths might contain in their concern that they would morally corrupt those who heard or read them.

Many of the Greek myths taught man to accept his limitations, including his mortality. They illustrated, by example, the ideas that the Greek poets later expressed, showing mortal man that he was not a god and could not excel the gods in any respect, including wisdom, wealth, the arts, or beauty. The gods lived eternally and without change, whereas man soon faded away as if he were only a shadow or a dream. Since he would inevitably die, he should make the most of his life. He should enjoy the happiness he found around him, for it could change without warning or reason.

Although man could not escape his fate, which was death, the Mycenaean Greeks believed that man was free, in the course of his life, to make many decisions that would determine the quality of his life. There was no authoritative, divinely inspired moral code to guide man's conduct. However, many of the Greek myths taught man how to behave in society and toward the gods by examining a mortal's choices, then presenting a decision and the consequences.

In spite of the absence of a divinely inspired moral code, man's obligations to himself, to society, and to his gods, was clear. He must strive for excellence (arete) in all aspects of his life. Yet, he must also remember to avoid extremes and, instead, to aim for the golden mean. He must be careful not to lose sight of his own mortality and human condition. He was not a god, and excessive excellence could lead to excessive pride (hybris), which would make man forget his humanity. He would become arrogant and insolent, showing little respect for either men or gods. The Greeks considered this temporary madness, or "áte." Inevitably, such a mortal, having lost his sense of reality, would bring destruction upon himself.

16 The Ages of Man

This myth, "The Ages of Man," reflects an attitude of pessimism. As the world becomes more advanced technologically, it becomes more corrupt morally. The myth looks back to the earliest ages as being the purest, reminiscent of a kind of Garden of Eden. The earliest age in the myth, that ruled by Cronus, is similar to the way people lived in a matriarchal society. They, too, lived off the land, although they worked very hard. They, too, felt no need to acquire and to exploit, pursuits that reflected the aggressive, warlike attitudes of the patriarchal society.

ANTICIPATIONS

1. In what ways is our age the best of times? In what ways is it the worst of times? Divide into two teams. One team will defend the idea that we are living in the best of times. The other will defend the idea that we are living in the worst of times. Which argument is more convincing?

THE MYTH

When Cronus was king of the universe, the deathless gods created a golden race of mortal men. These first mortals lived without hard work, without pain, and without sadness. The earth abundantly supplied them with acorns, berries, corn, honey, and nectar. They also had large herds of cattle. Thus, they could enjoy luxurious feasts without the back-breaking labor of farming. These people let their intelligence and conscience rule them. They chose to pursue the good life for its own rewards. They lived without fear, without crime, and without courts of law. Written laws were unnecessary since they did not need the threat of punishment to motivate proper behavior. They felt no need to explore, to acquire, or to exploit. They erected no walls or fences to separate their possessions from those of their neighbors. There were no sights or sounds of warfare. Wildflowers reigned in meadows and fields, and western winds maintained eternal spring. Old age spared them its weakness and misery. They enjoyed peaceful living and the love of the gods until they died. Then they became blessed guardian spirits.

After the first golden race of mortals had been buried and far-seeing Zeus had imprisoned his father Cronus, in Tartarus, the Olympian gods created a second, silver race of mortals. These men were far inferior to the golden race. They remained as children, helpless for a full century, and after they became adults, they lived for only a few more years. Their own poor judgment always brought them pain and suffering, for they could not refrain from violence and crime. In this age, summer, autumn, and winter appeared for the first time. Spring lasted only one-fourth of the year. The weather was often an enemy rather than a friend, producing blistering heat and icy snows. People were forced to seek refuge in caves or simple houses, and they now had to farm in order to have enough food to eat. Life was hard and unpleasant.

Next, Zeus created the third race of mortal beings—this was the age of bronze. These men were incredibly strong and equally violent in temperament. Their invincible weapons, their houses, and their occupations all depended upon bronze. Their very flesh seemed to be made of bronze. They brought their deaths upon themselves, dying from the violence by which they lived. After their deaths, they entered grim Hades' dismal kingdom where they spent eternity.

Last of all, Zeus, who thunders on high, established our[1] iron age. We, the fourth race of mortal men, live in a time of conquest. Great sailors have used seagoing vessels to claim more territory. We have forced the earth to supply us with metals as well as with food. We have fought with iron weapons for possession of more gold. People of our time must work hard every day and have troubled dreams at night. Only occasionally do we achieve success. Unfortunately for our iron race, moral behavior has begun to disappear and hospitality is coming to an end. Hosts may murder their guests, and family members may murder one another. We must be wary of our own behavior. For when children and their parents are no longer friends, when quarrels destroy the relationships between brothers and friends, when we deprive the aged of their rights and the respect they deserve, when we covet the possessions of our neighbors near and far, when we praise evil and violent behavior rather than actions which are good and peaceful, and when we have destroyed everything in our lives except pain and evil, then Zeus will destroy our race, and the last age of man will come to an end.

1. The time of the writer of this myth (about 700 B.C.).

1. Why did the Greeks believe there was more than one "age" of man?
2. What is the purpose of this myth? Does it relate to scientific reality?
3. This myth asserts that as mankind becomes more civilized technologically, his moral nature becomes more corrupt. Do you agree? Discuss.
4. Compare the fourth "age" of man with our own "age."
5. Complete this myth by creating a fifth "age" of man.

17 Prometheus

In most ancient cultures, man believed that his survival and his well-being depended upon pleasing the gods. Therefore, he offered his choicest food and sometimes human beings as sacrifices to his gods. Disobedience to the gods invited destruction and death.

Many of the myths of the ancient Greeks, like those of their neighboring cultures, reflected and promoted these ideas of dependence and subservience to divine authority. It is remarkable that the myth of Prometheus, which you are about to read, confronts and questions the traditional religious attitudes of its time.

Although every character in this myth is an immortal god, like all Greek myths, the story of Prometheus makes specific events reveal general truths about the nature of man and his relationship to the world in which he lives. Prometheus was the immortal who created man. He recognized that man was defenseless against the problems of cold and hunger. In order to assure the survival of man, Prometheus courageously dared to trick Zeus, the supreme ruler of gods and men. The idea that man is so important that a divine order should be disobeyed if it would destroy mankind may not seem strange to us. However, this was a daringly new idea in its time. In fact, the idea that man is very important and that, therefore, his survival and welfare are basic cultural values and goals is a debt we owe the ancient Greeks.

The myths of ancient Greece teach us that man may not claim more than the gods permit without receiving dire punishment or even total destruction. Prometheus raged against Zeus's inhumanity and evil, but he withstood it. Prometheus could not escape the punishment Zeus inflicted upon his body, yet through courage, defiance, and self-confidence, he remained strong in spirit.

1. In the following story, Prometheus is willing to risk personal suffering in order to live his life as he chooses. In order to direct your own life, you must be able to question and understand the values of those around you. You must also be able to decide whether it is worthwhile to risk popularity in order to pursue something significant. Sometimes it is not always possible to maintain social acceptance while achieving something new or defending a belief. This necessitates making a choice. What are *your* values?

   Rank the following in order of their importance to you.
   a. having the ability to influence other people's decisions
   b. owning things that other people wish they had
   c. having friends who sincerely care for you and for whom you care
   d. creating something that no one else has created
   e. having as much money as you want
   f. being a good athlete
   g. being a good student
   h. being liked by everyone
   i. having your own room
   j. working on a project by yourself
   k. working on a project with other people
   l. having free time
   m. having a variety of interests

2. When you read about Prometheus's actions in the following story, you might admire his tremendous courage. What enables Prometheus to be so courageous? Could you ever act with such inner strength and conviction? Because Prometheus likes himself, he is able to act with courage. Self-esteem is a necesary part of the courage required for self-assertion. Prometheus's self-esteem permits him to risk Zeus's punishment for defending mankind. What things make you feel good about yourself?
   a. personal appearance
   b. athletic activity
   c. intellectual ability
   d. creative ability
   e. sense of humor
   f. ability to entertain your friends
   g. being like everyone else
   h. being different from everyone else

3. Evaluate the choices you made in the above question and decide whether your feelings about yourself are determined by what others think of you or by your own satisfaction in your achievements.

The earth was young when Prometheus[1], the clever Titan, created all the living creatures from a mixture of earth and water. From his imagination, he fashioned birds for the air, fish for the sea, and animals for the land. However, from the image of the immortal gods, he fashioned man.

Gentle Epimetheus[2] observed his brother's creative activity with amazement and with envy. He also wanted to have some part in the creative process, so he pleaded with Prometheus to let him do something for each living creature. Because Prometheus loved his gentle brother, he decided to let him distribute the qualities that each of his creatures would need in order to survive.

With joy in his heart, Epimetheus set out to do his part. To creatures who were slow, he gave strength. To creatures who were weak, he gave great speed. Some creatures he armed with tusks, sharp claws, or stinging tails so that they could defend themselves. To other creatures, he gave either great or small size; the first to instill fright, the second to avoid detection. When he had assured himself that the land, sea, and air creatures were suitably defended, Epimetheus proceeded to protect them from the hazards of their natural environment: heat, cold, and starvation. Depending upon the climate, he gave them skins of thin leather, or of heavy fur. He gave creatures the ability to climb, to dig, or to stalk their food. He proceeded thoughtfully from creature to creature until he had distributed all of the qualities that each would need in order to survive upon the earth.

He was feeling quite proud of his accomplishments when suddenly he came upon man. Man was naked and defenseless. He, alone, of all Prometheus's creatures, had received no gifts. How would he ever survive? Gentle Epimetheus did not know what to do. He stood there, gazing at man, and hoped that somehow everything would be all right.

Epimetheus was still standing there when his clever brother joined him. Prometheus had followed Epimetheus, and had been very pleased with the distributions his brother had made. However, with one glance he understood the terrible problem.

"There isn't anything left for man, is there?" he questioned softly, trying to remain calm in the face of his tremendous disappointment. Slowly, gentle Epimetheus shook his head, tears welling up in his eyes as he realized the magnitude of his mistake.

Of all his creations, Prometheus most loved man. He resolved to do whatever was necessary to insure man's survival, regardless of the risk to himself. During the next moonless night, the clever Titan stole up to Mount Olympus, home of his cousin Zeus and the other immortal gods. He knew that the Lord of Olympus would not help him. However, he realized that Zeus's children, strong-armed Hephaestus and grey-eyed

Athena, would sympathize with him, because they, too, were creators. The clever Titan immediately went to their workshop.

Even though they feared Olympian Zeus's thunderbolts, Hephaestus and Athena risked their great father's wrath in order to help their fellow creator. Silently and secretly they taught Prometheus their knowledge of arts and crafts so that he, in turn, could impart this knowledge to humankind. As a parting gift, Hephaestus, the lame smith, gave Prometheus fire[3] so that mortals could use their new knowledge.

Prometheus returned to earth to become humankind's great teacher. He taught mortals to understand their environment, to calculate, to read and to write, to build houses and sailing ships, and to tame wild animals for food, labor, and protection. He showed them treasures within Mother Earth: copper and iron, silver and gold. He taught them how, with the gift of fire, mortals could use these treasures to improve and beautify their lives. Thus it was that man, frail as he was, became master of his environment. Once mortals had this knowledge, they became aware of the gods. They worshipped the gods by building altars, by making images, and by offering sacrifices.

Then Prometheus became concerned that mortals would give the gods the best fruits of their labors, leaving little for their own uncertain existence. Therefore, the clever Titan designed a scheme whereby mortals would be able to offer pleasing sacrifices to the gods and still eat well themselves.[4]

Prometheus carefully carved the carcass of a great ox, dividing the parts into two sacrificial piles. Into one pile he put the rich organs and the nourishing meat, craftily hiding them away in the ox's stomach. He then covered this sacrifice with oxhide. Into the second pile, he wrapped layers of white fat over the bare white bones of the ox, covering this sacrifice also with oxhide. Then the wily Titan called upon great Zeus, Lord of Olympus, to choose which portion should be for the eternal gods and which portion for humankind.

As Zeus lifted up the hide that covered the fatty portion, he was quite impressed with the quality of the sacrifice. Clearly, mortals had not skimped in their efforts to please the gods. However when the Lord of Olympus raised the hide that covered the second sacrifice, he was repulsed by the appearance and the smell of the ox's stomach. Searching no further, he made the natural decision, announcing, "From now on, the fatty portion will be for the immortal gods, and the stomach portion for humankind!"

Then, anxious for some of the tender, tasty meat, the Lord of High Thunder quickly unwrapped the fat and found *bones!*

With new insight, Zeus sought the eyes of his crafty opponent. Even under his great cousin's scrutiny, clever Prometheus could not hide the joy he felt in having succeeded in his deception.[5]

Zeus's mind became clouded with rage, and he thundered at Prometheus, "Wily schemer and deceiver! You have given man good meat to eat, but from now on he will have to eat it raw. I forbid man the use of fire!"

Then Olympian Zeus gathered up all fire, and returning to Mount Olympus, hid its flame from man.

Prometheus knew that man could not survive without fire. In spite of the devastating power of Zeus's thunderbolt, clever Prometheus tempted the great Olympian's rage by daring to steal fire from the gods a second time. This time he succeeded by hiding its bright flame within a huge, hollow fennel stalk.[6]

When Zeus looked down from Mount Olympus and saw fire gleaming among Prometheus's mortals, he controlled the fury in his heart. With cruel laughter he decided how he would punish both Prometheus and humankind.

He called his son, Hephaestus, the renowned smith, and commanded that he bind the rebel Prometheus to Mount Caucasus far in the north, in Scythia.

Although Hephaestus felt great admiration and sympathy for the clever Titan, he obeyed his great father's command. Against his will, he took Prometheus through the pathless wilderness of the far north until they reached the high-ridged, winter-bitten, and rocky gorges. There, the renowned smith fastened the defiant Titan to the icy cliffs with unbreakable stone chains. He then drove an equally strong stake through Prometheus's chest for additional security. Thus, able to move only his head, Prometheus was condemned to be parched by the blazing sun each day, and frozen by the icy winds each night.

Having completed his terrible task, strong-armed Hephaestus tried to leave Prometheus with a few comforting words. "Dear friend," he said, "remember that the Lord of Olympus has just acquired the supreme power of his father Cronus. In time his nature might change."

To this, the shackled prisoner replied, "Hephaestus, although the Fates have denied me the blessing of death and the ability to foresee my own future, Olympian Zeus, too, is also subject to their will.

"My mother has given me secret knowledge[7] that will either humble his pride, or destroy him. The Lord of Olympus is destined to pursue a goddess, whose name I shall not reveal. This goddess is destined to give birth to a son who will become greater than his father. If his father is Olympian Zeus, then this son will hurl Zeus into the darkness of Tartarus, just as Zeus once hurled his own father, Cronus.

"Far-seeing Zeus can avoid this prophecy only by freeing me, for without my advice, he is surely doomed. Until then, he can devise no cruel torment or evil scheme that will force me to divulge this knowledge."

As soon as strong-armed Hephaestus had reported this information to his illustrious father, the Lord of Olympus sent his swift-footed son, Hermes, to Prometheus's side.

"Prometheus, thief of fire! Look at me when I speak to you!" Zeus's herald commanded. "The father of the gods demands that you declare the secret knowledge that will destroy him."

To these words, the unconquerable Prometheus replied, "Nothing in your great father's power will force this knowledge from me unless he unshackles these chains of bondage. Therefore, let Zeus hurl his thunderbolts upon me! Let his tempests lash the earth until its subterranean foundations quake and crack! He cannot force me to prevent his downfall. It is not my nature to fear the immortal gods."

"Then I must warn you," replied Hermes, "that the Lord of High Thunder will send wave after wave of tortures upon you. First he will strike this rugged ridge with his thunderbolts, splitting the rock apart so that it will enfold you within its darkest depths. Only after many ages have passed will you return to the world of sunlight.

"Then you will face an even more horrible torture. For Olympian Zeus will set his predatory eagle upon you. Each day, this greedy vulture will tear open your body and gorge his voracious appetite upon your defenseless liver. Each night your liver will regenerate itself to provide a renewed feast for the eagle on the following day.

"So consider my message, defiant friend. Loud-thundering Zeus does not lie. His wishes become deeds. You can escape from this agony only if some immortal, of his own free will, chooses to give up his own immortality and take your place in the depths of Tartarus.[8] No matter how you twist and turn in the attempt to lessen your torture, just as you are handcuffed and staked to this cliff, so you are chained to your fate. As brilliant as you are, you are not ingenious enough to outwit Olympian Zeus!"

"Return to your great father, Hermes," commanded the strong Titan. "No immortal can intimidate me. Let Zeus shake the atmosphere with violent storms and flaming thunderbolts! Let his great wrath hurl my body down into the darkness of Tartarus! I will endure even his mighty, ravenous eagle! For although Zeus may batter my body, he cannot shatter my spirit."[9]

Suddenly the sky clouded over and became black and ominous. Swift-footed Hermes quickly sped away as a fierce wind began to batter the lonely figure chained to the frostbitten cliff.

1. The name Prometheus means "forethought." Ironically, he had the ability to see all future occurrences except those that happened to him.
2. The name Epimetheus means "afterthought." Epimetheus couldn't forsee the consequences of his actions.

3. The early Greeks thought that fire originally was divine in origin. Because it belonged in the heavens, man had to explain how he came to possess it.
4. Religious sacrifice was an important ritual, and in order to avoid feeling guilty, mortals needed to justify why they could keep the meat needed for survival.
5. When Prometheus dared to trick Zeus, he defied traditional religious attitudes by making mortals more important than his gods.
6. Fennel is an edible plant which grows in Europe and Asia. It is still used in parts of Greece to transport fire from one place to another. Greek islanders have a torch race called the "Prometheia," which celebrates the importance of fire to mankind. The winner is the person who wins the race with the original flame still burning within his fennel stalk.
7. Prometheus's mother was an oracle, or prophet. She confided to him the special information that if Zeus (or anyone, for that matter) married the sea-goddess, Thetis, any son born would become greater than his father.
8. Heracles accidently wounded the immortal centaur, Cheiron, who prayed to Zeus to remove his suffering by permitting him to die. Zeus heard Cheiron's prayer and permitted the centaur to take Prometheus's place in Tartarus.
9. Eventually, when he needed Prometheus's help (secret knowledge), Zeus directed his son, Heracles, to kill his eagle and to free Prometheus.

REFLECTIONS

1. What characteristics do Hephaestus and Prometheus share? How are their personalities different?
   a. Do you have any friends who are like Hephaestus?
   b. Do you know anyone who is like Prometheus?
2. What motivates Prometheus to revolt against Zeus? Which is more important to Prometheus, his great love for humankind or his desire for independence or freedom from the gods? Who wins the contest of wills, Prometheus or Zeus? What motivates you to study? To create? To make friends?
3. Think of people in history whose courage or suffering remind you of Prometheus. Compare and contrast Job and Prometheus, Jesus and Prometheus.
4. Choose a figure from public life or from the media who has risked his or her reputation for the good of society. Prepare an oral or written project in which you adopt this person's view and defend his or her actions.
5. Do you sympathize more with Zeus or with Prometheus? Why? Is Prometheus a hero or a villain? Within the classroom, set up a jury-trial in which Prometheus must defend himself and must be judged to be guilty or innocent of treason against Zeus.
6. The Prometheus myth contains many *paradoxes*. The word "paradox" is Greek in origin. A paradox is an idea that combines two opposites, each of which is true. For example, Prometheus is both a hero and a villain. What paradoxical situations or events can you think of?

7. Prometheus risked Zeus's rage in order to enrich humankind. Which of the following risks are *you* willing to take?
   a. Trying something new for its own sake, regardless of the consequences
   b. Trying something new because it might be dangerous
   c. Trying something new because it is safe and it might increase your knowledge or experience
   d. None of the above

HUMAN EXPERIENCE

We may see the tyranny of Zeus in our own lives as a dominating person, or group of people, who insist that we share their values, ideas, and habits. Such people exert subtle pressures upon us to conform in dress, language, and ways of behaving. When these people are our friends, it is difficult to withstand their demands to conform to their standards if these differ from our own. In order to become independent or autonomous, it is necessary, sometimes, to rebel against the prevailing values of our peers.

The most important creation of anyone's life is one's own life. Prometheus, the creator and the sufferer, makes us realize that we, too, must sometimes suffer in order to create our own lives. We learn through experience what our own personal value systems are. It is sometimes necessary to stand alone in order to defend them.

Prometheus rebels against Zeus because he likes what he creates and is eager to defend it, even at the cost of a lifetime of agony. He is a committed creator. We, too, must invest ourselves fully in what we do, so that we may achieve something significant and thus feel a sense of self-esteem.

Success is the ability to fail and continue trying. We have foresight if we can see the consequences of our actions. To be able to judge or evaluate these actions, however, we must be able to look ahead. We also must be capable of looking back on our actions so that we may change by observing them. Prometheus and Epimetheus, together, represent those qualities which are essential for all of us if we are to observe and judge our behavior. Living life creatively requires both of these perceptions—both looking ahead and looking back. They are ways of knowing the world and ourselves.

Prometheus stands up to the wrath of Zeus and accepts his punishment. He controls his own destiny in the sense that, knowing the punishment to come, he does not refuse the task at hand. We, too, control our own destinies in this way. Either we can see opportunity as a risk, and therefore refuse it, or we can welcome the challenge of growth, even though it will bring changes that involve decision-making or commitment.

Prometheus does what he thinks is in the interest of humankind, regardless of the cost in personal suffering. In our own lives, what is sometimes a fearful journey can disclose a discovery, if we are willing to tackle the situation or problem directly.

Sacrifice

The Greeks had many forms of sacrifice, but in each case, they offered meats or animals to the gods that appealed to them, in order to find favor with them, or to appease their wrath.

Sacrifice is really the act of giving up something for the sake of something else. Most of us make small sacrifices on a daily basis; we give up some immediate pleasure for responsibility or achievement, whether this means homework, household chores, or other duties.

In another sense, whenever we grow, mature, or develop, (from infant to child, child to adolescent, adolescent to youth, or youth to adult) we *give up* some of the pleasures we have experienced at an earlier age in order to grow into the next.

Life is process, or continual change. People who are unable to handle the sacrificing of old, familiar, pleasures and childish behavior never permit themselves the pleasure or risk of handling change and achieving new goals.

Such people may also be unable to cope with loss, either through the death of a loved one, or through some other significant separation, such as war, divorce, or loss of friendship. Another kind of loss that sometimes occurs in life is the result of changing our status. In marriage, one may have momentary yearnings to be free, or experience the feeling just before achieving a goal. At such a time, people who have never sacrificed in small ways may have the feeling that they are moving backward, or have lost something valuable by moving ahead.

We know that children have a sense of wonder about the world that adults regard as fresh and desirable. Adults would like to have this for themselves. Yet the adult, in having to sacrifice his or her sense of wonder, gains new insights into him or herself and acquires deeper understanding of the world. We all need these insights because as we become older, our problems become more difficult to solve.

Another example of sacrifice is donating to charity, which is a sacrifice of money, or time, for the benefit of less fortunate people. What are one's motives in donating to charity? Is it to call attention to one's self in order to be thought wealthy by the community, or is it a genuine interest in giving? Without seeing one's real goals in sacrificing, we do not know whether our actions are valid as sacrifices or whether they are for the sake of exhibiting one's assets to others. This problem arises again when we question whether a parent assumes responsibility for the welfare of his or her children out of genuine love and interest in their well-being, or other motives. Among these might be the need to see the child as an extension of the parental ego, or, even more unhealthy, is the perverse wish to be a martyr in the name of parenthood. We develop the capacity to sacrifice in significant ways when we are able to measure *reality* in such a way that we can determine for ourselves with clarity why we act.

If we act for reasons that are not related to our own integrity, we are offering the ritual and not the feeling or the conviction. If we can assess reality and use it as a means for testing our real motives and reasons for our sacrifices, we will be able to handle both the internal and the external worlds objectively, and direct our actions accordingly. Then and only then can we move from the *pleasure principle* to the reality principle, which is a modification of the former. It is at that point that we develop feelings of confidence in ourselves that permit us to trust ourselves through our own, growing rational abilities.

18 Pandora

Long before the time of Hesiod,[1] who tells this story, Pandora was a Mother Goddess or a Great Goddess. As such, she was all-giving. She gave birth to and nourished all life, and, as Mother Earth, she received the dead for rebirth in the spring.[2]

Mankind worshipped earth goddesses such as Pandora under many different names; for example, Athena in Athens, Aphrodite on Cypress, and Artemis on Crete. However, no matter which name was used, the earth goddess was worshipped in order to assure the human family health, prosperity, and fertility in personal and in agricultural terms.

In these pre-Mycenaean societies, women were considered to be representatives of the local, reigning Mother Goddess. Consequently, women held a superior position to men in society. Women dominated the society's religious, social, and legal customs.

This changed between approximately 1900 B.C. and 1600 B.C. when invading Greek-speaking peoples, the Mycenaeans, brought their male-dominated religion into Greece. Thereafter, men took over the leadership roles in society.

Like the other Greek myths, this story illustrates the attitudes of a male-dominated society.[3]

1. Hesiod lived in approximately 700 B.C.
2. A more detailed account of the matriarchal religion can be found in the introductory chapter, "Religious Background."
3. Hesiod took the common theme of the curious wife and molded it into an explanation of why women bring both blessings and sorrow to men. He created this myth as opposed to retelling an older version.

ANTICIPATIONS

1. Today, both men and women question the truth of Sigmund Freud's statement, "Anatomy is destiny." What does this expression mean?

2. Interview the male and female members of your family, including parents, brothers, sisters, aunts, uncles, and grandparents.
   a. How do or did they earn a living?
   b. What influenced their vocational decisions? Interest? Financial reward? Job availability? Finances? Other influences?
   c. Were they discouraged by anyone from their *own* career choices?
   d. What would they have wanted to become?
3. Traditionally, women were expected to care for home and children.
   a. Do you think anything limited their lives?
   b. Did they think their lives were limited?
4. Society has different expectations for its women than for its men in many areas of life. What effect did or do such expectations have on each sex's
   a. need for approval?
   b. self-esteem?
   c. ability to be honest about feelings?

THE MYTH

While Prometheus, the courageous Titan, was enduring his punishment far to the north in Scythia, Zeus who delighted in thunder, proceeded with his next objective, the punishment of man. Once again he called upon his son, Hephaestus, the smith.

"Hephaestus," he commanded, "I want you to create a beautiful woman from the same ingredients that Prometheus, the clever Titan, used to create his beloved mortals. I want her to be beautiful enough to be a blessing, yet evil enough to be a punishment for mankind."

Strong-armed Hephaestus obeyed his great father's order, giving the girl the face of a goddess but human voice and strength. Then grey-eyed Athena dressed her in silver clothing and placed an embroidered veil upon her head. Hephaestus crowned her with a golden wreath of intertwined wild animals, a marvel which he, alone, could devise. When they had finished, the children of Zeus led the mortal girl out among the immortal gods.

The Olympians gasped in admiration at the beautiful creature the renowned smith had created. The Graces placed golden necklaces around her neck, while the Seasons placed spring flowers among the golden animals of her crown.

Then the Lord of Olympus directed golden Aphrodite to give her the qualities of love and desire. Finally, in order to insure that woman would be a source of sorrow to man, Olympian Zeus instructed his cunning son, Hermes, to give the girl an inquisitive and deceitful nature.

As far-seeing Zeus commanded, all obeyed. Swift-footed Hermes decided that this mortal girl should be called Pandora[1] because so many Olympians had given her gifts. Finally, as his gift, the Lord of High Thunder gave Pandora a sealed jar[2] and told Hermes the Wayfinder to accompany her down to earth, where he should present her to gentle Epimetheus from the immortals.

Epimetheus could not resist such an appealing gift. Even though his brother Prometheus had warned him never to accept any gift from Mount Olympus because it might prove to be a source of evil, gentle Epimetheus could not believe that anyone as beautiful and as appealing as Pandora could bring anything but delight. Therefore, he immediately married her.

Soon, thereafter, Pandora became curious about what the sealed jar contained. No sooner had she broken the seal and lifted the lid from the great jar than its contents flew out into the air, scattering everywhere. Olympian Zeus had filled the jar to the brim with evils for man, thousands of sorrows and sicknesses that now hovered, some to attack by day, and others to steal in by night. Only one spirit remained behind in the jar. Hope had become caught under the rim, and it could not fly away before Pandora replaced the lid.[3] Through the contents of the jar, the Lord of High Thunder completed his terrible revenge against Prometheus, thereby warning both gods and mortals not to challenge his authority.

1. Pandora means "all gifts" or "all-giving."
2. Pandora opens a jar rather than a box because the ancient Greeks used clay jars for storage purposes.
3. Hesiod created this myth. He does not indicate the significance of Hope's confinement in the jar. Modern retellings of the Pandora myth interpret Hope as a blessing. If so, then Hope is the only blessing in the jar. Moreover, as Hesiod tells the story, Hope is caught under the rim of the jar and remains within it. Therefore, humankind may or may not have been given Hope.

REFLECTIONS

1. What is a stereotype?
2. Find examples of stereotyping in
   a. TV programs
   b. movies
   c. advertisements
   d. books
   e. magazines
   f. quotations from politicians
3. In what ways is Pandora a stereotype?
4. In what ways did the myth of Pandora lead to a feminine stereotype?
5. Traditionally, the myth of Pandora always follows the myth of Prometheus. Why?

6. Is curiosity a blessing or an evil?
7. Since Hope is left in the jar, does this mean that man is denied Hope? Since the jar contains only evils, was Hope meant to be an evil or a comfort?
8. Tell the story of Pandora from Epimetheus's point of view.
9. The following women were among those responsible for bringing the cause of the rights of women to public attention. Write a short biography of one of them and present it to the class.
   a. Susan B. Anthony
   b. Elizabeth Pankhurst
   c. Simone de Beauvoir
   d. Gloria Steinem
   e. Betty Friedan
10. A television interviewer has scheduled Pandora to appear on his or her talk show. You, as Pandora, will be asked, among other things, why you opened the jar, by one of your classmates playing the interviewer. Defend your actions and then reverse roles with the interviewer.

HUMAN EXPERIENCE

Pandora, given to man in this myth as a punishment, is seen both as an earth-mother figure and as a demonic force portraying the dangers associated with beauty and curiosity. She represents both the good woman and the evil woman. She is both dangerous and desirable because of her beauty. She is the first woman in a world that has consisted only of men, and therefore the responsibility for the seduction of men is placed upon her. She causes evil in the world through her curiosity about the contents of the jar. Pandora is, therefore, a two-sided figure: beautiful and fruitful on the one hand, evil and destructive on the other.

To our modern eyes, it appears that Pandora was created as the *dangerous woman.* Since the gods put the evils into the jar and gave Pandora all her "gifts," it might be argued that they are responsible for her nature. In any case, Pandora takes her place in a human tradition that condemns women as hazardous because they are attractive to men. Fear or hatred of women has a long history. This was partly due to men's feelings of anger and jealousy toward women who were capable of bearing children. Because men feared these powers of women, they turned their anger and fear into feelings of superiority, which then enabled them to control and dominate that which they feared. Thus, sometimes men made women responsible for all the evils, including physical desire. They felt safer when they were in control of women, subordinating them within the areas of work, marriage, and religion. Women's "powers" then seemed to be counterbalanced by their inferior status in society.

The Women's Liberation Movement in contemporary society has strongly criticized these attitudes and practices. They have pointed out that women have traditionally behaved in expected "female" patterns of behavior. For instance, they cry when they are hurt. Men, on the other hand, have been expected to behave as if they are strong and invulnerable, even when they don't feel that way. Women's Liberation supporters have suggested that it is limiting and degrading to force people to behave in expected roles rather than as individual people. Men who feel the need to control women cannot truly love them; nor are they free, themselves, of the yoke of tyranny. To be *in control* makes spontaneity and freedom impossible both for the one who controls and the one who is being controlled.

Today social institutions are in the process of responding to federal legislation that makes women an equal force in the labor market. However, the status of women is in flux, and while greater opportunities are present than ever before in some career choices, other fields have not yet opened their doors to women. Women, themselves, have in large numbers refused to be suppressed in any area of their lives, and they are fighting for recognition and equality as never before in history.

19 Lycaon
The Flood
Dawn of the New Era

INTRODUCTION

Each of the following three myths relates closely to one another. The first myth, "Lycaon," dramatizes a situation that was a crime against both humankind and the immortal gods. The second myth, "The Flood," describes divine retribution for that crime. The third myth, "Dawn of the New Era," involves the reconciliation between gods and mortals, and provides for the continuity of the human race.

ANTICIPATIONS

1. How is mankind punished for evil behavior today?
2. Mankind has always wanted to create new life. What examples can you find of this activity in our own age?

INTRODUCTION

Lycaon

The myth of Lycaon taught the ancient Greeks that their great god, Zeus, did not want *human* sacrifice, and that he would not tolerate the practice of cannibalism.

The ancient Greeks knew that there had been cannibalism in Attica (the southeastern Greek mainland). Every eight or nine years, a human being, perhaps the sacred king, was killed and dismembered. His inner parts were then mixed with animal meat and served to worshippers.

This myth is a good example of the way a myth can substitute for a divine commandment. It is a dramatic presentation of Zeus's attitude toward human sacrifice and cannibalism. The message leaves no doubt as to how man should conduct himself.

THE MYTH

A bronze race of mortals once inhabited the earth. They were arrogant and cruel, and they were disrespectful to the deathless gods. Zeus, who delights in thunder, heard rumors of their behavior and vowed that, if these rumors were true, he would destroy this race. So that he could evaluate for himself how religious, righteous, and law-abiding mortal man actually was, Zeus decided to travel over the earth in the disguise of a humble mortal.

Zeus, as a humble traveler, wandered south past the mountains in Arcadia, which are known for their wild beasts, past Mount Cyllene, where his son, Hermes of the Golden Wand, was born, and into the pine forests of Lycaeüs.

As dusk drew on the dew-covered chariot of Nyx (Night), the humble traveler entered Lycaon's palace. Lycaon was the king of Arcadia and the father of fifty sons. Zeus had heard rumors that these were the most arrogant and disrespectful mortal men on the face of the earth. Now he would see for himself if these rumors were true.

It was time for the evening meal when the humble traveler entered the great assembly hall, and Lycaon had gathered his extensive family about him for the festive occasion. Upon finding an uninvited stranger in their midst, and a humble one at that, King Lycaon met the stranger with hostility. He questioned him even before he fed him, which had not been the socially accepted practice in Greece among earlier races of man.

"Who are you, and what do you want here?" he roared.

"I am one of the deathless Olympian gods," the humble traveler responded. "I have come down to Arcadia from the mountains in the north. I seek hospitality in the name of far-seeing Zeus, who is the protector of strangers and beggars."

At this, Lycaon looked at the traveler and grinned. Then his scornful laughter revealed what he thought of this preposterous assertion. "We will determine whether you are as immortal as you say you are," he responded. "From your appearance it seems more likely that you share our mortal destiny. However, I invite you to share part of our meal with us."

While his fifty sons and their many wives and children looked on expectantly, Lycaon announced to one of the attending servants, "Bring forth that young Arcadian boy."

When the child was brought forth, bound, the king slit his throat and then cut him into many pieces. He had certain pieces of flesh boiled and the other pieces broiled over the blazing flames of the hearth. Then he had the cooked flesh and the mutilated fragments of bone laid upon a platter and served along with the rest of the meal.

"Oh, we shouldn't forget to sacrifice to the immortal gods, should we!" Lycaon exclaimed as he gave the observant stranger a humorous glance. "We'd better do this before we eat, so just be patient everyone," he requested. "It won't take long."

Lycaon, having been educated in the old religious customs, called for a cow. When a servant brought one, Lycaon slit its throat, dismembered it, and roasted the meat. Then he whispered directions to another of the servants, who left the room and returned immediately with a bowl filled with body organs.

Lycaon took the roasted flesh, mixed the heart, liver, pancreas, and other organs among the meat and set the platter down before the humble stranger.

He knew that if their strange guest were a god as he proclaimed himself to be, he would not touch this sacrifice. Lycaon had composed it as a test of his guest's true identity. The organs provided the clue. If the humble stranger were truly an Olympian god, then he would recognize the organs as those of a mortal, in this case, one of Lycaon's own grandchildren. If not, he would not be able to recognize the source of these morsels once they had been chopped and mixed with the chunks of meat.

As soon as Lycaon placed the sacrifice in front of his humble guest, he announced, "This portion is for Zeus, Lord of Olympus, and the other deathless gods. May they eat heartily and well, as we sit down to our own fragrant food."

The stranger regarded the sacrifice on the platter before him with complete contempt. The royal family had forgotten his presence as its members ravenously attacked the food upon their own tables. They did not feel that this fuss over a stranger should have delayed their meal. Therefore, in their attention to their own food, they did not witness the transformation that was occurring only a few feet from them.

By the time they felt the tremendous heat and the blinding white light, it was too late to escape. Zeus suddenly overturned the feast and rocked the palace with the blasts of an awesome thunderstorm. Lightning bolts struck the roof and walls, engulfing the palace in raging flames and killing every occupant except Lycaon.

Lycaon, being the most educated in religious practices, had made an effort to protect himself as he took the calculated risk of the deceptive sacrifice. He alone had kept one eye upon the humble stranger. Therefore, as he watched the stranger recoil at the sacrifice and begin to loom larger and brighter in the darkened hall, Lycaon fled from his palace.

The Arcadian king hid in the fields. The darkness and the cool breeze felt good upon his skin. He decided to warn his neighbors that the deathless gods were wandering the earth, and that they were ready to avenge the disrespect that had developed in the land. He opened his mouth to speak out, but his tongue would not obey his mind. All he could do was howl.

Terrorstruck, Lycaon examined himself. He was suddenly aware that instead of running in the manner in which he was accustomed, he was using his arms, as well as his legs. He found that he no longer could stand upright. His skin and robes had become covered with long hairs of silver and grey. As he licked his dry lips, he could see a longer, more pointed tongue. He had become a wolf!

The terrible stranger had avenged Lycaon's ridicule and cruelty. Yet, in many ways, Lycaon had not changed at all. His eyes still sparkled, although in a narrower space. His mouth still grinned maliciously. He continued to slaughter beasts in his bloodthirsty, furious way, delighting as much in killing his prey as in eating it.

Thus the Lord of Olympus avenged upon one family a fate that the whole human family at the time deserved. Mortal man had become monstrous and was guilty of unmatched evils.

As Zeus, who delights in thunder, returned to Mount Olympus, he thought about mortal man's inhumanity to his fellow man and his disrespect for his gods. The thought of Lycaon's royal family rekindled his wrath. Feelings of rage and vengeance overcame his sighs of sorrow and pity. Far-seeing Zeus was to seal the fate of this race of man.

INTRODUCTION

The Flood

Sometime in the third millenium B.C. (3000–2000 B.C.), there was a great flood in Mesopotamia. This cataclysmic event produced three great flood records; the Sumerian, the Biblical, and the Greek myth contained in this chapter.

All three tell of mortals saved by a divinity who had advised them to build an ark, which ultimately landed safely upon the top of a mountain. In the case of both the Greek and Biblical records, the divinity caused the flood to punish man for immoral behavior. However, unlike God and Zeus, the Sumerian gods acted impulsively. Such gods are much more frightening because they bring ruin even to the virtuous.

THE MYTH

The Olympian gods gathered upon Mount Olympus to hear far-seeing

Zeus's judgment upon mortal men. He had told them about the way in which the royal family of King Lycaon lived, recounting in detail their treatment of both mortals and immortals. All of the gods agreed that humankind must be punished. Yet, they grieved for the total destruction of mortals. What would happen to the earth without their presence? Who would sacrifice to the immortals if no mortal was left to worship the deathless gods?

Olympian Zeus comforted their fears by assuring them that once he had destroyed this race, he would create a new race of mortals to supply their altars with fragrant sacrifices.

Loud-thundering Zeus prepared to use his fearsome weapons to destroy man. However, he became concerned that his lightning and thunderbolts might so engulf the earth and seas in flames that even Mount Olympus and the heavens would be destroyed. Therefore, he determined to destroy man by water, rather than fire. He dared not burn the earth, but he certainly could flood it in safety.

Zeus imprisoned Boreas, the north wind, in the cave of Aeolus, the keeper of the winds, so that Boreas would be unable to freeze the flood waters into ice. With Boreas, he imprisoned Zephyrus, the west wind. Otherwise, Zephyrus might dispel the storm clouds before they had brought their devastating rains.

With these winds confined, the Lord of Black Clouds then set the south wind loose upon the earth. Bringing with him the storm clouds that frighten mortals, the south wind flew over the earth. His body was covered by terrifying black clouds, while his white hair, his robe, and his wings were all streaming with rain. As he flew, he clenched the storm clouds in his hands, crushing and squeezing all the moisture from them. The heavens roared with peals of Zeus's thunder, and a deluge drenched the earth.

Meanwhile, Iris, rainbow-clothed messenger of Hera, descended to earth. There she collected water from the seas and brought this nourishment up to the weeping clouds to further increase the rainfall. The corn bent earthward beneath the onslaught of the deluge. Farmers wept over the loss of their crops. Yet, it never occurred to them that they, too, would perish.

Loud-thundering Zeus looked down from Mount Olympus and decided to increase the devastation, since the disaster was not yet sufficient to erase mortal man from the earth. Therefore, the king called upon his brother, the Lord of the Sea, for help.

Poseidon, the Earthshaker, was delighted to receive permission to exercise his own full authority. He assembled all the river gods and sea gods and instructed them: "Unlock your gates and the doors to your houses. Remove whatever restrains your waves so that nothing obstructs the movement of your waters. Then, give them the freedom to flow wherever they choose." The water gods proudly exercised their new powers. They returned to their underwater homes and followed Poseidon's commands.

Meanwhile, as the sea swelled with fury, the Earthshaker struck the earth with his terrible trident. By causing the land to tremble and crack, the great sea lord opened new passages for the rising rivers and seas.

The flood now rushed over the land, burying the orchards and the open fields of grain. As it roared along, it gathered sheep, cattle, farmers, entire trees, and houses, tearing them apart with its swirling force. Even temples dedicated to the deathless gods, with shrines containing sacred fires, were destroyed in the deluge. Buildings too strong to fall were buried beneath the waters, which now ran rampant over the earth. Slowly but surely the rising waters swallowed even the tops of towers and hills.

Men frantically tried to escape doom. Those who lived by the sea tried to rescue their boats, but, as often as not, they had not foreseen the extent of their peril. The raging seas had smashed their boats or had cast them loose before they could occupy them. Those who were able to launch their boats died of starvation on the endless sea. Those who lived inland took to the hills and mountains, desperately climbing higher and higher until there was nothing left to face except their inevitable fate.

The deer's swiftness was powerless against the torrential flood waters, and the wild boar found his terrible tusks no protection against this formidable new enemy. The birds frantically beat their wings as they wearily searched in vain for a resting place. When finally exhausted, they plunged into the endless sea.

Afterwards, all was still. Sea monsters relaxed their bulky bodies where mountain goats had recently grazed, and the sea nymphs swam in wonder among submerged houses, palaces, and temples. Dolphins invaded the woods and groves, chasing one another around mighty submerged tree trunks. Except for those creatures whose home was the river or sea, all earthly life had perished.

Dawn of the New Era

The following myth continues the story of the Greek flood by introducing the two mortal survivors, Deucalion and Pyrrha. The myth combines ideas from earlier oral versions, one dating from the matriarchal period, when the oracle was Themis rather than Apollo, and the other dating from the patriarchal period, since a male god, Zeus, caused the flood.

Deucalion and Pyrrha obeyed Themis's commands and did not look behind them to see what was happening to the stones. Traditionally, gods did not permit mortals to observe miracles. In the *Bible*, when Lot's wife disobeyed God's command, He punished her by turning her into a pillar of salt.

In this myth, stones were transformed into people, an idea that could have arisen in Asia Minor. In mythology, man usually was created from the most abundant local material. Because Greek soil was very rocky, the new race of mortals was created from stones. In the Navajo religion, "First Man" and "First Woman" were created from two ears of corn. The first Norse man and woman were created from two trees.

THE MYTH

Before the deluge occurred, Prometheus had realized his great cousin's intentions. From his imprisonment upon the cliffs of Mount Caucasus far to the northeast, the clever Titan called out to his son, Deucalion, warning him of the impending disaster. He advised his attentive son to construct a sturdy boat, fill it with provisions, and then enter it with his wife, Pyrrha, the daughter of Prometheus's brother, Epimetheus. Finally, Prometheus commanded Deucalion to revere the Lord of Olympus and the other deathless gods in the coming time of terror.

Deucalion obeyed his loving father in every respect, so that when the great rains arrived the couple was well-prepared. They floated over the floodwaters for nine days and nine nights, surrounded by an endless sea of desolation. Finally the deluge ceased, and they found that their boat had drifted near the twin peaks of Mount Parnassus. These peaks had evaded the flood because their tremendous height transcended the clouds and reached the starry heavens.

When loud-thundering Zeus looked down from Mount Olympus and saw that the earth had become one vast sea, he was satisfied. Then he noticed that one small craft had survived the devastation, and that its occupants were the last living representatives of humankind. As he examined them more closely, he recognized that they were the children of his Titan cousins. He knew that, of all their race, these two were innocent. They were humble and kind, and they respected the deathless gods. Therefore, he was content to let them remain the sole survivors of the great catastrophe.

Far-seeing Zeus then freed Boreas, the north wind, and Zephyrus, the west wind. Zephyrus dispelled the threatening storm clouds, and Boreas blew upon the waters to encourage them to recede. Next the Lord of Thunder commanded his great brother, Poseidon, to put aside his trident and calm the turbulent surface of the sea.

The Lord of the Sea obeyed his brother's wishes and, in turn, commanded his immortal son, Triton, to calm the waters by blowing on his horn-like shell. Triton emerged above the waters at his father's summons, took his shell, and blew a sharp blast. The signal was heard from the far eastern point, where Helius rises out of the ocean with his chariot of the sun at the break of day, to the far western point, where he descends into the ocean at the end of the day.

The sea and the river gods obeyed Triton's order and retreated from their newly acquired dominions, reluctantly returning to their customary homes. Thus, the waters gradually receded from the face of the earth, revealing the hills, trees, mountain valleys, streams, and the shambles of a civilization that had existed only a short time before. Far-seeing Zeus had restored the earth, but it had become a silent and desolate wasteland, devoid of humans to populate it.

As the waters receded, Deucalion's boat became beached upon the mountainside which appeared beneath it. The lonely couple moored their boat and sacrificed to the deathless gods, first to Olympian Zeus, who is the God of Escape, and then to the local mountain gods.

Then Deucalion announced, "Dearest Pyrrha, do you realize that we are alone upon the earth? We are the only living creatures Helius beholds as he travels each day from east to west. The great sea has buried everyone else.

"We share love and now danger, for we cannot be certain that the terrible deluge will not return. I am thankful that we have survived together. Could either of us have borne this terrifying experience alone? I think not. Without your companionship and comfort, I would have let the waters engulf me.

"I wish that I had my cunning father's talent for creation! If he could inspire me, perhaps I, too, could model clay into mortals and implant life within my creations."

Weeping for the loss of their entire race and for the desolation around them, Deucalion and Pyrrha again offered thanks to the deathless gods for their own survival. Then they decided to pray to the great Pythian oracle, Themis, because of her reputation for justice. The receding waters had disclosed her temple, and it was now accessible to them. They carefully made their descent to the Cephissus River, crossed its turbulent waters, and then cleansed themselves. They now were ready to enter great Themis's temple.

The flood had left the sacred building filthy with mud and moss, its holy altar without its sacred fire. However, Deucalion and Pyrrha humbly prostrated themselves and kissed the cold stone floor. They then prayed to the great Mother Goddess and prophet:

"Oh, Themis, lover of justice, if the deathless gods have exhausted their fury, if they can forgive us and be kind to us, then tell us how we can reestablish our mortal race. Help us in our despair and desolation."

The Great Goddess heard their prayer and replied to them: "Leave my temple, both of you. Let your clothing hang loosely, ungathered and unbelted. Hide your faces with your clothing, and as you bend down to the earth, throw the bones of your mighty mother over your shoulders and behind your backs."

Deucalion and Pyrrha heard the words of the great oracle in stunned silence. What exactly had Themis commanded them? Pyrrha spoke first. "I must not obey the Great Goddess," she said. "If I were to remove my mother's sacred bones from her tomb, I fear that her shade would suffer in the Kingdom of the Dead."

"Would Themis request us to perform a sacrilegious act?" asked Deucalion. "The oracle must have had a different message in mind." Consequently, Deucalion and Pyrrha repeated the mysterious advice, hoping to discover another explanation.

Suddenly, Deucalion announced, "I think I have found an interpretation that will disturb neither the living nor the dead. The earth is our great mother, and the rocks and stones with which she abounds are her bones. Therefore, we should throw rocks and stones over our shoulders and behind our backs."

Pyrrha was not certain that Deucalion was correct. She replied, "I am hopeful, yet, I am afraid. The idea seems safe. What harm would it do to try?"

Consequently, they loosened their clothes and veiled their heads, as the oracle had directed them. Then, they left the temple and collected rocks and stones, tossing them over their shoulders and behind their backs. When they had thrown as many as they could find and lift, they paused. The earth seemed to be stirring behind them. Since their task was finished, Deucalion and Pyrrha cautiously unveiled their heads and turned around. They gaped in wonder at the sight which met their eyes. Themis had answered their prayers.

The mountainside above them was strewn with rocks in various stages of transformation. Those closest to them had already become softer. As their natural hardness left them, the rocks had swelled and elongated, gradually taking the shape and dimensions of mortal men and women. The first stones they had thrown were in the most advanced stages of transformation. Yet even these did not show signs of being alive. Instead, they stood upon the earth like rough-hewn marble statues, which their sculptor had not quite finished sanding and polishing.

The parts of the rocks that contained any moisture had been transformed into the blood and body liquids necessary for nourishment and life. The solid parts of the rocks had been transformed into bones. The veins which had been present in the stones, remained in the newly created mortals. As more time passed and their newly developed bodies warmed into life and motion, the rocks, which Deucalion had thrown, became mortal men, and those Pyrrha had thrown became mortal women.

This new race was destined to lead a hard, laborious life. However, having been developed from stone and rock, it was born with the innate ability to bear its burdens. These mortals became known as "people" (*laos* in Greek) because they had been created from stones (*laas*).

Then Helius once again warmed the earth with his sunshine, causing the moist land to become warm. Seeds from within the earth swelled and ripened into new life. The earth thus restored to life all the forms that had existed prior to the flood, and new ones as well.

REFLECTIONS

1. Write a science-fiction myth depicting the destruction of the world, its cause, and the recreation of man.
2. What does Zeus's attitude about Lycaon's crime reveal about the development of Greek religion?
3. Why do you think cultures throughout the world have "flood myths"?
4. If there were going to be a flood today, what do you think Deucalion would put into his ark? Discuss.
5. When Zeus punished mankind with a flood, what do you think was revealed about his values? Discuss.
6. Write an essay on why the gods created a new race of man.

20 Arachne

INTRODUCTION

Arachne had achieved excellence *(areté)* in her weaving. However, she was not satisfied to be known as the best mortal weaver. She believed she was a better weaver than any of the gods. She lost her sense of perspective, and forgot that she was human. She became arrogant and insolent, even to the old woman who gave her advice. This is an example of excessive pride or *hybris*, which leads to catastrophe. The Greeks called this abdication of the rule of reason *áte*. Therefore, when Arachne's emotions controlled her actions, she brought destruction upon herself. The appropriate nature of the punishment adds to the appeal of this myth.

ANTICIPATIONS

1. Discuss whether you think all people need to feel proud of themselves. What happens when they appear to feel too proud of themselves?
2. Where do you draw the line between healthy pride and arrogance? Give examples.
3. How do you think a talented, attractive person avoids arrogance?
4. Why do you think some people behave arrogantly when they appear to have no reason to do so?

THE MYTH

Arachne's only claim to greatness was her weaving. Neither her humble birth, nor her country of Lydia was remarkable in any way. Yet, through her extraordinary ability as a weaver, Arachne had earned great fame among her own people and among the neighboring countries as well. The nymphs of Mount Tmolus often left their vines, and the nymphs of the Pactolus River their streams, just to admire Arachne's work. They enjoyed observing every aspect of her performance, from the spinning of the soft mass of wool into yarn, to the designs she made with her shuttle. They marveled at the completed tapestry. Everyone thought that only grey-eyed Athena, the patron goddess of arts and crafts, could have taught Arachne to be such a skillful weaver.

Yet, Arachne was a particularly proud and independent young woman. She arrogantly denied that she had ever received any aid from the grey-eyed goddess. In fact, she boasted that she was far superior to Athena in the art of weaving. "Let battle-stirring Athena appear and contest her skill with mine," Arachne challenged. "If she wins, I shall accept whatever punishment or shame she chooses to impose upon me."

The grey-eyed daughter of Zeus was outraged at Arachne's disrespect. "I deserve praise from mortals, not their contempt," she exclaimed. "My powers of revenge surely will achieve what my gifts have not."

Determined to restore her own authority and reputation, Athena decided to punish Arachne. She transformed herself into a white-haired old woman, who hobbled along with the support of a staff. In this disguise, she appeared before Arachne and spoke kindly to her.

"Young lady, I hope I may interrupt you. Old age deserves respect. Long years bring a person broad experience. Therefore, do not ignore my advice. Strive for fame and glory against other mortal women, but recognize and accept the superiority of the immortals. If you humbly beg the goddess Athena's pardon for your arrogance, she will forgive your misconduct."

Arachne's eyes blazed with rage. Her weaving shuttle dropped to her lap in her temptation to strike the presumptuous stranger. However, her judgment somewhat controlled her temper, and she let her words express the feelings her hand resisted.

"You old fool!" she exclaimed scornfully. "Your idle, prying tongue betrays the curse of old age. Maybe your own daughter or your son's wife will bother with your wise words, but I have no interest in your guidance. No advice of yours will change my mind. I shall continue to do just as I please. As for the Great Goddess, why hasn't she appeared? Why has she delayed our contest? Let Athena accept my challenge, the sooner, the better."

"Oh, she is coming," asserted the old woman, and as she spoke, she became transfigured with a divine radiance. Emerging from her disguise, Athena commanded awe and reverence from all who saw her.

Only Arachne remained fearless, yet even she self-consciously blushed against her will. However, she remained stubborn, and in her defiant determination to win the contest, Arachne hastened her own fate. No longer did the goddess try to dissuade Arachne with helpful advice. No longer did this great daughter of Zeus evade the challenge.

The contestants immediately settled into their preparations. Carefully they set up their looms, tying the long, fine, vertical warp threads to their loom beams and dividing these threads with reeds. When they had completed this task, they tucked up their skirts in order to permit quick, unhampered movements, picked up their threaded shuttles, and began to work. Each weaver moved her shuttle swiftly and skillfully through the threads, enjoying the labor she performed so well. Each wove wispy clouds shimmering with sunlight and a magnificent rainbow shining in a thousand blending colors. Finally, each weaver artistically wove into her tapestry golden threads which accentuated brilliantly the stories she portrayed.

The grey-eyed daughter of Zeus depicted the twelve Olympian gods enthroned above the Areopagus[1] in Athens. There the immortals debated the merits of the argument between Athena and Poseidon over which of them should be considered the city's patron god. In her tapestry, the Lord of the Sea had just struck a rock with his three-pronged fish spear, the trident, splitting it and causing a fountain of salty waters to spring forth from the fissure. He based his claim to the area upon the value of this miraculous gift. The goddess Athena pictured herself armed with her crested golden helmet, her breastplate and shield, and her shining spear. She had just struck the earth with her spear, causing a leafy green tree, completely covered with olives, to emerge fully grown. She based her claim to the area upon the value of her miraculous gift. Although the deathless gods admired both gifts, they decided that Athena's gift was more useful than Poseidon's and, consequently, awarded the city to her.[2]

The goddess decorated the four corners of her tapestry with four miniature scenes, each depicting the terrifying fate of arrogant women who had been disrespectful to the gods. In one corner, the gods punished two women by transforming them into snow-covered mountains. In the second corner, golden-throned Hera transformed another woman into a crane, while in the third corner, Hera, again, punished a female by transforming her into a stork. In the fourth corner, the gods punished a man's daughters by turning them into marble steps leading up to a temple. With these illustrations of divine retribution, Zeus's great daughter Athena hoped to warn Arachne about what she could expect for her pride and presumption.

Meanwhile, Arachne used her great talent to ridicule the immortal gods. With dazzling artistry, she depicted Olympian Zeus's many love affairs. Among them were his transformation into a bull for Europa, into a swan for Leda, into a golden shower for Danaë, and into the husband, Amphitryon, for Alcmene. As if this were not enough to document her point, Arachne also illustrated the romantic exploits of Poseidon, the Earthshaker, and those of far-shooting Apollo and of loud-roaring Dionysus.

When each had completed her tapestry, Athena inwardly appreciated

Arachne's remarkable skill, but she could not tolerate the mortal woman's disrespect. Because Arachne had taunted the gods with her scornful sense of humor, Zeus's grey-eyed daughter tore apart her tapestry and struck her three times upon her forehead with the shuttle.

Arachne, in defeat and despair, knit a rope around her neck and tried to hang herself. However, the Great Goddess took pity upon her and prevented her suicide by catching her falling body. Yet she did not release Arachne from further punishment. "Live, wicked wretch," grey-eyed Athena commanded, "but hang forevermore. Let my curse remain even upon your children and their children to the end of all your race."

As she left, Zeus's great daughter sprinkled Arachne with juice taken from the leaves of a poisonous aconite plant. As the drops touched Arachne, they completely altered her appearance. Her flowing hair shed and fell to the ground. Her nose and her ears vanished. Her head shrank, and the rest of her body diminished also, until all that remained of her was a large belly with spiny, jointed fingers where her legs and arms had been.

Thus, like the other mortal women who had offended the gods, Arachne found herself transformed. As a spider,[3] she would weave eternally.

1. A rocky hill near the Acropolis in Athens, which became the location of the first Athenian court, composed of an aristocratic council of elders.
2. Poseidon flooded the region of Attica in his rage over his decision, and the Athenians continued to honor both gods.
3. Arachne has donated her name to the family to which spiders belong: the arachnids.

21 Niobe

INTRODUCTION

Niobe, like Arachne, brought destruction upon herself. She, too, had achieved an extraordinary kind of excellence, in the birth of her many beautiful and handsome children, and like Arachne, Niobe became too proud of her achievement. It made her unreasonable. She insisted that she was a goddess. This is another indication of the temporary madness (*áte*) that comes from *hybris*. Her foolish attitude and her outrageous behavior brought ruin upon her and her family.

THE MYTH

Everyone in Lydia and Phrygia, on the west coast of Asia Minor, was discussing Arachne's arrogant actions and grotesque punishment. The news was so spectacular and intimidating that it traveled west, across the Aegean Sea to the Greek mainland. There, Niobe, the queen of the Boeotian city of Thebes, also heard about Arachne. The news should have impressed Niobe, first because she had known Arachne when they were young maidens in Lydia, and also, because Niobe's personality was very similar to Arachne's. However, possibly because this similarity was so great, Niobe did not learn from Arachne's experience. Consequently, her own arrogant attitude brought about her ruin and the ruin of her family.

Niobe had much to make her arrogant: Her father was King Tantalus of Lydia; her husband was King Amphion of Thebes; and most important to her, she was the mother of fourteen glorious children.

Niobe's arrogance worried the daughter of the blind Theban prophet, Teiresias, who was similarly gifted in prophecy. Being concerned about the vengeance that the deathless gods take upon those mortals who do not honor them adequately, the prophetess walked through the streets of Thebes crying:

"Women of Thebes, dedicate sacred rites to the power of great Leto and to her mighty twins, Artemis of the Raining Arrows and Apollo of the Silver Bow. Mix sweet-smelling incense, and bind your foreheads with sacred wreaths of laurel. Great Leto bids me to offer you this counsel."

Every woman in Thebes hastened to obey the urgent summons, paying tribute to Leto and her deathless children. They wound the sacred laurel leaves around their foreheads; they fed their sacred fires with incense; and they prayed to the immortal gods as the prophetess had commanded them.

Queen Niobe appeared among the female worshippers with her royal guard in attendance. She was the picture of beauty and wealth in her gold-embroidered Phrygian cape. However, her fair face was clouded with rage. Her long hair trembled with her anger as she observed the religious ceremonies with haughty eyes and increasing fury.

"Women of Thebes!" she exclaimed. "You are mad to prefer the deathless gods to the mortal ones! Why are you worshipping Leto instead of your earthly queen? Leto is nothing but a feeble creation of mortal minds. She is invisible and impotent, whereas I am the daughter of King Tantalus of Lydia, who was the only mortal ever invited to feast with the immortals on Mount Olympus.[1] My mother, one of the Pleiades, is the daughter of the great Titan, Atlas, now the mightiest mountain, on whose high shoulders the starry heavens rest. Zeus is both my grandfather and my father-in-law.

"My power commands both Boeotia and Phrygia across the Aegean Sea. My royal palace contains infinite riches. As if all this were not sufficient reason to worship me as a divine being, look at my face. I am as beautiful as any of your deathless goddesses.

"Finally, as the jeweled crown of all my joys, I am the mother of seven beautiful daughters and as many handsome, accomplished sons. When they marry, I will have twice as many children. Is this not ample justification for my pride? Is it not ample reason for you to worship me?

"How dare you then worship Leto before you worship me? No one else respects her. Neither the sky nor the seas gave this banished goddess refuge. Even the earth refused to give her a place to bear her children. She was nothing more than a vagabond until the floating island of Delos accepted her and gave her its unstable land beset by waves. Moreover, after all her wanderings, she only gave birth to two children, whereas I have fourteen.

"Who doubts that I am happy? Who can doubt that I shall remain powerful? I am so rich and powerful that adversity cannot hurt me! No matter how much Misfortune might destroy, she would have to leave much more behind, so much do I possess. For example, suppose that a few of my children were to die. I have so many of them that Misfortune could not possibly reduce them to a small number. Even then I could compete successfully with your Great Goddess, Leto. Her unimportant accomplishment of two children almost brings upon her the shame of a childless woman.

"So, women of Thebes: Remove your laurel wreaths, and turn away from these foolish religious rites."

The timid Theban women regretfully obeyed their arrogant queen. They stopped their sacred observances and removed their sacred laurel crowns. Yet, in their hearts they continued to adore their deathless goddess, Leto, and her immortal children, the Archer Goddess and the Lord of the Silver Bow.[2]

Meanwhile, high on Mount Cynthus, great Leto observed this insult to her divine honor and became enraged with Niobe. The goddess immediately sought her twin children and shared her impassioned fury with them.

"I am filled with grief and fury. Niobe of Thebes has publicly humiliated me. She is causing mortals to question my power as a goddess. Unless I am revenged, I shall lose all religious honors among mortal men.

"Furthermore, this cursed child of Tantalus dares to consider her own mortal children superior to you. She even calls me childless because I have borne only the two of you, whereas she has fourteen children. May she become childless as retribution for her wicked words."

Leto would have pressed on with further furious complaints, but far-shooting Apollo interrupted her. "Stop," he declared. "We have heard enough. More talk only will delay our planned revenge." His twin, Artemis, spurred by quick anger, agreed.

Then the children of Leto, Apollo of the Silver Bow and Artemis of the Golden Arrows departed from their aggrieved mother and glided swiftly through the air down to the Boeotian city of Thebes. They concealed their shining divinity beneath dark clouds and landed secretly upon the towering walls of the city. Apollo planned to make his long silver bow sing as he shot the seven sons of Niobe. Artemis would then rain her golden arrows down upon Niobe's seven daughters. Nothing diverted these deathless gods from their divine vengeance.

The spacious plain which lay in front of Thebes was dusty from the trampling hooves of the horses which young men daily exercised there, and from the tracks of chariots driven by other young men as they practiced their skills in warfare. Here the deathless twins found two of Niobe's seven sons. Wearing clothes of Phoenician purple, the young princes sat upon golden saddles as they practiced their riding skills.

Ismenus, Niobe's oldest child, was the first victim of the divine assault. He was reining his horse as he rounded a corner of the riding area when an arrow flew through his breast. He gave a sudden cry, and the reins dropped from his dying hands. He slipped slowly off his horse and sank down upon the sand, lifeless.

Next, Niobe's son, Siphilus, heard the rattling sound of the arrow case and frantically tried to outrace his own death. However, his effort was in vain, for the arrow overtook him and struck him from behind, penetrating his neck and throat. Because he had been leaning low over his horse's mane, he plunged headlong over the head of his blood-smeared horse and died upon the sand.

Phoedemus and young Tantalus, having completed their own exercises, were practicing their wrestling skills. With well-oiled limbs they pressed against each other's power, their athletic bodies locked in an embrace. One arrow pierced both of the brothers' bodies as they stood locked in one another's mighty grip. Together they cried out in pain and fell bleeding upon the sandy earth, breathing their last.

Their brother, Alphenor, observed what had happened to the wrestlers and horrified, rushed to help them. However, he was too late. As he embraced their cold corpses, furious Apollo aimed his silver bow once again and severed the thread of Alphenor's life.

Niobe's sixth son, Damasichthon, was killed by a double wound. After being shot in the knee, he had bent over in an attempt to dislodge the arrow, when a second arrow fatally pierced his neck.

The last son, Ilioneus, in great terror raised his arms in prayer to the immortal gods. He addressed his plea to all of them since he did not understand the cause of this divine retribution.

"Oh deathless Olympians," he pleaded, "have pity upon me and excuse me from your fatal arrows!" Far-shooting Apollo heard the prayer, but his oath of divine vengeance was irrevocable. However, he made certain that his arrow killed Ilioneus instantly and painlessly.

When Niobe received word that her sons had been destroyed in their prime by shining arrows, she recognized the handiwork of Leto's mighty children. She was amazed that the deathless gods would dare to touch her sons, and enraged that they could and would wield such power.

Niobe's husband could not bear such sorrow. Hoping that death would release him from his plight, he plunged a dagger into his own breast and joined his sons in the kingdom of the dead.

Niobe now was pitied even by her enemies. Divine vengeance had taken its toll so quickly. The day before, the queen had proudly walked the streets of Thebes arrogantly flaunting her wealth and power, suppressing great Leto's sacred rites. Now, the deathless gods had made Niobe a widow and bereaved mother of seven children. As Niobe fell upon the cold corpses of her beloved sons and kissed them all for the last time, she raised her arms to the sky and cried:

"Cruel Leto. Feast upon my grief. I am filled with anguish over the seven lives you have taken from me. I hope my deep sorrow will satisfy your wild fury.

"Yet, do not think that you have won any victory over me. In the end, I will prove to be stronger than you. I do not have as many children as before, but I still have my seven daughters, and that is many more children than you have, vindictive goddess!"

Niobe hardly had finished speaking when the bow string vibrated again. Arrow-raining Artemis had begun to kill Niobe's daughters. At the ominous sound of the bow, every heart felt the chill of terror except Niobe's. Her arrogance made her stubborn and insensitive as she sat, stunned, in the presence of her seven murdered sons.

Niobe's seven daughters, clothed in long black robes of mourning, their long hair unbound, stood weeping before the funeral biers of their brothers. One daughter was unsuccessfully attempting to withdraw an arrow from her brother's side when she, herself, was suddenly struck. As she kissed her brother, she died upon his cold corpse, amazed by her fate.

A second daughter, who was trying to comfort her mother's grief, suddenly became speechless as she died breathlessly from an arrow in her throat. A third daughter fell to her death as she tried to flee from her fate, and a fourth fell upon the corpse of one of her sisters, making that lifeless body her deathbed. A fifth daughter was fatally struck as she attempted to run from her deathless pursuer, while the sixth died shrieking in terror over the deaths of her five sisters.

To shield her last daughter, Niobe threw her own body over the child as a protective shield.

"Oh save this child," she cried. "She is the youngest, the last of many, and the only one for whom I plead for life."

However, the Archer Goddess slew the daughter in the midst of her mother's plea.

There Niobe sat, surrounded by death. Her husband, her seven sons, and her seven daughters were all dead. Niobe was now the Queen of Sorrows. Hardened by her grief, she was a statue of desolation. The wind did not disturb a hair upon her head. The roses in her cheeks faded into the pallor of grief. Her eyes did not move in her lowered head, nor did her mouth move, or her pulse beat. Her neck lost its ability to turn, her arms to move, her feet to walk. As Niobe sat, completely lifeless and still, she became transformed into a statue of solid stone. Only her tears remained warm and liquid, as they streamed down her marble face.

A whirlwind swept Niobe away from Thebes and across the Aegean Sea to her own country of Lydia, where it placed her upon the summit of a great hill. There from her marble cheeks, tears of mourning flow eternally, night and day.[3]

Such divine revenge struck fear into every heart. With renewed zeal, mortal women brought offerings to great Leto's sacred altars and proclaimed her awesome power.

1. Tantalus is best known for his famous punishment. In return for tricking the gods, he was chained forever to a tree in Tartarus, beneath luscious fruit he couldn't reach and up to his chin in water that turned to dust whenever he tried to drink it.
2. Artemis and Apollo.
3. There is a human-shaped cliff in Lydia which appears to weep in winter when the sun strikes its snowy summit and melts the snow.

REFLECTIONS

1. Compare and contrast Niobe and Arachne.
2. Arachne and Niobe meet in the market place. Role-play a conversation that would be consistent with each character.
3. Would Athena have punished Arachne if Arachne's tapestry *had* glorified the gods? Explain your answer.
4. Would Athena have let Arachne feel superior to all other mortals as long as she respected the gods? Explain.
5. Niobe was excessively proud of her possessions. Do you think wealth inevitably corrupts a person's values? Explain.

22 Erysichthon

Erysichthon was another mortal who was punished for his *hybris* and *áte*. Like Arachne and Niobe, he caused his own ruin by his attitude and actions. Erysichthon had no respect for another's property and, in this case, the property was sacred to a god. When he was given an opportunity to change his ways, like Arachne, he refused. He saw no difference between himself and a god. In fact, he must have considered himself superior to the gods in order to have felt that he had the right to destroy the sacred grove.

His punishment convinced anyone who might have been tempted to lose sight of his mortal condition, that the gods did not tolerate *hybris*. Man must know himself and know his place in the universal scheme. Once again, the fact that the "punishment fits the crime" augments the appeal of this myth.

THE MYTH

Fair-wreathed Demeter dearly loved her sacred grove of trees in Thessaly, and spent many happy hours in its shade. Therefore, she became furious when Erysichthon, an impious young prince, decided to desecrate the sacred grove by building a palace with the sacred trees.

The prince gathered twenty gigantic servants, who together possessed the strength to uproot an entire city. He armed them with hatchets and with double-bladed axes and led them to great Demeter's sacred grove, commanding them to fell the trees. He announced that he himself would begin with the giant oak tree in the center, whose branches seemed to reach to the heavens. When he noticed that his servants reacted with reluctance, the prince announced that he would behead anyone who disobeyed his command.

"Even if this giant oak tree were the great goddess Demeter herself," Erysichthon boasted, "I would cut her down and sweep the earth with her crown of branches."

The dryad[1] who lived within this giant oak tree screamed in apprehension. Great Demeter heard her cry and exclaimed angrily, "Who dares to destroy my sacred trees?" Disguising herself as the mortal who was her chief priestess in the area, Demeter approached Erysichthon and cautioned him: "Young man," she said, "Do not mutilate trees that are sacred to the immortals. Order your servants to refrain from this impious task. When you desecrate great Demeter's sacred grove, you anger her."

Erysichthon was not intimidated by this advice. Glaring at the priestess more belligerently than a mother lioness faces a fearless hunter, he replied: "Leave me to my ways, or I shall fell you with my eager axe! With these great logs, I intend to build a strong house where I shall feast my friends in great style."

As he raised his arms to strike the tree, the oak trembled with fear. Its leaves and acorns grew pale, and its branches became covered with dew. When the wound it received from Erysichthon gushed purple blood, the prince and his servants gaped in amazement. With mounting terror they heard a voice from within the oak proclaim, "I am the dryad who lives within this sacred tree. With my departing life I prophesy that vengeance for your irreverent action is near."

The giant oak crashed to the ground, crushing its fellow trees beneath its huge trunk and crown of branches. The servants of the prince deserted their master so quickly that only the bronze axes lodged in the sacred tree trunks betrayed their participation. The disguised golden-wreathed goddess shook her shining hair in anger. However, she excused the attendants from their insult to her honor because they had committed their crime in obedience to their master's commands.

Her rage toward their prince was implacable. She emerged, resplendent from her disguise, towering over the irreverent prince as her head appeared to soar toward the heavens. "Build your splendid house, you dog," she advised, "and hold your sumptuous feast within its walls, for you shall dine frequently for the remainder of your life."

With these words, great Demeter turned her back upon Erysichthon and disappeared from sight. Then the fair-haired goddess summoned a nymph and commanded, "Take my chariot with my harnessed dragons, and go to the frosty land of Scythia far to the north. In that forlorn and barren area near Mount Caucasus, which bears neither corn nor fruit, you will find the starving creature, Famine. Bid her carry out my vengeance by infecting Erysichthon's mortal body and devouring all his nourishment."

When the nymph arrived in the wasteland of the Caucasus, she found sad Famine sitting in a stony field tearing futilely at the barren ground with her nails and her teeth. Her sunken eyes looked pale and dead. Her lips were white with slime, her teeth coated with rust. Her skin stretched so tightly over her bones that it revealed her inner organs.

Keeping her distance from this emaciated creature, the nymph relayed great Demeter's message. Even from a distance the gnawing sensation of Famine was contagious, so the nymph left the area immediately.

Famine obeyed the fair-wreathed goddess's command. Carried through the skies by a wind, she arrived in Thessaly and entered Erysichthon's palace through the roof. There she lay beside him while he was fast asleep and embraced him in her arms. Breathing upon his face and his chest, she caused his body to rage with hunger. Then, having performed her task, Famine forsook the fertile earth and returned to her native, barren land.

Meanwhile Erysichthon continued to sleep soundly, but now he dreamed of feasts, chewed imaginary foods, and swallowed the air. He awakened feeling ravenously hungry and rushed to his first of many huge meals.

Erysichthon soon felt himself consumed by a terrifying disease. He demanded the fruits of the sea, the heavens, and the earth. Yet he was condemned to the perpetual torment of unappeased hunger, for no matter what foods or how much of them he ate, he was still hungry for more. Twenty servants prepared each meal, and twelve more servants poured his wine, for Dionysus shared the Great Goddess's vengeance.

The king and queen were so embarrassed by this outrageous affliction, they hid their famished son from society. To some, they announced that Erysichthon was off collecting debts or that a boar wound had made an invalid of him, and to others that he was off acquiring a wife.

Meanwhile, Erysichthon was hidden within the palace eating everything anyone could supply him. Yet food that would have fed entire towns and nations could not satisfy Erysichthon's large appetite. In fact, the more food he consumed, the more food his greedy stomach craved. No matter how the servants attempted to satisfy his desires, he remained more dissatisifed than ever. Moreover, even with all the food his wealth could provide, his body wasted away without the sustenance it desperately demanded. Before long, his enormous appetite reduced his family to poverty.

As long as the palace storehouses could supply his needs, only the royal family was aware of the embarrassing curse. However, once the prince had exhausted the provisions within the palace, he sat down in public among the local garbage sites and begged for any morsels other people were discarding from their meals. There he remained, an object of ridicule and fear to the townspeople.

His sisters moaned, his mother wept with grief, and his father called upon the great Earthshaker,[2] Erysichthon's grandfather, in his distress.

"Great father, if you truly are my father, look upon your grandson and help him. I wish that far-shooting Apollo had struck him with one of his unerring arrows and that I had buried him. Instead, my son is cursed with this insatiable appetite. My storehouses have been exhausted in the attempt to appease his hunger. My barns have sacrificed their animals to his gluttony. He has even eaten the laboring mules, the race horses, the war horses, and the household pets. So if you are my father and Erysichthon's grandfather, either remove this dreadful affliction from his body or help me find some way to feed him."

The Lord of the Sea heard his son's prayer. When Erysichthon could no longer supply his body with sufficient food, the starving prince compulsively began to devour his own flesh and blood. Thus he consumed himself and died. Fair-haired Demeter was avenged.

1. A tree spirit.
2. Poseidon.

REFLECTIONS

1. Write a character sketch of Erysichthon. Based upon what you know of him, discuss how you think he would act in other situations.
2. Put yourself in Erysichthon's life and keep a diary beginning with the day you met Demeter's priestess until your death.

23 Midas

Midas was a foolish king, not an arrogant one. Therefore, this myth is more humorous than many of the other Greek myths. The source of the humor is exaggeration. Midas's wish, when fulfilled, was carried to its logical conclusion. The punishment by Apollo was also a form of exaggeration; the god disproportionately enlarged Midas's weakness. It is interesting that the Greek gods were more lenient with foolish behavior than they were with arrogant or insolent behavior. Dionysus forgave Midas, and Apollo's punishment was moderate, given his fondness for the silver bow.

ANTICIPATIONS

1. If you were granted one wish, what would it be? Why?
2. Make a list of the products you see advertised on television over a weekend. What do these ads reveal about the values of our society?
3. What do you view as the goal of most adults in your community?
   a. money
   b. fame
   c. more than one car
   d. owning property
   e. being the boss
   f. having an important career
   g. other

THE MYTH

Dionysus, the ivy-wreathed god of wine, cultivated the vineyards on Mount Tmolus which grew near the clear waters of the Pactolus River in

Lydia. One day when the maenads[1] and satyrs[2] who always followed him gathered nearby, Dionysus noticed that Seilenus,[3] his dearest friend and advisor, was not present.

Seilenus, who was old and drunk, had danced about the fields and had lost his way. Phrygian[4] peasants had found him, playfully had bound him with greenery, and had taken him to their king, Midas, while a wreath of ivy still covered his head.

In the past, King Midas had learned the rites of loud-roaring Dionysus from the great minstrel, Orpheus.[5] Therefore, when he observed the wreath on the old man's head, Midas recognized that Seilenus was a companion of the wine god and entertained him royally for ten days and nights. On the eleventh day, King Midas took Seilenus through the Lydian fields until they found the ivy-wreathed god.

Dionysus was overjoyed to be reunited with his dear friend. Gratefully, he told King Midas to name his wish and, swearing upon the waters of the River Styx, the god swore that he would grant the king whatever he asked. It was a wonderful opportunity, but the wine god offered it to a person whose choice showed poor judgment.

King Midas responded, "Let everything my body touches change into gold." Dionysus was disappointed that the king could think of no better wish than this foolish one. However, having sworn to grant whatever Midas requested, the ivy-wreathed god kept his word.

King Midas was overjoyed with Dionysus's gift. He left the god with a smile lighting his face. He could not contain his desire to experiment on the nearest object to see if, in fact, the ivy-wreathed god had truly given him his wish. Therefore, Midas cautiously plucked a green-leafed twig from a low-hanging branch of a slender oak tree. Scarcely believing what his eyes and touch revealed, the little branch quickly glittered with tinkling, golden leaves. Next, the king grabbed a lump of earth. In his hand, the dirt became transformed into a chunk of gold ore. Passing a farmer's field, Midas tore off a stalk of corn. He found himself holding husks of gold which bent to reveal row upon row of tiny, golden kernels within. Pulling an apple off a nearby tree, the king felt as if one of the immortal Hesperides[6] had given him one of Hera's golden apples. Upon arriving home, Midas carelessly placed his hand upon a marble pillar. To his delight, even the fluted stone blazed with a golden light.

King Midas had returned home with a hearty appetite. In preparation for dinner, a servant entered carrying a basin and a pitcher of water. As the servant poured water over the king's hands so that he could wash them, a shower of golden rain streamed into the basin below. Midas was bedazzled by his new power. While his imagination dwelled among these golden wonders and dreamed of even greater miracles to come, his servants spread a lavish meal of bread and meats before him. The smell of freshly baked bread was irresistible.

Midas's gleaming dreams dispersed as he picked up a roll. He found himself holding a shining mass of gold. Next, he tried to eat the meat. It looked invitingly tender and tasty upon the platter, but it became solid gold plate between his teeth. It was beautiful to the eye, but absolutely inedible. Becoming frantic, the king decided to drink his wine. Since it was already in a golden goblet, he was certain that at least he could satisfy his increasing thirst. However, once the liquid touched his mouth, it, too, became transformed into gold. There Midas sat, with liquid gold running down the sides of his sad face. His servants tried not to laugh at the remarkable, yet pitiful sight.[7]

Cursed with his golden touch, King Midas felt poor in the midst of incalculable wealth. He was starving for food, yet his riches could not feed him. He was parched with thirst, yet his wealth could not satisfy his need. He began to detest the gold he had desired and to loathe the power he had acquired. Raising his arms, he prayed to the god who had given him his wish.

"Oh, ivy-wreathed Dionysus, help me! I have erred. I have used your generous gift unwisely. Pity me, and free me from this golden curse!"

Dionysus pitied the repentant king and released him from his golden touch. "Go to the crystal waters of the Pactolus River," he directed, "that flow by the Lydian city of Sardis. Walk upstream toward the river's source. There, where the waters issue forth from their rocky bed like a foaming fountain, dive in. Let the waters wash the golden touch from your body."

King Midas obeyed the god's commands. As he cleansed his body of the golden gift, he transferred the charm to the waters of the river. To this day, the waters of the Pactolus contain flecks of gold which wash their shores with glistening, golden grains.[8]

Thereafter, Midas hated the wealth that had caused him such pain and spent his time out-of-doors enjoying nature. His companions became the Shepherd God, Pan,[9] and the nymphs who lived in mountain caves and played in the woods and meadows. However, changing his environment did not improve the king's judgment.

The Shepherd God delighted in playing simple little melodies on his reed pipes for the pleasure of Midas and the nymphs. Resting on the side of Mount Tmolus one sparkling day, Pan bragged to his companions that his music was superior to great Apollo's. The Lord of the Silver Bow heard this boast and agreed to contest his musical skills with Pan. Both gods agreed that Tmolus, the Mountain God, would be their judge.

Tmolus, quite regal in appearance, sat upon his mountain which seemed to brush the sky. He raised his head above the murmuring trees in order to clear their branches from his ears, and he wore, as his crown, an oak wreath whose acorns dangled on his brow. When both contestants were ready, Tmolus announced, "Pan, God of Shepherds, now your judge listens. Begin to play."

Pan tuned his pipes and blew a simple melody. His music pleased the taste of all the nymphs, and also Midas, who was listening nearby. Then the mountain judge turned to far-shooting Apollo. As Tmolus turned, his woods followed his movement and also stood at attention.

The Lord of the Silver Bow had bound his long, golden hair with laurel leaves. His robe, dyed with Phoenician purple, swept the ground. With his left hand, he raised his lyre of Indian ivory set with precious jewels. In his right hand, he held the plectrum. His relaxed yet regal stance indicated the presence of a master musician. As great Apollo played, he pleased the ear and calmed the heart of the judge.

When he had finished, Tmolus announced, "Pan, you must concede your rustic reed to far-shooting Apollo's lyre."

The audience applauded the verdict of Tmolus, except for King Midas. The foolish king argued that the decision was unjust since he, Midas, preferred the Shepherd God's country music.

Apollo took revenge upon Midas for his poor taste and his even poorer judgment. He wanted to expose the king's stupidity to everyone. Therefore, thinking that Midas's ears did not deserve their human shape, he transformed them into a shape which he felt more appropriately indicated their owner's sensibilities. He lengthened the king's ears, covered them with long grey and white hairs, and made them so unstable where they attached to Midas' head that they flopped about whenever the king moved in any way. The rest of Midas's appearance remained human, for the god intended to punish only the part of the king which had displeased him. Consequently, from that time until his death, Midas was forced to wear a pair of ass's ears upon his head.

King Midas covered his shame with a red turban. However, he could not conceal the source of his embarrassment from the servant who always cut his long hair.

The poor servant now knew a secret which he could hardly contain. He did not dare reveal his king's deformity; yet he could not bear to remain silent. Therefore, the servant found an isolated area where he dug a shallow pit. Kneeling down upon the ground, he leaned over the hole and whispered into it that his king wore ass's ears upon his head.[10] Then he replaced the dirt he had removed and quietly left the area.

In time, a group of whispering reeds grew upon that spot. By the end of the year, they had become large enough to disclose the king's secret whenever the light south winds rustled them. To this day, the reeds repeat the servant's words and make the secret of Midas's ears known to anyone who will listen.

1. Female worshippers of Dionysus who carried *thyrsi* (poles twined with ivy or grape-vines and topped with a pine cone) and dressed in animal skins.
2. Active young men who followed Dionysus. They had goats' legs, horses' tails, small horns or pointed ears, and were woodland creatures.

3. An older, wiser, drunker, satyr-like companion of Dionysus.
4. Phrygia: a large area of Asia Minor with flexible boundaries. Arachne's area of Lydia was originally part of Phrygia. Thus, Mount Tmolus and the Pactolus River may appear in either country.
5. A famous minstrel who is connected with the worship of Dionysus. His myth appears in this section.
6. The Hesperides were nymphs who guarded a grove, sacred to Hera, in which a tree bore golden apples. This grove appears in Section IV, The Heroes in the myths of Perseus and Heracles. It is also described in Section II, The Olympian Family, in Hera's myth.
7. In the original myth, Midas does not turn his daughter, or any other human being, into gold. The great American author, Nathaniel Hawthorne, rewriting the Greek myths for children, created his own golden touch.
8. The golden touch represents Midas's wealthy kingdom and the gold to be found in the Pactolus River.
9. Pan, the Shepherd God, is either the son of Zeus or of Hermes. He had the horns and legs of a goat. He loved to dance, sing, and play his reed pipes for the nymphs who were his companions.
10. Egyptian gods carried a reed scepter to which a pair of ass's ears were attached at the top as a symbol of royalty.

REFLECTIONS

1. Write a parallel to the Midas myth in which the major character gets his or her wish and must live with it.
2. Why do you think Midas is a foolish king?
3. Write a want ad for the local newspaper under the name of King Midas. Explain why you want the golden touch.
4. What are King Midas's redeeming qualities? Do you think these qualities help him in any way?

HUMAN EXPERIENCE

The wish for wealth is a motivator for everyone to some extent. We all have needs (food, shelter, clothing) and wants (luxuries). We know many people, however, whose craving for gold (wealth) far exceeds their basic needs. Sometimes they want wealth for its own sake or to impress other people. It gives them a feeling of power, because they assume that anything they want in life can be paid for with great wealth. Such persons are called "materialists." They see wealth as power. They say "If I am wealthy, I can have everything." What sometimes happens, however, is that they discover that wealth cannot buy the things most people really want, such as love, friendship, respect from others, or self-esteem.

Having things and experiencing feelings do not always go together. One can, like Midas, literally starve for food (symbolically, food and love are substitutes for each other) while being able to turn everything one touches into gold. On an unconscious level, some people equate wealth and love.

Sometimes a person who *only* craves wealth, really wants love and thinks that since he, himself, is not gifted in loving, he must be made more attractive through wealth. When this happens, people feel hopelessly disconnected from their feelings and are unable to stop their incessant gold-hunt. They may work hard, but find it difficult either to find satisfaction in loving or to form loving human relationships. They starve, as did Midas, for what they *really* need.

It is to be hoped that people like Midas will realize the shallowness of their lives. Sometimes they never do.

The second part of the myth deals with assessing one's own ability to judge reality. King Midas has a quality of self-importance that puts him in a position to make the wrong choices—he takes upon himself those god-like qualities which mortals can never have. He does not know himself well: he is a king, not a musical scholar. Is mortal man equipped to play the critic to the music of the gods? On another level, when *we* insist on the universal acceptance of our own, personal tastes, we deserve the fate of Midas.

The myth is also telling us something amusing. It was Midas's only wish, when he could have had anything he wanted, that everything he touched turn to gold. Aren't the gods saying that when we want something in *excess* of our needs, that wish has consequences that may lead to punishment and suffering?

24 Daedalus and Icarus

Daedalus's career as an architect, engineer, and sculptor may have recorded the spread of these aspects of civilization throughout the Mediterranean area. Since Daedalus's major travels began after he left Crete, the myth may have indicated, in particular, the spread of Minoan culture.

Daedalus represented the golden mean in Greek thinking. His behavior was reasonable and moderate. He flew neither too high nor too low. Icarus, on the other hand, suffered from *hybris*. Once he realized that he could fly as he wished, he became too proud of his ability. He threw reason and caution away and did as he wished. This rule of emotion (*áte*) caused his death (*nemesis*).

ANTICIPATIONS

1. Daedalus's desire to escape from prison forces him to think in a new way. What really provokes a person to create?
   a. Necessity or survival?
   b. The challenge of solving a problem?
   c. The need to express feelings?
   d. The wish to communicate a point of view?
2. Why aren't more people innovators? What circumstances *prevent* creativity? Rank the following in order of importance:
   a. Fear of criticism from others.
   b. Preference for what already exists.
   c. Need to be like everyone else.
   d. Fear of failure.
   e. Conviction of one's mediocrity.
3. In the story, Daedalus commits a crime because he is jealous of his nephew's creative ability. How do you solve your *own* problems of

jealousy in terms of
   a. Popularity
   b. Material possessions
   c. Athletic ability
   d. Intellectual ability
   e. Talent
4. In the story, Daedalus feels responsible for his son. To what people do you feel responsible? List them.

THE MYTH

Daedalus was the master artisan of his time. A member of the royal house of Athens, he received the art of craftsmanship from Athena. He achieved great fame as an architect, an engineer, and a sculptor. He was the first artist whose statues had open eyes, arms swinging free from their sides, and legs separated from each other in a stride. These sculptures were so human in appearance and so varied in their gestures that they seemed to be able to move by themselves.

Daedalus's sister sent her talented young son to Daedalus as an apprentice. Perdix[1] was indeed a young genius. Finding a snake's jawbone, he used it to saw a thin piece of wood. Next, using the backbone of a fish as a model, he notched a series of teeth in a sharp iron blade, thus inventing the first saw.[2] Perdix also was the first to invent the draftsman's compass by fastening the ends of two straight metal arms together so that one arm stood still while the other drew a circle around it.[3]

Daedalus envied his nephew's superior inventiveness. He became obsessed with the fear that his nephew would outshine him and that he would die in obscurity. Under the guise of showing Perdix the view from the top of Athena's temple on the Acropolis,[4] he pushed Perdix off the roof. For this, Daedalus was tried on the Areopagus[5] by a council of elders and condemned to exile for the crime of murder.

Some writers say that grey-eyed Athena saved Perdix from death. Clothing his arms with feathers while he was still in midair, she changed him into a partridge. To this day, the partridge avoids heights and precipices. Instead of soaring high into the air and building its nest in trees, it flutters along the ground and lays its eggs in bushes.

Daedalus took refuge with King Minos on the island of Crete. Even though he came as an outcast, Minos treated him with great respect because he was an inventor—a valuable addition to the royal household. When Pasiphaë, Minos's queen, fell in love with the Cretan Bull, Daedalus agreed to help her win its love by constructing a lifelike wooden cow.[6] In addition, it was Daedalus who, upon Minos's request, constructed the Labyrinth for the Minotaur.[7] Furthermore, Daedalus agreed to help Minos's daughter, Ariadne, save Theseus' life by showing her how Theseus could emerge safely from the Labyrinth once he had killed the Minotaur.[8]

When Minos learned of Theseus's escape, he blamed Daedalus. As punishment, he imprisoned Daedalus and his young son, Icarus, in the Labyrinth. However, Pasiphae, remembering Daedalus's helpfulness, secretly unchained the father and son.

Imprisonment made Daedalus weary of Crete and his long exile. Anxious to return to his native land, he thought: "Misfortunes often provoke ingenious solutions. Minos can prevent escape upon the earth and the sea, but the air surely is free. I will dare to attempt a path through the sky, for although Minos rules the world, even he cannot possess the air. Olympian Zeus, forgive my plan. While I do not intend to reach the stars, this is the only way I can escape."

He turned to ideas never before explored by man. How could he and Icarus use the air as a means of escape? He searched the sky, hoping to find an answer. Could the sea gulls, gliding above his head, provide a clue? The anatomy of their wings provided him with the necessary inspiration. Copying the designs of nature, Daedalus arranged a row of feathers. Beginning with tiny ones, he gradually increased their lengths in order to create an edge that sloped upwards. Then he fastened the feathers together in the middle with threads of flax, joining the bottom stems with a softened wax. When Daedalus had arranged the feathers in this way, he bent them into a gentle curve which imitated the arch of natural wings.

As Daedalus worked upon his invention, his young son, Icarus, unaware of his father's serious purpose, playfully caught the floating feathers which the breezes tossed about. Thus, Icarus continually interrupted Daedalus's progress.

When Daedalus finished his invention, he fitted one pair of wings upon himself, slowly raised himself into the air, and practiced using his new wings to balance his body in the air. There he hovered, moving his feathered arms up and down, continuously fanning the air so that it would support him.

Once he felt secure, Daedalus instructed his son. "I warn you to be careful," he advised. "You must follow a course that is midway between the earth and sky. If you fly too low, the waves will soak your dragging feathers and make them too heavy. If you fly too high, the sun will scorch your feathers and melt their wax. Therefore, be sure to fly halfway between the two. Just follow me. Pay no attention to the stars. I will teach you the rules for our flight and will guide you along the pathless way. We will only succeed if we fly with the winds."[9]

As Daedalus advised Icarus, he tied the second set of feathered wings to his son's shoulders and showed him how to move them. As he worked, tears broke from his eyes and dripped down his cheeks; his busy fingers trembled with fear.

When all was ready, Daedalus kissed his young son, embraced him, then flew upward with his light wings. Like a hovering mother bird, Daedalus urged Icarus to follow close behind him. He continued to instruct his son by demonstrating the movement of his own winged arms and by carefully supervising his son's motions.

A fisherman beside a silent stream, a shepherd leaning on his staff, and a farmer resting upon his plow all stared in amazement at what they saw traveling through the air. They believed that these gliding figures must be gods since no human being could find a way through the sky.

When Icarus felt sure of his wings, he shed his fears and began to fly more courageously. In his eagerness to reach the sky, he boldly deserted his guide and soared higher and higher until he approached shining Helius's chariot. The sun's heat dissolved the wax that bound his feathers together. As the feathers floated away, Icarus continued to move his barren arms up and down, but in vain, for without their feathers his arms could not support his body in the air. He looked down at the sea, frightened.

"Oh, Father! Father! I am finished!" he cried, as he tumbled down to the sea below. Even as he called his father's name, the dark sea stopped his breath and swallowed him.

Lonely Daedalus, a father no longer, cried out: "Icarus! Where are you? Which way have you flown? In what region should I search for you?"

As Daedalus frantically flew about calling his son, he spied Icarus' feathers scattered upon the sea below. Then he cursed his inventive skill for bringing him such deep sorrow.[10]

Daedalus descended to the nearest island to recover and bury Icarus's body and to perform the customary funeral rites. As he grieved, a partridge looked on, chirping joyfully at Daedalus's sorrow. Perdix was avenged.[11]

King Minos, who had never intended to part with Daedalus, proceeded to search the Mediterranean islands and coastal nations for his escaped prisoner. In order to increase his chance of finding Daedalus, Minos arrived at each seaport accompanied by his powerful navy. He presented each king with a spiral seashell, offering a huge reward to the king who could successfully draw a thread through it. As Minos had expected, no one could perform this apparently impossible task.

Meanwhile, Daedalus had found refuge with King Cocalus on the island of Sicily, where he was living in fame as an accomplished architect. When Minos arrived in Sicily, King Cocalus announced that he would be able to thread the shell, but he requested permission to take the shell and return it to Minos the following day. Minos agreed. Then

Cocalus secretly gave the shell to Daedalus, knowing that he would be able to thread it. When Cocalus returned the successfully threaded seashell as promised, Minos was overjoyed with his discovery.

"He's here!" he exclaimed. "Only Daedalus is clever enough to solve my puzzle. How did he ever do it?"

Cocalus explained how Daedalus had bored a hole in the shell and had fastened the end of a thread on an ant. The ant had entered the shell and had pulled the thread through it.

Minos demanded that Cocalus surrender Daedalus to him immediately. Some writers say that Cocalus courageously refused to surrender Daedalus, that Minos declared war on Cocalus, and that Cocalus killed Minos in the fighting which ensued. Others say that Cocalus agreed to return Daedalus to Minos that evening after a feast in his honor. However, in preparation for the festive occasion, Cocalus's daughters, who were fond of Daedalus, helped bathe their guest of honor the king, and murdered him by pouring scalding water upon him.

After the death of Minos, Daedalus remained in Sicily for many years. He was last seen in Sardinia. He never returned to Athens.

1. The name Perdix means *partridge*.
2. The Minoans had delicate saws for their fine work.
3. Bronze smiths used compasses to draw circles for bowls, helmets, and masks.
4. The highest part of Athens. This temple existed before the Parthenon was built (approximately 900 years earlier).
5. The location of the early Athenian court, near the Acropolis.
6. See myth of Theseus (Section IV, The Heroes).
7. See myth of Theseus (Section IV, The Heroes).
8. See myth of Theseus (Section IV, The Heroes).
9. Daedalus was aware that, at the time, sailors used the winds for navigation and were often at their mercy.
10. Some writers say that Pasiphaë helped Daedalus and Icarus escape from Crete in small boats, for which Daedalus invented sails. They outsailed Minos's fleet, but Icarus capsized his boat, fell into the sea, and drowned.
11. Daedalus or Heracles renamed the island Icaria in memory of Icarus's burial there. The waters into which Icarus fell became the Icarian Sea.

REFLECTIONS

1. We learn about people's characters from the choices they make. We learn as much by what a person *could* say, but chooses *not* to say as we learn from what he does say. We also learn as much from what he chooses *not* to do as we learn from what he does.
   a. What did we learn about Daedalus when he chose to fly away with Icarus?
   b. What other choices did he have?
   c. If he could foresee the possibility of failure, should he have made a different decision?

2. Daedalus was similar to Prometheus in many ways. Both were clever, inventive people who were willing to take risks in order to create. In what way was Daedalus different from Prometheus? Whom do you prefer and why?
3. Why isn't Icarus's mother mentioned in the story?
4. What was Daedalus's attitude toward his invention? How did Icarus feel about his father's invention? How does the attitude of each affect his actions?
5. Rewrite this myth from Icarus's point of view. Explain how he felt as he watched his father work on the wings. Explain his attitude toward the escape. What went through his mind as he flew?
6. Put Daedalus on trial for the murder of his son. Divide the class into defense attorneys and prosecutors. Have each lawyer write a brief in which he uses the available evidence to convince the jury as to Daedalus's guilt or innocence. The class will be the jury.
7. Do you think a scientist should consider the social, political, and economic effects of his or her invention?
    a. Should a scientist forego inventing something that could be used to the detriment of mankind?
    b. Do you think a scientist or artist should create for a dictator?
    c. Do you think drugs should be used to control human behavior?

HUMAN EXPERIENCE

Daedalus and Icarus were opposites in every way. Daedalus was a gifted creator and had judgment and wisdom. Today, we would call him an artist-scientist, one who is courageously dedicated to his art. Icarus, on the other hand was daring, trusting, and became emotionally carried away either with the joy of flying or the joy of thwarting authority. Daedalus had foresight and could see the possibilities and results of his work, the dangers as well as the potential for freedom. He was able to caution Icarus, to advise him, to instruct him. He possessed a talent and used it. He was an innovator. He felt free to create.

Icarus was a youth who felt omnipotent and lived for the joy of the present, heedless of his father's cautionary words to take the middle road, to fly neither too high nor too low. He was willing to sacrifice a future gain for a present pleasure. Icarus felt free to disobey.

In this myth, Icarus represents the wishes we all have to be in control of our lives without heeding the advice of our parents, teachers, or friends. We, like Icarus, want to "try everything." With Daedalus as a guiding figure, the pair represent the internal conflict within man between achieving great heights by throwing caution to the winds and overreaching, and understanding limits and reality.

Experience, however, cannot be passed on; it must be lived and felt. We must all learn by doing, even if we fail or injure ourselves. This does not mean we must shun risk or avoid achieving success. On the contrary, we should enter into some new experiences with a sense of ourselves, or we will never learn to master the rules of any game. Icarus was Youth, the problem unsolved; Daedalus was Experience, the problem mastered. Daedalus had learned the wisdom of judgment. It is judgment that decrees whether or not we are being grandiose in setting our goals. Sometimes we learn judgment by experiencing the consequences of flying too high or too low.

Daedalus's wish to fly was motivated by his frantic need to escape the Labyrinth. He used his technical knowledge to enter the air, a new medium, by applying the principles of aviation he saw birds using.

Man thinks there is something godly about creation, but frequently creators are punished in some way for bringing new ideas to mankind. Man, in his thoughts, has always wanted to fly. Today, we are physically able to fly in gigantic planes, but we are also concerned about the misuse of technology, either through accident or malicious direction. We, too, have built-in punishments that await us as a result of our flights—flights to the moon, into space and extraterrestrial life, and into technology.

Everyone must undergo in his or her own experience Icarus's fall from the heights to Daedalus's experience of mastery. Sometimes this mastery can only occur after we have learned to heed the advice of Daedalus to Icarus. His admonishing of the lad not to fly too high or too low was "middle-of-the road" advice, and was called by the Greeks the *golden mean*. It means that one must temper emotion with reason and do everything, not in excess, but in moderation.

However, in order to reach Daedalus's maturity, like Icarus, we too, must *want* to soar. For this, we need some ideas, dreams, or wishes. We must want to find a way to escape the tedium of the known, in order to find the creative inspiration to convert the givens of our lives into gifts, achievements, or innovations.

A real creator must think and feel *beyond* what has already been done. He or she must be able to soar in his or her thoughts. The artist or other creator fashions new ways to do things and transforms reality by creation. Creation lifts the spirit, and we who see it respond by feeling elevated, improved, and enriched. Great art and high achievement have the power to inspire everyday life, to lend depth to our vision.

Creativity

Creativity is one way people free themselves from the limitations of conditioned responses. It is a means by which people free themselves also, of ordinary choices. It enlarges the universe by discovering new dimensions. It also enriches people by enabling them to experience these dimensions inwardly.

Creativity is not an attribute of great people only, even though there have always been creative masters—the geniuses of history. Creativity is not necessarily always a rewarding achievement. It may end in frustration or in anger at society, friends, or family. Sometimes, not even the results of creative activity are fulfilling: a creator may think that perhaps his or her work is not good enough, or that society does not acknowledge the greatness of his or her work.

Creativity, in any form, requires imagination—the capacity of the mind to produce or reproduce several symbolic functions without a deliberate attempt at organization or censorship. It can be a way of living, or of solving problems, and we can all be creative in our lives.

We know some things about the creative personality by understanding what *prevents* creativity. Such things as sticking to previous habit, self-discouragement, and timidity tend to inhibit creativity, whereas traveling, playing games, solving puzzles, pursuing hobbies, reading, and writing promote creative activities.

There are some conditions or attitudes under which creative endeavor thrives. One of them is, surprisingly, aloneness, or being able to be alone without being lonely so that one can be in touch with one's feelings. This does not mean withdrawing from society, but simply remaining by one's self periodically, without anxiety. Discipline and alertness are also needed. They are useful tools for recognizing that something previously dismissed as insignificant or meaningless can be important. Other circumstances that seem to promote the creative process are inactivity and daydreaming.

Creative people can usually see similarities between unrelated things. For example, Daedalus watched birds flying and made an analogy, or a comparison. He saw a connection between the flight of the birds and their liberation and his own ability to create a similar type of freedom for himself through flying. That he dared risk the potentially dangerous results of flying was a good part of his creative thrust. He knew the risks and the reallities. He knew he was not meant to be a bird, but his simulation of their achievements made him an outstanding scientist-artist in terms of innovation. He took the *risk* of bringing something new to mankind.

In order to be creative, we must want to be able to put what we have discovered into action. Without action, all our pretenses and our reactions are meaningless. Creative process dies when it is not employed concretely.

The creative process is a way of finding or inventing a new object, state of mind, or experience that is not easily attained. Such a process brings about a desirable enlargement of human experience by establishing a bond between us and the creative act or product. When we respond to great works, the creativity in which we participate, makes us appreciate not only the innovations bestowed upon us, but gives us a heightened awareness of our individual potential for creative activity.

We can, through identification with the artist or his work, re-experience some of the same emotions that gave rise to that work. We can also enter into the particular way in which the artist makes feelings, imagination, process, and content part of a larger scheme of things. The artist, through his or her work, provides us with a mirror in which we see reflected what we would like to *be* as well as what we *are*.

25 Phaëthon

INTRODUCTION

Phaëthon suffered from the temporary madness (*áte*) caused by *hybris*. He intended to take over his father's role, a clearly impossible task. Disaster was inevitable with such an irrational attitude. He would not listen to his father's arguments. Phaëthon was beyond help, and Zeus had to destroy him in order to save the universe.

Phaëthon could have represented the annual sacrifice of a sacred king's son in the Mother Goddess religion. He was king only for a day, and then he died. After his death, the original sacred king, his father, came out of seclusion and resumed the throne. In Corinth, the sacred king or his substitute was killed by a horse-drawn chariot. The human sacrifice was attached to the back of the chariot and dragged behind it until he died. This kind of a death sprinkled the blood immediately over whatever soil the chariot traveled over. For its purpose, it was very efficient.

This myth also explained the existence of certain natural phenomena, such as the location of particular deserts and of human beings who have very dark skin.

ANTICIPATIONS

1. Rank the following in the order in which they would give you prestige.
   a. a ten-speed bicycle
   b. a large house or apartment
   c. expensive clothes
   d. an expensive car
   e. travel to unusual places
2. What ways do students gain prestige in school?
   a. athletics

b. academic achievement
c. theatrical performances
d. student council
e. extracurricular activities

THE MYTH

Phaëthon was fond of bragging that his father was none other than shining Helius, the deathless God of the Sun. He realized, by the amused look in their eyes, that some of his friends did not believe him, but as long as they appeared to accept his boast as fact, he ignored their skepticism.

One day, however, a friend publicly confronted Phaëthon with the question of his paternity. "Your arrogance is disgraceful, Phaëthon. You are foolish to believe your mother. She is obviously exaggerating or fabricating about your father. Accept the fact that your father is no deathless god, but an ordinary mortal. You are really no better than we are."

Phaëthon blushed at his friend's censure, then became enraged that a youth should dare to criticize him. He quickly sought his mother, Clymene, and determined to resolve any doubts about his father's identity. "Mother," he implored, hugging her. "If it is true that shining Helius[1] is my father, you must give me some tangible proof so that my friends will not dare to ridicule me."

Clymene was sensitive to Phaëthon's plea and was infuriated that her word, too, was being disputed. Therefore, she raised her arms to the starry heavens, through which the shining chariot of the sun now coursed, and declared:

"Phaëthon, I swear by the shining sun, that Helius, who illuminates and warms the universe, is your father. If I am not speaking the truth, may his light which now shines upon us be the last light my eyes ever see.

"However, if my oath has not convinced you, your father's eastern palace is not far from here since he ascends the heavens from our land. You have my permission to go there and meet your father. He will confirm to you that what I have told you is true."

Phaëthon was delighted at this opportunity. He longed to drive his father's chariot and usher in the daylight as his father did. His youthful imagination played with these desires as he traveled to his father's palace.

Upon his arrival, he was awed by the brilliance of the palace. It soared to the heavens on lofty columns. It dazzled his eyes with the luster of its gold and sparkling jewels, its ivory roof, and its double silver doors, designed by the renowned smith, Hephaestus.

Looking all about him, Phaëthon slowly ascended the palace steps and entered the building. There he saw shining Helius, the god whom his mother claimed was his father, clothed in purple robes and seated upon an emerald-studded throne. He longed to approach the radiant figure, yet the brightness of his father's light hurt his own mortal eyes and forced him to remain at a safe distance. Beside deathless Helius, arranged in two rows, stood the Hours, Days, Months, Years, and Ages. Phaëthon even noticed the Seasons there. Fragrant Spring wore a crown of flowers and Summer a crown of wheat. Autumn's forehead was stained from grape juice, while Winter's head was white with frost.

All-seeing Helius noticed the entrance of the astonished youth who now stood apart, apparently intimidated by the presence of all these immortal gods.

"What has brought you here, Phaëthon?" he asked. "Is there something I can do for you, dear son?"

Phaëthon replied, "Oh great giver of light, oh Father, I need some token that will prove my birth and remove from my mind the doubts I have about my mother's word."

Removing the crown of shimmering rays from his head so that his mortal son could approach him, all-seeing Helius welcomed his son and embraced him.

"You are indeed my son," the god announced, "by merit as well as by birth. Your mother has spoken the truth.

"But, to put an end to your doubts, ask me for any favor, and I swear on the dark waters of the River Styx, the irrevocable oath of the deathless gods,[2] that I will grant your wish, no matter what you request."

"Oh, Father," replied Phaëthon, breathless with anticipation, "I wish to drive your chariot and bring in the new day just as you do."

Now Helius sighed deeply with remorse and greatly repented the oath he had so solemnly sworn. Shaking his head regretfully, he said, "Your imprudent wish causes me to regret my equally rash offer. You are requesting the one favor I would deny you, yet I am eternally bound by my sacred oath to grant whatever you wish.

"I hope I can dissuade you from your desire, for your wish hastens your death. You have neither the age nor the physical strength to drive my chariot as I do. In your ignorance, you are pleading for a task which even the immortals would not dare to undertake. If the dreaded Thunderer who rules Mount Olympus[3] cannot drive my chariot, do you not realize how impossible the challenge would be for a mortal youth?

"The initial assent is so steep that my horses can barely climb it early in the day when they are well rested and refreshed. As they travel through the highest heavens at noon, even I am filled with fear if I dare to look down upon the distant earth and sea. Thereafter, the horses need a strong, steady rein, for the descent is steep, and they forge ahead with almost uncontrollable speed. As I bring each day to a close, immortal Tethys, whose seas will greet me, worries that I might lose control and fall into her dark waters.

"Moreover, you will find no cities, no marble altars laden with wealthy offerings to the deathless gods, no restful groves of olive trees along your way. The stars in the heavens are not friends, but foes. Often I must drive my chariot against the direction they travel, expending all my energies in order to continue along my own prescribed path. Their monstrous shapes dangerously line the way. I must be certain to travel between the Bull's sharp horns and past Cheiron the centaur with his poised bow, meanwhile avoiding the angry claws of both the Scorpion and the Crab and the jaws of the roaring Lion. You are not strong enough to keep the chariot on this rugged course.

"Furthermore, my fiery horses are naturally impulsive and unruly. Once they have reached their stride, they exhale blazing flames from their nostrils and mouths and chafe at their repressive harnesses. They barely tolerate my guidance; they are not apt to recognize your authority.

"Therefore, lest my gift should cause your death, I beg you to change your mind. What you are requesting is not a favor, but a terrifying punishment. If you yearn for a sign which confirms that I am your father, my fear for your safety reveals my paternity. My heart is troubled over your decision; my face reflects my concern. I wish that you would remain safely on the earth and choose among the wide array of wealth it offers."

However, shining Helius counseled in vain. Phaëthon, enthusiastic about heavenly glory, refused to compromise his desires. Therefore, his father reluctantly conducted his imprudent son to the dazzling chariot which the renowned smith, Hephaestus, had created of hammered gold and silver, and inlaid with brilliant jewels. As Phaëthon admired its workmanship, Selene, the moon goddess, hid her silver horns, and dawn with rosy fingers made the sky light. Shining Helius realized that it was now past time for his journey. He directed the Hours to harness his fiery horses immediately. Meanwhile, the shining god covered his son's face with ambrosia in order to protect it from the crown of flames. Then Helius placed the shimmering rays of the sun upon Phaëthon's head.

With a sigh of foreboding, he addressed his last counsel to his determined son.

"Phaëthon," he pleaded, "listen to my final words of advice and heed them. You must handle the reins with strength for otherwise the horses will run too fast. Once you permit them to determine their own speed, you will not be able to control them. Follow the broad pathway through the middle zones, and avoid the poles at the extremes. The well-trodden tracks will guide the wheels of your chariot. Do not climb too high or descend too low lest you ignite either the heavens or the earth with your raging fires. For this too, it is best to chart a middle course.

"But, I have said all I can. Night has disappeared and dawn with rosy fingers has made the day light. The journey must begin. Step into the chariot and gather the reins, or while you still have a choice, accept my counsel and refuse my chariot. I implore you to let me illuminate the world while you remain behind in safety."

In reply, Phaëthon jumped into his father's chariot and grabbed the reins. Feeling courageous and certain of his skill, he thanked his father for the adventure of his dreams.

Meanwhile, shining Helius's horses neighed impatiently, striking their hoofs upon the barriers which confined them and blasting the air with the heat from their fiery nostrils. As soon as the Titan Tethys had removed their restraining barricades, they galloped forth toward the heavens, their soaring feet quickly cutting through the intervening clouds and outpacing the eastern wind. Sensing the transport of a lighter chariot and a weaker driver, the horses welcomed their freedom and chose uncharted paths, forcing the chariot to jump and jolt at their mercy.

Meanwhile, Phaëthon did not know how or when to direct the horses, and even if he had known, they would not have obeyed him. Having climbed unusually high in the heavens, the fiery rays of the sun ignited the stars. Phaëthon forgot his father's warning and, from the height of the heavens, he gazed down upon the earth. He shuddered with terror as he became aware of his own location. No longer did he care about proof of his paternity. No longer did he care to drive the shining chariot of the sun. No longer did he thank his immortal father for granting his wish. He longed instead for the comfort of the earth, and he wished that he were the son of his mother's mortal husband.

Phaëthon did not know what to do. Too much of the path was behind him for him to retreat, yet too much distance lay before him for him to continue forward. In his terror and despair, he frantically stared about him at the frightening heavens. The threatening Scorpion so intimidated him that his trembling fingers inadvertently dropped the reins.

As soon as they felt the passive reins upon their backs, the horses charged wildly through the heavens, furiously climbing first toward the stars and then descending steeply toward the earth, always transporting the blazing sun behind them. The moon goddess Selene stared in amazement when she beheld her brother's horses beneath her own, his sun's rays igniting the clouds. Then as she watched, the sun's flames attacked the earth. They ignited the trees and crops, and burned them to ashes. They consumed the cities of the earth, devouring men, animals, and buildings indiscriminately.

The mountains, too, suffered from the sun's destructive rays. Mount Aetna blazed with twice its flames, Mount Parnassus moaned beneath its two fiery peaks, and even Mount Caucasus, to the north in frozen Scythia, sweated with unaccustomed heat. Libya became a sandy desert, and the Ethiopians developed burned, black skin.

Phaëthon's chariot had become a flaming coal which transported him through clouds of fiery smoke and ashes. Even his protective ointment could not save him from the tortures of the scalding air. With every breath he took, he gasped anew in agony. Engulfed in a holocaust, Phaëthon could not see where he was. His wild horses dragged him at their whim.

Major rivers were engulfed by flames and evaporated. The ocean, too, became a victim of the sun's fury and retreated, leaving new mountain ranges and sandy deserts where once its waters had flowed. Fish sought refuge upon the ocean floor, while sea monsters, caught upon the surface, boiled to death and floated lifelessly there upon their backs. The sea deities hid from the perilous rays by diving beneath the scalding waves, while the Lord of the Sea[4] thrust his furious face and his arms in protest above the flaming waves three times, only to be repelled by the blaze each time.

Gaea felt her body crack from the intense heat and heard the dark Lord of the Dead[5] exclaim with fright at the blinding light. She thrust her head into the fiery air, shielding her scorched forehead with her hand as she appealed to her grandson[6] for help.

"If you intend to destroy me, Olympian Zeus, then why are your lightning and thunderbolts inactive? For if I deserve to perish by fire, then I want to be destroyed by your own flaming weapons. Look! Even as I try to speak, ashes and flames are choking me. Smoke has blinded my eyes. Burning cinders have scorched my face. Rampant fires have singed my hair! Is this how you repay me for making the earth fertile? Was it for this purpose that I have nourished man and beast and have provided immortals with banquets of sacred sacrifices?

"Even if I have provoked your wrath and my own ruin, of what crime is the Lord of the Sea guilty? His power equals yours, yet his kingdom is rapidly diminishing.

"However, if you feel no pity for me or for your brother, then lament the fate of your own kingdom. The north and south poles are already smoking, and their destruction heralds the ruin of your power. If the earth, the sea, and the heavens are destroyed by fire, then Chaos will return. So, quench these flames and end our agony before the universe is beyond repair."

Gaea became silent. Her tongue had become so scorched that she could not speak. The smothering smoke had become intolerable. So, without further admonition, she drew within her own great body and took refuge in dark Hades' dismal kingdom.

Meanwhile, Zeus quickly responded to her plea. Roused to action, the Lord of Olympus assembled the gods. They all agreed that unless the Lord of Thunder[7] prevented their imminent destruction, the mortal Phaëthon would demolish the universe.

Then, far-seeing Zeus climbed to the highest of his towers and searched for clouds which could smother the fires upon the earth with a deluge of rain. However, even they had perished in the heat.

Zeus, who delights in thunder, took his weapons and with unerring aim, he hurled his lightning bolts at the youth in the shining chariot of the sun. He had no other choice. With one mighty blow, the Lord of Olympus removed Phaëthon from his life and from shining Helius's fiery crown and chariot. His body was hurled helplessly through the air, and it blazed a trail down to earth as if he were a falling star. The River Po in Italy extinguished the flames from his burning corpse, and its nymphs buried him. The terrified horses and the remains of the chariot dashed wildly to their stables, returning the crown of the sun to shining Helius's palace.

Phaëthon's father, shining Helius, spent a day secluded with his own grief, while the renowned smith, Hephaestus, fashioned a new chariot. However, blazing ruins so illuminated the earth that the absence of the sun was no deprivation. Phaëthon's mother, Clymene, searched the earth for the remains of her son. Upon finding his marble tomb, she tearfully embraced his epitaph, which proclaimed, "Here lies Phaëthon, who died because he dared to drive shining Helius's chariot."

1. Ovid gives Apollo as Phaëthon's father, because at the time Ovid wrote his version of the myth, Apollo had assumed the role of sun god in Rome.
2. The oath on the River Styx is explained in Section I, In the Beginning—The Rule of Zeus.
3. The Dreaded Thunderer is Zeus.
4. Poseidon.
5. Hades.
6. Zeus is the grandson Gaea is calling.
7. Zeus.

REFLECTIONS

1. Who do you think was more responsible for Phaëthon's fate, Helius or Phaëthon?
2. Should Phaëthon have risked death in order to drive his father's chariot? Explain.
3. In what other ways do you think Phaëthon could have achieved the prestige he sought?
4. Become Phaëthon. Write a letter to Icarus explaining why your father was or was not a good father. In your opening paragraph, discuss what is meant by a "good" father.
5. Compare and contrast Phaëthon and Icarus. List the ways they were alike in one column and the ways they were different in another. What conclusions can you draw from your lists?

26 Pygmalion

Pygmalion is mentioned in Greek myth as a king of Cyprus. However, the great Roman writer of myths, Ovid, created the following romantic version about him. The myth is very short and simple. It is provocative because it ends just as the interesting part could begin, leaving the rest to the reader's imagination.

ANTICIPATIONS

1. We all like to think that we approach the roles in our lives with a sense of completeness and commitment to the values we have. We admire "perfect" things: "perfect" beauty, "perfect" scenery, "perfect" meals. We ourselves sometimes try hard to become "perfect" in one way or another. Is there such a thing as "perfection" in human beings? What is the result of searching for it?
2. How many kinds of love are there in the world?
3. Sometimes our desire for perfection gives rise to a feeling of dissatisfaction. Rank the following things in the order of importance to you:
   a. orderly bedroom
   b. knowing your daily schedule in advance
   c. doing homework assignments on time
   d. household chores
   e. being selective about television programs
   f. accepting the foibles of your friends

THE MYTH

Pygmalion was a man who was frightened by women because he believed they had evil qualities. Consequently, he chose to remain unmarried. He spent his time carving an ivory statue of a woman who was more beautiful than any mortal woman he had ever seen.

Gradually, Pygmalion fell in love with the statue. Unlike real women, his statue was perfect. He began to treat it as if it were real. It felt so real to him that Pygmalion even thought it returned his kisses. He touched the statue carefully so as not to hurt it and spoke flattering words to it. He gave presents to the statue of precious jewels, birds, and flowers. He dressed it in rich robes and placed rings on its fingers. He also adorned the statue with necklaces and earrings.

One night, Pygmalion placed the statue upon his bed. Its head rested upon a goosedown pillow; its body lay upon a rich spread of Phoenician purple. Fondly Pygmalion kissed the statue and called it his wife.

The day of the festival of golden-wreathed Aphrodite was a solemn one on her sacred island of Cyprus. On this day, white cows, their horns decorated with gold, were sacrificed at the altars of the goddess. Standing before Aphrodite's altar, Pygmalion asked that the statue become his wife. Aphrodite heard his prayer.

When Pygmalion returned to his statue, he lay upon the bed and held the statue in his arms, kissing it. Suddenly he found that its lips were warm and its body soft. His fingers imprinted themselves on the ivory surface. He doubted still whether or not it was real. The statue, however, had become a real warm-blooded woman.

Pygmalion joyfully thanked golden Aphrodite. The living statue felt the kisses and saw Pygmalion as her lover. Joyfully Pygmalion made this extraordinarily beautiful woman his wife[1], and Aphrodite blessed their union. In time they had a daughter named Paphos.

1. Modern writers have called Pygmalion's live statue Galatea.

REFLECTIONS

1. Did the creator of this myth want you to believe that once she is human, Pygmalion's wife would be perfect?
2. This myth could be the dream of a dissatisfied husband, because it is opposite to what he has in his life in reality. The dream could also be called "wish-fulfillment." Seen this way, this myth is a "fantasy," or a wish. What, if anything, are the limitations of this story, in terms of real life?
3. In what ways do you think this myth is more like a fairy-tale than a myth? What are its characteristics?
4. Write a continuation of the myth.

27 Narcissus and Echo

Both Echo and Narcissus underwent transformations. Echo lost her bodily form and remained only a voice, also known by the name of Echo. Narcissus, upon his death, became a flower that bears his name. Thus, both myths provided a non-scientific explanation for a phenomenon in nature. The myth of Echo explained why a person's words could be repeated in certain circumstances. The myth of Narcissus explained the origin of a particular flower.

In addition, both myths described how readily the Greek gods punished those who offended them, and how uniquely appropriate their punishments were. When Echo helped Zeus pursue his extramarital relationships, she miscalculated Hera's reaction. As always, Hera's vengeance was swift and harsh. Hera turned Echo's greatest asset, her *areté*, her excellent conversational ability, into her punishment.

Narcissus's *areté* or excellence, was his physical beauty. He attracted so much admiration that he became excessively proud of his appearance. The Greeks called this kind of pride *hybris*. Narcissus felt so superior to other people that he became arrogant. He believed that those who loved him did not deserve to receive his love. Such extreme pride produced *áte*, "temporary madness." Narcissus's love of himself became his punishment (*nemesis*), and it destroyed him.

ANTICIPATIONS

1. Do people usually like other people who are more like them or who are more *unlike* them? Why? Are your friends more like you than unlike you?
2. Do you think anyone can love another human being if he or she doesn't think much of him or herself? Explain.

3. Do you think the saying, "opposites attract" is true? Support your answer with examples.
4. Do you think self-interest is fostered by
   a. advertisements?
   b. politics?
   c. family life?
   d. career?
   e. other?
5. What do you think is the difference between self-love and self-esteem?
6. In what ways are you certain that your comments, opinions, and values are strictly your own and not those you have heard?

THE MYTH

The river god, Cephissus, loved a beautiful sea nymph, Leiriope, in his watery dwelling. She gave birth to a beautiful baby boy and named him Narcissus.[1] Leiriope inquired of the blind Theban prophet, Teiresias,[2] whether her newborn son would live a long life. Teiresias replied, "If he never knows himself." Leiriope, not fully understanding what the words of the prophet meant, kept all mirrors away from him. She reared him so that he would never be able to see what he looked like.

Narcissus was a very handsome young man and many youths would have liked to love him. He, however, scorned them all, including the nymph Echo.

Echo was a companion of golden-throned Hera on Mount Olympus. Many times when Hera might have stopped Olympian Zeus from courting other nymphs, Echo would engage Hera in long conversations until the nymphs had time to run away. When Hera realized that Echo was helping her husband in his amorous pursuits, she said, "I shall stop the powers of that tongue which has tricked me! For this abuse, your tongue, from this point on, shall be of little use."

She carried out her threats. Thereafter, Echo was condemned to repeat the last words spoken, and give back only the sounds she had heard.

Echo discovered Narcissus while he was hunting deer in the forest. As he chased the deer into nets, Echo pursued him. The closer she came, the more she burned with love of him, as a match burns when it approaches fire. She longed to pursue him with words of love, but her punishment did not permit her freedom of speech. She could not initiate a conversation with him; she could only repeat his last words.

Finding herself despised by Narcissus, Echo sadly retreated to the woods and hid herself in caves. Her soul still longed for Narcissus, and her grief at his rejection increased. Her body become withered, and her blood converted to air. Soon, nothing was left of her but her voice, for her bones became stones.

Another youth whom Narcissus scorned prayed that Narcissus, himself, might experience the same heartache he had so heartlessly inflicted upon others. This prayer was heard by Nemesis, the Goddess of Retribution. Because she felt this prayer was justified, she consented to its fulfillment.

There was a spring in the middle of the woods whose silver waters were as clear and as smooth as a polished mirror. It was totally secluded. Neither bird nor beast disturbed its surface. Narcissus, one day, wandered to it, tired and overheated from his hunting. He lay down upon the grass and quenched his thirst at the spring.

Soon another kind of thirst arose within him. He gazed into the still water and beheld a form which gazed back at him. He fell in love with the image he saw in the water. He became completely distracted with love for the reflection. He lay by the water's edge, still as a marble statue. He continued to admire the beauty of this image, totally unaware that it was his own reflected beauty that had captivated him. In return, the reflection in the spring admired his beauty and appeared equally charmed by Narcissus.

Narcissus tried to kiss the flattering image within the spring and thrust his arms down into the water in an attempt to circle the neck of his beloved. Whenever he did this, however, the image would slip away from his embraces. Neither sleep nor hunger could induce Narcissus to leave his lover in the spring.

Finally, lifting his head toward the trees, Narcissus asked, "You, woods, which spread your branches round about, was there ever such an unfortunate lover as I am? You have seen many pairs of lovers. Have you known of any other lovers to pine away as we do?"

If he had only turned aside, the reflection would have faded away, and Narcissus might have known that his own reflection was what he loved—that his love had no independence from himself.

However, he continued, sadly, "I am not separated from my love either by sea or mountain, walls or roads. Only a little water separates us. My love himself," he continued, "desires to be loved. When I lean down to kiss him, his lips meet mine. Why can't we touch each other?

"Ah love," he said, looking into the pool, "come forth, whoever you are. Why do you evade me? Why do you disdain me? Nymphs have often loved me in vain. Somehow you seem to encourage my hopes and to desire the hand I offer you. You smile at my smile and cry when I cry.

"Ah!" he said, suddenly, "You are I. Now I plainly see that it is my *own* shadow which has bewitched me. It is love of myself which tortures me. What can I love, since what I desire I already have? Too much love of this kind has made me poor.

"Oh, gods!" he cried. "Disjoin me from myself. I want to be separated from what I love. Grief is destroying me. It does not grieve me half so much to part with life, itself, for my grief will find its perfect cure in death."

Gazing sadly upon his image again, his tears created troubled circles upon the water, which made his image vanish. He begged it to stay and beat himself upon the breast. Seeing this action reflected in the water, he could no longer bear his sorrow. As wax dissolves with heat or morning frost melts with the sun's warmth, so Narcissus melted away from the fire of his hopeless love.

Echo, watching him waste away, remained in the woods. Although she still felt anger because he had spurned her, she pitied Narcissus, and whenever in his sorrow he cried, "Alas!" she repeated, "Alas!" His last words were, "My hopeless love, farewell." And Echo repeated, "Love, farewell."

Then Narcissus lay down, and Death's cold hands shut his self-admiring eyes. The water-nymphs, in mourning for their dead brother, spread their clipped locks of hair upon his body. Then they grieved over the death of Narcissus, and Echo pined in every closing phrase of sorrow.

When the funeral pyre was built, no one could find Narcissus's body. In its place was a yellow flower with tufts of white petals, which came to be called the narcissus. Narcissus's shade entered the Underworld, where, for eternity, he gazes upon his reflection in the waters of the River Styx.

1. The word narcissus comes from the Greek *narkissos*, a plant which produces narcotic effects. The word *narcotic* can also mean *sleeper* and *numbness*.
2. Teiresias was blinded by Hera for taking Zeus's position in an argument. Zeus compensated Teiresias for this cruel punishment by giving him the power of prophecy and an unusually long lifetime. Teiresias first gained his reputation by accurately predicting the future of Narcissus.

REFLECTIONS

1. Take turns being Narcissus or the interviewer on a popular talk show. What questions would you ask Narcissus? As Narcissus, how would you respond?
2. Write an essay or poem expressing your feelings about Narcissus or Echo.
3. Write a new ending for the myth of Narcissus.
4. Write a diary that Echo might keep. Explain her feelings about Hera's attitude and actions, as well as the attitudes and actions of Narcissus.

HUMAN EXPERIENCE

The word *narcissism* has come to mean self-love. Those people who derive pleasure only from their own physical or mental attributes to the exclusion of interest in others are called *narcissistic*. Another word for narcissism is *egotistical*. In Latin, the word *ego* means *I*. Narcissism is a normal state in infants. If a child has loving parents, he learns to trust them and realize that he is different from them. As he matures, he is able to realize that there are other people in the world he can also trust and love. If people reach adulthood, still unable to trust others, they remain *narcissistic*. They see others only as extensions of themselves, rather than as separate individuals. They also may demand that others be like them, or may be uncomfortable or unable to understand people who are different from themselves. Often, they even marry people who are mirror-images of themselves, and they may be intolerant of differences. Frequently, narcissists cannot put their trust in other human beings at all. When this occurs, they can turn only to themselves, feeling that other people will always disappoint them.

Love for a narcissist is a strange phenomenon. He is unable to form close bonds with other people. He will search for someone exactly like himself (a *self-object*). The normal, mature adult will be able to love someone else quite different from himself (a *love-object*). Narcissists cannot love others as distinctive persons but only if the qualities of the other person reflect themselves either as they are or as they would like to be.

One of the reasons for the relationship between the Greek *narkissos* or narcotic, and narcissism is that when one is entirely devoted to himself, he becomes numb or stuporous to the outside world and hence, anesthetized to it, and to the needs of others.

Narcissus feels he is the center of the universe. His flaw is abnormal self-love. Fascinated by his own beauty, he feels superior to others. No one, he feels, is good enough for him, and this excessive pride causes his downfall. In the myth, Teiresias correctly prophesies that Narcissus will live to an old age if he does not know himself. When Narcissus first looks into the pool, he does not recognize the reflection with whom he falls in love as himself. Later, he realizes that he is in love with his own image, and not that of another.

He literally withers away, transformed into a flower. People who do not recognize that their lives leave no room for caring for others, cannot live full lives. Narcissistic love is felt as nonreciprocal. The narcissist feels rejected by most people, but in some ways, he rejects others because behind the facade of loving himself "too much," he really does not have enough self-esteem. He is afraid that if he gives love, he will have it taken from him.

The Narcissus and Echo myths are told together because each character has similar problems. Narcissus is over-involved with himself to the exclusion of others, and Echo only repeats the final words of others. She has lost her uniqueness, her individuality, her sense of self. Echo reflects the voices of others, while Narcissus reflects himself and loses others.

Originally intended by the Greeks, perhaps, as a way of explaining the natural phenomenon of the echo, the myth of Echo, today, has many more implications in our daily lives. We adopt the speech and slang of our friends, sometimes, in order to be loved or accepted. This practice can abolish free or imaginative communication and we lose not only our ability to express our own feelings, but limit ourselves to the expressions of others, thus deadening the uniqueness of our own personalities.

28 Orpheus and Eurydice

INTRODUCTION

The *aretē* of Orpheus was his voice. He sang so magnificently that he charmed the Sirens on the voyage with Jason to recover the golden fleece, and also the gods and shades in Hades' dismal kingdom. The ancient Greeks believed that excellence could lead to *hybris* or excessive pride. This was true in the case of Orpheus. Although his *hybris* did not become insolence as it did with Arachne and Niobe, he was as arrogant as they were. Orpheus believed that, because he loved Eurydice, the inevitability of death should not apply to her.

The "átē" (temporary madness) of Orpheus revealed itself in his refusal to recognize that he was not a god. He forgot his human limitations. He abandoned the *golden mean* when his emotions usurped the powers of rationality, intellect, and reason.

The gods punished Orpheus by showing him that his own weakness (his inability to obey the command of the gods) forced Eurydice to return to the kingdom of Hades. Orpheus was forced to learn that, being human, he could not control the universe, and that, in fact, he could not even control himself.

Yet, even after he was punished, Orpheus did not regain his dignity. He accepted the death of Eurydice, but his emotions continued to rule his life. Because he was ruled solely by passion, he lost the ability to command admiration from others. The kind of a man he was became more important than his excellent voice.

The ancient Greeks realized that life and happiness were unpredictable for everyone. One's blessings could evaporate, and death could come at any time. The story of Orpheus shows that the inability to accept and to cope with the crises of life produces great misery. Without Eurydice, Orpheus could have returned to a meaningful life in society. He could have received the pleasure that came from giving of oneself, and receiving in return. Instead, he became a misanthrope, and as a result, his excellent voice was no longer valued or admired.

His violent death may indicate that Orpheus was either a sacred king in a matriarchal society or a youth who represented Dionysus in the ritual drama of the wine-god's death and rebirth. In either role, Orpheus would have been dismembered and eaten.

ANTICIPATIONS

1. How do you react to a crisis?
   a. get sick (headache, stomach ache, and so on)
   b. get angry
   c. pretend it hasn't happened
   d. dream about it
   e. prepare for it
   f. talk about it with someone
   g. other

THE MYTH

Orpheus was a master poet of Thrace, a country to the east of Macedonia. His beautiful voice and accompanying lyre could charm man and beast, and some said it could even move stones.

But alas! When Orpheus married Eurydice, catastrophe followed. As his bride walked with the river nymphs along the Hebrus River, a serpent bit her on the heel. It killed her instantly, separating her from her devoted husband.

Orpheus was overcome with grief. He neither ate nor slept. Finally, in a desperate attempt to recover his wife, he descended to the Underworld by the road from Taenarum in southern Greece. In order that his misery might move the deathless gods, he sought fair Persephone and her husband, grim Hades, Lord of All beneath the Earth.

Upon his arrival, Orpheus tuned his strings. Then the great poet sang to the song of his lyre before the dread rulers of the dismal land:

"Your powers that sway the world beneath the earth, that last land of all mortal men, hear me. I wish to tell the truth. I have not come here merely to explore the Underworld out of curiosity. Nor have I come to find scowling Cerberus, who, barking, shakes his triple heads. I am only searching for my wife. Only for love of her do I suffer these terrors. My unfortunate, young wife stepped upon a snake's head, and it bit her in the heel. Thus she has suffered an untimely death. I have striven to bear her loss, but I cannot endure it.

"Eros," he continued, "is a god well-known above. Perhaps he is known here, also. For if Fame truly reports all passions," he said darkly, "the Lord of the Underworld has also felt its flames.

"By these prayers of mine," Orpheus implored, "reverse Eurydice's too hasty fate. Restore her to me. After a short stay on earth, early or late, we must all come to your kingdom. Here we throng, assigned to our last home. So Eurydice, too, when her time on earth has expired, will again be yours. If the Fates deny me and you will not postpone her death, my second choice is to abide here. So rejoice in both our deaths, or return us both to life!"

While he sang these words, the bloodless shades silently wept. Springs no longer tempted Tantalus,[1] Ixion's[2] whirling wheel of fire stood still, and Sisyphus[3] sat listening upon his stone. Even the Furies, who never wept, now were seen to weep, while the triple jaws of Cerberus opened wide with wonder.

Fair Persephone yielded to the powerful plea of Orpheus, and grim Hades, too, felt pity for him.

From among the lately arrived shades, they called Eurydice. She arrived, still limping from her painful wound. The Lord of the Underworld gave her to Orpheus with this decree, "Until you pass the entrance to the world of light, you may not look back to see Eurydice. If you disobey, you will lose what you have, and your wife will remain a lifeless shade here, forever."

Together, Orpheus and Eurydice left grim Hades' kingdom. With difficulty, they climbed the steep and rugged ascent, dark and thick with fog. Finally, they approached the light of the upper world. Fearing to lose Eurydice, yet longing for the sight of her, the impatient lover Orpheus felt compelled to look behind him in order to see her face.

Three times the Underworld shook with thunder. Eurydice, instantly dying, slid back to the dismal kingdom beneath the earth. "What madness has destroyed us, Orpheus?" she asked. "The Fates draw me into the grip of Death, and eternal sleep closes my eyes.

"Farewell, Orpheus. I am enveloped in endless night. I reach for you, but I no longer belong to you. I cannot see beyond the dismal mist which blinds my eyes." Fearing that he would lose her forever, Orpheus tried to grasp her. However, his hands closed upon air, not flesh.

Eurydice, dying a second death, did not blame her husband, for what could she complain of but his love. She managed to utter one last farewell, but so softly that Orpheus scarcely heard her voice.

Orpheus was now desolate and grief-stricken. He realized that through his love for her he had lost Eurydice once more. He returned to the Underworld and pleaded with Charon to help him, but the ferryman angrily refused to take him across the River Styx.

Orpheus sat forlorn upon the banks of the River Styx for seven months, abstaining from any kind of food or drink. Grief and tears filled his days and nights. He called the gods of the Underworld severe. He complained of the cruel Fates and railed against all those who had deprived him of his love.

Orpheus and Eurydice   173

At length, he went to the snowy mountains of Thrace. There Boreas, the north wind, blasted him mercilessly.

In the years that followed, Orpheus refused the company of women. He fled from them, either because of his marriage vows or because of his wife's fate. A group of wild maenads, under the influence of Dionysian revels, became furious at his rejection of them. Ferociously, they retaliated by tearing his body limb from limb and scattering the pieces over the land.

The shade of Orpheus was now free to join his beloved wife in the Underworld.

1. Tantalus was a king of Lydia who tricked the Olympians by serving his son Pelops to them for dinner. In Tartarus, he was chained to a tree, up to his neck in water he could not drink, and within reach of fruit he could not eat.
2. Ixion murdered his father-in-law by throwing him into a fiery pit. He also tried to seduce Hera. In Tartarus, he was chained to a revolving, fiery wheel.
3. Sisyphus spied on a romantic affair of Zeus and told the river nymph's father. He was condemned to spend eternity in Tartarus pushing a huge boulder to the top of a steep hill. Just as the rock approached the summit, it rolled down again.

    Sisyphus, Ixion, and Tantalus are the three most famous criminals in Greek mythology.

REFLECTIONS

1. Discuss whether or not you think Orpheus is a heroic character. To what extent was his behavior admirable?
2. Write this myth from Eurydice's point of view.
3. Write the myth as a play and perform it.
4. What motivated Orpheus to go down to the land of Hades in search of Eurydice? Discuss the importance of
   a. his wish to die.
   b. his wish for immortality.
   c. his wish to be with the woman he loves.
   d. his wish to become a hero.

HUMAN EXPERIENCE

The character of Orpheus was ruled by emotion. He was a poet and a musician. He bemoaned his fate both when he lost Eurydice initially, and when he lost her as a result of his compelling desire to look back at her, heedless of warnings.

It was a value of the Greeks to temper emotion with reason. Orpheus was not heroic when he attempted to keep Eurydice with him by pleading for her to join him on earth, or offering to join her in the Underworld. His problem can be seen as his inability to accept the fact that man cannot control the universe. Man is subject to accident, death, catastrophe, and above all, reality. Reality can sometimes be painful, but in most of our lives, we are required to live with more than one force, drive, goal, or wish at a time. This causes conflict within us, and results, at times, in our inability to deal sensibly with a catastrophe, such as death, or the life-forces we *all* feel that carry with them the need to choose our acts wisely, to accept the full responsibility for making own own choices, and to accept their results. This myth asks us to question how we really react to a number of external stimuli: to love, to death, to orders from others, to loss, to the disappointment of imperfection in ourselves, and in the world.

It is interesting to note that although the myth contains the names of both lovers, Eurydice is virtually a concept rather than a flesh-and-blood woman. At the beginning she was already dead, so the story focuses on the way Orpheus handled his fate. Eurydice's death was a major catastrophe in his life. Orpheus is either a hero because he did *not* accept his fate, or he was a flawed human because he could not live with life as it was.

Our experience usually teaches us that we have certain alternatives in life. We must either learn to accept what we are powerless to change, or to remain in a constant state of misery, or die. These three alternatives inevitably face us in our lives at one time or another. No one escapes the necessity of making choices that affect our lives—our fate, in one sense.

Orpheus looked back either because of weakness, love, or predistination. If we "look back," as did Orpheus, in our own lives, we can learn from past mistakes and correct them. The philosopher Santayana said, "He who never learns history is bound to repeat it." Looking back over our own lives is not the deadly act it is in this myth. It is a continual process in which we try to change our futures for the better by getting to know (having insight into) our past behavior.

Orpheus was given some choices that he resolved in an ambiguous manner: he could have accepted the Fates and not plead for Eurydice's rebirth, he could have chosen to die, or he could have remained alive and miserable. Orpheus, in rejecting every other woman, symbolically rejected life, itself. He did not deal *actively* with his life. Each of us has the ability to choose ways of handling matters of life and death. Usually the Greek notion of using reason to temper feelings brings us into balance with our feelings and lends perspective to our choices.

29 The Calydonian Boar Hunt

Although Meleager is considered to be one of the famous Greek heroes, his fame is connected principally with the boar hunt he organized. Boar hunts were a frequent and popular activity among Mycenaean royalty. Although the Mycenaen religion emphasized Zeus and the Olympic gods, this myth also illustrates matriarchal values from the older worship of the "Great Goddess."

This boar hunt may have become famous because it caused members of a family to kill one another. No society would condone such a crime, but the family-dominated matriarchal society especially considered any crime within the family unit to be dastardly. Moreover, the family unit was used to taking justice into its own hands. That Meleager's mother chose to avenge her brothers at the expense of her son reflects these cultural values.

The boar hunt may have represented the Mycenaean conquest of a matriarchal community, since boars were sacred animals in the matriarchal culture. The boar's tusks were curved like the moon, and the moon was sacred to the matriarchy. Its cycle determined the timing of all religious and secular events.

The events of the boar hunt, from start to finish, involved decision-making. This myth is interesting because so many people had a direct impact upon what happened. If any one of them had made a different decision, tragedy may not have occurred.

Meleager's fate was prophesied early in his infancy, in a way that reflected the attitude of the ancient Greeks toward the Fates and destiny. The Fates told his mother, Althaea, that her son would die *if* the log burned. They were not announcing that the log would burn, or when it would burn. That event was not predetermined. The divine prophecy was a warning to help mortal man make a decision.

Blaming Artemis as the main cause of the catastrophe robs the myth of its awesome power. In her anger, Artemis created a situation in which man would make choices that would destroy him. However, nature, not the gods, determines human destiny. In fact, Artemis played only a minor role in this myth. She sent the boar into Calydon in order to create the problem. She appeared only once, and at that time invisibly, in order to determine who would and who would not wound the boar. She left the rest to human nature.

It is possible to analyze the action without any reference to Artemis. The boar could have arrived on its own. Moreover, who hit and did not hit the boar could have been pure chance. It was all too easy for one of the heroes, or for any human being, to have felt that a god rather than his or her own ability or pure chance determined the success of personal actions. In the *Odyssey*, Zeus complained that mortals blamed the gods when it was their own poor judgement and greed that were responsible for their fate. Mortals must avoid the trap of excessive pride, but no Greek, mortal or immortal, asked human beings to surrender the control they had over their own lives through the process of decision making.

Meleager acted with independence when he invited a female to join a traditionally male activity. He courageously defended his action against those who reacted with typical, patriarchal, male chauvinism. Unfortunately, Meleager eventually let his emotions determine his actions, and *átē* ushered in his doom.

ANTICIPATIONS

1. Whenever we make a decision, we have made a choice.
   In what order do you do the following when you get up in the morning?
   a. Take a shower.
   b. Brush your teeth.
   c. Make your bed.
   d. Choose your clothes.
   e. Eat a full breakfast.
   f. Grab something to eat as you are leaving.
   g. Skip breakfast.
   h. Watch television.
   i. Other.
2. How do you determine what you will do with your free time?
   a. By what your friends are doing.
   b. By what your parents want you to do.
   c. By what you want to do.
   d. By what you are good at doing.
   e. By what you want to learn to do.

The circumstances surrounding the hero Meleager's birth were strange, and it was not determined whether his father was Oeneus, who was the king of Calydon, or Ares, the God of War.

When Meleager was seven days old, the three Fates, the immortal spinners of mortal destinies, suddenly appeared in Althaea's bedroom with their spinning wheel, their shears, and their flax, which was the substance of mortal life. Placing a meager measure of the essential flax nearby, the three goddesses set their wheel in motion. As they spun their flax into the thread of life, they predicted Meleager's future. First, Clotho (Spinner) chanted that Meleager would become a famous young man. Next, Lachesis (Distributor of Fortunes)[1] chanted that Meleager would become known for his great courage. Finally, Atropos (Inflexible), the most feared of the three sisters,[2] walked over to the hearth in which a fire cheerfully blazed. There, she chose an unlighted log which lay upon the hearth, raised it, and tossed it upon the flames. As the log began to burn, Atropos chanted: "Upon you and this blazing log, oh lately born babe, we confer an identical destiny."[3] As soon as Atropos had woven her power into Meleager's fate, Clotho stopped spinning, Lachesis measured the thread, and Atropos cut it. The three sisters then vanished from Althaea's room.

Althaea, terrified by the divine prophecy, immediately leaped from her bed, hastily snatched the blazing log from the fire, and extinguished its fatal flames. She preserved the log by putting it into a chest which she then hid in an inner closet deep within the palace. Her careful preservation of the log comforted her and made her confident that Meleager's future was secure.

Meleager was raised to become the next king of Calydon. Years passed, and the royal family prospered. Meleager became as noble and as brave as the Fates had foretold. Although he was young, he sailed with Jason and the Argonauts on their voyage to recover the golden fleece.

Not long after Meleager's return, King Oeneus committed a careless error which provoked Artemis's wrath and resulted in devastating consequences for himself, for his family, and for his kingdom. As was the custom when blessed with an abundant harvest, Oeneus sacrificed the first fruits of his corn fields to Demeter; olive oil from his orchards to Athena; wine from his vineyards to Dionysus; and the first sheep of his flocks to Pan. He then carefully proceeded to honor all of the other divine powers with generous offerings. However, Oeneus did not honor Artemis of the Golden Arrows.

Oeneus paid dearly for this neglect. Jealous of her reputation, the Archer-Goddess became furious when she saw that her altars remained barren while those of her relatives were well supplied with gifts. "When mortals dishonor me," she exclaimed, "I take revenge!"

Consequently, arrow-raining Artemis sent into Calydon a monstrous boar. Its stiff neck flaunted thickly set, thorny bristles which threatened enemies like a grove of spears. Its eyes glared with blood-red fires, while its grinding jaws spewed a boiling foam down upon its shoulders. It brandished gleaming, white tusks as menacing as an Indian elephant's, and its foul mouth bellowed thunder and lightning as if it were a transformation of immortal Zeus.

The boar ravaged Calydon. Incessantly on the rampage, first it burned the pastures with blasts of its breath. Then it invaded the corn fields, trampling down the tender young plants, and leaving nothing for the farmers to reap but shriveled leaves and mutilated stalks. Next it entered the orchards, shearing the heavily grape-laden vines of their fruit and leaving the unharvested grapes to rot upon the ground. It tore apart the leafy branches of the olive trees, strewing the ground with green olives. It ripped up entire apple orchards, felling the tall trees and destroying their roots, bark, blossoms, and fruit. Finally it preyed upon the flocks in the pens. Neither shepherds, nor dogs, nor even raging bulls dared to defend their herds. The country folk left their homes and fields and sought safety within the walled city.

The boar could not be captured or killed by even the bravest of men. Therefore, Meleager invited the most noble youths from all over Greece to join him in hunting for the boar. He promised to award the hide of the boar as a prize to the hero who killed it. This invitation was such an honor that no hero willingly refused the challenge. Only Heracles, who was committed to King Eurystheus for ten labors, could not join his friends. He had postponed his fifth labor in order to accompany Jason and the Argonauts; he dared not delay it further.

Thus Oeneus and Althaea were honored to entertain the greatest heroes of their son's generation. The best known of these included: Castor and Polydeuces, the famous "twin"[4] brothers of Helen of Troy; Jason, who initiated the famous voyage for the golden fleece; the inseparable friends, Theseus and Peirithoüs; Admetus of Pherae, who was Jason's cousin and friend, and the friend of Heracles as well; Iphicles and his son Iolaüs, who were Heracles' brother and nephew respectively; Peleus, later the father of swift Achilles, and his brother Telamon, later the father of the valiant warrior, Ajax; Nestor of Pylos, who was then a vigorous youth; and, finally, Laërtes, later the father of the renowned Odysseus.

Meleager courageously invited the celebrated huntress, Atalanta, to join this all male group. The beautiful maiden huntress was the last to arrive. She had a boyish face, although in a boy it would have looked feminine. She wore her hair simply arranged, bound in a knot at the back of her neck. Her simple clothing was clasped with a polished buckle. She carried her well-strung bow in her left hand, while an ivory quiver over her left shoulder held arrows which clattered as she walked. Meleager fell in love with her immediately, but his hopes were not destined to be fulfilled. "The man you love will be fortunate!" he exclaimed. He would have said more, but his sense of honor and his role as a leader of the expedition compelled him to attend to more serious matters.

Once everyone had arrived, King Oeneus entertained his guests with feasts and competitive athletic events for nine days. When the tenth day arrived and the heroes had finished their final preparations, some of the lesser known guests refused to hunt with Atalanta because they felt that a female had no right to participate in a traditionally masculine activity. However, Meleager exerted his authority as the leader and persuaded them to join the hunt.

First the group had to climb through a virgin forest which covered the mountainside and rose above the plain. They unleashed their hunting dogs upon the boar's scent and searched for its footprints. They eagerly anticipated the encounter and actively sought this danger in order to achieve fame and glory. Each hero thought about how skillfully he would distinguish himself once he had confronted the enemy.

As they tracked the boar, the group came upon a moist and marshy valley, annually fed by generous spring rains. Here the hunting dogs discovered and provoked the boar, which immediately rushed among the youths as jagged streaks of lightning. In its frantic fury, it felled young trees, shaking the ground and causing the forest to echo with sounds of destruction. The dogs, fearful of the boar's terrible tusks, scattered.

The youths, however, shouted with excitement and inspired courage in each other. Taking a firm stand, they positioned their metal-tipped spears for the throw. Jason threw his spear with great strength, but it flew past the boar's side. Another youth asked for Apollo's help before he threw his spear. "If I have honored and do honor your divine power," he prayed, "help make my throw successful, and let me hit the boar."

Apollo guided the spear, but Artemis of the Showering Arrows removed the iron point from the flying wooden shaft so that when the spear struck the boar, it did not wound the boar but, instead, incited the boar to even greater wrath. It violently assaulted the hunters as if it were a boulder that a catapulting machine had hurled against a fortification. As it charged its enemies, its malicious eyes shone blood-red, and its nostrils breathed flames of fire. Some youths received deep wounds. Nestor would have perished long before the Trojan War if he had not prudently used his lance to vault into a nearby tree.

Meanwhile, the raging boar sharpened his brutal tusks upon the stump of an oak tree and, confident of his power, threatened total slaughter.

Castor and Polydeuces, conspicuously dressed in white and mounted upon white horses, together had poised their spears overhead and had taken aim when the boar retreated into a web of underbrush, concealing itself from the pursuit of any horse or weapon. Telamon, showing admirable persistence, rushed into the dense thicket, so intent upon the chase that he stumbled upon an exposed root and fell. Atalanta quickly drew an arrow from her quiver, took aim, and let the arrow fly. It flew accurately and struck the boar beneath its left ear, thereby staining bristles with a steaming trickle of blood. Atalanta blushed with pride.

Meleager, who was the first to notice Atalanta's success, raised his voice in praise of the beautiful archer and called his friends' attention to the boar's bleeding wound. "Oh, most matchless huntress!" he exclaimed. "Your skill has exceeded your reputation. You shall receive the praise you deserve." Upon hearing this tribute to their female competitor, the men blushed with shame and jealousy. They roused each other's spirits with encouraging cheers, and being over-anxious to achieve, they threw their spears so quickly and haphazardly that some of their weapons collided in mid-air and none reached the boar.

Ancaeüs, one of the men who originally had protested Atalanta's presence on the hunt, then stepped in front of the other youths and, using both hands, waved his double-bladed axe menacingly in the face of the bloodthirsty boar. "Let me show you," he bragged, "how a man's weapon surpasses a woman's. This boar is now finished! Even if the Archer-Goddess Artemis were to raise her bow in order to protect her favorite against my skill, she could not preserve its life." Then, he leaned forward, his two-edged weapon ready to strike. However, like a sudden flash of lightning, the boar charged straight at him, and before his arms could lower the axe, the brutal beast had buried its tusks in Ancaeüs's groin. Down upon the earth he crumpled, his intestines strewn amidst his blood.

Undaunted by this grisly death, Peirithoüs approached the boar and ably aimed his lance. Theseus interrupted him by calling out, "Dearest friend, dearer to me than life, stay away from the boar! Wisdom is a necessary part of courage, and distance lends safety to heroism. Ancaeüs's foolish courage caused his death." With this advice, Theseus carefully aimed his heavy wooden lance with its bronze head. Then he hurled it so accurately that it surely would have dealt the boar its death blow if it had not been deflected by the leafy branches of a tall oak tree which stood between the hunter and his target.

Next, Meleager, a spear in each hand, hurled both with equal force. Although one spear hit the ground, the other sank into the boar's back. As the raging boar twisted and turned from side to side, hoping to eliminate the cause of his torture, it cast blood and foam upon earth and shrub. Meleager rushed in to finish the slaughter. Turning as the boar turned, ever more quickly, Meleager repeatedly thrust his spear into the boar's body, seeking the most direct path to its heart.

When the boar finally had fallen and breathed its last, everyone jubilantly congratulated Meleager. Then, the youths cautiously approached their formidable enemy as it lay lifeless amidst its blood and foam. The tremendous bulk of the vanquished beast astonished them, intimidating them more in death than it had in life. They extended their spears and dipped the metal points into their enemy's blood, as both a testimony to its power and a token of its defeat.

Next, as captain of the expedition, Meleager placed his foot upon the boar's bristly neck and announced the recipient of the prize. "Beloved Atalanta," he declared. "Permit me to share my labor and my glory with you and award you my prize." Then Meleager presented her with both the boar's gristly hide and its huge head, still armed with the tremendous tusks which had caused such dread and destruction.

Atalanta gladly received the gift. However, among themselves, the other youths quietly expressed feelings of resentment and envy. Meleager's uncles, Toxeus and Plexippus, brothers of his mother, were more forthright in their displeasure. They challenged Meleager's authority by attempting to intimidate Atalanta. "Put down those glorious prizes, woman," Plexippus commanded. "Do not expect to rob us of our hunting trophies. Meleager is no proper judge since love has blinded his judgment. By right of birth, if Meleager refuses his prize, it belongs to us. You have no valid claim. So, forget your beauty, and return the prizes. They belong to the men who earn them." As Atalanta listened, speechless, Toxeus grabbed the gifts Meleager had awarded her.

Meleager exploded with rage. He would not be deprived of his position of leadership, even by his mother's brothers. Placing love and public esteem above family relationships, he thundered, "You robbers of others' honors, now you will learn the difference between empty words and actual deeds!" He then approached Plexippus and quickly thrust his sword deep into his uncle's chest. While Toxeus watched in amazement, wondering whether he should avenge his brother's death or attempt to escape the identical fate, Meleager took advantage of his indecision and plunged the sword, which was still wet with the blood of one uncle, into the heart of the other. Then Meleager returned the disputed gifts to Atalanta.

Meanwhile, in the city of Calydon, Meleager's mother, Althaea, heard about the monstrous boar's death. As a gesture of thanksgiving for her son's victory, she brought gifts to the gods and sang hymns of praise to far-shooting Apollo. She was completely unprepared for the sight of her dead brothers, whom she recognized as their bodies were carried into the city. Overcome with grief, she immediately exchanged her ceremonial robes for funeral attire and filled the city with her anguished cries.

However, as soon as Althaea learned that her brothers had been murdered and that her son had killed them, her grief changed to a desire for vengeance. She returned to the palace, to the inner closet, and to the chest which she secretly had hidden within it. She resolutely removed the log from the chest, and, in the privacy of her bedroom, she kindled a fresh fire upon the hearth. Four times she offered the log of her son's life to the greedy flames, and four times she withdrew it. A sister's vengeance fought with a mother's love for control of the fatal log. Just as wind and tide may contend against one another, maneuvering a ship first with the breeze and then with the current, so Althaea vacillated between rage and pity, resolution and doubt, hatred and love.

Finally, the rage of a sister conquered the love of a mother. Holding the fatal log before the flames, she cried, "May my son's blood appease the ghosts of my slaughtered brothers." Then she bowed three times before the hearth and each time she called upon the three Furies.[5] "Come, come, come, you triple powers, you who avenge offenders against blood relatives, who pursue and punish guilty souls. Attend these rites of retribution. A sister is avenging the death of her brothers. I am punishing one crime by committing another, but one death must atone for another. Let this entire household collapse in ruin and arrow-raining Artemis's plague engulf us all.

"Shall Oeneus enjoy his victorious son while my father has been robbed of his two sons? It is better to sacrifice three lives than to let one go unpunished. So, ghosts of my dear brothers, accept my costly sacrifice, for with the life of my womb do I repay the loss of your lives.

"Oh, excuse a mother, dearest brothers, but I do not have the heart to kill my child. Although he deserves death, his mother should not be the one to kill him. But, then, he will live victorious, while you are abandoned shades! I will not have that!

"So, die, murderer! Let your father's hopes, his crown, and his kingdom die with you. Twice have I given you life; once upon your birth, and once by preserving this log. You have caused your own death, a just reward for your offense. Yet, my mother's heart is filled with pity. I would take revenge, yet I would not. Oh, my cursed indecision!

"You have won, my brothers! I cannot resist your bleeding wounds. Yet, while I comfort you, I shall avenge my son's death with my own."

With these final words, Althaea averted her face and dropped the fatal log upon the flames. The log seemed to sigh and emit a dying moan, and the flames themselves appeared to approach the log cautiously, as though reluctant to embrace it.

As the log fell upon the fire and ignited, in the forest, Meleager felt flames kindle within his body. He bore the agony with the inner strength and discipline of a hero, sorry only that his death was so undistinguished. He envied Ancaeüs, who had been slaughtered by the monstrous boar. At least the Fates had given Ancaeüs the opportunity to die using his skill in battle, with dignity and among his friends.

Meleager and the log were consumed as one by the blaze. Finally, when both were almost ashes, flames and pain flared briefly, then extinguished. Meleager's spirit vanished into the air, leaving charred coals beneath shrouds of ash to mourn him.

Now mighty Calydon had fallen. Meleager's mother, pursued by the Furies for murdering her child, appeased her guilt and personally avenged her son's death by thrusting a sword into her own chest.

Young and old, nobility and peasants, all grieved openly and without reserve. The women cut their hair, tore their clothes, and beat their breasts in sorrow and despair. King Oeneus covered his head with dust and lay stretched upon the ground, cursing life for bringing him such intolerable pain. However, even poets cannot adequately express the inconsolable grief of Meleager's sisters. They bruised themselves with their blows and mournfully embraced Meleager's ashes. When his tomb was erected, they wore away the stone inscription with their tears. Feeling pity for their grief, the Archer-Goddess transformed them[6] into birds. She accepted Oeneus's suffering as atonement for his insult to her honor. Artemis's vengeance was now complete.

1. Lachesis measured the thread of each mortal's life, determining its length.
2. Atropos used her shears to cut the thread of each mortal's life, thus determining his death.
3. In Celtic and Norse cultures, a person's life source also may be connected to an object outside of his body, such as to a plant or an animal. In each situation, whatever happens to the object happens to the person whose life is connected with it.
4. For Castor and Polydeuces, see myth of Nemesis, Section II, The Olympian Family.
5. The Furies, created by Gaea from Uranus's blood, punished a relative who killed a member of the family by driving the offender insane and causing his death.
6. Deïaneira, who was married to Heracles, was not present when her sisters were transformed into birds.

REFLECTIONS

1. Who do you think was most responsible for Meleager's death? Explain the role of
   a. Artemis
   b. Meleager's father
   c. Meleager's mother
   d. Meleager's uncles
   e. Atalanta
   f. Meleager
   In each case, explain what alternatives to the action taken the person might have had.

2. What do you think this myth reveals about the role of women in Mycenaean Greek society?
3. Write the story of the boar hunt from Atalanta's point of view.

Decision Making

It is difficult to make decisions that will change our lives. It is so difficult that many people let their lives run them. The cultural values of our society are changing at unprecedented rates of speed. Since our personal values are shaped in part by cultural or social practices, many of us feel that we live by a double set of values, those we would like to embody, and those that are shaped by our techno-cultural revolution.

We cannot make decisions unless we are able to do two things well; set priorities and establish personal values. *Values* are those qualities we find admirable in ourselves and in others. They represent the ways in which we believe; our preferences, beliefs, and ideals. The values we choose guide the way we feel about people, things, ideas, and places.

Decisions reflect values. If we value the expectations or the opinions of others more than our own, our decisions will reflect that value. If we value our own sense of responsibility to ourselves and to others, our decisions will reflect that fact. When we feel confused about decision-making, it is a result of having more than one goal or of conflicting values.

Some of us are rarely forced to make decisions until there is a crisis situation in our lives, which, by its nature decrees that we must find new ways, or alternatives, to live by if we are to grow successfully. This means changing not only some of our values but our priorities as well.

Most of our mistakes in decision-making come from the feeling that in order to make decisions, we should be more influenced by others than by our own inner guides. We lean on others in decision-making because we fail to make ourselves aware of *our* needs, because we move too quickly toward the familiar, and consequently do not make an *active* decision.

Having acted in this manner, we are uncomfortably aware that a decision *not* to choose is also a choice. We have made a decision even when we consciously or unconsciously "decide" not to do so.

Most of us feel that we "stand for something." However, when we stand so rigidly for a value that it obliterates the opportunity to try something new, or keeps us from reassessing our position in the light of new circumstances, new people or new times, then we fall back on habit.

In so doing, we may avoid the risk of changing our minds, but we are also closing ourselves to the possibility of change.

How can we find alternatives to old ways of decision-making and not rely only on the tried-and-true recipes we feel designate our past decisions? Obviously, all decision-making is based upon choice. Choice means eliminating all the alternatives but one.

Once that choice is made, it remains for all decisions to be put into action. Decisions are not active in a vacuum. They cannot influence our lives or create significant changes until we can commit ourselves to *acting* upon our decisions and living comfortably with the changes such action brings.

30 Atalanta

INTRODUCTION

When you read this myth, consider whether Aphrodite made Atalanta fall in love with Hippomenes. As in the "Calydonian Boar Hunt", a divinity structured a situation in which a person was clearly free to make a choice. In fact, except for the magical transformation at the end of the story, Aphrodite's power was unnecessary. Hippomenes could have thought up the trick of the golden apples himself. The goddess was invisible to everyone else.

Yet, it is human nature for people who are competitive in spirit to rationalize another person's success as "luck" or "the gods." In this instance, another suitor might have attributed the trick of Hippomenes to Aphrodite's help if he had not wanted to admit that Hippomenes was more imaginative or that Atalanta simply preferred Hippomenes.

THE MYTH

When Atalanta was born, her father was so disappointed that she was not a male child that he left her exposed in the countryside, hoping that she would die of starvation, illness, or from an assault by wild animals. However, a female bear found the infant and nursed her as if she were its own bear cub. Later, when hunters found Atalanta, they took her home with them and reared her.

Atalanta continued to live in the forest, and she became a famous huntress. Her skills in archery and in running were only equalled by her beauty. No matter where she went, her bow and arrows travelled with her. When two Centaurs attempted to rape her, she killed them with her weapons. Eventually she discovered the identity of her true parents, and returned to their palace and lived with them.

One day Atalanta asked the oracle of Apollo at Delphi whether the

Fates would permit her to take a husband. "A husband will cause your ruin," the oracle prophesied. "You will strive in vain against your fate and although you will continue to live, you will lose yourself."

Frightened by this advice, Atalanta drove all suitors from her, saying, "Unless you beat me in a foot race, I am a wife for no man. The suitor who loses will die."

Atalanta chose a large, enclosed athletic field as the site for the races. One at a time, she would contend with her numerous suitors. Each youth would receive a head start and would race unarmed. Then the maiden huntress would pursue her suitor, dressed in a full set of armor and carrying her bow and arrows. Atalanta would immediately shoot and kill any suitor she defeated in a foot race. She would decapitate the victim and place his head upon a pole. The pole would then be fixed on the circumference of the athletic field.

Even under these gruesome conditions, Atalanta continued to find many men who wished to marry her. She was so beautiful that many young men were eager to undertake that peril in the hope of winning her hand in marriage. Her face attracted suitors, while her feet destroyed them!

Watching one of these contests, Hippomenes[1] wondered at those who would so rashly risk their lives. "Must a man risk his life in order to gain the blessing of a wife?" he asked. Then he saw Atalanta and fell in love with her. "Forgive my doubts, you suitors who have died," he declared. "I did not know the merit of the prize."

Now Hippomenes envied the runners and hoped that none would win. Meanwhile, the current race ended and Atalanta won. Hippomenes watched as she shot the suitor with her well-aimed arrow.

"Why do you choose such easy victories?" he called to her, challengingly. "Contend instead with me! My victory will not detract from your glory."

In silence, Atalanta looked at Hippomenes, pleased with his appearance. She felt doubts and conflict and did not know whether she would be happier if she lost to him or conquered him.

"What god would destroy this youth who seeks to end his life if he can't marry me?" she wondered. "I am not worth your sacrifice," she mused, as she stood gazing at him. "What is it I feel for you," she asked herself, "Is it pity or love? I admire your courage and your contempt of death. You seem to be content to part with your life if the Fates deny me for your wife."

"Be gone, stranger!" she replied to Hippomenes, "Shun my bloody bed while you can. This race will loosen your head from your body. There is no maiden who would refuse to be your wife. Leave while you still can."

Then she thought, "Yet why do I think of you when I've killed so many others? Why does my heart beat for you alone? You have watched your rivals die. You must be weary of life to court death so intensely. Yet, must death be the payment for love? To destroy such a youth will shame my victory and cause hatred, but I am not to blame. Did I persuade you to run against me?"

Her thoughts ran on. "Oh! Would that you could avoid danger, or, since you are so foolish, would that you could run faster. Poor Hippomenes," she thought, "I wish you had never seen this place. You deserve to live. If the Fates would permit me to marry, you are the only one I would choose for my husband."

Now the king and crowds of people impatiently called for the race between Atalanta and Hippomenes to begin. Hippomenes fervently prayed, "Oh golden Aphrodite, favor my attempt to win the maiden huntress. Help me to win this race and to gain my love. Help the affections you have given me. You have inspired my love."

A gentle wind sped his prayer to Mount Olympus where golden Aphrodite heard his plea. She immediately descended to the earth and sought her sacred island of Cyprus. There, in the most fertile field grew a tree whose glittering leaves and branches shone with gold.

Aphrodite gathered three golden apples from that tree, and, invisible to all but Hippomenes, she delivered them to him and instructed him in their use.

At the king's command the trumpets sounded. Atalanta gave Hippomenes the customary head start. Swiftly, with agile steps they ran, their feet scarcely touching the surface of the sandy earth.

"Make haste, Hippomenes! Don't delay!" roared the crowd. "Don't be afraid! If you are bold, victory is yours!"

Both Atalanta and Hippomenes were delighted with the encouragement. Atalanta often purposely lagged behind, when she might have increased the distance between them. She would look fondly at Hippomenes, restraining her flying feet, then quickly resume the contest and overtake him. Their short breaths scorched the air; their mouths were parched.

The goal was still far off when Hippomenes threw the first of the three golden apples upon the plain.

Atalanta stopped and admired the unusual golden fruit. Anxious to possess the shining object, she turned aside and bent to catch the rolling, golden apple. It rolled right by her. While she was diverted from her course, the field resounded with shouts of joy as the crowd supported Hippomenes' lead.

Atalanta retrieved the apple. Running as swiftly as the wind, she overtook Hippomenes and soon left him far behind. Hippomenes cast the second golden fruit, this time throwing it farther than before. Again Atalanta stopped and retrieved the shining fruit. Again she overtook Hippomenes in the race.

As the great race approached the end, Hippomenes prayed, "Oh Giver of Golden Apples, help me! Give success to the love you've inspired within me." He then threw the last golden apple across the plain with all his strength, in order to cause Atalanta to detour and delay her victory.

Atalanta was doubtful as to what to do. In order to retrieve the apple, she would risk losing the race. However, conquered by love, Atalanta diverted her pursuit and acquired the shining fruit. The burden of the three heavy golden apples slowed down her speed. Atalanta could not recover the distance that separated her from Hippomenes, and he won the race. The crowd went wild with enthusiastic approval. Atalanta's father awarded his daughter to Hippomenes, and they were married.

However, Hippomenes did not give thanks or sacrifice to Aphrodite for his victory, and golden Aphrodite became provoked with sudden rage at his apparent contempt. She worried, lest other mortals slight her honor because of Hippomenes' example. Thus, golden Aphrodite took revenge upon them both.

One day, while resting from a hunt, Atalanta inspired Hippomenes with a passionate love. He was overcome with desire for her. In the deep forest, they found a grove that was sacred to Olympian Zeus. They entered the shrine and spent the night there.

They awoke to find that Aphrodite and Zeus had punished them for defiling the sacred grove. Atalanta noticed that a yellow mane surrounded Hippomenes' neck and fell upon his smooth shoulders. His arms had become legs, his fingers had turned to claws.

Hippomenes noticed similar changes in Atalanta.

Now, when they attempted to speak to each other, they heard only roars. As they left the sacred grove, their tails swept the ground. Together they moved through the woods, but now in the form of lions, feared by mortal men.

The great Titan goddess, Rhea, yoked them to her chariot. Forever after, they drew her chariot across the earth.

1. Another version of this myth says that Atalanta's suitor was Melanion.

REFLECTIONS

1. Why did Atalanta race against suitors? Why didn't she refuse to race, since she did not intend to marry?
2. Why did Atalanta let Hippomenes win when she knew that there was a prophecy against her marriage?
3. Compare and contrast Atalanta to Arachne and Niobe.

Atalanta tried to accept the prophecy of her fate by outracing her suitors until she finally fell in love. This, like other Greek myths, deals with the impact of fate on people's lives. The oracle, functioning as a good friend, showed a way to prevent the inevitable fate from occurring, usually by avoiding some temptation, or living with a dreaded beast. However, when Atalanta succumbed to human frailties, her doom was sealed.

Modern thought denies the existence of fate and insists that one's fate is unknown at birth. It also places great stock in the idea that a person can hope to become that which his intelligence and diligence strive to achieve.

It is, in other words, not fate which prevents our success, but our own limitations or laziness. When circumstances beyond our control influence our success or failure, they are rational or natural, as in the case of illness, unequal ability, economic upheaval, hurricanes, or war. Few modern thinkers believe that a particular person is singled out for special attention to be blessed or cursed. They believe that the story of our lives is written as we live it and unfolds as we, ourselves, create it.

IV

The Heroes

The Great Goddess Rhea (Cybele) is driving a chariot drawn by two lions, who are consuming a masked Giant. Heracles or Dionysus is standing behind Rhea and is attacking another masked Giant.

F ew mortals find it easy to become a hero. Yet, if a man can achieve honor and glory in his lifetime, his fame will live long after his death.

The Greek heroes were very human. They were born of mortal mothers. They may have received help from the gods, but they were responsible for their own behavior. They often committed serious errors of judgment or crimes, showing that they were not perfect beings. Yet, at their best, they were the defenders of the earth, the protectors of civilization, and the champions of the weak and helpless. In spite of their prodigious faults, they are eternally remembered for their suffering as well as for their accomplishments; being mortals ourselves, we sympathize with their human weaknesses.

One does not need to read many hero stories to realize that heroes shared many common experiences. All of the Greek heroes did not meet every part of the following composite description, but it is interesting to think about why so many factors apply to all of them.

The hero usually had an unusual birth. His father was often immortal while his mother invariably was mortal. He was born into royalty; his mother was a queen or a princess. There was often a prophecy about the hero's birth. The prophecy so frightened the family that they abandoned the infant soon after its birth, but the infant survived the ordeal, having been rescued by a family of lower social estate, or by an animal that reared him secretly.

Some accomplishment in his childhood indicated his potential, and as soon as he reached manhood, he chose a dangerous adventure. The adventure took him far from his home and forced him to perform at least one heroic feat, such as killing a powerful king, a monster, or a ferocious wild animal. In the course of these tasks, he made an area more civilized by providing safety, instruction, or settlement. He also came face to face with death by traveling into another world, such as the Underworld.

He returned from the encounter with death, having achieved honor and fame, and married a princess. His marriage, however, led to personal suffering. He made an error of judgment, caused by the excess of a basically admirable characteristic. Consequently, he lost the good will of mortals and immortals, and was forced to leave his country. He suffered, recognizing his error. He experienced a violent or unusual death, and his burial was without honor.

After his death, he was forgiven his errors and won immortal fame. However, his children did not inherit the throne. In the course of his life, he always had good intentions and kept his human dignity.

The Greek heroes lived at a time when society was changing from the matriarchal religious, social, and political organization to an organization based upon patriarchal principles. Therefore, the hero myths reflect the influence of both cultures.

The Greek heroes were destroyers as well as conquerors. They represented the aggressive warriors who invaded Greece and abolished the old ways. The monsters they fought were often female (such as Medusa), or were connected with the worship of females (such as Python or the other guardian snakes). These monsters represented some aspect of the matriarchal religion that was conquered and then replaced by patriarchal practices.

The female goddesses who helped the heroes may represent the training they received within the matriarchal society, which equipped them to compete for the great honor of sacred king.

The heroes may have been contestants, chosen as always from outside the reigning royal house, who had to perform special tasks in order to be chosen the sacred king. These tasks often involved a wrestling match, a chariot race, an archery contest, or the killing of particular wild animals, such as the boar, the lion, or the bull. The death of the hero may have reflected the brutal death of the sacred king. Thus, they could die by the spear or the arrow, at the hands of maddened women, dragged to death by a horse-drawn chariot, flung off a cliff, or burned to death. Given the ritual use of their blood and flesh, there would have been little left to bury.

The violent death of the hero reflected the imperfect nature of man and the world in which he lived. The hero, like any mortal, could not avoid his fate. However, he achieved greatness through the courage and wisdom of his actions. He became a model and an inspiration to other human beings.

1. Who are today's heroes in the fields of:
   a. science?
   b. politics?
   c. sports?
   d. the arts?
2. Greek heroes were people who helped society by making their world a better place in which to live. Read one news magazine (such as *Time*) and make a list of the people who might be considered heroic. List the people and state what positive contributions they are making to society.
3. What qualities would make a person a hero in ancient Greece? Discuss the importance of:
   a. courage.
   b. intelligence.
   c. physical strength.
   d. creative thinking.
4. Discuss the importance of each of the following:
   a. desire to please others.
   b. love of adventure.
   c. personal fame and glory.
   d. desire to improve society.

31 Perseus

The myth of Perseus is one of the earliest hero myths. In style, it most resembles the myth of Bellerophon. Both heroes depended exclusively upon divine magical aid for their success, and they both killed grotesque monsters. One hero killed Medusa; the other rode upon her winged offspring, the Chimaera.

Like the Chimaera, the Medusa that Perseus conquered represented a matriarchal culture. Priestesses of the Great Goddess wore hideous head masks during ceremonies in order to frighten away outsiders. Like the other Greek heroes, Perseus was a destroyer. He represented the patriarchal Mycenaean conquest of sacred shrines of the native earth-worshipping culture.

The death of Acrisius, grandfather of Perseus, indicated that man could not avoid his fate (his death). The later myths reflect the belief that while a man's fate may still be unavoidable, his life is influenced more by conduct than by chance.

When Acrisius and his brother Proteus divided their kingdom into two parts, they were solving the major political problem of accession to the throne in a constructive, peaceful way. Toward the end of matriarchal rule, sacred kings devised systems like this to remove the competition between one king and his successor.

THE MYTH

There were once twin sons named Proteus and Acrisius who lived in Argos. They quarreled constantly. As young men, they led rival armies in a civil war to determine who should be king of Argos. Although Acrisius won the war and banished Proteus across the Aegean Sea, Proteus eventually returned with his army and invaded Argos. The brothers then agreed that Proteus should rule the nearby kingdom of Tiryns and that Acrisius should remain in the kingdom of Argos.

When Acrisius found that he was growing older and yet had only one child, a daughter named Danaë, he went to the oracle and asked how he could become the father of a male child. The oracle terrified him by announcing: "One day, your daughter will give birth to a son, and he will kill you."

Although oracular prophesies were usually incomprehensible or ambiguous, there was no doubt in Acrisius's mind as to the meaning of these words. Desperately determined to avoid his fate, Acrisius did everything within his power to change his destiny. He built an underground bronze chamber, where he imprisoned his daughter. He knew that he would have nothing to fear if he could prevent her from having a child.

However, this scheme failed. In spite of her father's precautions, Danaë was loved both by her uncle, Proteus, and by Olympian Zeus. Proteus must have gained entrance as a trusted family relative. Zeus's entrance was much more spectacular. In order to meet the challenge of the bronze room, far-seeing Zeus transformed himself into a liquid stream of gold. Just as a shower of rain falls and becomes absorbed by the earth, so this golden shower penetrated the ceiling of the bronze room. Danaë found these riches pouring onto her lap.

Within the year, Danaë gave birth to a son, Perseus, and credited Zeus with his paternity. Acrisius, remembering the prophecy, determined to kill the child. He refused to believe that he was destroying Olympian Zeus's child, being privately convinced that the tale Danaë had told him was an inventive product of her imagination.

According to the unwritten code of hospitality, hosts did not murder their guests, and parents did not murder their children. However, it was acceptable to murder a person indirectly by placing him in a situation that would lead to certain death. Acrisius decided not to adopt the popular method of exposing the infant upon a mountainside to the ravages of weather, wild beasts, and starvation. Instead, he put both his daughter and his grandson into a carved wooden chest and sent them out to sea. He was certain that the dark, tempestuous waters would effectively foil the prophecy.

It did not occur to Acrisius that far-seeing Zeus would protect his family. Thus, Perseus and Danaë survived a perilous voyage which would have drowned ordinary mortals. No matter how the winds howled and the waves tossed them about, their chest neither swamped with sea water nor capsized. After a harrowing journey, the chest washed ashore upon the island of Seriphus, east of the Peloponnesus, in the Aegean Sea. Meanwhile, back in Argos, Acrisius sighed with relief. He was certain that he had cheated the Fates of their power.

Danaë and Perseus were rescued by a kind man named Dictys, who was the brother of the king of the island. Dictys took the mother and infant into his own home and reared Perseus as if the boy were his own son. Years passed, and Perseus became an impressive youth. He was intelligent, kind, brave, and an unusually fine athlete.

Polydectes, the king of Seriphus, fell in love with Danaë, but she did not reciprocate his affection. The king became determined to take her by force if she would not come willingly, and he knew that he could succeed with his plan only if Perseus were not available to defend her. Consequently, Polydectes began to devote his energy to devising a scheme whereby Perseus could be removed from the island of Seriphus.

The king announced that he intended to marry a foreign princess. Since it was the custom for a suitor to arrive with a number of impressive gifts for the woman of his choice, Polydectes gathered a group of friends about him, including Perseus, to solicit gifts from them. He asked his friends to donate horses to his cause. However, Perseus owned no horses.

Feeling self-conscious about his poverty in the presence of so many wealthy aristocrats, Perseus announced, "I have no family wealth to offer you, but I fearlessly offer you my services. For you, I would go anywhere on earth; I would even kill the horrible Gorgon Medusa in order to prove my loyalty and my courage."

King Polydectes smiled, but his eyes were cold and cruel as he said, "All right then, Perseus, I command you to bring me the severed head of the Gorgon Medusa . . . if you can."

The final words brought laughter into the assembly. Everyone knew that Medusa was the only one of the three Gorgons who was mortal, and that any of the three monstrous females would turn anyone who gazed upon them into a stone statue. Perseus had foolishly permitted himself to be manipulated into volunteering to die. Polydectes and his wealthy friends enjoyed observing Perseus's youthful pride and embarrassment. The opportunity for such entertainment did not present itself very often.

Far-seeing Zeus observed, with fatherly pride, his mortal son's courage. This young man had the potential of a hero. The Loud-Thunderer smiled as he imagined how Polydectes would react when Perseus returned from his adventure bearing the requested gift. The thought was too appealing to dismiss. Who was the king of Seriphus that he should ridicule a son of the Lord of Olympus?

Therefore, Zeus summoned the two immortals who could help his mortal son. Athena arrived first, shield in hand, her grey eyes meeting her father's expectantly. Behind her came smiling Hermes, hoping for adventure. Neither would be disappointed. For the Wayfinder, the realm of the Gorgons would be a welcome change from the shades in dark Hades' dismal kingdom, and he much preferred guiding live heroes to guiding dead ones. For Athena, the challenge was a special one indeed, for she was the goddess who had transformed Medusa into a Gorgon originally. Her final triumph over that arrogant girl would be to attach her severed head to her own great shield. Battle-stirring Athena was pleased with the idea.

Medusa had been a beautiful maiden, so lovely in fact that suitors had come from all over the Mediterranean area to ask her father for her hand in marriage. Most unforgettable had been her long golden hair, which Medusa had bragged equalled Athena's in beauty. The grey-eyed goddess remembered Medusa's vanity, watched her, and waited. When the Lord of the Sea fell in love with this mortal girl and slept with her in Athena's sacred shrine, the goddess's simmering rage exploded into a holocaust. If Medusa's hair was her best feature, Athena would begin with that!

Medusa awoke with the feeling that hissing, crawling creatures were using her head as a nest. As she reached up to feel the cause of her discomfort, she burned her fingers. Cautiously and with great fear she arose and reached for her hand mirror. For her, the nicest part of each morning was this quiet time when only the servants were awake. Then she could leisurely admire her own beauty as she combed her hair. To-day, her mirror confirmed a monstrous transformation. Where her long golden locks had shimmered in the firelight last night, long scaly dragons were exhaling flames into the sunlight. But that was not all. As Medusa noticed, with great relief, that her face, at least, was still untouched, large pointed teeth began to emerge above the sides of her mouth. She stared in silent horror as they gradually extended in front of her face with an upward curve as if she were some hideous wild boar.

Her one thought was to escape before anyone saw what had happened to her famous beauty. As she adjusted the position of her mirror, she noticed another gift: golden wings. At least the deathless gods would per-mit her to flee.

Medusa uttered a small prayer of thanks for the wings as she climbed upon the window ledge. By this time her hands were becoming stiff and heavy. She dared not think about additional transformations. She thought only about escape. Without a backward look, Medusa stepped off the ledge into the air, forsaking all that she had loved for the unknown. She was certain that only a goddess would have transformed her in this hideous way, and this same goddess would now lead her where she was destined to go.

Medusa was right. A wind propelled her winged body far to the west, over lands and seas, until finally it set her down in a wasteland beyond a towering range of mountains. She continued forward on foot through the rocky forests until she emerged by a seashore. The beach also was a rocky one, with scattered statues upon the coarse sand. Never before had Medusa seen such realistic sculpture. If she had not approached one or two of them and touched them, she would have thought that they were real people.

The thought of people turning into stone sculptures reminded her of a story she had heard long ago. As she remembered it, there were two monstrous immortal women who lived at the western end of the earth, not far from where the Titan Atlas held up the sky. They had snaky locks, boars' tusks, bronze hands . . . Medusa stopped. Her agonizing cry filled the air and echoed from the cliffs. "I have become a Gorgon!" She raged against her fate, futilely beating the air with heavy hands. Medusa wondered if she ever could resign herself to her fate: to her hideous appearance and to her dreadful loneliness.

Grey-eyed Athena and her swift-footed brother, Hermes, disguised themselves as adventurous young men who volunteered to accompany Perseus on his quest. Perseus had no difficulty in acquiring a small boat for his journey. King Polydectes was very accommodating. When Perseus had made his final preparations, he took leave of Dictys, the king, and finally, his mother. Danaë commended him to his great father's care, assuring him that the deathless gods, who had guided the little wooden chest safely through the tempestuous seas, would now guide him safely through his perilous task.

Once on board his boat, Perseus could feel his spirits lift. High adventure lay ahead, and he intended to make the most of it. When the horizon disclosed only the bright sky and the dark sea, Perseus noticed that his companions had become rather awesome. He could not explain to himself what had changed, for their appearance was the same. Yet, now they seemed more than mortal. Their eyes sparkled with an inner glow, and when they talked to him, he sensed that they knew his innermost thoughts.

In addition, without calling attention to the fact, they had taken charge of the voyage. They always included him in their discussions, yet Perseus felt that they were not fully disclosing all the knowledge they possessed, and that they were accustomed to working as a team. However, they were such delightful companions that he welcomed their presence and their encouragement and did not resent their relationship with one another.

They sailed upon the dark sea day after day. Perseus could tell from the shining journey of Helius each day that they were traveling in a westward direction. Since his companions remained cheerful and seemed to be satisfied, Perseus relaxed and enjoyed the voyage.

At long last, they reached their destination. Perseus had no idea where they were. They had left civilization far to the east. It was at this time that Perseus's friends finally revealed their real identity. He was delighted and awed.

Once they had beached their boat, the grey-eyed goddess began to tell him what he would have to do in order to kill Medusa. First he would need to find the three sisters of the Gorgons and make them reveal the location of certain nymphs who had equipment Perseus would need if he were to sever Medusa's head. Fortunately his immortal companions were able to help him locate the deathless old women. The three sisters lived beneath the Titan Atlas's northern cliffs, on a plain that was surrounded by mountains.

When Perseus first saw these women, he was shocked at their age. They were the oldest living creatures he had ever seen. When he commented upon this fact to Athena, she told him that they had been born that old. Among the three of them, they had only one eye and one tooth. These they passed from one to another in order to be able to see and to chew, each in turn.

When Perseus came upon the sisters of the Gorgons, they did not notice him. Once they acknowledged his presence, they refused to tell him the way to the immortal nymphs for fear that if they did so, their action could endanger their sisters in some way.

Perseus pretended to accept their decision and leave them. However, silently he crept away from the sight of the one eye and watched their behavior for a clue as to how to force them to obey his wishes. He found it sooner than he had anticipated. The crones were accustomed to sharing the eye and the tooth by removing them and passing them about from one hand to another. While the eye was out of a socket, the three immortals were totally blind.

Delighted with his discovery, Perseus crept as close to them as he dared. Then the next time a sister removed her eye from her head, he leaped in and grabbed it as it was changing hands.

The surprise attack was successful. When Perseus said that he would not return their eye until they told him the way to the nymphs, they realized that they no longer had a choice. If they did not help the mortal youth, they would spend eternity completely blind. Besides, they argued, if the young man were out to endanger their sisters, they would turn him into stone before he had a chance to hurt them. Therefore, they gave Perseus the directions he sought, and he, in turn, placed the lost eye in the palm of a groping hand.

Perseus found the nymphs much more attractive and much more helpful than the old sisters. They loaned him a pair of winged sandals, a leather bag that was worn on a shoulder strap, and the dark lord Hades' helmet, which made whoever wore it invisible.

When Perseus returned to his companions, the Wayfinder showed him how to use the bag and the sandals, which were similar to his own. The grey-eyed goddess told him to polish his bronze shield until it shone like the sea at sunset, for he would need it in order to kill Medusa without looking at her. If he looked at her directly, he would be turned into stone. Then Hermes loaned Perseus a strong, sharp, sickle-shaped sword, and Perseus put on the helmet of the Lord of the Dead.

Wearing his new possessions, Perseus and his companions flew to the ocean, where the three hideous Gorgons were sound asleep upon the seashore, surrounded by a collection of stone statues that were remarkably human in appearance.

The Gorgons were terrifying even when they were asleep. Their long, scaly dragons continuously slithered upon their heads, exhaling flames and smoke, and their boar-like tusks threatened immediate peril. Although a great distance still protected him, Perseus instinctively raised his shining shield.

Quietly they descended to the beach. While Perseus looked at the Gorgons' bright reflection in his polished shield, Athena guided him to Medusa. There, with Athena's hand upon his wrist and his own head turned aside to face the image upon his shield, Perseus beheaded the mortal Gorgon with one slice of his sharp sickle. Then, grasping the severed head by the snaky hair, he placed it inside the leather bag he was wearing upon his back.

As he picked up his shield and prepared to leave, he was amazed to see a winged horse emerge from Medusa's neck and fly off into the sky. The grey-eyed goddess later told him that this was Pegasus, the offspring of Medusa and Poseidon.

Perseus had just started to fly away when the immortal Gorgons opened their eyes. Seeing their mutilated companion, they were outraged and immediately flew into the air in search of the murderer, but the sky was empty. Perseus was wearing the helmet of invisibility.

Once it became clear to Perseus and his companions that they had escaped from the Gorgons, Perseus decided that he could fly home with Medusa's head without further aid, since he now had winged sandals to transport him and the sickle and the helmet to protect him. Athena and Hermes agreed to meet him on his return to the island of Seriphus after he had presented King Polydectes with the gift. Privately, the immortals decided to arrive early and unobtrusively observe the entertainment.

As Athena, the grey-eyed goddess, and her quick-footed brother left him, Perseus realized that shining Helius had driven his chariot into the sea. Although the sky was now ablaze with color, night was close at hand. Perseus did not feel comfortable flying over strange lands in the dark, so he decided it would be better to spend the night on the earth and to continue his journey in the morning.

As he looked below, inspecting the countryside for a good place to rest, he noticed the great Titan, Atlas, holding the sky upon his head and his shoulders. Nearby was the famous garden of the Hesperides, where the daughters of Atlas watched over Hera's golden apple tree. Thinking that the garden would be a lovely place to rest, he descended and approached the mighty Titan.

"Great Atlas," he asked, "may I spend the night in your garden? I shall be on my way again when dawn with rosy fingers makes the day light. If noble birth impresses you, a son of Olympian Zeus stands before you. If great deeds impress you, then admire the slayer of the Gorgon Medusa."

When brawny Atlas heard that the suppliant was a son of his loud-thundering enemy, he became wary and inhospitable. He remembered that the great oracle, Themis, at Pytho on Mount Parnassus had prophesied that, one day, a son of Olympian Zeus' would steal the golden apples from the trees in the garden his daughters protected. Fearing this theft, Atlas had enclosed the garden within walls of solid cliffs, making access by land impossible. In addition, he had put the monstrous hundred-headed dragon, Ladon, into the garden as a guard.

"Don't brag to me of your family and your deeds," Atlas replied. "Leave here at once, or I will throw you out."

Perseus was dismayed and discouraged by the giant Titan's hostile attitude. He knew that he could not pit his mortal strength against the strongest immortal, and yet he felt that he must rest here until dawn. When Atlas remained firmly opposed to his visit, Perseus responded:

"Since you refuse to let me rest here then accept my gift of eternal rest."

The mortal youth quickly turned his own head aside and pulled the head of Medusa from his leather bag. Atlas had no chance to avert his face. With only one glance at her hideous face, the great Titan was conquered by the severed head. His beard and his hair became transformed into bushes and forests. His hands, arms, and shoulders spread into ridges. His bones became hard rock, and his head became the summit of the mountain. In this petrified form, Atlas would support the starry heavens eternally.

Perseus then spent a peaceful night before he continued his journey.

Once shining Helius's light illuminated the earth, Perseus felt quite at ease in the air. He was flying over the land of Ethiopia when he noticed a maiden chained to a rock by the sea. She was so beautiful that she appeared to be an exquisite marble sculpture carved by a gifted artist. He could not resist the temptation to descend for a closer look. Although he was dismayed to see her anguished face washed by real tears, he was delighted with this proof of her mortality.

"Lovely maiden," he greeted her upon his approach, "Tell me, who are you? Where are you from? And why are you imprisoned here?" The girl blushed with fear and shyness as if she were unaccustomed to talking with strange young men. Then she gathered courage and responded.

"I am called Andromeda," she replied, "daughter of King Cepheus and Queen Cassiopeia of Ethiopia. When my mother bragged that she was more beautiful than the deathless Nereïds, these sea goddesses complained to the great Lord of the Sea. He avenged the insult by sending first a flood and then a ravenous sea monster upon our land. The people were terror-struck and consulted our oracle. He prophesied that if I were sacrificed to this sea monster, my death would appease the offended immortals, and our affliction would end. My father's subjects insisted that he obey the oracle, and, reluctantly he has done so."

As Andromeda was finishing her explanation the waves began to roar and pound upon the beach. The youth saw a monster extend its head above the waves and look about. Behind it, its immense body floated upon the sea. As the creature swam toward the shore, Andromeda screamed in terror. Her parents, hearing her cry, ran to comfort her. Perseus understood their anguish as they shared their daughter's terror. Yet, they were powerless to help her.

Therefore, Perseus announced, "You see before you the son of loud-thundering Zeus, born to Danaë from a golden shower. I have severed the Gorgon Medusa's snake-haired head, and I will rescue your daughter from this monster if, in return, you will promise she will be my wife."

Andromeda's parents eagerly agreed to the marriage and offered Perseus a kingdom as part of their daughter's dowry. Perseus took to the air, where he hovered above the monster's head. This enraged the beast, and it leaped vainly upon the shadow of Perseus it could see upon the water.

Perseus fought the monster from the air, making repeated descents in order to wound it. Finally, Perseus landed upon the weary monster's back and buried his sickle up to its hilt near the right fin. The monster roared with pain from this deep wound. In a wild fury it lurched about like a savage boar, now leaping into the air, now diving below the sea.

Perseus used his winged sandals to avoid the tempestuous waves and the monster's ravenous mouth. A torrent of blood gushed forth from the monster, and after a final convulsion, it died.

Safe upon the shore once again, Perseus constructed three altars. He sacrificed a calf to Hermes the Wayfinder on the left altar, a bull to loud-thundering Zeus on the middle altar, and a white cow to grey-eyed Athena on the right altar. He then accepted Andromeda as his bride, but he rejected the gift of a kingdom as unnecessary.

King Cepheus and Queen Cassiopeia gave Andromeda and Perseus a royal wedding. They decorated the palace with garlands, fed the sacred fires, and followed the ceremony with a lavish feast, which was accompanied by songs and music of the harp.

While Perseus was entertaining the wedding guests with tales of Medusa and her death, King Cepheus's brother, Phineus, entered, spear in hand, with a large group of armed men.

"Neither your loud-thundering father nor your winged feet, Perseus, can save you now!" Phineus proclaimed. "Andromeda belongs to me!"

King Cepheus, embarrassed at his brother's display of inhospitable behavior, responded, "Wait, Phineus. Is this how you thank Perseus for rescuing Andromeda? Blame the Nereïds and thunder-loving Zeus for your loss, not Perseus. If your love for Andromeda is so great that you will fight her husband for her now, then why didn't you prevent the sea monster from terrorizing her? Before your eyes she was chained, helpless, to a rock. The ravenous monster had opened his giant jaws to fill his belly with my daughter when Perseus, not you, risked his life and saved her."

Phineus was so infuriated by his brother's accurate criticism that he almost attacked him instead of Perseus. However, he threw his spear at Perseus and missed. When he saw Perseus aiming more accurately at him, he hid behind a sacred altar while his soldiers fought King Cepheus's guards.

Finally Perseus announced, "Friends of mine, beware!" He suddenly displayed Medusa's head for all his enemies to see, transforming two hundred foes into two hundred statues.

Phineus, from behind the altar, pleaded for help from his stone friends. When no one responded, he crept out and, no longer relying upon his eyes alone, he touched them. Medusa's power brought him to his knees before his enemy. "Oh, Perseus," he pleaded. "You have won the battle. Hide your weapon which transforms mortals into marble. Take everything but my life."

To these cowardly words, Perseus replied, "Faint-hearted Phineus, I will make your death quick and painless. Do not fear my sword." He then thrust Medusa's face into that of his cowardly suppliant, forever immortalizing in stone the glistening tears which dripped frozen upon the marble cheeks and the outstretched arms, poised to avoid the fatal blow.

When Perseus had returned to Seriphus with Andromeda, he found that Dictys and his mother, Danaë, had sought refuge from Polydectes by retreating into a sacred temple.

Perseus entered the king's palace and found him entertaining his friends. Polydectes was delighted to hear Perseus relate his adventures to the group. When the tale was over, the king laughed mockingly and requested another children's tale.

Perseus became infuriated by the king's scornful attitude. He and his mother had suffered enough from this arrogant king. "If you believe me, shut your eyes, friends," he announced. Then he turned his own face away and displayed Medusa's head for all the scoffers to see. All who met its gaze became marble statues.

Thus the reign of King Polydectes came to a dramatic end. Perseus appointed Dictys king. He returned the winged sandals, the helmet of invisibility, the leather bag, and the sickle to swift-footed Hermes, who, in turn, returned them to the nymphs. To grey-eyed Athena, Perseus awarded Medusa's severed head, which the goddess attached to the center of her great shield.

Finally Perseus was ready to return to Argos. He was anxious to meet his grandfather and assure him of his love and good will. He hoped that, by now, his heroic exploits would have preceded his arrival, and his grandfather would welcome him.

King Acrisius did hear about the heroic deeds of Perseus and of his impending arrival. Still fearing for his life, the king of Argos hastily left his kingdom in order to avoid the oracle's dreadful prophecy. He went to the city of Larissa, where for entertainment he spent one day observing some athletic contests.

Perseus, Andromeda, and Danaë also stopped in Larissa on their way to Argos. Noticing the athletic contests, Perseus decided to participate in the discus throw. When his turn came, Perseus skillfully threw the discus straight down the athletic field. Suddenly, however, the discus changed direction in the middle of its course and headed into the spectator area. There it struck King Acrisius and killed him instantly.

Perseus sadly buried the grandfather he never knew. He decided not to return to Argos because he was ashamed to claim the kingdom of a relative he had killed. Therefore, he decided to visit the son of Proteus, his mother's cousin, who was now the ruler of Tiryns. He hoped they could exchange kingdoms. They did, and Perseus founded a well-known line of kings, eventually becoming the great-grandfather of the hero Heracles.

1. The son of Zeus who will steal the apples is Heracles.

REFLECTIONS

1. Prepare a written biography on any hero of any time.
2. What effect does the use of magic and divine aid have upon the power of this myth? Discuss.
3. Become one of the two immortal Gorgons. Write a monologue describing the following:
   a. your life before Perseus's arrival
   b. the beheading of Medusa
   c. your response to the killing of your mortal sister Gorgon. Be sure to include your feelings along with your description of the events.

32 Bellerophon

INTRODUCTION

Before the conquest of Greece by the Mycenaeans, the native matriarchal society was peace-loving and trusting. Guests were welcomed and treated well. The Mycenaeans devised ways of circumventing this established moral code. For example, instead of killing Bellerophon, King Proteus sent him with his own death warrant to King Iobates who presumably would kill him. However, for the same reason that Proteus did not kill Bellerophon, King Iobates did not kill him directly, but instead tried to find a way to kill Bellerophon that would be socially acceptable.

The Chimaera may have represented the matriarchal society in Lycia that was conquered by the Mycenaean invaders. Its composite animals were important in the matriarchal religion.

Bellerophon is one of the famous Greek heroes, and his tale corresponds to the general heroic pattern set forth in the introduction to this group of myths. He achieved his *aretē* (excellence) from a divine gift. Yet, this gift led him to *hybris* (excessive pride). Bellerophon became arrogant. He forgot that he was mortal, not divine. He expected that, because he had received a divine gift, he was the equal of those who gave the gift. Like many other mortals, Bellerophon was conquered by *átē* (temporary madness). He suspended his reason, and let his emotions determine his actions. The decision he made caused the gods to destroy him (*nemesis*).

THE MYTH

Bellerophon was the son of King Glaucus of Corinth. When Bellerophon accidentally killed his brother, he was exiled. He came to King Proteus of Tiryns to be purified of the crime he had committed in Corinth, and remained a guest of the king.

While he was in Tiryns, the wife of King Proteus fell in love with Bellerophon. When he refused her advances, she told her husband, "You must kill Bellerophon. He lusts after me against my will."

This lie filled Proteus with rage, but he concealed his jealous anger. He did not feel it would be hospitable to kill Bellerophon outright.

So he sent Bellerophon to King Iobates in Lycia, across the Aegean Sea with the request written in code on sealed tablets that Bellerophon be killed. He commanded Bellerophon to show Iobates the tablets, thinking that Iobates would read the message and kill Bellerophon.

Guided by the gods, Bellerophon sailed to Lycia where he was well received and honored for nine days. When dawn's rosy fingers made the tenth day light, Iobates questioned his guest and asked to see the message from King Proteus.

King Iobates was amazed to read that King Proteus expected him to murder the youth who was now his guest. Iobates did not want to be directly responsible for murdering a guest. Therefore, instead, he commanded Bellerophon to fight and kill the Chimaera in order to free Lycia from its violent hold.

The Chimaera was a foaming, fire-breathing monster, the offspring of Typhon. It had three heads: one of a lion, one of a goat, and one of a powerful dragon. Its body was that of a lion in front, a goat in the middle, and a dragon behind. Its flames had devastated the country and all the cattle. This single creature had the power, therefore, of three beasts. King Iobates was certain that Bellerophon was no match for the dreadful beast.

Once Bellerophon had received King Iobates' order, he went to Polyeidus, the prophet of Corinth, for advice. The prophet told him to sleep on grey-eyed Athena's altar, which he did.

That night, Bellerophon had a dream. In his dream, Athena seemed to speak to him as he lay asleep. He saw the winged horse, Pegasus, in the meadow, running wildly. He recognized that this horse was the famous offspring of Medusa and Poseidon, the Lord of the Sea. It had emerged from Medusa's neck when Perseus had beheaded her.

In Bellerophon's dream, grey-eyed Athena mastered the wild horse herself. She put the bit into the horse's mouth and brought the golden bridle to Bellerophon. She told him to use the bridle to tame Pegasus.

Awakening from his dream, Bellerophon noticed the golden bridle. Gratefully he took the bridle and reported his dream to Polyeidus, who told Bellerophon to obey Athena's commands. Bellerophon lost no time in doing so. Arriving at the meadow where Pegasus romped, he threw the bridle over Pegasus's head and put the bit gently into his mouth. Then he mounted Pegasus, and was carried by him into the sky. From this position, Bellerophon was able to kill the Chimaera with his arrows.

When Bellerophon returned unscathed to Iobates, the king realized that Bellerophon had, in fact, rid the country of the terrifying monster, but he felt that he was still obligated to King Proteus to kill him. He gave Bellerophon two other tasks which he hoped would destroy him, but Bellerophon accomplished both. He killed a tribe of enemies called the Solymi plus the female archers called the Amazons. Later he killed all the Lycians who waited in ambush to kill him.

Finally, Iobates realized that Bellerophon was favored by the gods. He showed Bellerophon the tablets from Proteus and asked his forgiveness. He begged him to remain with him, to marry his daughter, and to receive all royal privileges. In addition, he offered Bellerophon the finest land, fertile with wheat and olives.

Later, Bellerophon became filled with tremendous pride. Considering himself to be the equal of the gods, he directed Pegasus to transport him to Mount Olympus so that he could reach the palaces of the gods and join them. He nearly accomplished his goal, but far-seeing Zeus made Pegasus throw Bellerophon off in mid-air. Bellerophon was killed by the fall.

In other versions of his death, Bellerophon brought his doom upon himself. Upon looking down from the heavens, he became so dizzy that he fell from Pegasus and was killed. Pegasus flew up to Mount Olympus where Olympian Zeus gave the winged horse a place of honor in the stars.

REFLECTIONS

1. Compare and contrast Bellerophon, Icarus, Phaëthon, and Perseus. What motivates each of them? To what extent is each heroic? Explain.
2. As a sportscaster, it is your job to broadcast the great fight between Bellerophon and the Chimaera. Create the details and cover the fight from beginning to end.
3. Create a new adventure for Bellerophon using Pegasus.

HUMAN EXPERIENCE

The Bellerophon myth, like that of Daedalus and Icarus, deals with the wish of a man to aim high, perhaps too high. There is a difference between a challenge, which forces people to grow in order to accomplish a new goal, and that striving to reach so much beyond themselves that they not only fail to achieve the goal, but destroy themselves.

There is a certain greediness in Bellerophon. Because he has performed his labors, he believes he is god-like and he actually attempts to fly to Mount Olympus, as if he were a god. Today we might say Bellerophon lacks humility and commits a thoughtless act. He is audacious and daring, but not brave. He is told exactly what to do in order to conquer his tasks. His flaw is that he mistakenly believes that if he succeeds he will be rewarded with godliness. The *over-reacher* sometimes does succeed in our society. However, it is not we who decide that we belong on Mount Olympus for our famous deeds. Greatness is judged by others through time. The judgment of our own greatness is not ours to make immediately, and if we do, we are punished for our vanity.

33 Heracles

Heracles (or Hercules[1]), was the most popular of the Greek heroes, and yet, his personality reflected nothing of the ideal *golden mean*. Everything about Heracles was excessive, except, and this is significant, that he did not suffer from excessive pride or *hybris*. He was unusually tall. He was so strong that, upon at least two occasions, his strength was greater than he realized, and he killed people unintentionally. He was an unusually emotional person. More than once he became afflicted with a temporary madness (*átē*). Then, upon recovering his sanity, Heracles was excessively remorseful for the deaths he caused. He imposed exile upon himself in situations where society had forgiven him. He was both a loyal friend, rescuing the wife of Admetus from death, and an implacable enemy, killing entire royal families for treating him badly years before. Moreover, after all these excesses, he was the only hero whom Zeus rewarded with immortality. It is natural to wonder why.

First of all, Heracles combined in his nature all the best traits (*aretē*) of mankind. He was warm, loving, and compassionate toward his family and his friends. He possessed great self-control. Once he realized that he had no choice, he managed to submit to the cowardly Eurystheus without complaint and with little hostility and, later, to serve Queen Omphale of Lydia as a slave (*nemesis*). Because of his great courage and physical strength, he literally defended the known earth against monsters of all sorts, permitting the growth of civilization. He was intelligent and creative in accomplishing his labors. He had a strong moral code. For example, he insisted that a person keep his word and deal honestly with strangers, and he punished numerous kings for failing to do so.

Moreover, Heracles accomplished his amazing deeds with little divine help. Athena supplied him with castanets, and Helius gave him a boat. This is minor, indeed, compared to what was given to Perseus and Jason.

Finally, the humanity of Heracles endeared him to mortals and gods alike. That he made mistakes only proved he was human. He was pure in heart. He did what he was compelled to do, not from a drive for personal power, or even for fame and glory. He carried out his labors because they were obligations. He appeared to represent a balance between the private person, whose personal standards and goals motivate behavior, and the public person, whose goal is to fulfill obligations to society.

Many of Heracles' labors represented tasks set before those who competed for the honor of sacred king in the matriarchal society. For example, such a candidate would have to: (1) participate in an archery contest; (2) fight wild beasts such as the lion and the boar; (3) clean and plow a hill or field in one day; (4) wrestle with the local champion; (5) bridle a wild horse; and (6) fight a bull or a man disguised as a bull. Wrestling with a bull was particularly important because the bull was thought to bring rain. Its roar sounded like thunder; its fiery breath was like lightning. If the sacred king could grab hold of its horn, the transfer of rain-making magic would occur, and the king's fertility powers would be enhanced. Scholars believe that Heracles embodied the heroism of a number of historical figures expanded into mythic proportions.

1. Hercules is Heracles' Roman name.

The Birth of a Hero

The Lord of Olympus wanted to father a mortal child who would become so strong and so intelligent that he would be able to defend both mortal men and the deathless gods against all their enemies. As far-seeing Zeus searched the earth for the mortal woman who could bear him such a great son, his eyes and his heart came to rest upon Alcmene, the granddaughter of the great hero, Perseus. Her father was King Electryon of Tiryns and Mycenae. Alcmene combined extraordinary beauty with equally extraordinary wisdom. Moreover, she was known for her virtue, being both loyal and compassionate.

On the same day that Zeus vowed to love Alcmene, she was married to Amphitryon. Before King Electryon had agreed to let Amphitryon marry his daughter, he had required him to promise not to sleep with his new wife until the king had avenged the death of his sons. However, before this happened, Amphitryon accidentally killed the king. He and the king had been standing near the cattle barns when a cow charged toward them. Amphitryon had quickly thrown a club at the animal in order to frighten it away. Unfortunately, the club had struck the cow's horns and had then rebounded against the head of the king, killing him.

For this crime, King Electryon's brother, Sthenelus, banished Amphitryon and then took the cities of Mycenae and Tiryns for himself.[1]

Recognizing that her husband had not murdered her father but had killed him accidentally, Alcmene accompanied her husband to Thebes, where King Creon purified Amphitryon of the crime. Amphitryon then left Alcmene in order to avenge the deaths of her brothers, who had been killed by pirates, for Olympian Zeus had commanded him to do this, and he dared not tempt the great god's wrath.

The Lord of Olympus knew that Amphitryon's absence would provide him with the perfect opportunity to love Alcmene. Realizing that Alcmene was virtuous, the great god decided to assume the appearance and personality of Amphitryon in order to accomplish his purpose. He then commanded dawn and shining Helius to prolong his pleasure with Alcmene by resting for three days until he returned to Mount Olympus. The unusually long night would foreshadow the tremendous strength and achievements of the child who would be conceived in Amphitryon's palace.

Zeus arrived at Amphitryon's palace at night. Alcmene, recognizing her husband, let him enter her private rooms. The disguised god told her all the news about Amphitryon's adventures and remained with her for three days.

The next night, the real Amphitryon returned to Thebes from his successful war. He immediately searched for his wife because he was so glad to be home. He was amazed to find that she was not surprised to see him. When he complained of her cool welcome, Alcmene explained that she had just been with him the previous night. Then Amphitryon realized that one of the deathless gods must have loved his wife in his shape. He sent for the blind Theban prophet, Teiresias, who confirmed that the queen's visitor had indeed been immortal, the Lord of Olympus himself.

When the time arrived for Alcmene to give birth, far-seeing Zeus announced to all the immortals that he intended to make the descendant of Perseus who would be born that day the future king of Mycenae. Zeus was thinking of Alcmene's son Heracles. However, golden-throned Hera, jealous as always of Zeus's other loves, wrecked this plan by sending her daughter, Eileithyia, down to earth to prolong Alcmene's labor. Eileithyia delayed the great infant's birth by sitting upon the threshold of Alcmene's bedroom with her legs and her fingers crossed, praying.

Realizing that golden-throned Hera's hatred was behind Eileithyia's strange behavior, Galanthis, one of the Theban matrons who was helping Alcmene, went out to Eileithyia and told her that she could rejoice, for Alcmene had given birth. Eileithyia jumped up in surprise, and as soon as she had straightened herself, the infant Heracles was born. Eileithyia transformed Galanthis into a weasel as retribution for this lie.

In the meantime, in Tiryns, Perseus's daughter-in-law, the wife of King

Sthenelus, had given birth two months prematurely to the infant Eurystheus. Great Hera's cunning scheme had been successful. In accordance with Olympian Zeus's sacred decree, Eurystheus, and not Heracles, would become the king of Tiryns and Mycenae.

Undaunted, the Lord of Olympus then contrived to win everlasting fame for his son by suggesting to golden-throned Hera that when these two children had grown to maturity, Heracles should perform for King Eurystheus any ten labors the king might choose, and that, after he had performed those tasks, Zeus would grant him immortality. The idea of ten labors, all of them difficult and many of them degrading or impossible, appealed to Hera, and she agreed.

Knowing Hera's great jealousy and fearing her wrath, Alcmene reluctantly placed the infant Heracles unprotected in a field, expecting that he would die of exposure, illness, starvation, or be killed by wild animals. However, Hera and Athena found the infant and were impressed with its strength and size. Fortunately for Heracles, only grey-eyed Athena recognized him as the son of Olympian Zeus. Athena persuaded Hera to attempt to nurse the infant. She tried, but found the infant too strong. Then grey-eyed Athena, who did not disclose to jealous Hera the identity of the infant, returned him to his own mother, Alcmene. She persuaded her to nurse and rear him along with his stepbrother, Iphicles, her son by Amphitryon, who had been born the night following Heracles' birth.

Heracles' Youth

In the evenings, Alcmene fed the two infants, washed them, and placed them in her husband's great bronze shield. In this cradle, she rocked them to sleep. One midnight, when Heracles was only eight months old, golden-throned Hera, suspecting that one of the two infants was Zeus's mortal son, sent two monstrous serpents down to the house of Amphitryon to devour Heracles. As they uncoiled their bodies and slithered forward, their eyes gleamed with raging fires, and potent venom spurted from their tongues. Far-seeing Zeus awakened the infants and caused the house to be fully illuminated as though it were broad daylight. Iphicles screamed when he saw the fangs of the malicious creatures above the rim of the shield, and he kicked off his lambswool blanket, hoping to crawl away from the danger.

However, Heracles sat up and immediately set out to kill the enemy. Using his little hands, he gripped each serpent securely by the throat. The snakes coiled about Heracles for a moment, but impending death soon relaxed their grip, and they died.

When Alcmene heard Iphicles' cry, she awakened her husband. She was so afraid that she urged Amphitryon to accompany her to the nursery in his bare feet. Seeing the house filled with bright daylight in the depths of the night chilled their souls. Amphitryon grabbed the nearest weapon. Then, the house became dark once again.

With servants supplying lamps, the household made its way into the nursery. There was little Heracles, clutching a serpent in each hand. With delight he laid them at Amphitryon's feet, harmless now that they were dead. Iphicles, however, had crawled into his mother's lap, where he was still shaking with terror.

At daybreak, Alcmene and Amphitryon summoned the great, blind, Theban prophet, Teiresias, and asked him to explain the significance of the events that had occurred in their house that night. Whether good fortune or evil, they were determined to learn the truth. Teiresias then informed them that their son Heracles would make them famous. Olympian Zeus had chosen them to rear the greatest of heroes. Teiresias revealed that Heracles would kill monsters upon the land and sea, aid the gods in their battle against the Giants, and that having accomplished twelve labors[2], his mortal body would die, but he would become immortal. He would become the husband of an immortal daughter of Olympian Zeus, and he even would be called a son by the deathless goddess who had tried to destroy him in his cradle. Teiresias then advised Alcmene to burn the dead serpents at midnight that night, because at that time on the previous night they would have killed her son. Then she was told to purify her house and sacrifice a boar to the great Lord of Olympus.

Eurytus of Oechalia, later the father of Iole, taught Heracles to bend the bow and to hit any mark he chose. Amphitryon, himself an expert charioteer, taught him how to drive the chariot. The clever son of Hermes, Autolycus, who was a famous wrestler, taught his skill to Heracles. The great warrior and horseman Castor, brother of Polydeuces and Helen, taught Heracles to become expert in the use of sword and lance, and in battle tactics.

Aged Linus, reputed to be a son of Apollo and of Calliope, the Muse, taught Heracles to read, to sing, and to play the lyre. However, when Linus beat him for being unmusical, Heracles became furious. He picked up his lyre and struck his teacher, killing him. Heracles defended himself against the charge of murder by arguing that he had hit Linus in self-defense.

The court acquitted him of the crime, but Amphitryon became concerned about his stepson's quick temper, given his great physical strength. Therefore, he sent him into the country to his cattle farm where he would have greater freedom. Heracles grew to be unusually strong and tall. Looking at his seven-foot frame, his flashing eyes, and his unerring excellence with the javelin and the bow, everyone who saw him acknowledged Heracles to be the son of Olympian Zeus.

When Heracles was eighteen years old, he heroically defended Thebes in battle. As a reward for his exceptional valor, King Creon of Thebes offered his daughter, Megara, to Heracles as his wife, and thereafter, treated him as if he were his real son.

However, King Eurystheus became jealous of Heracles' growing fame and commanded him to come to Tiryns and perform the promised labors. Heracles ignored the summons until his immortal father commanded him to obey. Heracles was still reluctant to subject himself to such degradation, so he traveled to the oracle of Apollo at Delphi and sought the Far-Shooter's advice. The oracle told him that the deathless gods had determined his fate. He could not avoid obeying King Eurystheus. For twelve years he must perform whatever ten labors the king demanded of him, but, afterward, he would be rewarded with immortality. It was the oracle of Apollo who first called the youth Heracles,[3] since Hera by sending her serpents, had given him the opportunity to prove his strength and attain glory (*kleos*). However, that had not been the goddess's intention.[4]

Heracles still loathed the idea of obeying an inferior being. However, he realized that he had no choice. Nevertheless, he still did nothing. Finally, golden-throned Hera decided the matter for him. She infected Heracles with temporary insanity. Thinking that his children were enemies, he killed them with his bow. Upon recovering, Heracles was overwhelmed with grief at the loss of his dear ones and the magnitude of his crime. He went into a self-imposed exile, and later, finally appeared before King Eurystheus.

Labor 1—The Nemean Lion

Eurystheus first commanded Heracles to slay the lion of Nemea, an offspring of Typhon, which lived near Mycenae. This creature spent its time ravaging the countryside. This huge beast could only be killed by hand, for neither stone, bronze, nor even iron could pierce its invincible skin. Its den was located in Nemea near a grove that was sacred to Olympian Zeus.

Heracles took his bow and arrows, and his stout club, which he had acquired by uprooting a wild olive tree,[5] and traveled until he reached the lion's den. The den was empty, so Heracles prepared his bow and waited. However, he could see no tracks, nor could he hear any roar.

Toward evening the lion returned to its den, blood spattered and content with the food its bloody pillage had supplied. From a secure shelter near the cave, Heracles aimed his arrow and let it fly, but the point could not penetrate the lion's flesh. A second arrow fared no better upon the lion's great chest. Before Heracles could send forth a third arrow, the lion entered the cave.

Noticing that the den had two entrances, Heracles closed up one of them with huge rocks in order to prevent the beast's escape. Then the son of Zeus entered the cave. The lion immediately charged its enemy.

With one hand, Heracles pushed his cloak and his arrows out of the way. With his other hand, he lifted his olive-wood club and slammed it down upon the lion's head with all his strength. The invincible beast's head broke the club in two, yet the blow stunned it with pain. Throwing his bow and quiver upon the ground, Heracles grabbed the lion from behind, encircled its neck with his arms, and squeezed the life out of it.[6]

Heracles then sacrificed to Olympian Zeus, giving thanks for his victory. He lifted the tremendous carcass upon his shoulders, and returned to King Eurystheus in Tiryns. The king was so frightened by Heracles' valor and strength and by the formidable carcass of the lion that he commanded Heracles to remain outside the walls of Tiryns upon completing each of his other labors. Eurystheus then commanded his craftsmen to fashion a giant bronze storage jar, and to bury it up to its neck in the earth. Thereafter, whenever guards at the city gate sent word of Heracles' return, the cowardly king would hide inside the jar and send a messenger to deliver his orders to the hero.

Heracles was furious that he had to obey such a weak-minded man, and one, who through Hera's scheme, had inherited a throne that was legally his own. However, he knew that the deathless gods had given him no choice.

When Eurystheus wanted no part of the Nemean lion, Heracles prepared to salvage the lion's skin as a trophy. However, the procedure required thought, for neither stone, nor bronze, nor iron could cut it. Then it occurred to Heracles to use the lion's own claws to remove the skin from its body. Shortly thereafter, the hero had cut free the giant skin. It would make invincible armor because no weapon would ever penetrate its surface. Thereafter, Heracles wore this lion skin as a cloak, with the lion's head either hanging behind him or covering his head as a hood.

Labor 2—The Hydra of Lerna

When Heracles returned to King Eurystheus, he was told to kill the Hydra of Lerna, another offspring of Typhon. The Hydra had nine long heads extending from its enormous body. It lived in a swamp whenever it was not busy destroying the countryside. Although eight of its heads were mortal, the middle one was immortal. Moreover, it was supposed to be invincible because whenever one head was cut off, two more emerged from the severed area.

Heracles' nephew, Iolaüs, drove him to Lerna in a chariot. They found the Hydra near its swampy den. Heracles first tried to kill it by shooting fiery arrows at it, but the Hydra only moved toward Heracles and, upon reaching him, curled itself tightly around one of his feet. Heracles next slammed his club upon its heads, but this weapon was also useless. With his sword, Heracles then began to cut off its mortal heads. However, this procedure produced predictably horrifying results, for as he had heard, wherever one head was removed, two more immediately sprouted from the gaping bloody wound.

Meanwhile, the Hydra's lone companion, a gigantic crab, emerged from the swamp and aided its friend by biting Heracles in the foot. Heracles was able to destroy the crab, but he realized that he would need the help of Iolaüs if he had any hope of destroying the Hydra.

He therefore commanded his nephew to make a burning torch from the nearby wood and join him with this new weapon. Heracles then proceeded to sever one mortal head at a time. Each time, Iolaüs was prepared with his torch to sear and seal the severed area with flames before any new heads could emerge. When only the immortal head of the Hydra remained, Heracles decapitated it and buried it beneath an immense rock.

Then the hero tore into the body of the monster and dipped the points of his arrows into its venomous blood. Thereafter, these arrows always brought their victims incurable wounds that resulted in certain death. Ironically, Heracles himself became such a victim many years later.

When Heracles had returned to King Eurystheus, the cowardly king refused to accept this labor as one of the ten, since Heracles had relied upon Iolaüs for help.

Labor 3—The Cerynitian Hind

King Eurystheus commanded that Heracles go to Arcadia, to capture alive and bring to Tiryns the sacred deer of Artemis, called the Cerynitian hind. This was a doe with golden horns, a reindeer[7] that lived in the far north. In order to avoid angering the Archer-Goddess, Heracles tried not to wound the sacred animal. He chased it across the northernmost regions of the earth for an entire year. Some writers say that he finally captured it while it slept, or that he set a net trap for it. Others say that he finally chased it south into Arcadia, where he shot it as it was about to cross the Ladon River.

Shortly thereafter, as he was carrying the wounded animal upon his shoulders, Heracles met the Archer-Goddess and her brother,[8] the Far-Shooter. They were furious with him because it appeared that he had killed the sacred deer. Heracles immediately showed them that the animal was alive and explained the purpose of his venture, blaming King Eurystheus for choosing the labor that the other deathless gods had compelled him to obey. Arrow-raining Artemis accepted his explanation and permitted him to continue his journey with her sacred animal. He promised to set it free once he had accomplished his task, and he did.

Labor 4—The Erymanthian Boar

For his next labor, Eurystheus commanded Heracles to capture the Ery-manthian boar, which lived on Mount Erymanthus in Arcadia where it ravaged fields, orchards, and farms. The king wanted him to bring it back alive to Tiryns.

In the course of this journey, Heracles became involved in a struggle with the Centaurs.[9] The Centaur, Pholus, was entertaining Heracles, when Heracles insisted upon opening a sealed jar of wine. The sweet smell attracted the other Centaurs and drove them out of their senses. They attacked Pholus in order to acquire the wine.

Heracles immediately stood against them in spite of their strength. They were fierce adversaries because they combined the strength of two men, the speed of a horse, and the experience and wisdom of a man. The Centaurs used, as weapons, entire pine trees, rocks, blazing torches, and axes. However, they could not intimidate Heracles, and he subdued those who were brave enough to continue the fight.

Others ran to the immortal Centaur, Cheiron, who was one of the wisest and best educated of living beings. Tragically, one of the Hydra-poisoned arrows meant for the mortal Centaurs wounded Cheiron in his knee. Although Heracles, in anguish over the accident, removed the arrow and applied the medicine Cheiron suggested, his effort was futile. Cheiron was doomed to spend eternity in unbearable agony. From his cave on Mount Pelion, the great teacher prayed to Olympian Zeus to remove his immortality so that he could escape the excruciating pain through death.

The Lord of Olympus heard his plea and pitied him. He permitted the immortal Centaur to relinquish his immortality and take the great Titan Prometheus's place in the darkest depths of Tartarus.[10]

Meanwhile, with a sad heart, Heracles proceeded with his journey. When he found the boar's tracks, his shouts frightened it from the thick underbrush where it lay hidden. Realizing that he would never catch the amazingly fleet animal upon its native terrain, Heracles chased it up Mount Erymanthus into the snowy, upper regions. There, its short legs were severely hampered by deep snow drifts, and it collapsed in exhaustion. The great hero tied it securely by the feet, slung it over his back, and returned with the living terror to the walls of Tiryns where, as usual, he was met by King Eurystheus's messenger.

Labor 5—The Augeian Stables

Possibly because Heracles interrupted his labors in order to accompany Jason and his friends on the heroic voyage to recover the golden fleece from King Aeëtes of Colchis, the fifth labor was designed by King Eurystheus to be distasteful and humiliating. The king commanded Heracles to clean the great stables of King Augeias of Elis in one day and without anyone's help.

Augeias owned such huge herds of cattle and goats that, years ago, he had stopped trying to clean up their droppings. Consequently, his stables were impassable and the dung-buried land surrounding them had become infertile.

Heracles approached the wealthy king and announced that he would clean the entire area in one day if Augeias would agree to pay him with cattle. Augeias was incredulous, but in the presence of his son, Phyleus, he gave his word. Heracles, meanwhile, never mentioned that he was obligated to perform this task for King Eurystheus.

Heracles then went into the surrounding high country where he dug new channels for the Alpheius and Peneius Rivers. Once he had dammed their customary channels, these rivers charged down from the heights and rushed through the yards and stables, carrying the hardened layers of dung with them. By the end of the day, the stable area was fresh and clean. Heracles then returned to the high country, removed the barriers he had constructed and rerouted the rivers into their previous channels.

Because Heracles had used his brain instead of his brawn in order to accomplish this task, Augeias refused to keep his part of the agreement. He would not pay Heracles for his work, even though Phyleus urged him to do so.

King Eurystheus refused to consider this labor one of the required ten because Heracles had performed it for pay. Heracles never forgave King Augeias for breaking his word. Years later, Heracles returned to Elis with an army. He captured the city, killed Augeias and all his sons, except Phyleus, and left the kingdom to the prince who had supported him.

Labor 6—The Stymphalian Birds

King Eurystheus next required Heracles to journey to Arcadia in order to remove the birds from the Stymphalian Lake and its surrounding woods. These birds shot their feathers as if they were arrows, killing humans and then eating their flesh. They were so numerous and so hidden that Heracles could not have defended himself. Therefore, grey-eyed Athena helped Heracles with this labor by requesting Hephaestus, the renowned smith, to make a pair of bronze rattles, or clappers, for him. When the goddess gave him the rattles, Heracles climbed up a nearby mountain and shook them. He used such force that the echoing noise thundered over the lake and woods, frightening all of the birds away. As they flew up into the air, Heracles shot them, one by one, from his position of safety.

Labor 7—The Cretan Bull

For the seventh labor, King Eurystheus commanded Heracles to bring to Tiryns, alive, the wild bull of Crete, father of the famous Minotaur. King Minos of Crete was willing to relinquish the beautiful animal because his wife had embarrassed him by developing a passion for it and had conceived a child by it.[11] Heracles caught the bull, tied it up, and returned to Tiryns with it upon his shoulders. Once he had displayed it outside the walls of Tiryns to Eurystheus's messenger, he set it free. The bull traveled through Sparta and Arcadia ravaging the countryside until it settled near Marathon, not far from Athens.[12]

Labor 8—The Mares of Diomedes
Admetus and Alcestis

As the eighth labor, Eurystheus commanded Heracles to bring the flesh-eating mares of the Thracian king, Diomedes, to Tiryns. These horses ate from strong bronze troughs and were kept fastened by iron chains because of their savage nature and their great power. Their food was supplied by unfortunate mortals who approached them, for they ate human beings.[13]

On his way to Thrace, Heracles traveled through the land of Thessaly, which was ruled by his friend, Admetus of Pherae. Admetus was honored by the deathless gods because he was unusually good and pious.

Once, as a punishment imposed by Zeus, Apollo had been the servant of King Admetus. These were the circumstances. When Apollo's son, Asclepius brought Theseus's son, Hippolytus, back to life,[14] Olympian Zeus killed Asclepius with a lightning bolt for his daring. Apollo avenged his son's death by killing the great Cyclopes who forged his immortal father's weapons. Outraged at his son's rebellion, the Lord of Olympus decreed a humiliating punishment for his son. He commanded that Apollo become the servant of King Admetus of Pherae for one year.

Admetus treated his servant with kindness and respect. In return, the Lord of the Silver Bow did everything in his power for his mortal master. Whatever herds he tended doubled in size.[15]

Admetus became a suitor for Alcestis who was the daughter of King Pelias of Iolcus. Because of her beauty, her goodness, and her piety,[16] Alcestis had many eligible suitors. Therefore, her father created a contest as the way of determining to whom he would award her. The suitor who won Alcestis for his wife would have to yoke a wild boar and a wild lion to a chariot and then drive it.[17]

Admetus asked far-shooting Apollo to help him, and he did. The Lord of the Silver Bow yoked the wild beasts for Admetus and then guided him as he drove the fierce team.

Admetus won Alcestis for his wife. However, in offering sacrifices of thanksgiving to the deathless gods upon his marriage, he forgot to sacrifice to arrow-raining Artemis.[18] Later, when he opened the door to the bridal bedroom, instead of his lovely wife, he found the bed filled with hissing snakes. Again, Admetus hurried to his friend Apollo. The Far-Shooter appealed to his twin sister to forgive the king for his mistake, and Artemis of the Golden Arrows agreed.

Moreover, as his greatest favor for the mortal who had made the humiliation of his earthly servitude bearable, far-shooting Apollo obtained a favor from the three Fates. He convinced them to release Admetus from the obligation to die if Admetus could find someone who would volunteer to die in his place.

The fatal day arrived long before Admetus had expected it. When Hermes the Wayfinder arrived to conduct him down to the Underworld, Admetus frantically sought volunteers to replace him. Thinking of those who loved him enough to sacrifice their lives for him, Admetus pleaded with his elderly father and then with his elderly mother. He felt certain that his parents were close enough to death and had lived long enough lives that one of them would make the sacrifice. However, neither one would do so. They reacted with little sympathy for his plea, stating that a person's life became even more precious as he or she neared death. Admetus would simply have to accept his fate as other mortals did.

Admetus never considered asking his lovely wife, for he would never have considered living without her. However, hearing of his plight, without a word to him, Alcestis voluntarily made the great sacrifice. She quietly drank poison and died.[19]

That was the day that Heracles arrived at his friend's house and was amazed to find it in a state of mourning. Heracles did not want Admetus to be obligated to entertain him under these circumstances, but Admetus was so fond of him that he told Heracles that no one of Admetus's blood had died. Thinking that a stranger was being mourned, Heracles agreed to be a guest and became noisily drunk. When a servant criticized his boisterous behavior under the sorrowful circumstances, Heracles learned from the servant that Alcestis had died.

Saddened and embarrassed, Heracles rushed to Alcestis's bier where he found grim Hades standing over her. Heracles persuaded the Lord of the Underworld to engage him in a wrestling contest in which the victor would win Alcestis. Grim Hades agreed and, after Heracles had won the contest, the Lord of the Underworld relinquished the shade of Alcestis. After restoring the devoted wife to her grieving husband, Heracles continued toward Thrace and the flesh-eating mares of King Diomedes.

Shortly after arriving in Thrace, Heracles was able to subdue and control these fierce horses by feeding them pieces of their master, the king. The death of Diomedes was appropriate since it had been this Thracian king who had taught these horses to eat human flesh. After the hero brought the mares to Eurystheus, the king of Mycenae and Tiryns dedicated them to his patron goddess, golden-throned Hera.

Labor 9—The Belt of Hippolyte

King Eurystheus commanded Heracles to seek the Amazons[20] and return with their queen's belt. The Amazons were a warlike, female-dominated society that lived near the southern shores of the Black Sea. Although they used men of neighboring communities to father their children, these women reared only their girls. The boys were returned to their fathers, enslaved, or emasculated. Each female had her right breast removed early in her life so that her anatomy would not interfere with her profession, which was throwing the javelin or the spear. The left breast was useful for nursing female infants. Ares, Stabber of Shields, had presented the queen of the Amazons, Hippolyte, with a special belt as a symbol of her superior rank. Since Eurystheus's daughter desired this belt, her father had commanded Heracles to acquire it for her.

When Heracles' ship arrived in the harbor of Themiscyra, Hippolyte visited Heracles and agreed to give him her belt. The idea of such an easy labor so infuriated golden-throned Hera that the goddess transformed herself into an Amazon. In this disguise, she approached Hippolyte's subjects, claiming that the strange seamen were abducting their queen. The Amazons immediately jumped upon their horses and charged the ship. Heracles, thinking that this was an ambush planned by Hippolyte, killed the queen and took her belt. Then he defended his ship from the invading force and sailed away.

On his return to Tiryns from the land of the Amazons, Heracles stopped at Ilium (Troy). He found the city suffering from the combined rage of far-shooting Apollo, and Poseidon, Lord of the Sea. One year earlier, these Olympians had decided to test the moral character of Ilium's king, Laomedon. They had transformed themselves into mortal men and in this disguise, they had been employed by Laomedon for one year. The Earthshaker[21] had surrounded Ilium with a huge defensive stone wall, while the Far-Shooter[22] had been the king's cowherd on the slopes of Mount Ida.

However, when the term of their employment had ended, King Laomedon refused to pay them the agreed upon wages. He threatened instead to chop off their ears with his bronze knife, bind their hands and feet, and sell them as slaves, if they did not leave immediately.

In retaliation, the Far-Shooter inflicted a plague upon the city, and the Earthshaker sent forth a dreadful monster from the depths of the sea. Carried into the countryside upon floodwaters, the sea monster seized the people it encountered and consumed them.

When the distraught king asked the oracle of Apollo at Delphi what he should do in order to rescue his city from this devastation, the oracle advised him to bind Trojan maidens upon the rocks by the seashore for the sea monster to devour. The Trojan people obeyed, and many of their fairest daughters met horrible deaths in this fashion.

The lot had fallen upon the princess Hesione when Heracles arrived. He agreed to kill the sea monster and release Hesione if, in return, King Laomedon would promise to give him his famous horses that could walk upon the waves of the sea. When Laomedon had agreed to these demands, Heracles killed the sea monster and delivered the princess to her father. Once again, however, King Laomedon refused to keep his word. Consequently, after threatening him with war, Heracles sailed away.

Years later, Heracles returned to Ilium with his friend, Telamon. Their army attacked and burned the city. They also killed its treacherous king. All but one of his sons were killed. Heracles gave the princess Hesione to Telamon as his wife, and he put Laomedon's infant son, Priam, upon the throne of Ilium.

Labor 10—The Cattle of Geryon

For the tenth labor, Eurystheus commanded Heracles to bring him the cattle of King Geryon of Erytheia, on the western coast of what is now Spain.[23] Geryon was a triple-headed giant who had the body of three men. These bodies all joined together at the waist, but separated into three again below the hips. He possessed a fine herd of red cattle that was guarded by his cowherd, Eurytion, and his two-headed watchdog named Orthus, an offspring of Typhon.

On his way, Heracles stopped in Libya, on the northern coast of Africa. Here he killed numerous wild animals that inhabited the land and deterred mortal men from living there. One of these animals was a snake that consumed the grain which grew along the banks of the Sagaris River and any mortals it encountered. Then he cultivated the desert land, introducing vineyards and olive orchards. When he left, Libya was prepared to take its place among the civilized countries of that time.

As Heracles continued his journey toward Geryon's kingdom, he arrived at the westernmost part of the Mediterranean Sea. There he erected two huge pillars: one on the continent of Africa, the other across the strait, on the continent of Europe. He extended the land supporting these pillars into the Mediterranean Sea so that the strait would be too shallow and too narrow to permit large ocean-dwelling monsters to enter the Mediterranean Sea.

Shining Helius's scorching rays had become so intense that, in self-defense, Heracles aimed his great bow at the deathless being as if he would shoot him. Helius admired the mortal hero's great stamina and courage, yet he commanded Heracles to be patient. Fearing the great Titan's awesome powers, Heracles obeyed and, as soon as Helius had driven his blazing chariot into the stables of the sea goddess Tethys, the Shining One[24] rewarded him with a huge golden goblet. In it, he sailed north upon the great Atlantic Ocean, toward Geryon's kingdom. While Heracles was sailing upon the open sea, great Oceanus tested him by making the goblet toss violently upon the ocean waves. Again Heracles prepared to shoot one of the immortals. However, Oceanus became afraid and calmed the sea.

Upon arriving safely in Erytheia, he was immediately attacked by double-headed Orthus. However, Heracles beat each head to death with his huge club. When Eurytion, the cowherd, tried to defend Orthus, Heracles killed him as well. Then, he took Geryon's cattle and started to return to his goblet ship. He might have left Erytheia without encountering Geryon if the cowherd of grim Hades' cows had not spied him and reported the news to Geryon.

Geryon tried to recover his cattle, but Heracles shot and killed each body of the triple-bodied king with his Hydra-poisoned arrows. Heracles then herded the cattle into shining Helius's golden goblet and sailed with them to Tartessus, which was a short journey. There he landed and gratefully returned the goblet to the shining god.

Returning overland toward Greece, Heracles traveled into Liguria, the southern part of what is now France. There, a large number of native warriors attacked him for Geryon's cattle. Heracles tried to hold them off with his bow, but he knew that his supply of arrows would never be sufficient. Frantically, he searched the area for anything he could use as a weapon, but the rich soil supplied no rocks.

In desperation, the great hero prayed to his Olympian father for help. Far-seeing Zeus responded to his plea by sending a shower of rocks down from the heavens. Heracles smiled with relief, grabbed the stones, and cast them at his enemies. Unable to withstand the onslaught, and terrified of the stranger's miraculous powers, the warriors hastily retreated.

Heracles continued his westward journey with Geryon's cattle, arriving in what is now Italy. He did not notice a dismal cave set deep within a rocky cliff. Yet a gigantic son of the renowned smith Hephaestus, named Cacus, lived in the sunless cavern. Cacus coughed black, volcanic fires, and was fond of eating human flesh. He would capture solitary strangers, slaughter them in front of his cave, and then hang their heads upon the entrance as testimony to his accomplishments. When Cacus spied the hero, Heracles, and his impressive herd of cattle, his eyes gleamed with delight and his stomach warmed in anticipation of his next good meal.

Ignorant of the impending danger, Heracles rested in the pleasant valley. Geryon's cattle spread out upon the banks of the river, glad to rest from the journey.

Stealthily, Cacus approached four splendid sets of cattle, male and female pairs, and silently pulled them backward by their tails into his dismal cavern, where he hid them deep within the recesses of his rocky home. Since their footprints faced the opposite direction from their actual destination, there was no way of tracking them to Cacus' cave.

When Heracles felt refreshed and the cattle had eaten and drunk their fill, the hero gathered Geryon's herd and prepared to leave the valley. The area echoed with the bellowing of the cattle as the animals slowly moved on their way.

Suddenly, Heracles heard the distant sound of a cow returning their cry. Amazed and angered, the hero furiously grabbed his huge wooden club and his bow. He set out in the direction of the sound, determined to locate the missing animal.

Cacus, realizing that one of the stolen cows had revealed his theft, hurriedly returned to his cave. Faster than the wind, he crossed the threshold and lowered and locked the rocky door which his father, the renowned smith,[25] had designed to protect his monstrous son's home.

Heracles followed, close upon Cacus's heels. However, when the hero arrived at the cliff, he was unable to discern an entrance, so cleverly had Hephaestus designed the door. His fury became frenzy as he walked along the cliff, futilely trying the strength of its rocky walls. Three times Heracles examined the fortress, and three times he returned to the valley to rest and think.

Suddenly, upon the same cliff, Heracles spied an area of sheer rock rising high into the heavens like a stone tower. Since it naturally leaned to the left, the hero climbed up to it and pushed from the right with all his strength. He wrenched it loose and hurled it to the valley below.

Then he looked into the gaping abyss he had uncovered. There, deep inside, lay Cacus's dismal den, with the monstrous subhuman creature cowering in fright at the invasion of unwelcome daylight.

Heracles now rained his arrows upon the monster, adding huge rocks and club-like branches as he found them. Unable to escape this deluge, Cacus vomited his sooty flames in order to surround himself with blinding smoke and ashes. Heracles, outraged at the camouflage, jumped into the flaming cavern. Discovering where Cacus had concealed himself, the hero gripped him by the neck until his eyes bulged from his head, his breath fought to escape. Cacus soon died of suffocation.

Heracles rushed to the entrance of the dismal den, tore the stone door from its fasteners, and led the cattle into the fresh, sparkling air. Then he returned to the cavern and dragged the corpse of Cacus into the daylight. Local farmers later celebrated the destruction of the fearsome criminal and honored Heracles as a hero.

Heracles continued westward, finally reaching the walls of Tiryns. There he gave Geryon's cattle to King Eurystheus, who, in turn, sacrificed them to his patron goddess, golden-throned Hera.

Labor 11—The Golden Apples of the Hesperides

Although Heracles had performed his first ten labors in the course of eight years, King Eurystheus had refused to count killing the Hydra and cleaning the Augeian stables as labors. Therefore, the king now commanded the hero to perform an eleventh task. He ordered Heracles to bring to Tiryns the golden apples of the Hesperides.[26]

Gaea had given this apple tree to golden-throned Hera upon her marriage to Olympian Zeus. Hera then planted the tree in the garden of the deathless gods near Mount Atlas in Libya. When the Hesperides, Atlas's daughters, could not resist picking the apples, golden-throned Hera placed as guard of the tree an offspring of Typhon, a huge hundred-headed dragon called Ladon. This dragon was a perfect watchman, never closing its eyes. Therefore, anyone who wanted the golden treasure would have to fight the terrifying monster.

In order to locate the route to these apples, Heracles sought the aid of the immortal nymphs, deathless daughters of the Titan goddess Themis and Olympian Zeus. The nymphs sent him to the ancient sea god, Nereus, the kind and just son of Gaea and Pontus. If he would, Nereus could tell Heracles where the famous garden of the immortals was located.

Heracles followed the nymphs' advice and captured the Old Man of the Sea[27] while he lay asleep upon the shore. Then Heracles held the god in his fierce grip while the immortal transformed himself into frightening shapes with the hope of terrifying his captor into releasing him. However, Heracles continued to grip the body he felt through the raging flames, the roaring lion, the slithering serpent, the rushing stream of water, and the menacing boar. Finally, realizing that he could not evade his captor's grip by his marvelous tricks, Nereus resumed his own shape and revealed the location of the garden. Then Heracles resumed his journey.

As he traveled through Libya, Heracles encountered its gigantic King Antaeüs, who was a son of the Earthshaker[28] and Gaea. Antaeüs won fame throughout the Mediterranean world for his prodigious strength and his great skill as a wrestler. The giant would force any stranger to wrestle with him. Whenever Antaeüs won, as he invariably did, he would kill his victim, decapitate him, and use his skull as part of the roof of the temple of his father, Poseidon.

With Heracles, Antaeüs met his match. Both wrestlers oiled their bodies, then covered them with sand in preparation for the deathly contest. Heracles, with his own great strength and skill was able to throw Antaeüs to the ground several times. However, the hero was surprised to find that each time, the giant arose from the earth with renewed vigor while Heracles, himself, was fighting off increasing fatigue.

Heracles realized that he would have to understand this phenomenon very quickly if he were to remain strong enough to conquer his formidable foe. Then Heracles remembered that the king was reputed to be a child of Gaea. Summoning all the strength he possessed, Heracles grabbed his opponent, gripped his body firmly, and raised the giant slowly off the earth. There he suspended his foe, away from his great mother's renewing powers, while he crushed him to death within the grip of his own mighty arms.

Upon reaching the Mediterranean Sea, Heracles again received shining Helius's golden goblet so that he could obey an urgent command from his Olympian father to cross the Mediterranean to the continent of Europe and rescue Prometheus from Mount Caucasus far to the northeast. Zeus of the Wise Counsels needed the immediate help of the great Titan whom he had punished 30,000 years ago. He had ordered Hephaestus, the renowned smith, to chain Prometheus with inescapable bonds to the cliffs of Mount Caucasus.[29] Now the Lord of Olympus could give further glory to his favorite mortal son, Heracles, by permitting him to shoot the eagle, another offspring of Typhon, which had continually devoured the liver of his great, early enemy. When Heracles freed humanity's great protector from his chains, he told him that Olympian Zeus had pardoned him and needed his prophetic advice.

The son of Zeus also informed the great Titan that, in return for his freedom, Olympian Zeus had decreed that Prometheus would have to wear upon his fingers a ring of stone and one of iron. The first material represented the cliff to which he had been confined, and the second material represented the chains that had bound him. These rings would remind him eternally of his rebellion against Zeus and the great suffering he had been forced to endure as its penalty.[30]

In appreciation, the crafty Titan advised Heracles not to attempt to gather the golden apples himself. Instead, he should temporarily take the heavens from the great Titan Atlas's shoulders and let him perform the task. Also, he advised Heracles that if he should need to do so, it was easy to trick Atlas as he was simple-minded.

When Heracles arrived at the garden of the immortals, he followed Prometheus's advice. Atlas was willing to relinquish the heavens to Heracles' care and to collect the apples for the hero. However, when the Titan returned bearing three of the golden fruit, he announced that it was so pleasant to be free of his weighty burden that he would take the apples to King Eurystheus himself while Heracles held up the heavens for him.

Heracles realized that if he let Atlas escape, the mighty Titan would never return. Thinking quickly, the hero devised a cunning scheme in which he pretended to agree with the Titan's suggestion. Heracles asked Atlas to hold the heavens while he put a pad upon his head. He had not prepared himself to hold up the heavens for any great length of time. The strong, but simple-minded Titan kindly agreed to Heracles' request. Placing the golden apples upon the ground, Atlas resumed his burden, and Heracles quickly gathered the golden fruit and departed for Tiryns.[31]

After Eurystheus had seen the apples, he permitted Heracles to return them to the garden of the immortals because he knew that the deathless gods would not permit them to remain away from their sacred tree. Grey-eyed Athena met Heracles and returned the apples to the Hesperides for him.

Labor 12—Delivery of Cerberus

As his final labor, King Eurystheus commanded Heracles to enter the dismal underworld kingdom of grim Hades and capture Cerberus, the dread hound that guarded the gates to that land. Cerberus, an offspring of Typhon, was a monster that had three dogs' heads, the tail of a dragon, and snakes' heads growing from its back. Unless he were satisfied with sweet food or intimidated by Hermes, the hound decided who could enter the kingdom and ate anyone who tried to leave.

Heracles took the road down to Hades' dismal land that he found near Taenarum, in southern Greece. Then, with the help of Hermes the Wayfinder, he entered the underworld kingdom.

There, the Gorgon Medusa looked so real that Heracles drew his sword in order to kill her, but Hermes assured him that she was nothing but a shade. Also near the gates, Heracles came upon Theseus and Peirithoüs, who were firmly attached to the rock upon which they were sitting.[32] The two friends immediately reached out to the hero in the hope that he could and would rescue them. Heracles grabbed the hands of Theseus and pulled him loose, but the Underworld shook beneath his feet as his hands reached Peirithoüs. Heracles realized that the dread rulers opposed freedom for Peirithoüs and let go of his hands.

Upon meeting grim Hades and his beautiful queen, Heracles explained the purpose of his visit. The Lord of the Underworld agreed to let the hero capture his hound as long as he refrained from using any weapons.

Heracles then returned to the bank of the River Styx, protected himself with his lionskin, and grabbed the monster in his powerful arms. Even when the hound's dragon tail bit him, Heracles maintained his deathly grip. Finally, the monster gave up the fight and let Heracles ascend with him into the world of daylight and living men. Once King Eurystheus had seen Cerberus from a safe distance, he permitted Heracles to return the dread hound to its underworld home.

After the Labors

When Heracles had finished his labors, he gave his wife, Megara, to his nephew, Iolaüs, as his wife. Because he had killed their children in the fit of insanity which Hera had caused, their marriage had suffered, and each was happy to begin a new marriage.

Heracles then wooed Iole, the daughter of King Eurytus of Oechalia. The king had decreed that he would award his daughter to the man who could beat him and his sons in an archery contest. King Eurytus was such a fine archer that he had been chosen to teach Heracles to shoot with bow and arrow many years before. Now Heracles won the contest. Nevertheless, the king refused to keep his promise because he feared that Heracles was emotionally unstable and might again become insane and murder his children. All of the king's children, except Iphitus, agreed with the king's decision.

In retaliation, Heracles drove away the king's horses. When Iphitus came to Tiryns searching for the horses, Heracles led him to the high tower of the palace, on the pretext of permitting him to look for them from the tower. Then, accusing Iphitus of falsely claiming that he had stolen the horses, Heracles threw him off the tower to his death.

After this murder, Heracles developed a disease. He asked the oracle of Apollo at Delphi how to become purified of the murder so that he would be cured of the disease. The oracle replied that he would have to be sold into slavery for three years and deliver the price of his purchase to the sons of Iphitus. Heracles obeyed, and Hermes the Wayfinder sold him to Queen Omphale of Lydia. His disease healed, but he was unable to attend Meleager's hunt for the Calydonian boar because of his commitment to Omphale.

While he was Omphale's slave, Heracles set out to punish all criminals in the land. He met fierce Syleus who enjoyed capturing travelers and killing them. Syleus would work them to death by forcing them to hoe his vineyards. Heracles killed Syleus with the hoe Syleus usually gave the travelers he captured. Omphale was so pleased with Heracles' bravery that, after she learned his history, she freed him.

Upon leaving Lydia, Heracles proceeded to travel from one country to another with the intention of avenging any previous insults to his honor. In each instance, Heracles killed those who had insulted him and rewarded those who had defended his integrity. He also established the Olympic Games in honor of his immortal father, Olympian Zeus. The games included a variety of athletic contests. A crown was awarded as the prize to each winner.

Heracles also helped the Olympian gods in their time of need. Gaea had given birth to a later race of Giants from the drops of Uranus's blood. These monstrous creatures were colossal in size, terrifying in appearance, and apparently unconquerable. Their heads and chins were hidden by thick clumps of hair; their feet were scaled like the skin of reptiles.

The Giants piled one mountain upon another in order to reach Mount Olympus. Then, they suddenly attacked the Olympian immortals. The outcome of this battle was uncertain. Gaea learned that an oracle had stated that the gods would kill the Giants with the aid of a mortal. The Great Goddess tried to acquire a drug which would protect her monstrous children from death. However, far-seeing Zeus heard of her intentions in time to prohibit Eos,[33] Selene,[34] and Helius[35] from appearing until, under cover of darkness, he had acquired the drug himself.

Olympian Zeus then commanded his grey-eyed daughter to bring Heracles to their aid. In the course of the ensuing battle, the Lord of Olympus and his great mortal son worked as a team. Zeus would subdue a Giant with his lightning and thunderbolts, and Heracles would kill it with his Hydra-poisoned arrows. Some Giants were blinded by Heracles and the Lord of the Silver Bow; other Giants were killed by Hephaestus, the renowned smith, who seared them with white hot iron from his forge. Ivy-wreathed Dionysus killed many Giants with his thyrsus.[36] The three Fates, in the meantime, killed two of the Giants by battering them to death with bronze clubs. Hermes the Wayfinder, wearing grim Hades' helmet of invisibility, confused the enemy. Golden-helmeted Athena hurled the island of Sicily upon one Giant, who remains buried there to this day. Finally, the battle-stirring goddess[37] killed the Giant, Pallas. She skinned him, using his skin to protect her own body in battle. This is how she earned the title of Pallas Athena.[38]

When Heracles returned to Tiryns, King Eurystheus accused him of trying to usurp his throne. He forced Heracles, his mother Alcmene, his brother Iphicles, and his nephew Iolaüs into exile. They finally settled in Calydon.

When Heracles decided to woo Meleager's sister, Deïaneira, he had to contest for her hand against the river god Acheloüs in a wrestling match. They oiled and sanded their bodies, and then each grabbed the other. It soon became evident to Acheloüs that Heracles was superior to him in wrestling skill. Therefore, the river god decided to win by using clever tricks. First, he transformed himself into a spotted snake, trying to frighten his foe with his hisses, and, failing that, tried to slither from his grasp. Heracles laughed and reminded the river god that he had strangled snakes when he was an infant. Acheloüs fared no better as a dragon, for Heracles told him how much more dreadful the Hydra had been. Next, Acheloüs transformed himself into a ferocious wild boar. Heracles conquered the god in that form as well and broke off one of his horns. Heracles presented the horn to the Hesperides who filled it with fruit. Then he married Deïaneira.

Heracles and Deïaneira had been married for three years when Heracles, while eating dinner in a friend's home, slapped a young servant for pouring water on his hands. The blow was so hard that Heracles unintentionally killed him. The boy's father forgave Heracles, realizing that the death had been an accident. However, as a self-imposed punishment, Heracles chose to exile himself, Deïaneira, and their young son Hyllus, from Calydon.

Arriving at the Evenus River, Heracles found the Centaur Nessus waiting for them. The Centaur announced that the deathless gods had awarded him the job of ferryman because he was so virtuous. Heracles and Hyllus crossed the river without his aid, but the hero accepted Nessus's offer to carry Deïaneira across since he was going to have to pay him anyway.

Nessus found Deïaneira so beautiful that once she was seated upon his back, he decided to rape her in midstream. Heracles responded to her call for help by shooting Nessus with one of his Hydra-poisoned arrows. Nessus retaliated for this mortal wound by confiding to Deïaneira that he would give her a love potion which would keep Heracles from loving any other woman. He directed her to gather in her hands the Hydra-poisoned blood which had clotted around his wound and to save it. When she wanted to administer this potion, she should rub it into Heracles' shirt. Deïaneira remembered this advice.

The day came when Heracles chose to complete his revenge against King Eurytus, Iole's father. King Eurytus had wounded Heracles' pride and honor by denying him Iole as his bride. Heracles had never forgotten this insult. Although King Eurytus was dead, Heracles fought his sons, killed them all, and left with Iole as his prisoner.

Afterwards, Heracles stopped to perform a religious rite to Olympian Zeus. Because he intended to offer a sacrifice, he sent his servant, Lichas, home to Deïaneira to obtain the special ceremonial shirt he wore on these religious occasions. When Lichas mentioned to Deïaneira that Iole was accompanying Heracles, Deïaneira feared that her husband still loved the beautiful princess. She remembered Nessus's advice and rubbed the Centaur's Hydra-poisoned blood into the ceremonial shirt as a love potion. Lichas, unaware of the history of the love potion, brought the garments to Heracles.

Meanwhile, soon after Lichas had returned to Heracles, Deïaneira noticed that, in smearing the Centaur's blood into Heracles' shirt, some drops had fallen upon the ground. She ignored them until she noticed that they burst into flames as the shining rays of Helius reached them. Suddenly Deïaneira realized that, in reality, the substance which Nessus had claimed was a love charm was the Centaur's cunning vengeance upon her husband. She quickly sent a servant to warn Heracles about the shirt. However, the servant arrived too late. When he returned with the news of her husband's torment, Deïaneira could not live tortured as she was by her guilt. Therefore, she hanged herself.

While Deïaneira was discovering that she had poisoned her husband, Heracles was preparing for the sacrifice. The heat of his body warmed the shirt and activated the Hydra's poison within the cloth. As the poison worked upon his skin, the poison-soaked cloth stuck to him, scorching him as if he were burning. Silently bearing the pain, Heracles leaped into a nearby stream in order to soothe his skin. Instead, the water caused his shirt to erupt into flames. Horrified, Heracles tried to tear off the shirt, but it stuck to his flesh. By removing one, he removed the other also, revealing lacerated muscles and bare bones.

The excruciating pain caused Heracles to become mad with rage. He blamed Lichas for the catastrophe since he had brought him the poisoned shirt. He grabbed the frightened boy and threw him far into the sea, where he drowned.

Heracles then sent his nephew, Iolaüs, to the oracle of Apollo at Delphi to ask how he could be healed. The oracle told Iolaüs to take Heracles with his weapons and armor to Mount Oeta and to build a huge funeral pyre there. The Lord of Olympus would decide Heracles' fate.

Heracles, no longer able to bear the pain, gave up hope of a cure and decided to put an end to his own life. While the forests resounded with his groans, he climbed upon the pyre and lay down. Then he asked anyone who approached him to ignite the pyre with a torch, but no one would comply with such a distasteful request. Finally, Philoctetes pitied his friend and agreed to kindle the pyre. Heracles was so grateful that he gave him his bow and arrows as a reward. As soon as the torch touched the wood, thunder rumbled and lightning struck the pyre. Its flames completely consumed the pyre and Heracles.

Later, Heracles' companions searched the area for his bones, but there were none. Only ashes remained. They then realized that far-seeing Zeus had claimed his heroic son. The flames had burned away the hero's mortal body, permitting the immortal part to join the deathless gods. At last, Heracles had received the immortality that the Delphic oracle had promised him so long ago.

When Heracles reached Mount Olympus, Zeus of the Wise Councils convinced his queen to adopt Heracles as her son. Golden-throned Hera agreed to replace her jealousy with love. As proof of her change of heart, she awarded Heracles her royal daughter, Hebe, as his immortal wife. Heracles the hero had become Heracles the god.

1. Princes and kings who kill someone, intentionally or accidentally, are quite common in Greek mythology, indicating the volatile nature of kingship and other roles involving power. Note: Perseus, Bellerophon, Theseus, and Jason as well as Heracles and the kings who provide the settings for these myths are examples of the political instability of the Mycenaean age. A person who committed homicide was exiled for about eight years, also the period of the reigning sacred king.

2. King Eurystheus actually ordered Heracles to perform twelve labors instead of the original ten because he was displeased that Heracles had received help with the second labor and had expected to be paid for the fifth labor.
3. Until then Heracles had been called Alcaeüs, after Amphitryon's father (i.e. Heracles' grandfather).
4. In an earlier, matriarchal culture, as the sacred king, Heracles would have protected Hera and thus, in fact, he would have been the "glory of Hera." It is very possible that he did, and that he was.
5. The wild olive tree traditionally was believed to frighten off evil spirits.
6. Combat with a wild animal, such as a lion, was part of the coronation ritual for a sacred king in Greece and in Asia Minor.
7. Reindeer is the only species of deer in which the female has antlers.
8. Apollo, the Far-Shooter.
9. Creatures with the heads, chests, and arms of men and the bodies and legs of horses.
10. See myth of Prometheus (Section III, The World of Man).
11. See myth of Theseus (Section IV, The Heroes).
12. See myth of Theseus (Section IV, The Heroes).
13. People in Thrace worshipped Dionysus. Terrible rites circulated about death of sacred kings and savage use of horses. See myth of Dionysus.
14. See myth of Theseus (Section IV, The Heroes).
15. Being a twin himself, Apollo was thought to have magical powers which would produce twins, particularly among herds and flocks, which he tended.
16. Alcestis was the one daughter of Pelias who refused to believe Medea's promises. See myth of Jason (Section IV, The Heroes).
17. Circling a race course in a chariot may have been a proof of royalty.
18. Because in the matriarchal society, Artemis had been hostile to the idea of marriage between one man and one woman, the Mycenaeans tried to appease her anger with wedding sacrifices.
19. There was a practice in Mycenaean times of having the wife and the husband die at the same time. When the first died, the second was expected to kill himself at the first's tomb.
20. The Amazons were also encountered by Bellerophon and Theseus.
21. Poseidon.
22. Apollo.
23. It was a Mycenaean custom for a husband to buy his wife with cattle. Each woman was valued at a particular number of cattle. Various myths reflect this idea.
24. Helius.
25. Hephaestus.
26. See myth of Perseus (Section IV, The Heroes).
27. The Old Man of the Sea: Nereus.
28. Poseidon.
29. See myth of Prometheus (Section III, The World of Man).
30. In honor of Prometheus's sacrifice, mankind has chosen to wear rings.
31. Some writers say that Heracles killed Ladon (even though Ladon was immortal) and collected the apples himself.
32. See myth of Theseus (Section IV, The Heroes).
33. Eos: dawn.
34. Selene: moon.
35. Helius: sun.
36. Dionysus's ivy—wreathed staff.
37. Athena.
38. This battle accounts for mammoth bones and volcanic fires; it is an explanatory myth.

REFLECTIONS

1. Discuss the development of the relationship between Heracles and Eurystheus:

a. What is their relationship before the labors begin?
b. What is Eurystheus's reaction to the labors?
c. How does Heracles cope with the fact that he has to obey orders?
d. What is their relationship after the labors?
2. What lessons does this myth teach? Discuss.
3. Why, of all the heroes, does Heracles become immortal? Does he deserve this distinction? Explain.
4. Write a thirteenth labor for Heracles set in ancient times.
5. Write a thirteenth labor for Heracles set in modern times.
6. Write a script dramatizing the myth of Admetus and Alcestis (Labor 8). Present it to the class.

34 Theseus

The myth of Theseus originated sometime after the Mycenaean Greeks invaded and conquered Crete in approximately 1450 B.C. The island of Crete contained a number of matriarchal communites, the major one being Cnossus, which was ruled by a priestess-queen and a sacred king called Minos (meaning *king*).

Minos left his kingdom once every eight years (the Great Year), and retreated to a cave where he conversed with his father, Zeus. Upon his return, he began another term as king. Presumably, in the interim, a substitute sacred king reigned and was sacrificed. It is clear that Minos wore the head of a bull on ceremonial occasions. A sacred symbol was the double axe (*labrys*), and the palace of Cnossus was called The House of the Double Axe or the Labyrinth.

By 1700 B.C., Minoan power had reached Greece. When Minos exacted the tribute of seven Athenian maidens and seven Athenian youths every nine years, this probably coincided with the Great Year. Consequently, it is possible that the Athenian tribute was a human sacrifice, a substitute for the sacred king who was in the cave. It is also possible that the young female and male acrobats in the frescoes on the walls of the palace at Cnossus were human sacrifices.

In 1450 B.C., Mycenaean Greeks invaded Crete. When they arrived at the palace of Cnossus, they must have been amazed by its tremendous height and huge, rambling expanse. They left communities of two-story, two room buildings. As they wandered through some of the many rooms in search of the king, they experienced a labyrinth in the sense that Theseus did. Therefore, when the invaders located the king, he was Theseus's Minotaur (*mino:* king; *taur:* bull). The Mycenaean invasion was surely an occasion on which the king would have worn his sacred bull headdress. Theseus's battle with the Minotaur reflects the ensuing battle between the Mycenaeans and the Minoans. In both myth and history, the Greeks won. The marriage of Theseus to Ariadne symbolizes a political peace treaty.

A separate Theseus myth developed in the Peloponnesus. There, Theseus followed his great competitor, Heracles, and undertook a perilous journey to rid society of monsters and criminals. Aegeus's sandals and sword were ancient symbols of kingship. A part of many Bronze Age coronation ceremonies involved drawing swords out of rocks. From one of the criminals, Theseus acquired a club of brass, similar to the olive tree club of Heracles. Like Heracles, Theseus wrestled with contenders and also captured the Cretan Bull. Later, the exploits of Theseus imitated those of Heracles by taking him to the Amazons and into the Underworld.

The myth of Theseus reflects more than heroism, however. It also provides insight into the complex and changeable political situations of his era. A king's position was tenuous, because many contenders for the throne claimed legal right by birth to this position of power and honor.

Theseus was a mixture of greatness and human frailty. The early part of his life was the highlight of his career. He showed great courage and physical strength and had great success (*arete*). Except for the help of Daedalus, Theseus accomplished his tasks on his own. He earned the acclaim he received as king of Athens, by being a creative, just, and courageous leader.

However, once Theseus left Crete, his personal life was marked by tragedy. He repeatedly displayed poor judgment (*hybris* and *áte*) that led to the deaths of his father and his son, and subjected his kingdom to war. Therefore, he died a disgraceful death (*nemesis*).

It is an indication of the objectivity of the ancient Greeks, of their unvarnished view of the nature of man and universe, that they later accepted Theseus with his faults and praised him for his achievements.

The myth of Theseus was resurrected and compiled in sixth century B.C. Athenian leaders wanted their city to have a great founding king, who would be comparable to the great hero of Argos (Heracles).[1] As Athens grew in prominence, its ancient hero shared in its glory. By the fifth century B.C., Theseus had become the legendary founder of Athenian democracy.

1. The title Argos was often used to describe the area which included Mycenae and Tiryns.

THE MYTH

Europa and the Bull

In the ancient country of Phoenicia, on the northern coast of Africa, lived the lovely princess Europa. One day as rosy dawn was about to rise, Europa dreamed that two women, one foreign and one Phoenician, were fighting over her. The Phoenician woman gripped her securely, saying that Europa belonged to her. However, the foreign woman announced, "Zeus, Lord of Olympus, has commanded you to be mine." Then she seized Europa and carried her away.

Europa jumped from her bed, her heart pounding with fear. "Which of the deathless gods has sent me these spirits?" she wondered. "What is the meaning of my strange dream?"

Europa then dressed, took her golden flower basket, and left the palace to search for the noble maidens who were her companions. She hoped that the presence of her friends would cause her to forget her disturbing dream, as dreams are usually powerless in the sparkling daylight. She found them heading for the meadows which lined the seashore, their flower baskets over their arms. As she joined them, Europa felt carefree once again. She delighted in gathering the beautiful, sweet-smelling flowers.

Meanwhile, on the snowy summit of Mount Olympus, Eros, son of gold-wreathed Aphrodite, noticed that far-seeing Zeus was watching the beautiful Phoenician princess. Eros could not resist the opportunity to use his awesome power. He quickly raised his bow, chose one of his most potent arrows, and then directed the shaft into the heart of Zeus.

Suddenly, the Lord of Olympus found Europa so beautiful that he could not resist loving her. He decided to tempt Europa's gentle heart. Because his immortal shape shone so brightly, Olympian Zeus knew that he could only appear before mortals in disguise. Otherwise, his light would blind their eyes and his fires would consume them. Therefore, the Lord of Olympus transformed himself into a great yellow bull, which had majestic curving horns, flashing eyes, and a shining white ring in the middle of its forehead. In this form he knew he could woo the lovely maiden without harming her. Then he commanded Hermes of the Golden Wand, to speed down to the Phoenician hills, find a herd of cows, and drive them down to the meadow by the sea where Europa and her friends were gathering wildflowers.

The maidens immediately noticed the magnificent bull that was grazing among the herd of cows. The bull smelled sweetly. In spite of its great beauty, the maidens at first kept a cautious distance, knowing bulls to be dangerous animals. However, the bull captured their interest with its gentle behavior. As soon as the maidens seemed less fearful, the bull left the herd and wandered toward Europa. Upon reaching her, it lay down at her feet. Europa began to feed it fragrant flowers. At this, the beast became so delighted that it licked her hands and frolicked with joy. As Europa gained more courage, she ventured to pet the bull and to decorate its horns with a garland of flowers. The bull lowed softly and sweetly. It seemed to encourage her to climb upon its back. By this time, Europa felt so safe in the bull's presence that she happily exclaimed, "Let's have some fun by riding upon this beautiful bull! Surely it will be willing to carry us upon its great back, for notice how gentle and kind it looks, quite unlike other bulls. Why it could be a person, except that it cannot talk."

Europa then climbed upon the bull's great back. Her friends would have climbed up behind her, but suddenly the bull, having obtained the prize it sought, rose to its feet and moved briskly toward the sea. Then, to Europa's astonishment, the bull rushed straight out to sea, traveling just enough above the waves to keep its hooves dry. Europa turned back and called out to her friends, but they could not help her. She was now a prisoner upon the bull's back.

The sea beneath them became calm as Poseidon, the great Lord of the Sea, created a pathway for his bull-shaped brother. Europa remained seated upon the bull's back. With one hand, she grasped one of its horns. With her other hand, she held her long robe above the water. The purple cloth of her gathered garment caught the wind behind her like a large sail. Soon Europa no longer could discern the pale mountains of her homeland silhouetted in the receding distance. There was only the endless sea below, and the eternal sky above. Europa sat spellbound as the immortal Nereïds, granddaughters of Oceanus and Tethys, rose out of the water and rode alongside her on the backs of playful sea animals. Dolphins leaped and dived nearby, while Tritons blew wedding music from their tapered shell horns.

"Who are you and where are you taking me?" Europa asked the bull.

The great bull replied to her in her own language:

"Be at ease, gentle maiden. There is no need to be afraid of me nor of the water, for I am Olympian Zeus who loves you. Before long, we shall reach the island of Crete, which nursed me when I was an infant. There we shall be married and have children who will become famous rulers of mortal men."

Soon after Zeus had spoken, the island of Crete appeared before them. There Zeus assumed a majestic human shape, married Europa, and became the father of her children. Europa bore the Lord of Olympus three sons: Minos, Rhadamanthys, and Sarpedon.

In accordance with Zeus's wishes, Europa then married Asterius, the king of Crete. Asterius, who had no sons of his own, adopted Europa's children. Although two of Europa's sons eventually left Crete, Minos remained on the island and married the immortal Pasiphaë, daughter of shining Helius, Titan god of the sun.

Minos and Another Bull

When old King Asterius died, Minos claimed title to the throne of Crete, but rivals disputed his right to reign. Minos responded by asserting: "The gods have chosen me to be king of Crete! As proof of my divine right to the throne, whatever I request, the gods will provide."[1]

Then he prayed. "Poseidon, earth-shaking guardian of this island, I call upon your great name and ask you to confirm my regal authority by sending forth a bull from the depths of the sea. I promise to show my gratitude by sacrificing the bull to you."

The Lord of the Sea heard Minos's prayer and caused a handsome bull to emerge from the waters. Its miraculous arrival confirmed that, indeed, Minos had divine approval for his kingship. Thereafter, no one contested his rule. Cretan civilization developed and prospered. With the help of Olympian Zeus, Minos established a civilized code of laws on Crete that were later adopted by the Greeks.[2] His powerful navy enabled Crete to dominate most of the Mediterranean island communities. Thus, Minos earned a reputation as a worthy king and was respected by the major civilizations of his age.

Time passed and Minos prospered, but the great bull still lived. Minos could not bring himself to kill the magnificent beast. Finally, instead of sacrificing it to Poseidon as he had promised, he added the bull to his royal herds and sacrificed a lesser bull in its place.

For this affront to his honor, the Lord of the Sea became furious with Minos and severely punished him for breaking his word. First, Poseidon transformed the treasured bull into a raging beast. Then, he humiliated Minos by making Queen Pasiphaë fall in love with it. Pasiphaë's passion for this bull became so intense that she craved its love in return. She begged Daedalus, who was then living with the royal family, to help her win the bull's desire.

Daedalus readily agreed to help her. He constructed a wooden cow, hollowed out the inside completely, covered the outside with cowhide, and placed it, with wheels under its hoofs, in the meadow where the bull usually grazed. Daedalus then helped Pasiphaë hide inside. When the bull appeared in the meadow, it noticed Daedalus's incredibly realistic cow. Believing it to be alive, the bull mounted it and impregnated Pasiphaë. In time, Pasiphaë gave birth to a monster that had a bull's head and a human body. Its name was Asterius, but it became known as the Minotaur.

Minos was so embarrassed by this monstrous proof of his wife's perverted passion that he commissioned Daedalus to construct a place where the Minotaur would be hidden. Daedalus responded by creating the Labyrinth, a huge room containing countless, confusing passages so structured that no one inside the enclosure could find his way out. There Minos imprisoned the Minotaur.

It was at this time that the oldest son of Minos, Androgeus, won every honor in the festival which King Aegeus held in Athens. Resentment of Androgeus's victory soon led to his death. Some writers state that a group of jealous athletes, who soon would have had to compete against

Androgeus in the Theban games, ambushed and murdered him. Other writers state that King Aegeus caused the death of Androgeus by enticing him to kill the Bull of Marathon[3] that killed him instead.

Outraged at his son's murder, Minos sought revenge by waging war against the Athenians. However, Minos found that Athens was stronger than he had expected. The Athenians and Cretans were so evenly matched that the war dragged on without prospect of victory for either side. In desperation, Minos prayed to his father, Zeus, for help. The Lord of Olympus heard the prayers of his Cretan son. Angrily, he devastated the Athenians with plague, drought, and famine.

Terror now reigned in Athens. When ordinary sacrifices appeared useless, the Athenians obeyed the ancient oracle of Apollo at Delphi, who demanded the lives of four Athenian maidens. Yet this human sacrifice apparently did not appease the gods, since the devastation continued unabated. Therefore, the Athenians again asked the Delphic oracle what they must do. The oracle responded that they must satisfy Minos by letting him decide how he would punish them. Once the Athenians had made peace with Minos, the oracle assured them that the anger of the gods also would be appeased.

Unable to cope with further disaster, the Athenians reluctantly informed Minos that they would submit to his power. Minos was jubilant at the prospect of finally avenging his son's death. He agreed to establish peace with Athens on one condition: Once every nine years, for as long as the Minotaur lived, the Athenians must send to Crete seven young maidens and seven young men, whom Minos would feed to the Minotaur.[4] Defeated, the Athenians agreed to send Minos this human sacrifice.

This was the world into which the hero Theseus was born.

1. In ancient history, a leader was not accepted by the people unless he could perform "magic tricks" or "miracles." Minos's father, the god Zeus, helped Minos as Poseidon will help Theseus.
2. Approximately every eight years, Minos left his throne and spent a short time in a cave on Mount Ida (where Zeus was reared) conferring with his immortal father. Minos would report to Zeus, and Zeus would instruct him. These visits coincided with the Athenian tribute.
3. The wild bull of Crete that Heracles had subdued and brought to King Eurystheus on the Greek mainland now was called the Bull of Marathon and was ravaging the countryside near Athens.
4. Minoan sources disclaim the existence of the Minotaur. Athenian youth were simply imprisoned in the Labyrinth. The winner of the Androgeus Games won these youths as a prize and may have made slaves or servants of them or may have freed them.

The Early Years

The circumstances surrounding the birth of Theseus were very unusual. King Aegeus of Athens was worried about the future of his kingdom because he had no son to inherit the throne. Meanwhile, his brother,

Pallas, had fifty sons. Therefore, Aegeus was certain that, unless he had a son, his brother's family would inherit the throne of Athens.

Aegeus traveled to the oracle of Apollo at Delphi and asked her how he could have a son. The oracle replied, "Do not open the mouth of your wineskin until you return home to Athens." Aegeus could not understand this prophecy. Therefore, he traveled from Delphi to the city of Troezen in order to ask King Pittheus,[1] one of the wisest men of his time, to explain its meaning.

King Pittheus immediately understood the mysterious prophecy. He interpreted it to mean that Aegeus should neither drink wine nor make love until he had returned to Athens, because when he next did so, he would father a son. However, Pittheus could not resist the opportunity to have a grandson who would combine the blood of the two major royal families of Greece.[2] Therefore, instead of helping Aegeus, he craftily took advantage of him. He made Aegeus drunk and encouraged him to sleep with his daughter Aethra. Thus, Theseus was conceived in defiance of the oracle's prophecy.[3] Unknown to Aegeus, Poseidon also slept with Aethra that night.

Before returning to Athens, King Aegeus provided for the son Aethra might bear him. With Aethra as his witness, Aegeus secretly hid a sword and a pair of sandals in the hollow beneath a huge rock.[4] He commanded that, when the boy grew strong enough to lift the great rock and remove his father's gifts, Aethra secretly should sent their son with these symbols of his royal birth to his father in Athens. There, Aegeus would recognize and welcome his heir. Meanwhile, Aegeus ordered Aethra to raise their son without telling the boy that Aegeus was his father. Secrecy would prevent his brother Pallas and his sons from discovering the boy's existence and murdering him.

In time, Aethra gave birth to a son, whom she named Theseus. She raised him, fatherless, in his grandfather Pittheus's palace in Troezen. Pittheus told everyone that Theseus's father was Poseidon, since the people of Troezen worshipped Poseidon as the protector of their city.

Theseus first displayed his heroic nature when he was seven years old. Hearing that his cousin,[5] Heracles, was visiting King Pittheus, Theseus brought some friends into the palace in order to meet him. Heracles had taken off his lionskin in order to eat dinner. When the children came upon the lionskin, it looked so alive that everyone except Theseus ran away. Theseus, thinking that it was a real lion, quickly grabbed an axe from one of the attendants, approached the lionskin, and fiercely attacked it.

Theseus grew up to be strong, able, courageous, intelligent, and wise. He became a superb wrestler by using strategy as much as strength to bring him victory. The idea of using intelligence in wrestling was new at that time.[6] Even Heracles depended upon his physical size and strength to make him victorious.

When Theseus was fifteen years old, Aethra brought him to the rock, where she revealed to him his true birth and the instructions of his father Aegeus. Theseus was so strong that he easily lifted the rock. With great pride, he removed the objects his father had hidden there and put them on.[7]

Theseus's courage was as great as his strength. Although he would obey Aegeus's command to go to Athens, he refused to take the safe sea route. Instead, he became determined to choose the perilous land passage from the Peloponnesus across the Isthmus of Corinth to Athens. The land route sheltered such a frightening collection of robbers and murderers that no man dared to rule them. Pittheus tried to dissuade his grandson from this decision by describing each of the predators and his villainous deeds, but without success. Theseus so admired Heracles' heroic deeds that he, too, longed to achieve such fame and honor. He felt that he would disgrace his father Poseidon if he chose to avoid the kind of struggles that Heracles purposely sought. He knew his father in Athens would prefer a son who had the strength and courage to bathe his sword in the blood of public enemies. He wanted his worthy deeds to prove his noble heritage. However, he determined to hurt no man unless he was forced to defend himself.

The first criminal Theseus encountered, in Epidaurus, was the fearsome robber Periphetes, called Corynetes, or "Club-carrier," because his solitary weapon was a huge bronze club. Reputed to be either a son of Hephaestus or of Poseidon, Periphetes was accustomed to murdering all travelers who passed his way. He had directed only one blow at Theseus when he found himself caught in a losing struggle for his life. Theseus was particularly pleased to win Periphetes' club[8] because he could carry it with him ever afterwards as proof of his strength in battle, just as Heracles carried the lionskin.

Next, near Corinth, Theseus met the clever fiend, Sinis, called Pityocamptes or "Pinebender." Sinis forced any traveler he could beat in a fight to help him bend two pine trees until their tops touched the ground. Then, sometimes Sinis forced his victim to hold down the tree tops until his strength disappeared. At other times, Sinis let the pine trees rebound suddenly as soon as his victim had taken hold of them. Either way, the action of the pine trees hurled Sinis's victim through the air to his death. Often Sinis would tie his victim to the bent pine trees. As the two trees would spring upright, the victim would be split in two or would be torn limb from limb, his pieces scattering over the countryside. Theseus wrestled with Sinis, overpowered him, and put him to death in the same manner Sinis had employed with his victims.

Then Theseus killed the wild, huge sow of Crommyon Phaea, an offspring of the terrible monster Typhon and named after the old woman who fed it. It was so ferocious that it killed humans as well as crops and beasts. Theseus initiated this attack, thinking it a noble pursuit to risk his life by assaulting and killing savage beasts.

Afterwards, near Megara, Theseus came upon the scheming robber Sceiron, reputed to be either a son of Pelops, or of Poseidon. Sceiron lived high upon the cliffs which bore his name. After robbing travelers, he enjoyed forcing them to the steep seaward side of the cliff where he compelled them to wash his feet. Once the travelers stooped to do this, Sceiron suddenly would kick them off the cliff down to the sea below. There a giant sea tortoise hungrily waited for Sceiron's human gifts. As Theseus pretended to wash Sceiron's feet, he seized Sceiron by the feet and threw him over his head. Sceiron sailed over the cliff, down to the rocks below, where he, too, was consumed by the hungry tortoise.

Upon reaching Eleusis, Theseus encountered King Cercyon, who forced all travelers to wrestle with him.[9] Once Cercyon pinned his victim beneath him, he would kill him. Until Theseus's arrival, no traveler had survived a wrestling match with Cercyon. However, Theseus lifted the king up into the air and then killed him by slamming his body down upon the ground. Theseus had pitted his wrestling skill against Cercyon's strength and had won.

Soon thereafter, Theseus met the last villain, Damastes or Procrustes, the "Stretcher." Also reputed to be a son of Poseidon, Damastes owned an inn beside the road. He would wait outside, hospitably offering travelers a place to rest. Inside the inn, Damastes kept two beds prepared for his guests, a small one and a large one. He would put short men into the large bed, where he either would attach weights to stretch them, or he would beat them with a hammer until he had made them the same length as the bed. On the other hand, Damastes would put tall men upon the small bed, proceeding to saw off the parts of their bodies that extended over the frame.[10] Theseus slew Damastes by stretching him out upon the large bed until he was even with the bed's length.

Thus, singlehandedly, Theseus made land travel safe between Troezen and Athens. He had earned fame and honor. Now he was ready for King Aegeus to acknowledge him as the lawful heir to the throne of Athens.

1. King Pittheus of Troezen was a son of Pelops and Hippodameia. Pelops was the greatest king of the Peloponnesus and was Theseus's great-grandfather.
2. Like his cousin Heracles, Theseus was the descendant of the greatest families in Greece. Aegeus was related to Erechtheus the Great and the first people who lived in the region of Attica.
3. Aegeus later dies because he thinks his son Theseus is dead. If he had heeded the oracle, he would have had no son, or a different one. This might have prolonged his life.
4. These signs of kingship apply also to the medieval heroes, Arthur and Sigfried.
5. Theseus and Heracles were cousins because Theseus's grandfather (Pittheus) and one of Heracles' grandmothers were both children of Pelops.

6. Theseus invented the *art* of wrestling, and, later, established the instruction of wrestling as a skill. Previously, wrestling had involved strength but not strategy. Being a small man, Theseus needed strategy to bolster his own strength.
7. The ancient Greeks considered this to be Theseus's first heroic deed. They commemorated it with a bronze statue of Athena on the Acropolis of Athens.
8. Heracles also carried a club, one he had made from an entire olive tree.
9. Heracles also wrestled during the course of his labors, his most famous match being against the giant Antaeus.
10. From Procrustes, the word *procrustean* has developed. It refers to any argument which is distorted in order to suit the purposes of the person using it. It may also refer to the arbitrary means a person uses to achieve conformity.

The Cretan Experience

When Theseus arrived in Athens, he found everything in a state of turmoil. Pallas and his fifty sons were threatening Aegeus's rule. The sorceress Medea[1] was living with Aegeus and had given him a son. Being jealous of Theseus's claim to the throne and hearing of his impending arrival in Athens, Medea convinced Aegeus that an enemy was on his way. Aegeus had become so suspicious and fearful that Medea easily persuaded him to let her poison their guest at the feast they planned to hold in his honor.

Theseus attended this feast without disclosing who he was. Yet, in order to give his father an indication of his true identity, when servants placed meat upon the table, Theseus drew out Aegeus's sword as though to slice it.

With horror, Aegeus immediately recognized the stranger's sword as his own. He realized that this stranger was not his enemy but his long-awaited son. No wonder Medea had been so anxious to poison him! As the sudden vision of his son's death flashed through Aegeus' mind, he hurriedly pulled out his own sword and overturned the cup of poison before it reached his son's lips. Aegeus lovingly embraced Theseus and expelled Medea and her son from Athens. Then he publicly acknowledged Theseus as his son and legal heir to the throne.

Because of his heroic accomplishments, the people received Theseus with great joy. However, now that Theseus was heir to the throne, he had to fight Pallas and his sons. Pallas considered his claim to the throne more legitimate than Aegeus's, since Aegeus was an adopted son and, consequently, not related by blood to the royal family of Athens. With the help of an informer, Theseus killed half of the rebels while they were lying in ambush. The rest dispersed and accepted his legitimacy.

Then, considering it necessary to impress the Atheneans with his courage and skill, Theseus volunteered to capture the fearsome Bull of Marathon.[2] This bull created endless destruction by ravaging the countryside and killing whomever it met. Like Heracles, Theseus captured the bull alive and brought it through the streets of Athens so that everyone could see it and acknowledge his own heroism. Then he sacrificed the bull to Apollo.[3]

Shortly thereafter, Minos arrived from Crete for the third Athenian tribute. It was customary for the fourteen victims to be chosen by lot. The atmosphere in Athens was full of dread. The Athenians angrily accused Aegeus of being the cause of their trouble, but immune to their suffering.

Theseus understood these complaints and, therefore, willingly volunteered to be one of the fourteen sacrifices and share the fate of the victims of the lottery. He publicly offered to be devoured by the monster or slain and sacrificed upon the tomb of Androgeus if his courage and skill failed to kill the Minotaur. The Athenians loved him for his courage and honor, but Aegeus did not want to lose his son.

Knowing that none of the victims would ever live to return to Athens, the Athenians had always sent them to Crete in a ship bearing a black sail, symbolizing their death. Because Theseus was so confident that he would kill the Minotaur, Aegeus gave the captain of the ship a white sail, to be hoisted in place of the black one upon the return voyage if Theseus's mission were successful.

Aided by Athena and Boreas, the north wind, the dark-prowed ship carrying King Minos, Theseus, and the other thirteen Athenian captives sailed swiftly toward the shores of Crete. Then Eros, son of gold-wreathed Aphrodite, conquered Minos's heart with his love-inspiring arrows. Then the Cretan king no longer could resist one of the Athenian maidens and lovingly touched her beautiful face. In distress, the maiden called upon Theseus to protect her from her royal captor.

Theseus's face darkened with rage. Carefully controlling his fury, he addressed King Minos:

"Son of Olympian Zeus, the Fates will determine our future. You may be an esteemed king of divine descent, but I myself claim a father among the deathless gods, one who, as your father's brother, also wields great power. So, restrain your amorous nature and ignore these Athenian maidens. Otherwise you will force a son of the Earthshaker to display his power."[4]

All who listened to Theseus's courageous words stood in silent wonder at his daring. How would the Lord of Cnossus respond to his bold captive?

Minos, always a clever king, cloaked his anger and said, "Father Zeus, far-seeing and loud-thundering Lord of Olympus, hear my plea. If I am your son by Europa, whom you carried to Crete and married, then prove it with a divine sign. Let your lightning bolt flash, and let your thunder roar in the presence of shining Helius, as an indisputable sign of your paternity.

"As for you, Theseus of Athens, if Zeus, who delights in thunder, answers my prayers, prepare to prove that you are the child you say your mother bore to the great Earthshaker.[5] Notice the golden signet ring I am removing from my finger. Watch closely as I toss it overboard into the depths of the boundless dark sea. If you are indeed a son of deathless Poseidon, as you declare yourself to be, then you will have no fear as you dive into these fathomless waters and swim down to your great father's palace. No doubt the Lord of the Sea will help you recover my ring."

Loud-thundering Zeus listened with pride to his clever son's prayer and could not resist acknowledging his paternity. He blazed his lightning across the noonday sky so that all who saw it would honor Minos, his great mortal son.

The King of Crete smiled, delighted with this divine acknowledgement. His eyes sparkled their challenge as he said: "Theseus, you have seen Olympian Zeus respond to my claim. Now it is your turn. Dive into the roaring sea after my glittering gift and return it to me with the Sea Lord's blessing."

Theseus did not refuse the invitation, but immediately and confidently plunged off the deck into the sea. Minos concealed his surprise and ordered the seamen to turn the ship into the wind in order to hold it nearby. However, Boreas, the north wind, blew the ship quickly onward, while the Athenian captives tearfully mourned the certain death of their hero.

Meanwhile, the dolphins carried Theseus down to his father's palace in the depths of the sea. There he saw the dancing Nereïds and his father's regal wife Amphitrite. The Queen of the Sea covered him with a purple linen robe, lay a shimmering wreath upon his hair, and placed Minos's ring in his hand.

Theseus then swam to the surface of the sea and emerged completely dry by the stern of the dark ship. The Athenian captives cheered his victory and thanked the Earthshaker for his safe return, while Minos beheld his gleaming god-given attire with great awe. The Cretan king respectfully accepted his signet ring and sadly gave up his claim to the Athenian maiden. The captive Theseus was indeed the great Earthshaker's son and the treasure of Athens.

At this time each year, Minos held athletic games in memory of his son, Androgeus. Theseus asked to participate and was granted permission to do so. Minos's daughter, Ariadne, fell in love with Theseus as she watched him surpass all other athletes in strength. She could not bear the thought that such an impressive youth soon would be sacrificed to the Minotaur. Therefore, after the contests, Ariadne secretly approached Theseus and offered to help him if he would promise to take her to

Athens as his wife. When Theseus agreed, Ariadne begged Daedalus for a means to save Theseus. Daedalus gave her a ball of thread and suggested an ingenious way for Theseus to escape.

When the time came for the fourteen Athenian captives to enter the Labyrinth, Ariadne gave Theseus the ball of thread along with Daedalus's instructions.

Upon entering the Labyrinth, Theseus fastened one end of the ball of thread to the door and unrolled it as he followed the winding passages toward the Minotaur. However he became weary and discouraged by the endlessly twisting and turning paths. He had given up ever finding the Minotaur, when, suddenly, he spied his enemy within arm's reach.

As soon as the Minotaur caught the scent of the stranger, it lowered its head and hurled itself with full strength upon him. Theseus instinctively used his wrestling skills to combat his enemy. He grabbed the Minotaur by its horns and threw the ferocious monster to the ground. Then he beat it to death with his fists.

Elated with his victory, Theseus eagerly rewound the ball of thread and followed its lead to the entrance of the Labyrinth, where the other captives had been anxiously awaiting his return.[6] Together, they left the Labyrinth, met Ariadne, and silently located their ship. Then, under cover of darkness, they sailed away to the island of Naxos.

When Minos heard rumors that the Athenians had escaped, he rushed down to the waterfront. He was amazed to find that their ship was no longer moored in the harbor. However, his astonishment became outrage when he learned that, before their flight, the Athenians had punctured his entire fleet. Pursuit was now impossible.

All writers agree that Theseus deserted Ariadne and returned to Athens without her.[7] Many writers say that Theseus left Ariadne on the island of Naxos where either loud-roaring Dionysus married the forsaken princess and carried her off to the island of Lemnos, or she married a priest of the ivy-wreathed god and remained on the island of Naxos.

When Theseus's ship approached the coast of Greece, it was still bearing the black sail. Aegeus, who anxiously was awaiting its appearance, saw the black sail upon the horizon. Grief-stricken at the thought of his son's death, Aegeus hurled himself off the Acropolis to his death.[8]

With the death of Aegeus, Theseus became king of Athens. He refused to have sole power, only remaining in charge of waging war and preserving the law. He united the different villages surrounding Athens into a city-state and persuaded many people to move there by offering them the freedom and privileges of natural born citizens. He gave the farmers, the craftsmen, and the noblemen equal voices in the government. Finally, just as Heracles had instituted the Olympic Games in honor of Zeus, Theseus established the Isthmian Games in honor of Poseidon. Theseus became as great a king as he had been a hero.

1. The background information regarding Medea's arrival in Athens is found in the myth of Jason and The Golden Fleece, Section IV, The Heroes. Aegeus agreed to give her refuge if she gave him a son, which she did.
2. The capture of the Cretan Bull was one of Heracles' labors (See myth of Heracles, Section IV, The Heroes). This bull was the father of the Minotaur. After Eurystheus saw the bull, Heracles released it. Because it settled near Marathon, it became known as the Bull of Marathon.
3. Presumably, Theseus sacrificed the bull to Apollo rather than to Poseidon, because Apollo tended sacred herds of cattle.
4. These leaders contested for preeminence by competing with "magic tricks" or "miracles." Each god helped his son. It is not clear that one of these two was the winner, but neither lost. When Moses and Pharaoh competed, Moses won. The idea was customary among ancient peoples.
5. The Greek heroes traditionally have both a mortal father and an immortal father in order to satisfy the need for them to be human beings who are able to accomplish extraordinary deeds. Their mortal parents make them real men who live in the real world. Their immortal fathers (Zeus, or in the case of Theseus, Poseidon) may not be their fathers at all. These gods may be attributed to the heroes in order to account for the extraordinary tasks they are able to perform.
6. According to some writers, who refused to accept miracles, Theseus defeated a general whom King Minos hated, in a wrestling match. Minos was so delighted that he released Theseus and the other Athenian prisoners and cancelled all further tribute from Athens.
7. Two explanations relate Ariadne's death. Some writers say that Theseus left her in Crete, where she hanged herself since Theseus and her family had abandoned her. Others say that she died of a broken heart on Naxos because Theseus had fallen in love with a nymph.
8. Three other explanations are offered for the black sail and Aegeus' death. One involves Theseus' excitement over his safe return. One involves the curse Ariadne placed upon Theseus as revenge for her abandonment. Finally, the Athenians write that Aegeus tripped because he ran too quickly, thus absolving their hero Theseus of any blame.

The Late Years

During the last part of his life, Theseus did many foolish things that brought unhappiness to himself and to Athens. First, he organized an expedition against the Amazons[1] in which he abducted their queen Antiope.[2] To avenge the abduction, the Amazons attacked Athens but were defeated. Later, Antiope bore Theseus a son, Hippolytus.

Theseus left Antiope in order to marry Ariadne's sister, Phaedra. In order for Phaedra's children to become the legal heirs to the throne of Athens, Theseus sent Hippolytus to Troezen, where he was to be reared to become the successor to Theseus's aged grandfather, King Pittheus.

Shortly thereafter, Theseus killed Pallas and the last of his sons for their attempt to assassinate him. Some writers say that Theseus was tried for murder by an Athenian court but was acquitted because the court considered his crime justified.[3] Other writers say that, as punishment for his crime, the Athenian court exiled Theseus from Athens for one year, and that, consequently, he took Phaedra with him to Troezen.

It was in Troezen that Phaedra met Hippolytus and fell in love with him. Because Hippolytus was her stepson, she felt ashamed of her feelings, but nevertheless, she could not resist her passion for him. Hippolytus, in turn, could not love her because she was his stepmother. In fact, Hippolytus did not love any woman. He only loved hunting and was dedicated to the worship of Artemis, who was the goddess of the hunt and of chastity.

Phaedra became obsessed with the fear that Hippolytus would tell his father about her passion for him. Therefore, she devised a cunning scheme that would punish Hippolytus for his rejection of her. She wrote Theseus a note that stated that she had been forced to take her own life because Hippolytus had raped her. Then, clutching the note, she hanged herself.

Theseus returned home to find his wife dead. He read the letter, believed Phaedra, and was filled with rage against Hippolytus. Refusing to listen to anyone else's point of view, Theseus immediately banished his son from Athens and Troezen and prayed that his father Poseidon would kill Hippolytus.

The Lord of the Sea fulfilled Theseus's wish. While Hippolytus was driving his chariot along the seashore, away from Troezen into exile, Poseidon sent forth another bull from the sea. This beast terrorized the horses that were pulling Hippolytus's chariot. The horses bucked and reared in spite of Hippolytus's expertise as a horseman. They finally upset the chariot and tossed Hippolytus to the ground. Hippolytus became entangled in the reins, and the hysterical horses dragged him to his death.[4] Thereafter, Theseus belatedly realized his mistake and mourned the death of his son. Theseus then returned to Athens.

In order to meet the hero Theseus and to test his courage, King Peirithoüs[5] led a small group of men that stole a herd of oxen grazing near the walls of Athens. However, instead of killing Peirithoüs, Theseus was so impressed with his courage that they pledged eternal friendship. Thereafter the two kings were inseparable.

Searching for adventure, Theseus and Peirithoüs decided to kidnap and marry daughters of Zeus. Together they went to Sparta, where they captured twelve year old Helen.[6] They drew lots to see whose wife she would become. Theseus, who was fifty years old at this time, won Helen as his bride by lot, but, because of her youth, he left her to be reared by his mother in Aphidnae, a town near Marathon, until she was old enough to marry.

Peirithoüs then decided to abduct Persephone, the beautiful queen of the Underworld. The two men were able to enter the Underworld, but grim Hades quickly conquered them with a trick. Pretending to offer them something to eat and drink, he invited them to be seated. He maneuvered them into the Seat of Lethe (Forgetfulness) to which they became permanently attached. They were bound to it by coils of snakes. Their flesh stuck to it. Try as they would, neither could free himself. Soon, they both forgot the world they had left.[7]

Peirithoüs remained in the land of Hades, forever bound to the Chair of Forgetfulness. Theseus, however, was saved from his friend's fate by Heracles, who rescued him when he entered the Underworld in order to perform his last labor. Seeing Heracles appear suddenly before them reminded the two men of their former lives and of their hopeless enslavement. Desperately they stretched their arms out to him, imploring him to save them. Heracles was able to pull Theseus free, but when he tried to rescue Peirithoüs the earth shook. Interpreting this to mean that the gods were determined to punish Peirithoüs, Heracles sadly let go of his hand.

While Theseus was imprisoned in the Underworld, Helen's brothers, Castor and Polydeuces, invaded Athens with the strong Spartan army in order to rescue their sister. Not finding her there, they angrily burnt and destroyed all of Attica. Fearing the destruction of Athens, Menestheus[8] counseled the Athenians to befriend the invaders. It was good advice. Castor and Polydeuces spared the city and placed the wise Menestheus upon the throne of Athens. When Helen's brothers found her with Theseus's mother Aethra, at Aphidnae, they rescued Helen, enslaved Aethra as her servant, and burned the town to the ground. Then they returned to Sparta.

Thus when Theseus returned home, many Athenians hated him for causing the Spartan invasion, and would not permit him to regain his throne. Fearing for his life, he left Athens for the island of Scyrus, where he hoped to be received with hospitality by its king, Lycomedes. However, he met with treachery instead. Hoping to gain favor with Menestheus and being jealous of Theseus's great reputation, Lycomedes decided to kill his guest. On the pretense of showing Theseus an impressive view, Lycomedes took him high above the sea to a rocky area, where he pushed him off the cliff to his death.

Years later, in the battle of Marathon, many Athenians thought they saw Theseus leading them to victory against the Persians. During the Persian Wars, the oracle of Apollo at Delphi commanded the Athenians to return Theseus's bones to Athens and honor them. Cimon, the conqueror of Scyrus, tried to locate Theseus's grave. He saw an eagle picking and scraping away at a mound of dirt, and thinking that this might be a divine sign, decided to search there. He uncovered a tomb containing the body of a large man that had been buried with a bronze spear and a sword. Cimon returned to Athens with the body and the weapons. The Athenians received these items with sacrifices and celebrations. They forgave Theseus's errors of judgment that had brought war to Athens. They remembered only the heroism of his life and the glory of his kingdom.

1. The Amazons were a matriarchal society. They lived on the southern shores of the Black Sea and practiced the art of war. The right breast of each woman was removed so that it would not interfere with her ability to aim weapons and fight in wars.

2. Some writers say that the Amazon queen was named Hippolyte.
3. Before Theseus's acquittal, anyone who killed someone either was forced into exile for about eight years (the reign of the sacred king) or was killed in a manner that fit his crime.
4. Some writers say that Theseus learned the truth from Artemis in time to bury Hippolytus with honor. Other writers say that Apollo's son, Asclepius, the great physician, returned Hippolytus to life, and, in return for this expertise, Zeus killed him.
5. Peirithoüs was the son of Ixion, one of the three greatest Greek criminals. Ixion murdered his father-in-law by throwing him into a fiery pit, and later he tried to seduce Hera. The son appears to have resembled his father in character.
6. Helen, later of Troy.
7. Classical Greeks moved Theseus's Underworld adventure to Egypt, keeping the names of Hades, Persephone, and Cerberus, in order to make this adventure one which could actually have occurred.
8. Menestheus is a descendant of the royal house of Athens, through Erechtheus.

REFLECTIONS

1. Why does Theseus volunteer to kill the Minotaur?
   a. to please others?
   b. love of adventure?
   c. personal fame and glory?
   d. to improve society?
   e. sense of justice?
2. Why does Theseus join Peirithoüs in his venture to abduct Persephone?
   a. desire to please Peirithoüs?
   b. love of adventure?
   c. personal fame and glory?
   d. other?
3. How does the death of Theseus affect his heroic stature?
4. To what extent should a leader's private life affect his public position?
5. Discuss whether you would want Theseus as your:
   a. father
   b. friend
   c. neighbor
   d. teacher
   e. president
6. Who is the more sympathetic character: Theseus or Heracles? Explain.
7. Become Theseus. Keep a diary or journal describing any one of the following events:
   a. lottery for tribute to Minos
   b. sea voyage to Crete
   c. battle with Minotaur
   d. abandonment of Ariadne
   e. return to Athens

35 Psyche and Eros

INTRODUCTION

The story of Psyche and Eros is found only in one source, a book called *The Golden Ass* by the Roman, Lucius Apuleius. It is more of a folk tale or a fairy tale than a myth, and it is not Greek. It is included here because it is a good story, and scholars who are interested in human behavior have given it unusual attention.

Psyche and the Greek heroes were similar in some ways, yet different in other significant ways. Consider Psyche's personality, the nature of her tasks, and the role of the gods. At the end of the story, compare these aspects to any of the myths about Greek heroes. The comparison will point up the distinction between a myth and other types of stories.

ANTICIPATIONS

1. Many young people feel that they are capable at a fairly early age of establishing and sustaining a close relationship with a boy friend or girl friend. During this time, sexual attraction may be understood or felt as love. How does one make the distinction between sexual attraction and love?
2. In this tale, it is prophesied that Psyche's fate will be to marry a serpent. Why do you think that particular animal was selected to be Psyche's mate?

THE TALE

There was once a king who had three daughters. Two of them were pretty, but the third, Psyche, was a breathtaking beauty. People came from all over in droves to see her face. So extraordinarily beautiful was she that people began to call her "the new Aphrodite." Soon, she became so famous that people began to neglect the goddess Aphrodite. Instead of offering her sacrifices, they worshipped Psyche instead. This made the goddess angry and she called her winged son, Eros, to her side.

"My dear child," she said, "revenge the injury that has been done to me. Pierce the heart of Psyche with your love-inspiring arrows so that she may fall in love with the most miserable creature living. Make sure that he is the poorest, the ugliest, and the most wretched man imaginable."

Meanwhile, Psyche, with all her marvelous beauty praised by everyone, was not courted by any man. Her two sisters were royally married to two kings, but Psyche sat home alone. She lamented her solitary life and was disquieted in mind and body. Although she pleased the world, she hated her own beauty.

Her father, suspecting the gods of envying her, went to the oracle of Apollo at Delphi, where he prayed and offered sacrifices in exchange for a husband for his daughter. The oracle told the king that Psyche would not have a mortal husband, but would marry a winged serpent feared even by the gods. She should be set upon a rock on a mountain-top to await the beast. Upon hearing this prophecy, the king returned home, sad and sorrowful. Psyche's family wept together and spent their days in sorrow.

The time approached for Psyche's marriage. Black torches were lighted, and, instead of singing, everyone was moaning. Psyche was extremely unhappy. Finally, she turned upon her father and mother and cried, "Why do you waste your time crying for me? You see the reward for my beauty? Take me to what fortune has named as my destiny. Place me on the top of the rock. I want to see my husband. Why should I delay?"

Her family pitied Psyche and brought her to the rock on a high hill, then departed. Torches were put out and the people went home. The miserable parents, consumed with sorrow, resigned themselves to everlasting darkness.

Poor Psyche, alone and weeping on top of her rock, was blown by the gentle air of Zephyrus, the west wind. She was carried from the hill by him to a deep valley where she was placed upon a bed of sweet flowers. Here she slept and rose with a peaceful mind. She saw around her a pleasant forest with a river as clear as crystal. In the middle of the wood was a handsome mansion. It was so finely wrought that it seemed to have been built by Hephaestus, the renowned smith. The pavement was made of precious stones, and every room glittered with treasures.

Psyche decided to enter the house, and after examining the riches, noticed there was no lock to keep the treasures safe. Suddenly, she heard a voice that said, "Why do you marvel at such great riches? They are all for you. Whatever you want, you shall have. We whose voices you hear will be your servants and will tend to any desire you have. We shall also serve you royal meats and great delicacies."

Psyche bathed herself and lay upon the bed. Then she noticed a table laden with all sorts of divine meats and great foods. When she sat down, all sorts of unusual food and wines were brought in, not by a person, but, it seemed to her, by a wind, for she could see no body. She could only hear voices on every side. Some of these voices sang to her; invisibly, another played a harp. However, Psyche saw no one.

After she enjoyed all these pleasures, Psyche went to bed. She was fearful because she was alone. An unknown, unseen husband came to her bed and loved her, but he rose in the morning before daylight and departed. Psyche never saw his face.

The servants continued to present her with everything she desired including music. During the time that Psyche was in this place of pleasure, her parents wept and lamented, and her two sisters tried to comfort them.

The following night, Psyche's husband spoke to her, saying, "Your sisters think you are dead. They are returning to the rock where they left you. Beware! Do not talk with them. If you do, you will bring great sorrow to me and to yourself." Psyche, hearing her husband, did as he commanded.

When he had left and the night passed away, Psyche lamented and cried all the following day. She thought that now she was past all hope of comfort. Virtually imprisoned and deprived of human conversation, she had been commanded not to aid her sorrowful sisters, or even to see them. Thus she wept all day and went to bed without dinner.

That night, her husband was angry. "If all you can do is to weep," he cried, "Go! Look upon your sisters, but remember my warning." Psyche begged her husband to grant her permission to speak with them and comfort them.

At length he was contented, and he told Psyche to give her sisters as much gold and jewels as she wished. "However," he added, "do not be moved by your sisters' advice or by your curiosity. If you disobey you will deprive yourself of all this wealth."

Psyche thanked him and said, "Sweet husband, I would rather die than separate from you. For whoever you are, I love you as if you were love-inspiring Eros. I would be so happy if you could command your servant, Zephyrus, the west wind, to bring my sisters down into the valley as he brought me."

Then she kissed him, and he agreed to her wish. When morning came, he had departed as usual.

Her sisters had by now reached the rock where they had last seen Psyche, and, not finding her there, they wept. They called their sister by her name and when Psyche heard their cries, she commanded Zephyrus to bring them to her. With gentle breezes, he lifted them up and placed them softly in the valley.

All three cried with joy when they were reunited. "Come into our palace," said Psyche. She showed them the treasures and they, too, heard the voices who were Psyche's servants, and who drew her bath and prepared her meal.

When they had eaten every delicacy, they became envious of Psyche. One of them demanded to know her husband's name. However, Psyche, remembering the promise she had made to her husband, pretended that he was a handsome young man with blonde hair. Before she divulged too much, she filled their laps with gold, silver, and jewels. Then she commanded Zephyrus to carry them away.

After the wind took them back to the mountain, they returned home muttering, "It is wrong that we, the elder two sisters, are married to ordinary husbands, whereas our younger sister has so much treasure. What great jewels! What flattering robes, what gems were there! She must be married to a god. No one but a goddess could have winds that obey her or voices to serve her!"

Both sisters compared their own husbands to the unseen husband of Psyche and began to plot ways to harm her. They hid the treasures she gave them, and in front of their parents, they wept false tears. When their father and mother saw them lament, their own grief doubled. The evil sisters, however, devised schemes whereby they could destroy their sister.

Meanwhile, Psyche's husband warned her that her sisters intended to do harm to her and would insist that she behold his face. "If this once happens," he said, "you will see me no more. Therefore, if these nasty hags do come again, do not talk to them. Let them speak what they will. If you can restrain yourself and have no communication about me to them, the young and tender child in your womb will be born an immortal god, but otherwise it will be a mortal creature."

"Dear husband," Psyche answered, "you have experienced my faith and honesty all this time. Why do you question that I will change now? Therefore, command your west wind, Zephyrus, that he may do as he did before, and I may comfort myself with the sight of my sisters."

Her husband yielded to his wife once more and departed in the morning as was his custom.

The sisters arrived upon the rock and, deciding not to wait for Zephyrus, they leaped down, daringly, from the hill themselves. Zephyrus, however, according to divine command, brought them down and placed them in the valley without any harm.

The sisters then burst into the palace without leave. They flattered

Psyche for the treasure she had given them. Craftily, they told her, "We know the infant you nourish within you will be like his parents, and if that is true, there is no doubt that a new god shall be born."

Thus, little by little, they won Psyche's confidence. Gradually, they demanded to know who her husband was and of what parentage. Instead of answering them honestly, Psyche told them that her husband was a middle-aged, somewhat gray-haired merchant. Quickly, she filled their laps full of gold and silver and bade Zephyrus to bear them away.

The sisters could not understand how Psyche could have told them that her husband was a young man one time and a middle-aged man another. Either she had lied, they decided, or else she had never seen him. They reminded Psyche of the oracle's prophecy that she would marry a fierce serpent.

"We will protect you," they told her, "and you will live with us when you have had your child. Otherwise, you will both be swallowed by this serpent."

The fearful words drove the promise Psyche had made to her husband out of her mind. She thanked her evil sisters and admitted that she had never seen the shape of her husband. Because he disappeared by day, she had reason to suspect he was a beast. "Therefore, my loving sisters," said Psyche, "if you have any wholesome remedy for me in my danger, give it to me at once."

One of them said, "Take a sharp knife and put it under the pillow of your bed. See that you also have an oil lamp hidden. When he comes to your bed to sleep, arise secretly, and with your bare feet, go and take your lamp. With the knife in your right hand, cut off the head of the poisonous serpent. After he is dead, we will marry you to a handome man." Then the west wind again bore them back to their rock.

Once Psyche was alone, her mind tossed like the sea waves. She wavered and hesitated; she doubted and feared. Soon after her husband came and kissed her, he fell asleep.

Then Psyche took hold of the lamp and the knife. As she approached the bedside, she saw the sweetest of all beasts, love-inspiring Eros, himself. When Psyche saw such a glorious body, she fell upon her knees, trembling with fear and love. Her husband was, indeed, the god, Eros. His fair hair, his quiver of bow and arrows which lay at his feet, everything about him was god-like. Filled with curiosity, Psyche took one of the arrows out of the quiver and accidentally pricked herself. The arrow inflamed her love. She kissed Eros again and again.

But alas! While Psyche burned with love for Eros, and as she stared at his face, a drop of burning oil from the lamp fell upon the right shoulder of the god.

Eros awakened, realized that Psyche had broken her promise and fled without a word from his unhappy wife. She reached up to catch him by the right thigh and held him fast as he flew above her. Finally, she had to let him go, and she fell, exhausted, upon the ground.

Eros lighted on the top of a cypress tree and angrily told her, "I disregarded my mother Aphrodite's command to have you marry a man of base and miserable condition. Indeed, I came from Mount Olympus to love you myself. Did I seem like a beast to you that you should want to cut off my head with a knife? I, who have loved you so well? Your sisters will be punished for their part in this. As for you, your punishment will be my absence."

When he spoke these words, he flew into the air. Psyche gazed after her husband until she could see him no longer, weeping piteously. Then she threw herself into the nearest river, but did not drown. Fearful of retribution from Eros, the river tossed her upon its bank.

The Shepherd God, Pan, who was teaching Echo songs, saw Psyche's misery. He counseled her to continue adoring Eros and to win him back by a promise of service.

Psyche decided to go to the city where one of her sisters lived with her husband. Upon seeing her sister, she reminded her of her evil advice to kill love-inspiring Eros. She told her sister what had befallen her when she tried to see her husband. Psyche added that her own punishment was that Eros would marry her sister.

Leaving Psyche, her vain, jealous sister went to the mountaintop on which Psyche originally was left and called Eros to take her as his more worthy wife. She tried to fly off from the mountain, but was dashed by the rocks when she fell, headfirst, into the valley. The birds and wild beasts fed upon her, a fate which she richly deserved. The same fate befell Psyche's other sister.

Psyche began to travel around the country seeking her husband, Eros, but she could not find him. He was in his mother's room, nursing the wound which the oil had left.

A white gull found Eros's mother, golden Aphrodite. It told her that her son had been burned and was in danger of death. Aphrodite begged to learn the name of Eros's love. "Madame," said the bird, "I know only that she is called Psyche." On hearing this, golden Aphrodite began to search for Psyche in order to punish her.

Fair-wreathed Demeter warned Psyche of the search. Psyche, grateful, asked the Great Goddess if she would hide her among the sheaves of corn until Aphrodite's anger had passed. Great Demeter, however, had made a peace treaty with golden Aphrodite and refused to permit Psyche to live in the temple with her.

Then Psyche, driven by despair to a forest within a valley, saw a temple, which she approached. Riches and letters of gold were inscribed with the name of golden-throned Hera, to whom they were dedicated. Psyche knelt down and begged the Queen of Olympus to help her.

Great Hera heard Psyche's prayers and appeared before her. Hera said that she would gladly help her but did not wish to do anything contrary to the will of golden-wreathed Aphrodite. Psyche was now cast off by Hera as well as by Demeter. She did not know where to go or what to do.

She decided to pray to Aphrodite for help. Meanwhile, golden Aphrodite was also searching for Psyche. Imploring Hermes, the Wayfinder, to conduct a worldwide search for the girl, she told him that should any man find Psyche, Aphrodite would reward him with seven sweet kisses.

When the Wayfinder announced this reward, every mortal was inflamed with desire to search for Psyche. However, Psyche was discovered by one of golden Aphrodite's servants, who angrily dragged her by the hair before the goddess.

Aphrodite decided to torment Psyche cruelly. She tore her dress and threw her to the ground. Then she took quantities of millet, barley, poppy seed, wheat, lentils, and beans and mixed them together. She told Psyche that if she ever expected to have a husband, she must separate all the grains into piles and be finished by nightfall. However, Psyche sat still and did nothing. The task seemed completely beyond her ability.

A small ant took pity on Psyche and called upon his friends to help her by dividing the grain.

When golden Aphrodite saw that the grains had been divided, she told Psyche that she didn't believe that this was the work of Psyche alone, but rather of her lover's. She said to Psyche, "See that forest that extends to the river? There are great, golden sheep there. I command that you go and bring back some of their fleece." Psyche arose, not to obey this command, but to throw herself into the river to end her sorrow.

However, a divinely inspired green reed told her to wait until the sheep had drunk at the river. Then, it said, they would lie under the bushes, and she could easily gather their gold fleece.

When Psyche had accomplished this task, gold-wreathed Aphrodite announced that she did not believe that Psyche had performed this labor by herself. Aphrodite now gave Psyche a vessel and demanded that she bring it back from the summit of a nearby mountain, filled with water from the river that flowed into the great River Styx.

Psyche climbed to the summit of the mountain, no longer caring whether she lived or died. When she approached the ridge, she realized the impossibility of her task. Terrible dragons guarded a fountain of water that gushed into the valley below. The black waters warned her to run away, or she would be killed.

Olympian Zeus's bird, the eagle, took pity on Psyche. Flying above the cruel dragons to Psyche, the eagle took the vessel, filled it with the river's black water, and then returned the filled vessel to her.

Joyfully, Psyche returned to golden Aphrodite and gave her the vessel filled with black river water. Still, Aphrodite was not satisfied.

"You must be a witch to be able to do all these things by yourself," she said. "You will do one more thing for me. Take this box and go down to Persephone in the Underworld. I want her to send me a little of her beauty because I've lost some of my beauty since Eros became ill. But return quickly, as I must dress and go to the theater of the gods."

Psyche was now certain that all her good fortune had ended. She did not see how she could ever return from the Underworld. So without hesitation, she climbed a high tower in order to throw herself off, thinking that this was the easiest way to reach the Underworld. But the tower spoke to her and said, "Poor girl! Why do you want to kill yourself? Don't you know that once you are dead, you can never return to life?"

"You are not far from the city of Sparta," it said. "There you will find the hill, Taenarus, where you will see a road that leads down to the palace of grim Hades.

"But be careful that you do not make the journey empty-handed," the tower went on. "Take with you two cakes made of barley and honey in your hands, and put two obols in your mouth. When you have gone a long way along this road, you will see a lame ass carrying wood, driven by a lame man. This man will ask you to give him the sticks that have fallen to the ground. You must pass by and not help him.

"In time," the tower continued, "you will come to the great river of the Underworld, the River Styx, where Charon is the ferryman. You will have to pay him the fare of one obol before he will take you across the river. Let him take this coin from your mouth. Then, as you sit in Charon's boat, you will see an old man swimming in the river, reaching out to you for help. Ignore his pitiful cry.

"Once across the river, you will see some old women spinning. They will ask you to help them. Do not help them," the tower warned. "For all of these are traps designed by golden Aphrodite to make you drop one of your cakes. Do not think that keeping these cakes is a trivial thing, for if you lose one of them, you will never again be able to return to the land of the living.

"Next," said the tower, "you will see a great and marvelous three-headed dog, Cerberus. Day and night he lives by the gates of the Underworld, determining who may enter and who may leave. If you give him one of your two cakes, he will not harm you and will let you enter."

The tower continued, "When you reach grim Hades' palace, his queen, fair Persephone, will entertain you with delicious meat and drink. However, you must sit upon the ground and request only brown bread," the tower advised.

"Then, declare your message and receive whatever beauty the goddess gives you. Upon your return to the world of the living persuade Cerberus to permit your return by feeding him the second cake. In order to cross the River Styx, give your second obol to the boatman, Charon. Then return to the upper world by the road you originally took. Most important of all," the tower warned, "do not look into the box fair Persephone gives you and do not be curious about the treasure of divine beauty."

Thus the tower spoke to Psyche and advised her. Immediately, she took two obols and two cakes and journeyed toward the Underworld. She passed the lame ass, paid Charon one obol, ignored the old man swimming in the river, refused to help the women spinning, and filled Cerberus's greedy mouth with a honey-cake.

Upon reaching Queen Persephone's chamber, she refused to sit in a royal seat or to eat delicious food. Instead, she knelt at the goddess's feet, ate coarse bread, and delivered her message. After receiving the sealed box, she returned to the world of the living by feeding Cerberus the second cake and paying Charon with the second coin.

When Psyche returned to earth, she decided to take some of the divine beauty to make herself more beautiful and to please her husband. However, when she opened the box, she could find no beauty within it. Instead, a deadly sleep invaded her body and she fell to the ground as if lifeless.

By this time, Eros's wounds had healed. Unable to endure Psyche's absence any longer, the god flew toward his loving wife. When he found her, he wiped away the deadly sleep and helped her deliver the box to his mother.

Having fulfilled all her labors, Psyche's reward was that Eros fell more and more in love with her. The gods prepared a marriage feast. Olympian Zeus commanded Hermes the Wayfinder to bring Psyche to Mount Olympus. When she arrived, Zeus gave her a cup and said, "Drink from this cup of immortality, Psyche, so that you will become immortal, and so that Eros will remain your eternal husband."

Thus Psyche and Eros were married. Together, in time, they had a child named Pleasure.

REFLECTIONS

1. Contrast Psyche's personality with the personalities of Heracles and Perseus.
2. Contrast Psyche's tasks with those of Heracles and Perseus.
3. Compare Aphrodite in this story with Hera in the myth of Heracles.
4. Why is this story more like a fairy tale than like a myth?
5. Why doesn't Eros tell Psyche who he is?
6. Take one scene from this story and dramatize it.

36 Jason

The voyage of the Argo provided one of the few occasions on which the independent Mycenaean kings united in a common effort to bring about trade with nations near the Black Sea. As was the case in their later voyage to Ilium, economic issues were important enough to motivate these kings to submit to group decisions. Sometime between 1300–1200 B.C., about fifty representatives from every palace-state accompanied Jason on the voyage. The historical foundation for this myth was probably the desire to obtain the precious stone, amber, rather than any supposed golden fleece.

Jason did not appear to possess *aretē*, (excellence) in the conventional sense. He was not the independent, aggressive type of hero that both Heracles and Theseus were. His skills were organization and delegation. He was able to assemble the greatest heroes of his time and take them on a long voyage with a minimum of rivalry and dissension among them.

Jason treated Medea as he treated the heroes: he let her do what she did best. Medea's great talent, however, was magic, and Jason's failure as a human being was in his assumption that he and his quest were worth the evil that was caused by her magic. His fault was *hybris*; his permissive attitude toward Medea's atrocities reflected an exaggerated opinion of his own importance.

Jason's ambition knew no bounds. Later, ungratefully and without thought, he cast off Medea, to marry a young, beautiful princess who was socially more acceptable and politically more advantageous. His complete insensitivity to Medea's feelings became Jason's *áte*, (temporary madness) and led to the destruction of everything he loved, including his reputation.

Medea, too, became a victim of *hybris*. She fell madly in love. Self-confident and proud of her witchcraft, she did not hesitate to perform the most vile deeds in the service of her passion for Jason. *Hybris* made her arrogant. Nothing was sacred except her love for Jason. When Jason deserted her, she became equally mad with hatred. These passionate emotions were *átē* and caused her to murder innocent people, including her own children.

It is possible to blame Jason's and Medea's behavior upon Hera, for Hera used Jason to avenge Pelias's insult to her honor. However, this view makes Jason and Medea mere puppets in the hands of powerful immortal deities. Again, as with Meleager, such an interpretation robs the myth of its vitality and is not an accurate representation of the view of mortal man held by the ancient Greeks. Hera never helps Jason more than he himself, or luck, could have helped him. Medea, of course, could have fallen in love with Jason without Aphrodite's help. To a large extent, the gods merely represent the emotions and ideas of Jason and Medea. Jason and Medea were responsible for their own actions, even though their fate, given the nature of their personalities, was inevitable.

THE MYTH

Jason was the son of Aeson who was the rightful king of Iolcus in Thessaly. However, Aeson's brother, Pelias, had usurped the throne. Failing to have any son, Pelias feared that Aeson, or Jason as son of Aeson, might reclaim the throne.

As soon as Jason was born, his parents, fearing that Pelias would kill him, pretended that he had died, and they darkened their home as if in mourning. Secretly, they sent him away at night, clothed in purple, to be reared by the famous teacher, the immortal Centaur Cheiron.[1] There he lived for twenty years.

At the time that Jason was growing into young manhood, Pelias consulted an oracle, which warned him of a dreadful fate: his death would be near if a stranger came toward him with one foot bare.[2] At first, Pelias did not understand the oracle. However, while he was performing the annual sacrifice to Poseidon, its meaning became clear.

All the citizens of Iolcus and the surrounding countryside were invited to the sacrifice to the Earthshaker. Golden-throned Hera waited near the Evenus River, disguised as an old crone, testing all strangers to see if they would offer to carry her across its swollen waters. No one offered until Jason, arriving from Cheiron's cave on Mount Pelion, did so. Golden-throned Hera, angry at Pelias for neglecting to sacrifice to her as well as to Poseidon, caused Jason to lose one sandal in the muddy river bank. In order to arrive promptly at the sacrifice, he hurried on without it.

Pelias immediately noticed the young man who had one bare foot and asked him his name. Jason revealed his identity, to Pelias's secret horror. Jason stated that he had come to recover, for his father the throne of Iolcus which rightfully belonged to him.

Pelias pretended to acknowledge Jason's claim but told him that the spirit of Phrixus summoned the Greeks to rescue the golden fleece from the barbarians. He swore by Olympian Zeus that he would relinquish his kingdom if Jason would retrieve the fleece. Jason was delighted because he knew that Perseus and others had gained glory from tasks they had performed in various lands, and he was eager to earn fame for himself.

What was this golden fleece that Pelias wanted Jason to seek? It had a fascinating history. Before Jason was born, a king and queen named Athamas and Nephele ruled in northern Boeotia. They had two children, a boy, Phrixus, and a girl, Helle. Later, Athamas married a second wife, Ino, who plotted against the life of Phrixus so that her own children could inherit the throne. In order to save the children from their cruel stepmother, their mother Nephele procured the aid of Hermes the Wayfinder. By magic means, the god brought with him an immense, winged ram with golden wool. He placed the children on the ram's back instructing it to carry the children to Colchis, a kingdom near the Black Sea.

While the ram was crossing the narrow strait of water which separated Europe from Asia, the girl, Helle, fell off and was drowned. Ever since, this strait has been called the Hellespont in her memory. Phrixus managed to hang onto the ram and eventually reached Colchis. Its king, Aeëtes, gave him a royal welcome and decided to sacrifice the golden ram to gold-helmeted Ares, in honor of its successful flight.

First, of course, he carefully preserved its fleece and nailed it to a tree in a sacred grove, placing it in charge of an enormous, menacing dragon, which never slept.

From that time on, all brave Greeks longed to restore the golden fleece to Greece. They regarded it as a magnificent object, now lost to the barbarous King Aeëtes of Colchis.

Aeëtes was inhospitable to strangers because an oracle had told him that he would die whenever strangers arrived to remove the golden fleece. Therefore, Pelias, in deciding to send Jason to retrieve this valued object, believed that Jason would never return home. Hence, his own life and kingdom would be spared.

Proudly accepting his mission, Jason summoned Argus, the son of Phrixus, who, on Athena's advice, built a fifty-oared ship, named the *Argo* after its builder. The ship was built near Mount Pelion, the site of Cheiron's cave. Grey-eyed Athena had given Argus timbers from one of the oak trees in Dodona to use as the prow of the *Argo*. These trees, sacred to Zeus, would make sounds that could be interpreted as prophecies. Thus it was said that the prow of the *Argo* could speak. Moreover, it surpassed in size and equipment any other ship of its time.

When it was finished, Jason consulted an oracle that told him to gather together most of the renowned young men of Greece for his crew. Jason sought the best men he could find. They called themselves the Argonauts and there were fifty-four of them.

Among those who volunteered were: Heracles, the great mortal son of Zeus; the minstrel, Orpheus; Zetes and Calaïs, sons of Boreas, the north wind; Castor and Polydeuces, brothers of Helen of Troy; the brothers Telamon and Peleus, who would become the fathers of Ajax and Achilles; Laërtes, one day to become the father of Odysseus; Atalanta, the maiden huntress; Admetus of Pherae; Meleager of Calydon; and Argus. They all wanted Heracles to be their leader, but he declined because it was Jason's expedition.

Jason stood upon the deck of the *Argo*, and, holding a golden goblet in his hands, called upon Olympian Zeus to make their voyage successful. As a good omen, thunder peeled from the clouds and lightning flashed in response. The wicked Pelias glowed with delight when the Argonauts, with Jason as their captain, set sail for the island of Lemnos.

Lemnos was a strange place. No men lived on it. The women of Lemnos had murdered all their sons, husbands, brothers, and fathers because they wanted the island for themselves. Some writers say that because the Lemnian women had ignored gold-wreathed Aphrodite, she had caused their bodies to emit a foul odor, and for this reason their husbands had taken captive women from nearby Thrace and made love to them. In retaliation, the Lemnian women had murdered their men. Here the Argonauts spent a few days resting and relaxing.

Upon leaving Lemnos, the *Argo* ran into a ferocious storm, and the rowing was hard. Heracles, straining at his oar, broke it, and the Argonauts decided to make an emergency landing at Mysia, an island near the Sea of Marmara. There, Heracles went into the woods to cut a new oar from a tree. His best friend, Hylas, who was sent to fetch water, was seized by nymphs. Concealed beneath the water's surface, they dragged him down to them. Heracles would not leave without Hylas. Polyphemus heard Hylas shouting and thought that he was being pursued by pirates. While Heracles and Polyphemus searched in vain for Hylas, the ship sailed away. Heracles returned to King Eurystheus at Tiryns. Polyphemus founded a city in Mysia and became its king.

The *Argo* sailed to Bebryces, which was ruled by Amycus, a son of Poseidon the Earthshaker. Amycus was a strong man who took great delight in compelling all strangers who arrived in his country to box, thereby killing them. He challenged the Argonauts to choose their best boxer to fight him. Polydeuces accepted the challenge and struck him on the ear, thus killing him.

Next they came to Salmydessus in Thrace, where the blind prophet Phineus lived. Phineus was said to have been blinded by the gods for revealing the future to mortals and for telling the sons of Phrixus how to sail from Colchis to Greece. Not only was Phineas blinded; he was tormented by the Harpies. These were hideous birds with the faces of young girls, sharp claws, and the bodies of vultures. They were constantly hungry, and, since they had wings, whenever Phineus prepared to eat a meal, they descended to his table and snatched most of his food, leaving the rest with a disgusting odor. Consequently, the unfortunate Phineus was always on the verge of starvation.

Phineus welcomed the Argonauts and promised to tell them how to find their way through the treacherous waters if they would free him from the Harpies. In order to trap the Harpies, the Argonauts placed Phineus's dinner before him. When the Harpies flapped their wings over the table and snatched Phineus's food, they had to reckon with Zetes and Calaïs, the two winged sons of the north wind. These two brave Argonauts fought off the Harpies and chased them into the heavens.

This so frightened the Harpies that they never returned, and Phineus was saved. Freed from the monstrous birds, he charted the course of the Argonauts and warned them about the dangerous, gigantic Clashing Rocks. Whenever the winds drove these rocks against each other, no ship could pass between them. When the rocks were shrouded by mist, not even a bird could penetrate the space between them. Phineus's advice was to send a dove between the rocks, and to sail on only if the bird had flown through safely.

The Argonauts thanked Phineus for his advice and resumed their journey. Approaching the rocks, they released a dove given to them by grey-eyed Athena. The bird passed safely between the rocks, but lost the tip of its tail as they closed behind it. The Argonauts waited until the rocks had separated again and then rowed with all their strength in order to pass through safely. Since then, the Clashing rocks have not moved, for they were destined to remain fixed once a ship had sailed safety between them.

The Argonauts sailed past Mount Caucasus and arrived at Colchis. When the ship anchored, Jason found Medea, the daughter of Aeëtes, wandering by the seashore.

Medea was extremely beautiful and tall, with glowing, dark eyes and dark hair. As a young girl, she was well-known for her knowledge of witchcraft. A skillful sorceress, she was familiar with herbs and potions and their effects. She came to these arts partly by heredity, for she was the niece of Circe, the best-known enchantress of the age.

As part of her plan to take revenge against King Pelias for neglecting to sacrifice to her, golden-throned Hera decided that Medea's magic could be useful to Jason. So she had the gold-wreathed Aphrodite ask her son Eros to cast a spell upon Medea, causing her to fall in love with Jason. Also at Hera's request, love-inspiring Eros flew to Colchis, found Medea, and planted one of the invisible arrows in her heart. Immediately, Medea fell in love with Jason.

Meanwhile, Jason approached King Aeëtes and told him that King Pelias of Iolcus had commanded his to rescue the golden fleece. It was like Jason to ask for the golden fleece openly, instead of trying to steal it. Aeëtes, remembering the prophecy that he would die when strangers removed the golden fleece, was enraged by Jason's request. Pretending to agree with Jason, Aeëtes told him that if he performed certain labors, the fleece would be his. Privately, Aeëtes expected that the labors would kill Jason.

Jason's first labor was to yoke the fire-breathing bulls with bronze feet. Hephaestus had given these bulls to Aeëtes. Fortunately, Medea was there to help him. She covered his body with an ointment that would protect him from both fire and iron. As she did this, she explained to Jason how he could perform the tasks her father had demanded of him. Jason then vowed that he would marry her and keep her as his wife as long as he lived. The ointment kept the fire from burning Jason's body, so he was able to seize the fiery bulls by the horns and yoke them to the plow. Without Medea's help, he would have burned to death.

After the yoking of the bulls, Aeëtes commanded Jason to plant some dragon's teeth. When he did this, Medea told him, men would spring up from the ground, fully armed, to attack him. This labor Jason also performed. When he saw the men spring from the dragon's teeth, he followed Medea's instructions to throw stones into their midst from a distance. While they fought each other, he attacked them, killing them as they fought among themselves.

Even though Jason had performed these three labors, Aeëtes withheld the golden fleece, intending to kill the Argonauts and burn their ship. He did not reckon with Medea, who had anticipated her father's evil intentions. She led Jason to the sacred grove of Ares where the golden fleece was hung and drugged the dragon that forever guarded it. This permitted Jason to rescue the fleece. Then Medea boarded the *Argo* with him, taking her brother along with her. The *Argo* sailed that very night.

When Aeëtes realized what had happened, he took to a ship and pursued the *Argo*. As the ship drew near, Medea, fearing that Aeëtes would capture the *Argo*, realized that its capture would mean certain death for herself and for Jason. She would have to act quickly. Seizing her brother, who was standing nearby, she quickly killed him and cut up his body. The pieces of his corpse she threw into the dark sea.

Her ghastly deed accomplished its purpose. Aeëtes was forced to give up his pursuit in order to gather as many pieces of his son as he could find in the sea. He returned to Colchis in order to give him an honorable burial.

Not only Aeëtes, but the Argonauts as well, were horrified by Medea's unspeakable act. They protested to Jason that Medea must be a demon and a murderess. Jason was so much in love with Medea, that, although he was deeply shocked by her violent deed, he forgave her. He reminded his comrades that if it had not been for Medea, they would all be dead. Moreover, without her, they never could have captured the golden fleece.

Meanwhile, Aeëtes had sent all the natives of Colchis to look for the

Argo. He threatened them with the punishment intended for Medea if they failed to bring her back. Everyone took a different route and sought Medea in various places.

The Lord of Olympus, too, was enraged at Medea and battered the *Argo* with a furious storm, driving the ship far from its course. At this point, the prow of the *Argo* announced to the Argonauts that if they hoped to avoid further punishment by Zeus, they would have to be purified by Circe for the murder of Medea's brother. The Argonauts agreed to the purification, and set sail. They travelled past many islands until they came at last to Circe, who purified them by her sorcery. Orpheus, the minstrel, sang a song as they sailed past the Sirens. These were birds with women's heads and voices. He sang to drown the sound of the beguiling songs that the Sirens used to lure men and then to kill them.

After their encounter with the Sirens, the ship reached the channel that separates Sicily from Italy. There, they had to contend with the monster, Scylla, and the monstrous whirlpool, Charybdis. Scylla was a six-headed monster who snatched sailors off their ships and ate them. Charybdis was another female monster, who swallowed the sea waters and any ships upon them three times each day, only to regurgitate the timbers and the dead later. The problem for the Argonauts was how to avoid one monster without becoming food for another. Golden-throned Hera, however, summoned the sea goddess, Thetis, who conducted them safely through the monstrous gates.

When Medea's countrymen, the Colchians, were unable to find the ship, some settled in the countries in which their searches ended. A few came to the land of the Phaeacians, found the *Argo* there, and demanded Medea from King Alcinoüs. He told them that if Medea had already made love with Jason, he would not force Jason to give her up, but if they were not yet lovers he would send her back to her father. Alcinoüs's wife, Arete, immediately saw to it that Medea and Jason were married.

Thereafter, the Argonauts again set forth upon their adventures. Initially, they were prevented by Talus from landing at Crete. Talus was a man of bronze, who had a single vein extending the length of his body to his ankle, where a bronze nail was driven into the end of the vein. He guarded the island by running around the coast three times each day. On one of these trips, he spied the *Argo* sailing toward the island and attacked it by hurling stones at it. Medea put a spell upon him that caused him to scrape the vein in his ankle, his only vulnerable spot, against a jagged rock. All his immortal blood gushed out, and he died.[3]

Pelias, meanwhile, had concluded that Jason was dead, and he wanted to kill his brother, but Aeson requested permission to kill himself. The method he chose was to sacrifice a bull to Olympian Zeus, so as to drink all of the bull's blood and die. Jason's mother hanged herself.

When the Argonauts returned, Jason handed over the golden fleece.

After he learned of the dreadful wrong that Pelias had inflicted upon his family, he was filled with desire for revenge and asked Medea for a way to punish the evil king.

Medea went to the palace and told the daughters of Pelias that they could make their father young again through the use of certain drugs. In order to convince the girls, Medea butchered an old ram and placed its pieces in a bronze pot filled with boiling water and certain drugs. The lamb jumped out of the pot, alive and young. The daughters, convinced that their father could be rejuvenated, attacked Pelias in his sleep, cut him up, and boiled the pieces.[4] Infuriated by this unnatural deed, the people of Iolcus exiled both Jason and Medea.

Jason and Medea settled in Corinth, where they lived happily together for ten years and had three children. Jason adored his wife and children. In time, however, he became disenchanted with her beauty and ashamed of her previous deeds. He fell in love with the princess, Glauce, the daughter of King Creon of Corinth and asked the king's permission to marry her. Once the king consented, Jason tried to persuade Medea to leave him. He told her that this new marriage would be for the good of their children who would then be able to inherit the throne of Corinth. Medea refused and angrily called upon the immortal gods to defend her.

However, Jason married Glauce anyway, and King Creon forced Medea into exile, giving her one day in which to make her preparations.

In revenge, Medea sent her children to the princess bearing special bridal gifts which had been steeped in invisible poisons. When Glauce dressed herself in these lovely garments, they ignited and consumed her in their flames. King Creon, seeing his daughter's plight, tried to smother the blaze with his own body, thereby perishing along with her.[5]

Medea then took a savage revenge upon Jason. She became determined to murder the children he loved so that Jason would be left alone. She did, indeed, perform this gruesome task in the middle of the night. Then she fled from Corinth, taking refuge with King Aegeus of Athens where she was still living when Theseus arrived.[6]

Jason retreated to his ship, the *Argo*. While he sat there, remembering the days of his former glory, a rotten beam fell upon him and killed him.[7]

1. Cheiron also taught Apollo's son, Asclepius, and Achilles.
2. A man wearing one sandal was the mark of a soldier. Soldiers of more than one country fought their battles wearing a sandal only on their left foot, which was the shield side. This foot was advanced first and could be used to kick the enemy.
3. Two other accounts describe Talus' death. One version says that Medea drove Talus mad by means of drugs. Another states that one of the Argonauts shot Talus in the ankle with his bow and arrow, thus killing him.
4. When Medea convinces Pelias' daughter to boil him, she is advising a practice similar to that of the Celts. They killed their sacred king while he wore a mask of a ram, dismembered him, then cooked him for priestesses to eat.
5. Other writers say that Medea stole into the palace at night and set the building aflame with an unquenchable fire, thus killing Glauce and her royal father.

6. This event is described in the myth of Theseus, Section IV, The Heroes.
7. Other writers say that Jason, horrified and sickened by Medea's crime, committed suicide.

REFLECTIONS

1. Discuss:
   a. Why did Jason make no effort to deter Medea from committing any of her crimes?
   b. What alternatives did he have?
   c. Who is more admirable, Jason or Medea? Explain.
2. Become Medea and write a letter to Jason explaining your murder of the children.
3. You are a newspaper reporter who has accompanied the Argonauts on their voyage. Write a front page story dealing with one of their adventures.
4. Using the introduction to this Heroes section, make a chart of the characteristics of the typical hero. Apply these characteristics to:
   a. Perseus
   b. Heracles
   c. Theseus
   d. Jason
   Give each characteristic one point. Which hero accumulates the highest score?
5. What are the personality differences among each of the following heroes?
   a. Bellerophon
   b. Perseus
   c. Heracles
   d. Theseus
   e. Jason
6. Do you have to be self-centered to be a hero? Discuss.
7. Is there a price to pay for being a hero? If so, is it worth the price to be a hero? Discuss.

HUMAN EXPERIENCE

Jason is, in many ways, a symbol of the predicament and responses of modern man. If one were to consider Medea and Jason as one person —they seem to embody the pulls in opposite directions present in us all. These pulls produce conflict and ambivalence.

Ambivalence means feeling two different ways at the same time about the same thing, or person. In human relationships this is sometimes called *love-hate*. It is difficult for us to realize that parents, for example, are not perfect. This makes them human, but it may also incur our anger when we see their flaws. We become ambivalent about them.

Ambivalence often makes us try to compensate for the unacceptable hate-feelings in our *love-hate* by becoming too obviously loving, and even smothering in our efforts to love. Thus the hate becomes repressed and may break through when one feels betrayed by the loved one. Then love can be replaced by relentless hate. Murders inspired by passion are usually the outcome of failing to understand that we, as human beings, are all subject to feeling ambivalent.

By understanding and acknowledging the feelings of ambivalence we have, we can often resolve them. In order to do this we must learn that when one of the two components of the feeling remains repressed, it may give rise to anxiety and guilty feelings. A person caring for an invalid member of his family, for example, may have mixed feelings. One feeling may be love, of wanting to be helpful, but another, of which he may not be conscious, could be that of annoyance and hostility. The manner in which most people handle such antagonistic feelings is to repress or minimize them, thus defending themselves against the fear and anxiety these feelings could generate if admitted.

In the Jason myth, this process of ambivalence is enacted by the two central figures. Jason turns against Medea, thus vanquishing his own repressed, murderous instincts. Hera, originally a goddess of fertility, can be seen as the rebirth in all of us of our potential ability or talent. In the myth, she only decrees Medea's love for Jason, not their single or dual fates. She, like other gods, becomes the catalyst for the actions of mortals by placing men in situations where they act freely, in accordance with their own personalities.

Most of us have, at some time, endowed someone else with our own feelings of rage or rejection, and so on. This is called *projection*. It is a process which seems to get us off the hook because it can feel good to blame someone else for our own weaknesses. It is one way, also, of dealing with ambivalence.

However, it never solves the problem for us no matter how hard we try to convince ourselves that "It was not my fault. He did it." Some unconscious understanding of the truth makes us unhappily aware that we are *projecting* our own anger or ambivalence, rage, or rejection onto other people, and this realization causes us to lose self-esteem.

To gain back our lost self-respect, we try to resolve our conflict. In so doing, it helps to know that it is sometimes appropriate to have mixed feelings toward people we think we should love, such as parents, brothers, sisters, friends. In order to feel comfortable about such feelings, we can try to comprehend their causes and bring to consciousness, if possible, the repressed or unacceptable set of feelings. We may not be able to abolish ambivalence altogether, but we can realize that it represents two sides of the same coin before it erupts into violence, guilt, and blame.

The Hero

Since people have always needed heroes, they appear in the mythology of every culture. Their hair-raising adventures are thrilling to us and their modes of overcoming adversity inspire us.

Just as people created stories to explain creation and other phenomena, they also felt the need to create great heroes whom they could extol and admire. Especially when they felt unequal to the monumental tasks that confronted them or to dangers they could not defeat, they wished for a great leader who would have the power or means to vanquish their foes and protect them. The mythical hero, then, was endowed with superhuman power that equipped him for the enormous struggles he had to endure. He was often the composite fantasy of groups of people who shared a common heritage and aspirations, and based in part upon the great deeds of historical figures.

In many myths, the hero has a noticeable weakness in his power, strength, or cunning that appears early in the story. Being human, he needs some help from another to guide his development. Thus Jason has Medea and Hera; Theseus has Ariadne; and Perseus, Bellerophon, and Heracles have Athena.

These figures teach the hero or lend him their shrewdness through an apprenticeship, so that he can ultimately emerge victorious. Their special role in the heroic myths is similar to those of parents or leaders who help the young person develop the skills that will enable him to cope with the problems of his existence. As he achieves a sense of autonomy, he no longer requires the guardianship of helpful figures. He is now an active and combative adult.

Why does a hero wish to be a hero? What motivates him to leave his comfortable home and strike out for the difficult, dangerous unknown? One of the reasons lies in our yearning for immortality. Forced to accept the end of earthly existence, we have wanted to leave some token of ourselves behind when we die, telling those who live after us that we once existed. For example, the goal of the Greek heroes was to meet the demands that the gods and society made upon them with dignity, courage, unselfishness, and excellence. This was the road to fame. It earned the hero the respect and tribute of society while he lived, and fame and immortality after his death.

Another group has been able to achieve immortality by reason of their royal birth. Thus, kings, queens, and nobles have built elaborate tombs and statues commemorating themselves. For them, fame was easy to acquire. They were born with the power and the wealth to perpetuate themselves in stone.

Those people born with less power and wealth than royalty have sought immortality through achievements. This invariably has involved risk and danger. Yet, history and literature recount numerous people who sacrificed their lives in order to achieve greatness, and, with it, immortality. These people confronted the inevitability of death and decided that it was more important how they lived and died than how long they lived.

Finally, there are people who become heroes, but fame and immortality were not their original intention. For example, most artists, musicians, scientists, and writers who have achieved fame—and with it, recognition after death—have not been driven in their pursuits by the need or desire for public acclaim. They have been inner-directed people who have been motivated to achieve. They created for the sake of the value of their art and the pleasure of pursuing it.

In all cases, heroes became heroes in the process of overcoming adversity. They demonstrate a persistent drive toward mastery and achievement. Neither passive pawns of outside forces nor of their own instincts, they are persons who organize their existence, foresee their goals, and initiate their moves in order to face challenges and problems.

Other motivations for heroes include the wish to conquer or to succeed in mastering their own environment, with a consequent heightened sense of self-esteem. Initially, in human nature, self-esteem comes from the approval of parents, whom we internalize in the form of self-love or self-approval. If we do not receive the respect and admiration of our parents (who are our gods, when we are young), we often seek it some place *outside* of the self and often in unhealthy ways. An example of this is to overvalue what others think or feel about us. This we do instead of having the capacity to evaluate our value from within ourselves.

The concepts of retaliation and revenge, so much a part of the hero's task, are readily understood by young people who often feel mistreated, misunderstood, or abused in the face of adult authority. When a child is punished or treated angrily by adults, he may feel helpless in dealing with his feelings. Conflict grows out of his need and love for them *and* his rage toward them for overpowering him.

Children who are punished for misdeeds may reverse their real situation, because it is too painful. Instead of seeing *themselves* as angry and vengeful, they attribute to another person the anger they feel. In so doing, their fantasies make them become the larger-than-life figures of authority and power who do bloody and violent deeds. In this way, they show their feelings in an acceptable way.

Going from our personal lives to our lives as members of the human race, the monsters and foes we must contend with today are as formidable as those of the mythical hero. Disease, poverty, pollution, inflation, depression, and warfare are our enemies. They will require heroic efforts on the part of all of us if we are to overcome their disastrous effects. Growing up in a world with such enemies acquaints us with our tasks. Grappling with them successfully will make each of us heroes in our time. In fact, the value and appeal of the hero myth increases with the realization that we are all heroes in miniature. Although we do not possess all, or even most of the characteristics of the mythical hero, and our achievements will soon be forgotten, each of us must undertake tasks that are difficult, and appear at times to be impossible. We face death in every fear that threatens to make us retreat from the challenge of living. If we are courageous and master our emotions, we are able to perform the tasks before us, one by one, and will emerge from the trials with self-confidence and justifiable pride. The wish to achieve and to excel still requires persistence, work, and the mastery of obstacles. The ultimate victory we win is our own maturity.

Beasts and Demons

Today, demons and evil spirits are as active as they were in Greek times, but are located in ourselves, not always in the outside world. They are the powerful drives within us. Myths represent these drives—love, sex, power, or ambition—in the symbolic form of beasts and monsters. In the myth, as in our own lives, monsters may represent the repressed areas of ourselves of which we feel ashamed, or that we feel may not be socially acceptable. These may be motives or deeds that are not controlled by our consciousness. In other words, mythical demons, like unacknowledged feelings, are projections of our emotional impulses symbolized by animal forms. Contemporary *demons* have many guises. Some of them are the product of modern life. We live in an increasingly depersonalized world in which the individual feels himself to be less important than he ever was in his society and even in his own home.

It is not unusual for people to *separate* or *distance* themselves from others, or to be distanced by them. It is not unusual for people to experience divided feelings in the experience of loving.

There is much stress, tension, and anxiety in our fast-changing world. Many of us have, at some time, felt the *inner demons* of such moods as boredom, depression, loneliness, hostility, aggression, and maliciousness. These moods occur frequently as a result of conflict, crisis, or frustration. They can bedevil us when we have more than one goal and find decision-making difficult. They can appear when we fail to acknowledge feelings. Boredom, for example, is not always a failure of outside stimulation. Sometimes we become bored when we are uncomfortable about recognizing other feelings, so we *turn off* and tell ourselves that the world is not playing host to our needs. It is important to recognize these moods and feelings and to try to understand their causes in ourselves.

If we like what these contemporary demons produce in our lives, and they conform to our wishes, we call them good luck. If they go against us, we either blame others who "arouse the beast in us" and may provoke us to behave in ways we regret, or we call them bad luck.

Today's demons, like the mythical monsters, also have insatiable appetites. Our demons crave alcohol, drugs, cigarettes, and too much food.

Excessive and habitual dependence upon food or artificial stimulants for satisfaction, not for nourishment, may create patterns of self-destruction for the user. These demons are not, in themselves, harmful, but the reactions they produce do not come from the individual, himself, in a natural way. We delude ourselves into thinking that we need these things for the purpose of bringing fun and joy into our lives through their use.

However, the feeling of joy, when it is spontaneous, is the combination of well-being and security. It cannot be bought and sold; it does not come in a bottle. When it *is* natural, it is infectious and creative; it has the power of cheering the hearts of others.

Carried into the community and the world in excessive form, our individual, internal demons, when experienced by an entire culture, can result in rebellion, crime, war, and cruelty to other human beings.

As long as we are human, we will have our demons in some form or other. It is not the demons that matter to us. It is how we handle the challenge of dealing with them and what we learn about ourselves as we do that is important.

Symbols

Man has been called a symbol-making creature. A symbol is an object that represents something else. In ordinary life, the most common symbol is the word. Another common source of symbols is the image; for example, a flag can symbolize the country for which it stands.

In mythology, it is primarily the people who become symbols because the focus of the myth is on human behavior. Therefore, we think of mythical heroes or mortals as representing certain personality types. When we speak of a *Herculean task*, it brings to mind that which is nearly impossible to achieve. *Augean stables* have come to mean messy rooms. The names themselves, in most cases, have become household words and have travelled into our language as adjectives or nouns. *Nemesis* has become the adversity a person cannot conquer. *Narcissism* has come to symbolize inordinate self-love. A *Procrustean bed* is the term that symbolizes the effort to make the truth fit the argument. A *hydra* is usually used in terms of the unmanageability of a bureaucracy. When one opens a *Pandora's box*, one is symbolizing the unleashing of all the mysterious evils or troubles upon the world. The *Midas touch* symbolizes the acquisitive personality, or one who has a craving or gift for making money.

Symbols are an excellent means of communication because they represent what might be called *emotional shorthand*. They absorb, encompass, convey, and release emotions that are understood because of their simplicity. They permit us to select from a mass of data one single representation or significant feature, such as an image, a slogan, or a tune. Through the process of association, which means permitting one's self spontaneous chains of thought or feelings without censorship, this single feature can be transferred to the individual. It can also be transferred to the culture or group to which an individual belongs, furnishing a common framework.

We arrive at an understanding of symbols through intuition, or unconscious wisdom, and the imagination. When we finally perceive the nature of the symbol, the thing for which it stands is isolated and clarified in our minds. This leaves us with the image, either visual or auditory.

The results of the understanding of a symbol or symbolic thinking is often the formation of a *concept* or a general notion that embraces all the attributes common to individual members of a group. For example, the concept of chair is a general notion that applies to all chairs. Concepts are a form for describing what we see or know. Clusters of concepts convey more abstract values, such as faith, loyalty, patriotism, love, or friendship.

Emotions and concepts are intertwined. They are both internal and help us to answer the question, "What is it?"

Man also produces symbols in the form of dreams. No one can understand everything he sees or hears. Whatever we see, taste, hear, touch, or feel is limited to and depends upon the quality of our senses. No matter how we try, however, we reach a point beyond which conscious knowledge cannot go. Symbols appear to us in dreams, and may, in fact, be called the language of dreams.

The images or symbols produced in dreams are generally more vivid than experience itself. One reason for this is that only in dreams can concepts or images express their true unconscious meaning. Although most of us have fallen, for example, falling in a dream takes on a different feel than falling in reality.

Symbols have been utilized in advertising, traffic signs and signals, mathematics, music, and art. They are an immediate source for our attention and our interest because there is nothing shadowy about them on a conscious or a visual level. They are frequently universal in their appeal, and at the same time more deeply personal than any other mode of knowing.

GLOSSARY

A

Abas (AHB us)—boy punished by Demeter for his insolent attitude. *(Ch. 13)*

Acheloüs (ahk ah LOW us)—river god who wrestled with Heracles for Deïaneira and lost. *(Ch. 33)*

Achilles (ah KIL eez)—greatest Greek hero in war against Ilium (Troy). *(Chs. 29, 36)*

Acrisius (ah KRIS ee us)—ill-fated grandfather of the hero Perseus. *(Ch. 31)*

Acropolis (ah KROP uh lis)—highest part of Athens; contained temple of Athena. *(Chs. 24, 34)*

Admetus (ad MEE tus)—friend of the hero Heracles; husband of Alcestis; king of Pherae; an Argonaut, hunted the Calydonian boar. *(Chs. 29, 33, 36)*

Aeëtes (ee EE teez)—king of Colchis; father of Medea; possessor of the golden fleece. *(Chs. 33, 36)*

Aegean (ee JEE un)—sea that divides Greece from Asia Minor; named after the hero Theseus's father who plunged into it. *(Ch. 34)*

Aegeus (EE jus)—king of Athens; father of the hero Theseus. *(Ch. 34)*

Aeolus (EE uh lus)—keeper of the winds. *(Ch. 19: F.)*

Aeschylus (ES kuh lus)—Greek writer of tragic plays. (525 to 455 B.C.). *(Ch. 14)*

Aeson (EE suhn)—lawful King of Iolcus; father of the hero Jason. *(Ch. 36)*

Aethra (EE thruh)—daughter of King Pittheus of Troezen; mother of the hero Theseus. *(Ch. 34)*

Aetna, Mount (ET nuh)—volcanic mountain on the island of Sicily; imprisons monster Typhon. *(Chs. 5, 13, 25)*

Agamemnon (ag uh MEM non)—husband of Clytemnestra; king of Mycenae during the Trojan War. *(Ch. 15)*

Aglaea (uh GLEE uh)—one of the three Graces; daughter of Zeus and Eurynome. *(Ch. 7)*

Ajax (AY jaks)—son of the hero Telamon; great hero in the Trojan War. *(Chs. 29, 36)*

Alcaeüs (al SEE us)—name given to the hero Heracles upon his birth. *(Ch. 33)*

Alcestis (al SES tis)—wife of King Admetus of Pherae; pious daughter of King Pelias of Iolcus. *(Chs. 33, 36)*

Alcinoüs (al SIN oh us)—king of the Phaeacians who helped the hero Jason. *(Ch. 36)*

Alcmene (alk MEE nee)—wife of King Amphitryon; mother of the great hero Heracles. *(Chs. 20, 33)*

Alpheius (al FEE us)—river used by the hero Heracles to clean the stables of King Augeias of Elis for his fifth labor. *(Ch. 33)*

Alphenor (al FEE nor)—one of Niobe's seven sons. *(Ch. 21)*

Althaea (al THEE uh)—wife of King Oeneus of Calydon; mother of the hero Meleager. *(Ch. 29)*

Amaltheia (al mal THEE uh)—goat that nourished Zeus when he was an infant on the island of Crete. *(Ch. 2)*

Amazons (AM uh zonz)—tribe of warrior women living near the Black Sea in the age of Heracles and Theseus. *(Chs. 32, 33, 34)*

Amphion (am FEE on)—king of Thebes; husband of Niobe. *(Ch. 21)*

Amphitrite (am fi TRI tee)—queen of the Sea; wife of Poseidon; helped the hero Theseus. *(Ch. 34)*

Amphitryon (am FIT ree on)—grandson of hero Perseus; mortal father of the hero Heracles. *(Chs. 20, 33)*

Amycus (AM ih kus)—king of the Bebryces who challenged the Argonauts to a boxing match. *(Ch. 36)*

Ancaeüs (an SEE us)—member of the Caledonian Boar Hunt who angered Artemis with a disastrous result. *(Ch. 29)*

Androgeus (an DRO jih us)—son of King Minos of Crete; the Athenians were blamed for his death. *(Ch. 34)*

Andromeda (an DROM uh duh)—daughter of King Cepheus of Ethiopia; rescued by the hero Perseus. *(Ch. 31)*

Antaeüs (an TEE us)—giant son of Gaea and Poseidon who wrestled with the hero Heracles. *(Ch. 33)*

Antigone (an TIG uh nee)—daughter of King Oedipus of Thebes; revolted against the law of the palace-state. *(Intro. R.B.)*

Antiope (an TEE uh pee)—Amazon queen captured by the hero Theseus; mother of Theseus's son Hippolytus. *(Ch. 34)*

Aoede (ay EE dee)—one of the three early Muses; daughter of Mnemosyne and Zeus. *(Ch. 7)*

Aphidnae (ah FID nee)—town in Attica near Marathon where Theseus hid young Helen of Troy after he abducted her. *(Ch. 34)*

Aphrodite (af ro DY tee)—goddess of love and beauty; daughter of Uranus or of Zeus and Dione. *(Chs. 5, 8, 13, 15, 18, 26, 30, 35, 36)*

Apollo (uh PAHL oh)—god of music, medicine, and prophecy; son of Leto and Zeus. *(Chs. 1, 4, 5, 10, 12, 20, 21, 23, 33)*

Apuleius, Lucius (ap yuh LEE us)—creator of the tale "Cupid (or Eros) and Psyche." *(Ch. 35)*

Arachne (uh RAK nee)—an excellent but arrogant weaver; punished by Athena. *(Ch. 20)*

Arcadia (ar KAY dee uh)—interior region of the Peloponnesus; home of the barbaric King Lycaon, the Stymphalian birds, and the Cerynitian

hind. *(Chs. 19:L., 33)*

Areopagus (er ee OP uh gus)—rocky hill next to Athenian Acropolis; location of first Greek court of law. *(Chs. 15, 20, 24, 34)*

Ares (AY reez)—god of war; son of Zeus and Hera. *(Chs. 4, 9, 29, 36)*

Arete (ah REE tee)—wife of King Alcinoüs of Phaeacia; helped the hero Jason and Medea. *(Ch. 36)*

areté—possessing excellent ability or an excellent personality trait. *(Intro. Chs. 16, 33)*

Arges (AR jeez)—one of the three monstrous Cyclopes born to Gaea and Uranus. *(Ch. 1)*

Argo (AR goh)—the ship on which Jason and the Argonauts sailed to capture the golden fleece. *(Ch. 36)*

Argonauts (AR guh nautz)—heroes who sailed on the *Argo* to recover the golden fleece. *(Ch. 36)*

Argos (AR gos)—palace-state in the Peloponnesus; home of the hero Perseus's grandfather, Acrisius. *(Chs. 9, 31)*

Argus (AR gus)—builder of the famous ship on which the Argonauts sailed, the *Argo*. *(Ch. 36)*

Ariadne (er ih AD nee)—daughter of King Minos of Crete who helped the hero Theseus; sister of Phaedra, Theseus's wife. *(Chs. 14, 24, 34)*

Artemis (AR tuh mis)—twin sister of Apollo; goddess of the hunt; daughter of Leto and Zeus. *(Chs. 1, 4, 5, 11, 13, 21, 29, 33, 34)*

Ascalaphus (as KAL uh fus)—Underworld being who was punished by Persephone for revealing a secret. *(Ch. 13)*

Asclepius (as KLEE pi us)—son of Apollo; famous for his ability to heal. *(Chs. 33, 34, 36)*

Asia (AY zhuh)—continent visited by Dionysus; Asian nymphs raised him there. *(Ch. 14)*

Asia Minor—area east of Greece, across the Aegean Sea; home of King Midas, Arachne, location of Ilium (Troy). *(Chs. 20, 23, 33)*

Asterius (as TIR ih us)—king of Crete who married Europa and adopted her three sons. *(Ch. 34)*

Atalanta (at uh LAN tuh)—maiden huntress who joined the Calydonian Boar Hunt. *(Chs. 29, 30)*

Athamas (ATH ah mus)—king in Boeotia; husband of Nephele and Ino; father of Phrixus and Helle. *(Ch. 36)*

até(AH tay)—the state of temporary madness; exhibiting reckless behavior *(Intro. Chs. 16, 33)*

Athena (ah THEE nuh)—wise goddess of arts and crafts and defensive war: helper of heroes. *(Chs. 6, 9, 13, 17, 18, 20, 29, 31, 32, 33, 36)*

Athens (ATH enz)—palace-state in Attica; home of King Aegeus and his son, the hero Theseus. *(Intro.: H.B., Chs. 20, 34)*

Atlas (AT lus)—strongest Titan; condemned by Zeus to hold up the sky eternally; became Mount Atlas in Libya. *(Chs. 3, 31, 33)*

Atropos (AT roh pos)—"Inflexible;" the most feared of the three Fates; daughter of Zeus and Themis. *(Chs. 7, 29, 33)*

Attica (AT ih kuh)—southeastern part of Greek mainland; Athens located there. *(Chs. 20, 34)*

Augeias (au JEE us)—king of Elis who hired the hero Heracles to clean his stable-yards. (Heracles's fifth labor) *(Ch. 33)*

Autolycus (au TOL ih kus)—son of Hermes, taught the hero Heracles to wrestle. *(Ch. 33)*

B

Bacchus (BAK us)—Roman name for Dionysus, god of wine; son of Zeus and Semele. *(Chs. 5, 9, 14, 20, 23)*

Bebryces (BEB ri seez)—a tribe visited by the Argonauts on their voyage to capture the golden fleece. *(Ch. 36)*

Bellerophon (be LER uh fon)—the hero who killed the Chimaera and rode Pegasus. *(Ch. 32)*

Black Sea—general location of the Caucasus Mountains where Prometheus was chained; area of the Amazons, and the golden fleece. *(Chs. 9, 17, 19: D.N.E., 33, 34, 36)*

Boeotia (bee OH shi uh)—region northwest of Attica; Thebes located there; home of Niobe. *(Ch. 21)*

Boreas (boh REE us)—god of the north wind. *(Chs. 19: F., D.N.E., 28, 36)*

Briareüs (bri ER ih us)—one of the three Hundred-handed giants; son of Gaea and Uranus. *(Chs. 1, 2, 3)*

Brontes (BRON teez)—one of the three Cyclopes; son of Gaea and Uranus. *(Chs. 1, 2, 3, 11)*

Bronze Age—the Mycenaean Age; age of the Greek myths. *(Intro.: H.B., R.B.)*

bull of Marathon—wild bull of Crete captured and set free by Heracles for his 7th labor, later renamed and killed by the hero Theseus. *(Chs. 33, 34)*

C

Cacus (KA kus)—fire-breathing giant; son of Hephaestus; killed by the hero Heracles. *(Ch. 33)*

Calaïs (KAL ay is)—one of the twin sons of Boreas, the north wind; brother of Zetes; an Argonaut. *(Ch. 36)*

Calliope (kah LY uh pee)—one of the nine Muses, daughter of Mnemosyne and Zeus; Mother of Orpheus. *(Chs. 7, 28, 33)*

Calydon (KAL ih don)—home of the hero Meleager. *(Chs. 29, 33)*

Cassiopeia (kas ih oh PEE uh)—mother of Andromeda, who was helped by the hero Perseus. *(Ch. 31)*

Castor (KAS ter)—mortal "twin" brother of Polydeuces; an Argonaut; hunted the Calydonian boar; taught the hero Heracles to use the sword. *(Chs. 15, 29, 33, 34, 36)*

Caucasus, Mount (KO kuh sus)—Prometheus was chained to these cliffs for 30,000 years. *(Chs. 17, 25, 33)*

Celtic (SEL tic)—religion in England with rites similar to those practiced by Medea. *(Ch. 36)*

Centaur (SEN taur)—creature having the head and torso of a man and the body and legs of a horse. *(Chs. 17,*

30, 33, 36)

Cepheus (SEE fus)—father of Andromeda; king of Ethiopia. *(Ch. 31)*

Cephissus (suh FIS us)—river in Attica where Deucalion and Pyrrha cleansed themselves before praying to Themis; father of Narcissus *(Ch. 19: D.N.E., 27)*

Cerberus (SER buh rus)—watchdog of Hades; three-headed offspring of Typhon; captured by the hero Heracles for his twelfth labor. *(Chs. 4, 28, 33, 35)*

Cercyon (SERK yohn)—king of Eleusis who forced all travelers, including the hero Theseus, to wrestle with him. *(Ch. 34)*

Ceres (SER eez)—Roman name for Demeter; goddess of grain; sister of Zeus; mother of Persephone. *(Chs. 2, 4, 13, 22)*

Cerynitian (ser i NISH i uhn)—(hind) doe with golden horns; sacred to Artemis; hunted by the hero Heracles for his third labor. *(Ch. 33)*

Chaos (KAY os)—the condition of the world before Creation occurred. *(Ch. 1)*

Charon (KER on)—ferryman across the River Styx of shades and visitors to the Underworld. *(Chs. 4, 28, 35)*

Charybdis (kuh RIB dis)—whirlpool in the strait between Sicily and Italy avoided by Jason and the Argonauts. *(Ch. 36)*

Cheiron (KI ron)—the immortal Centaur; teacher of Jason and Asclepius; wounded by Heracles. *(Chs. 17, 33, 36)*

Chimaera (ki MEE ruh)—offspring of Typhon; monster killed by the hero Bellerophon. *(Ch. 32)*

Chios (KI os)—the island where King Pentheus's visitor met Dionysus for the first time. *(Ch. 14)*

Cimon (SI muhn)—the person who located the hero Theseus's bones and returned them to Athens. *(Ch. 34)*

Circe (SER see)—famous sorceress who purified Jason and Medea of their crime. *(Ch. 36)*

Cithaeron, Mount (si THEE ron)—location of Dionysian rites in which King Pentheus was killed. *(Ch. 14)*

Clashing Rocks—rocks that prevented ships from entering the Black Sea until the *Argo* sailed through successfully. *(Ch. 36)*

Cleio (KLEE oh)—one of the nine Muses; daughter of Mnemosyne and Zeus. *(Ch. 7)*

Clotho (KLO tho)—"Spinner;" one of the three Fates; daughter of Zeus and Themis. *(Chs. 7, 29, 33)*

Clymene (KLIM uh nee)—daughter of Oceanus and Tethys; mother of Atlas, Prometheus, and Epimetheus; also mother of Phaëthon. *(Chs. 1, 25)*

Clytemnestra (Kli tuhm NES trah)—sister of Castor; wife of King Agamemnon. *(Ch. 15)*

Cnossus (Nos us)—palace of King Minos of Crete; contained a multitude of rooms, labyrinth-like to the invading Greeks. *(Chs. 10, 34)*

Cocalus (KO kuh lus)—king of Sicily who befriended Daedalus after he escaped from King Minos of Crete. *(Ch. 34)*

Coeüs (SEE us)—one of the original thirteen Titans; father of Leto. *(Ch. 1)*

Colchis (KOL kis)—palace-state of King Aeëtes (of golden fleece fame) at the eastern end of the Black Sea. *(Chs. 9, 33, 36)*

Core (KO ree)—special title for Persephone; daughter of Demeter and Zeus; wife of Hades. *(Chs. 13, 28, 33, 34, 35)*

Corinth (KOR inth)—location where the hero Theseus met Sinis, the "Pinebender," and where Jason and Medea settled. *(Chs. 34, 36)*

Corynetes (kor ih NEE teez)—the "Club-carrier" *Periphetes* who murdered travelers until he encountered the hero Theseus. *(Ch. 34)*

Cottus (KOT us)—one of the three Hundred-handed giants; offspring of Gaea and Uranus. *(Chs. 1, 2, 3)*

Creon (KREE on)—king of Corinth who permitted Jason to become engaged to his daughter Glauce. *(Chs. 33, 36)*

Crete (KREET)—large island, southeast of Greece, home of King Minos, the Cretan bull, and the Minotaur. *(Chs. 24, 35)*

Crisa (KRI suh)—the seaport Apollo used in order to reach Pytho (Delphi). *(Ch. 10)*

Crius (KRI us)—one of the original thirteen Titans; offspring of Gaea and Uranus. *(Ch. 1)*

Crommyonian (Krom i OH ni un)—(Phaea) a huge sow; offspring of Typhon; named after old woman who fed it; killed by the hero Theseus. *(Ch. 34)*

Cronus (KRO nus)—one of the original thirteen Titans; brother and husband of Rhea; father of the original six gods: Hestia, Demeter, Hera, Hades, Poseidon and Zeus. *(Chs. 1, 2, 3, 12, 16, 17)*

Cupid (KU pid)—Roman name for Eros; god of love; son of Aphrodite. *(Chs. 13, 28, 35, 36)*

Curetes (Ku REE teez)—Cretan youths who shielded the infant Zeus's cries from Cronus. *(Ch. 2)*

Cyclopes (SI klo peez)—three one-eyed offspring of Uranus and Gaea; became Zeus's servants. *(Chs. 1, 2, 3, 11)*

Cyclops (SI klops)—singular form of Cyclopes.

Cyllene, Mount (si LEE nee)—home of Atlas's daughter, Maia, and her infant son, Hermes. *(Chs. 12, 19: L.)*

Cynthus, Mount (SIN thos)—mountain from which Leto observed Niobe's insults. *(Ch. 21)*

Cyprus (SY prus)—island associated with the goddess Aphrodite. *(Chs. 8, 26, 30)*

Cythera (sy THEE ruh)—island associated with the goddess Aphrodite. *(Ch. 8)*

D

Daedalus (DED uh lus)—the master architect who designed the Labyrinth for King Minos of Crete in order to conceal the Minotaur. *(Chs. 15, 34)*

Damasichthon (dah mah SIK thon)—Niobe's sixth son. *(Ch. 21)*

Damastes (dah MAS teez)—the innkeeper called "Procrustes" who matched his guests to his beds until he met the hero Theseus. *(Ch. 34)*

Danaë (DAN ay ee) Dana'ë—mother of the hero Perseus; daughter of King Acrisius of Argos. *(Chs. 20, 31)*

Deïaneira (dee uh NI ruh)—second wife of the hero Heracles; sister of Meleager of Calydon. *(Chs. 29, 33)*

Delos (DE los)—birthplace of Apollo and Artemis; originally a floating island. *(Ch. 10)*

Delphi (DEL fi)—location of the oracle of Apollo on Mount Parnassus. *(Chs. 10, 30, 33, 34)*

Delphinian (del FIN ih un)—name of Apollo's altar; related to the word dolphin, a title of Apollo. *(Ch. 10)*

Delphinius (del FIN ih us)—dolphin in Greek, a title of Apollo, since he first appeared to his priests as a dolphin. *(Ch. 10)*

Demeter (dee MEE ter)—goddess of grain; sister of Zeus; mother of Persephone. *(Chs. 2, 4, 13, 22, 29)*

Deucalion (du KA lih un)—son of Prometheus; survived the Greek flood. *(Ch. 19: D.N.E.)*

Diana (di AN uh)—Roman name for Artemis; goddess of the hunt. *(Chs. 5, 11, 13, 21, 29, 33)*

Dicte, Mount (DIK tee)—mountain on island of Crete where Zeus was reared as an infant. *(Ch. 2)*

Dictys (DIK tis)—fisherman who protected the hero Perseus and Danaë on the island of Seriphus. *(Ch. 31)*

Diomedes (di oh MEE deez)—king of Thrace who fed his horses human flesh until the hero Heracles arrived to perform his eighth labor. *(Ch. 33)*

Dione (di OH nee)—one of the original thirteen Titans, mother of the goddess Aphrodite. *(Chs. 1, 8, 10)*

Dionysus (di oh NI sus)—god of wine; son of Semele and Zeus. *(Chs. 4, 5, 9, 14, 20, 23, 28, 29, 33)*

Dodona (do DO nuh)—1) location of grove of oak trees sacred to Zeus; one used to create the *Argo's* prow; 2) location of the oracle of the Titan goddess Dione, mother of Aphrodite. *(Chs. 8, 36)*

dryad (DRI ad)—a tree nymph or spirit. *(Ch. 22)*

E

Echo (EK oh)—a nymph who served Zeus as well as Hera and was punished for it. *(Ch. 27)*

Egypt (EE jipt)—where the Olympians went when they fled from Typhon and changed into animal shapes. *(Ch. 5)*

Eileithyia (i li THI yuh)—goddess of childbirth; daughter of Zeus and Hera. *(Chs. 9, 33)*

Electryon (ee LEK tri on)—king of Mycenae; father of Alcmene; accidently killed by Amphitryon. *(Ch. 33)*

Eleusis (ee LOO sis)—area in Attica dominated by the wrestler, King Cercyon, until the hero Theseus arrived; center for the worship of Demeter, and Persephone. *(Chs. 13, 34)*

Elis (EE lis)—home of King Augeias and his stables that Heracles cleaned for his fifth labor. *(Ch. 33)*

Eos (EE os)—Dawn, daughter of Titans Hyperion and Theia. *(Chs. 1, 12, 25)*

Epidaurus (ep ih DAU rus)—home of the robber Periphetes, the "Clubcarrier;" felled by the hero Theseus. *(Ch. 34)*

Epimetheus (ep ih ME thoos)—Titan brother of Prometheus; husband of Pandora; Father of Pyrrha. *(Chs. 17, 19: D.N.E.)*

Erato (ER uh to)—one of the nine Muses; daughter of Mnemosyne and Zeus. *(Ch. 7)*

Erechtheus (ee REK thoos)—honored, early king of Athens. *(Ch. 34)*

Eros (EE ros)—god of love; son of Aphrodite or one of the original three divinities. *(Chs. 1, 4, 8, 13, 28, 35, 36)*

Erymanthian (er ih MAN thi un)—boar captured on Mount Eryman-

thus by the hero Heracles for his fourth labor. *(Ch. 33)*

Erymanthus, Mount (er ih MAN thus)—mountain in Arcadia, home of the boar the hero Heracles captured for his fourth labor. *(Ch. 33)*

Erysichthon (er ih SIK thon)—an arrogant youth who dishonored Demeter and suffered the consequences. *(Ch. 22)*

Erytheia (er ih THEE uh)—home of Geryon who was the owner of the cattle Heracles captured for his tenth labor. *(Ch. 33)*

Ethiopia (ee thee OH pee uh)—kingdom of King Cepheus, father of Andromeda, whom Perseus saved. *(Chs. 25, 31)*

Euphrosyne (u FROZ ih nee)—one of the three Graces; daughter of Eurynome and Zeus. *(Ch. 7)*

Europa (u RO puh)—a love whom Zeus, in the form of a bull, carried off to the island of Crete. *(Chs. 20, 34)*

Eurydice (u RID ih see)—the wife of Orpheus, who died of snakebite. *(Ch. 28)*

Eurynome (u RIN uh mee)—daughter of Titans Oceanus and Tethys; loved by Zeus; mother of the Graces; helped rear the god Hephaestus beneath the sea. *(Chs. 7, 9)*

Eurystheus (u RIS thoos)—the cowardly cousin of Heracles for whom the hero performed twelve labors. *(Ch. 33)*

Eurytion (u RIT ih on)—the cowherd of Geryon's cattle until he met the hero Heracles on Heracles's tenth labor. *(Ch. 33)*

Eurytus (U ri tus)—trained young Heracles to use bow and arrows; father of Iole who was a love of Heracles's. *(Ch. 33)*

Euterpe (u TER pee)—one of the nine Muses; daughter of Mnemosyne and Zeus. *(Ch. 7)*

Evenus (ee VEE nus)—river where the centaur Nessus tried to carry Deïaneira away from Heracles; also where the hero Jason carried Hera in disguise, losing one sandal in the process. *(Chs. 33, 36)*

F

Fates (faytz)—three ancient goddesses, or daughters of Themis and Zeus, who determined the length of each mortal's life. (*Chs. 7, 29, 33*)

Furies (FUR eez)—three female creatures who drove those who killed relatives to their own deaths. (*Chs. 1, 2, 15, 29*)

G

Gaea (JEE uh)—the first Great Goddess or Mother Goddess in Greek mythology. (*Chs. 1, 2, 3, 5, 13, 25, 33*)

Galanthis (guh LAN this)—female servant who helped Alcmene give birth to Heracles. (*Ch. 33*)

Galatea (gal ah TEE uh)—the statue Pygmalion loved, which came to life. (*Ch. 26*)

Geryon (jee RI on)—a triple-headed, triple-bodied giant who owned cattle; the hero Heracles had to acquire him for his tenth labor. (*Ch. 33*)

Giants (JI untz)—monster children of Gaea and Uranus who fought the Olympians and Heracles. (*Ch. 33*)

Glauce (GLAU see)—daughter of King Creon of Corinth, whom the hero Jason intended to marry. (*Ch. 36*)

Gorgons (GOR gunz)—hideous female creatures who turned anyone who looked at them to stone; the hero Perseus beheaded the mortal Gorgon, named Medusa. (*Ch. 31*)

Graces (GRAY suhz)—three lovely daughters of Eurynome and Zeus. (*Chs. 7, 18*)

Great Goddess—or Mother Goddess worshipped as the major divinity in the matriarchal societies which existed in Greece before the invasion of the Mycenaeans. (*Intro: R.B.; Ch. Intros*)

Gyes (JI eez)—one of the three Hundred-handed giants; offspring of Gaea and Uranus. (*Chs. 1, 2, 3*)

H

Hades (HAY deez)—Lord of the Underworld; brother of Zeus; husband of Persephone. (*Intro: H.B., Chs. 2, 3, 4, 5, 13, 14, 28, 33, 34, 35*)

Harpies (HAR peez)—birdlike, female monsters who contaminated King Phineus's food as a punishment. (*Ch. 36*)

Hebe (HEE bee)—daughter of Zeus and Hera; cupbearer of the Olympians; married the immortal Heracles. (*Chs. 9, 33*)

Hebrus (HEE brus)—river in Thrace where a snake bit Eurydice resulting in her death. (*Ch. 28*)

Helen (HEL un)—famed for her beauty; daughter of Nemesis and Zeus; abducted by Theseus. (*Chs. 15, 29, 34*)

Helius (HE lih us)—Titan god of the sun; father of Phaëthon. (*Chs. 1, 9, 10, 12, 13, 25, 33*)

Helle (HEL ee)—daughter of Athamas: she fell off the ram with the golden fleece into the Hellespont which was named after her. (*Ch. 36*)

Hellespont (HEL us pont)—narrow strait named for Helle, who fell to her death there. (*Ch. 36*)

Hephaestus (hee FES tus)—god of metalwork; the renowned immortal smith. (*Chs. 4, 9, 11, 17, 18, 25, 33*)

Hera (HEH rah)—queen of Olympus; lawful wife of Zeus; goddess of marriage. (*Chs. 2, 4, 5, 9, 10, 12, 14, 20, 33, 35, 36*)

Heracles (HER uh kleez)—defender of the earth; most famous of all Greek heroes; performed twelve labors for King Eurystheus: 1) Nemean lion; 2) Hydra of Lernaz; 3) Cerynitian hind; 4) Erymanthian boar; 5) Augeian stables; 6) Stymphalian birds; 7) Cretan bull; 8) mares of Diomedes; 9) belt of Hippolyte; 10) cattle of Geryon; 11) golden apples of the Hesperides; and 12) Cerberus. (*Chs. 17, 33, 34*)

Hercules (HER ku leez)—Roman name for Heracles. (*Chs. 17, 33, 34*)

I

Hermes (HER meez)—son of Maia and Zeus; messenger of Zeus; guide of travelers; patron of merchants and thieves. *(Chs. 4, 5, 12, 13, 14, 15, 17, 18, 19, 31, 33)*

Hesiod (HEE si ud)—early writer of Greek myths. *(Ch. 18)*

Hesione (he SIH oh nee)—daughter of King Laomedon of Troy; rescued from a sea monster by the hero Heracles; married Telamon. *(Ch. 33)*

Hesperides (hes PER ih deez)—nymphs who guarded the golden apples in Hera's garden. *(Chs. 9, 23, 31, 33)*

Hestia (HES ti uh)—daughter of Cronus and Rhea; sister of Zeus; guardian of the home. *(Ch. 2)*

Hippodameia (hip ah dah MI uh)—wife of King Pelops. *(Chs. 3, 4)*

Hippolyte (hi POL ih tee)—queen of the Amazons whose belt Heracles needed to acquire for his ninth labor. *(Chs. 33, 34)*

Hippolytus (hi POL ih tus)—son of Theseus and the Amazon queen; died a tragic death. *(Ch. 34)*

Hippomenes (hi POM uh neez)—suitor and husband of Atalanta, the famous maiden huntress. *(Ch. 30)*

Homer (HO mer)—earliest author of Greek myths; "wrote" during the eighth century B.C.; very little is known about him. *(Intro.: H.B.)*

Hundred-handed giants—three monstrous offspring of Uranus and Gaea. *(Chs. 1, 2, 3)*

hybris (HOO bris)—excessive pride or arrogance. *(Intro. Chs. 16, 33)*

Hydra (HY druh)—monster offspring of Typhon; provided the hero Heracles with his second labor. *(Ch. 33)*

Hylas (HY lus)—friend of the hero Heracles; disappeared during the Argonaut's voyage. *(Ch. 36)*

Hyllus (HIL us)—son of Heracles and Deïaneira. *(Ch. 33)*

Hyperion (hi PIR ih un)—Titan god of the sun; son of Uranus and Gaea; father of Helius. *(Ch. 1)*

Iapetus (i AP uh tus)—one of the original thirteen Titans; father of Atlas, Prometheus, and Epimetheus. *(Ch. 1)*

Icaria (i KER ih uh)—island where Icarus was buried. *(Ch. 24)*

Icarian Sea—sea into which Icarus fell and drowned. *(Ch. 24)*

Icarus (IK uh rus)—son on Daedalus, who enjoyed flying too much. *(Ch. 24)*

Ida, Mount (I duh)—mountain on the island of Crete said to be the home of the infant Zeus. *(Chs. 2, 34)*

Iliad (IL ih ud)—Homer's epic about a portion of the Trojan War. *(Intro.: H.B.)*

Ilioneus (il ee OH noos)—Niobe's youngest son. *(Ch. 21)*

Ilium (IL ih um)—Troy, kingdom of Laomedon and, later, Priam. *(Ch. 33)*

Ino (I no)—helped rear the god Dionysus; tried to kill Phrixus and Helle. *(Chs. 14, 36)*

Iobates (i OB uh teez)—a king of Lycia who was supposed to kill Bellerophon. *(Ch. 32)*

Iolaüs (i oh LAY us)—nephew and companion of the hero Heracles; hunted the Calydonian boar. *(Chs. 29, 33)*

Iolcus (i OL kus)—legal kingdom of Aeson, father of the hero Jason. *(Chs. 33, 36)*

Iole (I uh lee)—daughter of King Eurytus whom Heracles, at one time, wished to marry. *(Ch. 33)*

Iphicles (IF ih klus)—step-brother of Heracles; hunted the Calydonian boar. *(Chs. 29, 33)*

Iphitus (IF ih tus)—brother of Iole; killed by Heracles unjustly. *(Ch. 33)*

Iris (I ris)—Hera's messenger; goddess of the rainbow. *(Chs. 4, 13)*

Ismenus (is MEE nus)—Niobe's oldest child. *(Ch. 21)*

Isthmian Games (IS mee un)—established by Theseus in honor of Poseidon. *(Ch. 34)*

Ithaca (ITH uh kuh)—home of the hero Laertes; father of Odysseus. *(Chs. 10, 29, 36)*

Ixion (ik ZI on)—father of Peirithoüs; one of the most famous criminals in Greek mythology; in Tartarus, chained for eternity to a flaming, spinning wheel. *(Ch. 28)*

J

Jason (JAY sun)—the hero who led the Argonauts to capture the golden fleece. *(Chs. 29, 36)*

Juno (JOO no)—Roman name for Hera, lawful wife of Zeus, queen of Olympus, goddess of marriage. *(Chs. 2, 4, 5, 9, 10, 12, 14, 20, 33, 36)*

Jupiter (JOO pi ter)—Roman name for Zeus, king of the Olympian gods and Lord of the Sky; judged disputes among the gods and maintained order in the universe. *(Intro.: H.B., R.B., Chs. 2–19, 24, 25, 30–36)*

L

Labyrinth (LAB uh rinth)—structure created by Daedalus to confine the Minotaur that the hero Theseus later killed. *(Chs. 24, 34)*

Lachesis (LAK uh sis)—"Distributor of Fortunes;" one of the three Fates; daughter of Themis and Zeus. *(Chs. 7, 29, 33)*

Ladon (LAY don)—offspring of Typhon that guarded the golden apples of the Hesperides. *(Chs. 9, 23, 31, 33)*

Ladon River (LAY don)—where Heracles captured the Cerynitian hind for his third labor. *(Ch. 33)*

Laërtes (la ER teez)—hero who participated in the Calydonian Boar Hunt and the voyage of the Argonauts; father of Odysseus. *(Chs. 29, 36)*

Laomedon (la OM uh don)—untrustworthy king of Ilium (Troy). *(Ch. 33)*

Lapiths (LAP ithz)—countrymen of Peirithoüs. *(Ch. 34)*

Larissa (luh RIS uh)—where the hero Perseus accidently killed his grandfather, Acrisius. *(Ch. 31)*

Leda (LEE duh)—mother of Castor and Clytemnestra; also reared Helen and Polydeuces, who were the offspring of Zeus and Nemesis; one of Zeus's loves. *(Chs. 15, 20)*

Leiriope (lee RI oh pee)—mother of Narcissus. *(Ch. 27)*

Lemnos (LEM nos)—island of women visited by the Argonauts. *(Ch. 36)*

Lerna (LER nuh)—home of the Hydra, which Heracles had to destroy for his second labor. *(Ch. 33)*

Lethe (LEE thee)—"Forgetfulness;" a seat to which Theseus and Peirithoüs were confined in the Underworld. *(Chs. 33, 34)*

Leto (LEE toh)—mother of Apollo and Artemis; one of Zeus's loves; enemy of Niobe. *(Chs. 10, 11, 21)*

Libya (LIB ih uh)—home of the giant Antaeüs, with whom Heracles wrestled; where Atlas held up the sky as Mount Atlas. *(Chs. 25, 31, 33)*

Lichas (LI kus)—servant who delivered death to Heracles in the form of a poisoned shirt. *(Ch. 33)*

Liguria (li GOO rih uh)—visited by Heracles on his return with Geryon's cattle; an unusual rain fell there. *(Ch. 33)*

Linear B (LIN ee ur)—early form of the Greek language found written on clay tablets on Crete and at Pylos. *(Intro.: H.B.)*

Linus (LI nus)—taught young Heracles the lyre and was killed by his pupil. *(Ch. 33)*

Lot (lot)—his wife wanted to witness the destruction of Sodom and Gomorrah. *(Ch. 19: D.N.E.)*

Lycaeüs, Mount (li SEE us)—mountain in Arcadia; homeland of the wicked King Lycaon. *(Ch. 19: L.)*

Lycaon (li KAY on)—the cruel king of Arcadia who did not obey the laws of hospitality. *(Ch. 19: L.)*

Lycia (LISH ih uh)—kingdom of Iobates, who had the task of killing the hero Bellerophon. *(Ch. 32)*

Lycomedes (li koh MEE deez)—the king who murdered the hero Theseus. *(Ch. 34)*

Lycurgus (li KER gus)—a Thracian king whom Dionysus drove to madness. *(Ch. 14)*

Lydia (LID ih uh)—homeland of Niobe, Midas, Arachne, and Queen Omphale, whom Heracles served as a slave. *(Chs. 20, 21, 23, 33)*

M

maenads (ME nadz)—female followers of Dionysus who dressed in animal skins and carried thyrsi. *(Chs. 14, 23, 28)*

Maia (MI uh)—daughter of the Titan Atlas; mother of Hermes. *(Ch. 12)*

Marathon (MER uh thon)—area near Athens where the Cretan Bull, set free by the hero Heracles, roamed and ravaged until the hero Theseus killed it. *(Chs. 33, 34)*

Marmara (MAR muh ruh)—a sea visited by the Argonauts on their journey to capture the golden fleece. *(Ch. 36)*

Mars (marz)—Roman name for Ares, god of war. *(Chs. 9, 29, 36)*

matriarchal (may tree ARK ul)—early religion in Greece involving worship of the Great Goddess or the Mother Goddess. *(Intro.: R.B.; Chs. Intros.)*

Medea (mee DEE uh)—daughter of King Aeëtes of Colchis, who used witchcraft to help the hero Jason and married him. *(Ch. 36)*

Medusa (muh DOO suh)–the mortal Gorgon whom Perseus had to behead. *(Chs. 31, 33)*

Megara (MEG uh ruh)—1) first wife of Heracles, whose children he killed in a fit of madness; 2) home of the robber Sceiron, whom the hero Theseus kicked to his death. *(Chs. 33, 34)*

Melanion (muh LA nee on)—suitor and husband of Atalanta; same as Hippomenes. *(Ch. 30)*

Meleager (mel ee AY jer)—organizer and hero of the Calydonian Boar Hunt. *(Chs. 29, 36)*

Melete (mel EE tee)—one of the first three Muses; daughter of Mnemosyne and Zeus. *(Ch. 7)*

Melpomene (mel poh MEE nee)—one of the nine Muses; daughter of Mnemosyne and Zeus. *(Ch. 7)*

Menelaüs (men uh LAY us)—husband of Helen of Troy. *(Ch. 15)*

Menestheus (MUH nes thooz)—king of Athens after Theseus was in disrepute. *(Ch. 34)*

Mercury (MER ku ree)—Roman name for Hermes; messenger of Zeus and guide of travelers; patron of merchants and thieves. *(Chs. 5, 12, 13, 14, 15, 17, 18, 31, 33)*

Metaneira (MET uh NEH ruh)—treated Demeter with kindness until she questioned Demeter's ability to rear children. *(Ch. 13)*

Metis (ME tis)—first wife of Zeus; known for her wisdom; mother of Athena. *(Chs. 2, 6)*

Midas (MI dus)—the king who learned that all gold does not glitter. *(Ch. 23)*

Minerva (mih NER vuh)—Roman name for Athena; wise goddess of arts and crafts, and defensive war; helper of heroes. *(Chs. 6, 9, 13, 17, 18, 20, 31, 32, 33, 36)*

Minoan (MIH noh un)—advanced ancient civilization on Crete named after king Minos. *(Intro.: H.B., R.B., 14, 24, 34)*

Minos (MI nos)—famous king of Crete. *(Chs. 10, 24, 34)*

Minotaur (MIN uh taur)—offspring of Minos's Queen Pasiphaë and a bull; had the head of a bull and the body of a man. *(Chs. 24, 34)*

Mneme (NEE mee)—one of the early, three Muses; daughter of Mnemosyne and Zeus. *(Ch. 7)*

Mnemosyne (nee MOZ ih nee)—mother of the Muses; one of the original thirteen Titans. *(Chs. 1, 7)*

Moerae (MEE ree)—the Fates: Clotho, Lachesis, and Atropos. *(Chs. 7, 29)*

Mother Goddess—or Great Goddess worshipped as the principal diety in the matriarchal societies which existed in Greece before the invasion of the Mycenaeans. *(Intro.: R.B.; Ch. Intros.)*

Muses (MYOO zez)—artistic children of Mnemosyne and Zeus. *(Ch. 7)*

Mycenae (mih SEE nee)—wealthy palace-state from the time of Perseus to the time of Agamemnon. *(Intro.: H.B., Chs. 31, 33)*

Mycenaean (mih see NEE un)—title given to the Bronze Age in Greece. *(Intro.: H.B., R.B.; Ch. Intros.)*

Mysia (MISH ih uh)—the Argonauts stopped there to repair an oar and to rest. *(Ch. 36)*

N

Narcissus (nar SIS us)—the young man who liked himself too much. *(Ch. 27)*

Navajo (NAV uh hoh)—American Indian tribe which states, in myth, that the first people were created from corn. *(Ch. 19: D.N.E.)*

Naxos (NAK SOS)—the island on which the hero Theseus left Ariadne. *(Chs. 14, 34)*

Nemea (NEE mih uh)—home of the lion the hero Heracles killed for his first labor. *(Ch. 33)*

Nemesis (NEM uh sis)—goddess of retribution; derivation of the concept of *nemesis.* *(Ch. 15)*

nemesis (NEM uh sis)—anyone or anything that prevents a person from achieving his or her goal; derived from the goddess Nemesis. *(Ch. 15 and Intros. Chs. 16, 33)*

Nephele (NEF uh lee)—mother of Phrixus and Helle, of golden fleece fame. *(Ch. 36)*

Neptune (NEP toon)—Roman name for Poseidon, Lord of the Sea. *(Intro.: H.B., R.B., Chs. 2, 3, 4, 10, 19: F., D.N.E., 20, 33, 34, 36)*

Nereids (NE rih ids)—sea nymphs. *(Chs. 1, 19:F, 25)*

Nereus (NER oos)—son of Pontus and Gaea; a sea god who had prophetic powers and who helped the hero Heracles. *(Ch. 33)*

Nessus (NES us)—the Centaur who took revenge upon Heracles for killing him. *(Ch. 33)*

Nestor (NES tor)—a wise hero, who participated in the Calydonian Boar Hunt long before he went to Troy. *(Ch. 29)*

Niobe (ni OH bee)—the mother who did not know when she should be satisfied. *(Ch. 21)*

Norse (nors)—myth states that the first people were created from trees. *(Ch. 19: D.N.E.)*

nymph (nimf)—immortals who live in streams or trees. *(Chs. 22, 27, 33)*

O

Oceanus (oh SEE uh nus)—one of the original thirteen Titans; husband of Tethys. *(Chs. 1, 6, 25, 33)*

Odysseus (oh DIS ih us)—hero of the Trojan War whose father, Laertes, was an earlier hero. *(Chs. 29, 36)*

Odyssey (OD ih see)—Homer's epic about Odysseus's return from the Trojan War. *(Intro.: H.B.)*

Oechalia (ee KAL ih uh)—home of King Eurytus, the famous archer who taught Heracles. *(Ch. 33)*

Oeneus (EE noos)—king of Calydon; father of the hero Meleager. *(Ch. 29)*

Oeta, Mount (EE tuh)—where Heracles died. *(Ch. 33)*

Olympic Games (oh LIM pic)—established by the hero Heracles in honor of Zeus. *(Ch. 33)*

Olympus, Mount (oh LIM pus)—home of Zeus and the immortal royal family. *(Chs. 3, 4, 5, 8, 9, 11, 12, 13, 14, 17, 27, 30, 32, 33, 35)*

Omphale (OM fuh lee)—queen of Lydia for whom Heracles served as a slave. *(Ch. 33)*

Oresteia (oh RES tee uh)—Aeschylus's group of three plays that dramatize the story of Orestes. *(Intro.: R.B., Chs. 1, 15)*

Orestes (oh RES teez)—son of Clytemnestra and Agamemnon who was pursued by the Furies because he murdered his mother. *(Intro.: R.B., Chs. 1, 15)*

Orpheus (OR foos)—son of the Muse Calliope; famed musician who could not live without his wife Eurydice; one of the Argonauts; taught Dionysian rites to King Midas. *(Chs. 23, 28, 36)*

Orthus (OR thus)—offspring of Typhon; two-headed dog which guarded Geryon's cattle until the hero Heracles performed his tenth labor. *(Ch. 33)*

Ovid (OV id)—a Roman poet (43 B.C. –17? A.D.) who retold the Greek myths and created myths of his own.

P

Pactolus (pak TO lus)—river in Lydia where Midas washed away the golden touch. *(Chs. 20, 23)*

Pallas (PAL us)—1) Giant killed by Athena, who then skinned him and used his skin for a shield; 2) competitor of King Aegeus and Theseus for the throne of Athens. *(Chs. 33, 34)*

Pan (pan)—the god of shepherds. *(Chs. 5, 23, 29)*

Pandora (pan DOH ruh)—first woman; wife of Epimetheus, whose curiosity won her fame. *(Ch. 18)*

Paphos (PAY fos)—daughter of Pygmalion and Galatea. *(Ch. 26)*

Parnassus, Mount (par NAS us)—site of the oracle of Apollo at Delphi where Deucalion and Pyrrha landed after the flood. *(Chs. 10, 12, 25, 33, 34)*

Pasiphaë (puh SIF ay ee)—wife of King Minos of Crete who loved a bull and gave birth to the Minotaur. *(Chs. 24, 34)*

patriarchal (pay tree ARK ul)—religion of Zeus in which males were given equality with or supremacy over females. *(Intro.: R.B.; myth Intros.)*

Pegasus (PEG uh sus) Pegasos—offspring of Medusa and Poseidon; the winged horse which the hero Bellerophon rode. *(Chs. 31, 32)*

Peirithoüs (pi RITH oh us)—king of the Lapiths and dear friend of the hero Theseus; hunted the Calydonian boar. *(Chs. 29, 34)*

Peleus (PEE loos)—brother of Telamon; father of Achilles; participated in the Calydonian Boar Hunt and the voyage of the Argonauts. *(Chs. 29, 36)*

Pelias (PEE lih us)—wicked king of Iolcus; enemy of Hera and the hero Jason; father of Alcestis. *(Chs. 33, 34)*

Pelion, Mount (PEE lih un)—home of the wise, immortal Centaur Cheiron. *(Chs. 17, 33, 36)*

Pelops (PEE lops)—son of Tantalus, who was cut up by his father and served to the Olympian gods for dinner; husband of Hippodameia. *(Chs. 3, 4)*

Peneius (pee NEE us)—Heracles rerouted this river as part of his fifth labor in order to clean King Augeias's stables. *(Ch. 33)*

Pentheus (PEN thoos)—a king of Thebes who investigated Dionysian revels too closely. *(Ch. 14)*

Perdix (PER diks)—nephew of Daedalus who was killed because his uncle envied his inventive ability. *(Ch. 24)*

Periphetes (per ih FEE teez)—one of the outlaws the hero Theseus killed; known as the "Club-carrier." *(Ch. 34)*

Persephone (per SEF uh nee)—daughter of Demeter and Zeus; wife of Hades; also known as Core; queen of the Underworld. *(Chs. 4, 13, 14, 28, 33, 34, 35)*

Perseus (PER soos)—the hero who beheaded the Gorgon Medusa. *(Ch. 31)*

Phaea (FEE uh)—(Crommyonian) the huge sow Theseus killed. *(Ch. 34)*

Phaeacians (FE ay SHI unz)—people who befriended the Argonauts, particularly Jason and Medea. *(Ch. 36)*

Phaedra (FEE druh)—daughter of King Minos of Crete; sister of Ariadne; married Theseus. *(Ch. 34)*

Phaëthon (FAY uh thon)—the young man who had to drive his father's chariot. *(Ch. 25)*

Pherae (FEE ree)—a palace-state in Thessaly, governed by King Admetus. *(Chs. 29, 33, 36)*

Philoctetes (fil ok TEE teez)—the youth who agreed to light Heracles's funeral pyre and, in return, received the hero's bow. *(Ch. 33)*

Phineus (FIN ih us)—1) brother of King Cepheus who fought against the hero Perseus for Andromeda; 2) a king who was punished by the Harpies for knowing too much, until the Argonauts arrived. *(Chs. 31, 36)*

Phlegethon (FLEG uh thon)—river of flames in the Underworld. (Ch. 13)

Phoebe (FEE bee)—one of the original thirteen Titans, mother of Leto. (Ch. 1)

Phoedemus (fee DEE mus)—one of Niobe's sons. (Ch. 21)

Phoenicia (fuh NISH uh)—land of Europa and of famous purple dye. (Ch. 34)

Pholus (FO lus)—a Centaur who entertained Heracles as the hero was traveling toward his fourth labor. (Ch. 33)

Phrixus (FRIK sus)—the youth who rode the ram with the golden fleece to safety in Colchis. (Ch. 36)

Phrygia (FRIJ ih uh)—land adjacent to Lydia. (Chs. 14, 21)

Phyleus (FI lus)—son of King Augeias of Elis who defended the hero Heracles against the king with regard to Heracles's fifth labor. (Ch. 33)

Pittheus (PITH oos)—grandfather of the hero Theseus. (Ch. 34)

Pityocamptes (pit ih oh KAMP teez)—the outlaw Sinis, known as the "pinebender" whom Theseus slew. (Ch. 34)

Pleiades (PLEE uh deez)—daughters of Atlas who were placed in the sky as stars; one was the mother of Niobe. (Ch. 21)

Plexippus (PLEX uh pus)—an uncle of Meleager who spoke out and regretted it. (Ch. 29)

Pluto (PLOO toh)—Roman name for Hades, Lord of the Underworld; brother of Zeus; husband of Persephone. (Intro.: H.B., Chs. 2, 3, 4, 5, 13, 14, 28, 33, 34, 35)

Po (poh)—river in Italy into which Phaëthon fell to his death. (Ch. 25)

Pollux (POL uks)—Roman name for Polydeuces; son of Zeus and Nemesis; brother of Helen of Troy; "twin" of Castor; hunted the Calydonian boar; an Argonaut. (Chs. 15, 29, 34, 36)

Polydectes (pol ih DEK teez)—evil king of Seriphus who wanted to be rid of Perseus. (Ch. 31)

Polydeuces (pol ih DOO seez)—"twin" of Castor; son of Nemesis and Zeus; brother of Helen of Troy; hunted the Calydonian boar; an Argonaut. (Chs. 15, 29, 34, 36)

Polyeidus (pol ih I dus)—the prophet of Corinth who advised the hero Bellerophon. (Ch. 32)

Polyhymnia (pol ih HIM nih uh)—one of the nine Muses; daughter of Mnemosyne and Zeus. (Ch. 7)

Polyphemus (pol ih FEE mus)—one of the Argonauts who was left behind along with Heracles when Hylas disappeared. (Ch. 36)

Pontus (PON tus)—along with Gaea and Eros, one of the first three divinities; the sea. (Ch. 1)

Poseidon (puh SI don)—Lord of the Sea; brother of Zeus. (Intro.: H.B., R.B., Chs. 2, 3, 4, 10, 19; F.D.N. F., 20, 33, 34, 36)

Priam (PRI um)—famous king of Troy; placed upon the throne by the hero Heracles. (Ch. 33)

Procrustes (pro KRUS teez)—the "Stretcher;" famous innkeeper who specialized in matching guests to his beds; killed by the hero Theseus. (Ch. 34)

Prometheus (pro MEE thoos)—the Titan who created and befriended humankind and whom Zeus punished for 30,000 years. (Chs. 12, 17, 33)

Proserpina (pro SER pih nuh)—Roman name for Persephone, queen of the Underworld; wife of Hades; daughter of Demeter and Zeus. (Chs. 13, 28, 33, 34, 35)

Proteus (PRO tih us)—1) mortal father of the hero Perseus; 2) King of Argos, who befriended the hero Bellerophon, then ordered the hero's death. (Chs. 31, 32)

Psyche (SI kee)—the mortal maiden who became the wife of Eros and gained immortality. (Ch. 35)

Pygmalion (pig MA lih on)—created the statue of a beautiful woman and fell in love with it. (Ch. 26)

Pylos (PI lus)—palace-state excavated in modern times; source of many Linear B tablets; kingdom of Nestor. (Intro.: H.B., Chs. 10, 12, 29)

Pyrrha (PIR uh)—wife of Deucalion; daughter of Pandora and Epimetheus; survived the flood. *(Ch. 19: D.N.E.)*

Pythia (Pith ih uh)—oracle of Apollo at Delphi. *(Chs. 10, 30, 33, 34)*

Pytho (PI thoh) original name of Delphi before Apollo took over the site from the Titan Themis. *(Chs. 7, 10, 19: D.N.E.)*

Python (PI thon)—snake which guarded the oracle of Themis at Pytho; killed by Apollo. *(Chs. 7, 10)*

R

Rhadamanthys (rad uh MAN thus)—son of Europa; brother of King Minos of Crete. *(Ch. 34)*

Rhea (REE uh)—daughter of Uranus and Gaea; wife of Cronus; mother of the first six gods: Hestia, Demeter, Hera, Hades, Poseidon, and Zeus. *(Chs. 1, 2, 3, 10, 13, 30)*

S

Salmydessus (sal mih DES us)—home in Thrace of the blind prophet, King Phineus. *(Ch. 36)*

Sardinia (sar DIN ih uh)—country in which Daedalus was last seen. *(Ch. 24)*

Sarpedon (sar PEE don)—son of Europa; brother of King Minos of Crete. *(Ch. 34)*

Saturn (SAT ern)—Roman name for Cronus, one of the original thirteen Titans; brother and husband of Rhea; father of the original six gods: Hestia, Demeter, Hera, Hades, Poseidon, and Zeus. *(Chs. 1, 2, 3)*

satyrs (SA terz)—followers of Dionysus; young men with horses's tails, goats' legs, and pointed ears or horns. *(Chs. 14, 23)*

Sceiron (SKI ron)—the bandit who liked travelers to wash his feet; killed by the hero Theseus. *(Ch. 34)*

Scylla (SIL uh)—female monster with six heads on long necks and dogs for legs, who ate sailors; seen by the Argonauts. *(Ch. 36)*

Scyrus (SKI rus)—island where the hero Theseus was murdered and where Cimon located the hero's bones. *(Ch. 34)*

Scythia (SITH ih uh)—land where Prometheus was chained to a cliff for 30,000 years. *(Chs. 17, 19: D.N.E., 25, 33)*

Seilenus (si LE nus)—old companion of Dionysus, found by King Midas and returned to the god. *(Ch. 23)*

Selene (se LEE nee)—Titan goddess of the moon. *(Chs. 1, 25, 33)*

Semele (SEM uh lee)—mother of Dionysus; became immortal; one of Zeus's loves. *(Ch. 14)*

Seriphus (se RI fus)—the island to which Perseus and Danaë floated and where they lived. *(Ch. 31)*

Sicily (SIS ih lee)—favorite location for Persephone because of its wild flowers. *(Chs. 13, 24, 33)*

Sicyon (SISH ih on)—location where Prometheus tricked Zeus into choosing the inferior sacrifice. *(Ch. 17)*

Sinis (SIN is)—the "Pinebender" whom Theseus killed as the criminal was accustomed to killing others. *(Ch. 34)*

Siphilus (SIH fuh lus)—son of Niobe. *(Ch. 21)*

Sipylus, Mount (SIP ih lus)—Niobe became part of this mountain and weeps forever there. *(Ch. 21)*

Sirens (SI runz)—bird-women who lured sailors to their deaths with their beautiful songs; avoided by the Argonauts. *(Ch. 36)*

Sisyphus (SIS ih fus)—one of the most famous criminals in Greek mythology; condemned in Tartarus to push a rock uphill repeatedly for eternity. *(Ch. 28)*

Solymi (SO lih mi)—tribe defeated by the hero Bellerophon as one of his tasks. *(Ch. 32)*

Sparta (SPAR tuh)—where Leda reared Castor, Polydeuces, Helen, and Clytemnestra. *(Chs. 15, 34)*

Steropes (STER oh peez)—one of the three Cyclopes; offspring of Uranus and Gaea. *(Chs. 1, 2, 3, 11)*

Sthenelus (STHEN uh lus)—banished Amphitryon from Mycenae and Tiryns and took over both himself.

(Ch. 33)

Stymphalian (Stim FA lih un)—birds which ate human flesh, with feathers sharp as arrows, that Heracles had to kill for his sixth labor. *(Ch. 33)*

Styx (stiks)—chief river of the Underworld; Charon would ferry shades and mortals across it. *(Chs. 4, 23, 25, 27, 28, 35)*

Sumerian (soo MER ee un)—Mesopotamian culture with a flood myth. *(Ch. 19:F.)*

Syleus (SI loos)—criminal who forced travelers to hoe his vineyards; killed by the hero Heracles. *(Ch. 33)*

Symplegades (sim PLEG uh deez)—the Clashing Rocks; kept ships from entering the Black Sea until the *Argo* sailed through successfully. *(Ch. 36)*

T

Taenarum (TEE nuh rum)—location in southern Greece of the road into the Underworld. *(Ch. 33)*

Taenarus (TEE nuh rus)—mountain which Psyche visited in order to take the road to the Underworld. *(Ch. 35)*

Talus (TAY lus)—bronze giant who guarded the island of Crete and was killed by the Argonauts. *(Ch. 36)*

Tantalus (TAN tuh lus)—father of Niobe; famous Greek criminal who killed his son Pelops and fed him to the Olympians, as a trick; condemned to spend eternity in Tartarus chained to a tree filled with fruit he cannot eat and up to his chest or chin in water he cannot drink. *(Ch. 28)*

Tartarus (TAR tuh rus)—the Underworld, or the darkest part of the Underworld where criminals spent eternity. *(Chs. 1, 2, 3, 4, 16, 17, 25, 27, 28, 33, 34, 35)*

Tartessus (tar TES us)—ancient city in what is now Spain where Heracles returned the goblet boat to Helius. *(Ch. 33)*

Teiresias (ti RE sih us)—famous prophet who counseled King Pentheus, the mother of Narcissus, and the parents of Heracles. *(Chs. 14, 21, 27, 33)*

Telamon (TEL uh mon)—friend of Heracles; brother of Peleus; one of the heroes in the Calydonian Boar Hunt and the voyage of the Argonauts. *(Chs. 29, 33, 36)*

Terpsichore (terp SIK uh ree)—one of the nine Muses; daughter of Mnemosyne and Zeus. *(Ch. 7)*

Tethys (TEE this)—Titan sea goddess; daughter of Gaea and Uranus. *(Chs. 1, 6, 25)*

Thaleia (THUH lih uh)—one of the nine Muses; daughter of Mnemosyne and Zeus. *(Ch. 7)*

Thalia (THAY lih uh)—one of the three Graces; daughter of Eurynome and Zeus. *(Ch. 7)*

Thebes (theebz)—home of King Pentheus and the prophet Teiresias. *(Intro.: H.B., Chs. 9, 14, 20, 33)*

Theia (THEE uh)—one of the original thirteen Titans; wife of Hyperion; mother of Eros, Helius, and Selene. *(Ch. 1)*

Themis (THEE mis)—one of the original thirteen Titans; a great prophet who commanded the oracle at Pytho before Apollo conquered it; reputed to be the mother of Prometheus. *(Chs. 1, 7, 10, 17, 19: D.N.E.)*

Themiscyra (them is KI ruh)—city of the Amazons on the southern coast of the Black Sea. *(Chs. 32, 33, 34)*

Theseus (THEE soos)—one of the most famous Greek heroes; killed the Minotaur; hunted the Calydonian boar. *(Chs. 15, 24, 29, 33, 34)*

Thespis (THES pis)—important person in the development of Greek tragedy; the first actor. *(Ch. 14)*

Thessaly (THES uh lee)—northeastern region of Greece; location of Iolcus, the Centaurs, and the Lapiths. *(Chs. 17, 30, 33, 34, 36)*

Thetis (THEE tis)—sea goddess who rescued and reared Hephaestus; destined to bear a son who would become greater than his father; mother of Achilles, the great hero of the Trojan War. *(Chs. 9, 17)*

Thrace (thrays)—home of Dionysus, Ares, Boreas, the north wind, and the barbaric King Diomedes who fed his mares with human flesh. *(Chs. 9, 14, 19:F, 28, 33)*

Thyone (thy OH nee)—name given to Semele when she became immortal. *(Ch. 14)*

thyrsi (THER sih)—plural of thyrsus *(Chs. 14, 23)*

thyrsus (THER sus)—pole twined with ivy and topped with a pine cone, carried by maenads and satyrs in Dionysian revels. *(Chs. 14, 23, 33)*

Tiryns (TIR inz)—sister palace-state to Mycenae; often ruled together. *(Intro.: H.B., Chs. 31, 33)*

Titans (TI tunz)—the earlier race of Greek immortals who were in charge before the gods were born and took over. *(Chs. 1, 2, 3, 4, 6, 7, 8, 10, 11, 12, 13, 14, 17, 18, 19: D.N.E., 21, 25, 33)*

Tmolus, Mount (tuh MOH lus)—scene of a musical contest between Pan and Apollo that was heard by King Midas. *(Chs. 20, 23)*

Toxeus (TOK soos)—brother of Plexippus; uncle of Meleager, who also died an early death. *(Ch. 29)*

Triton (TRI ton)—son of Poseidon and Amphitrite, who blew a shell horn to calm the seas. *(Ch. 19: D.N.E.)*

Troezen (TREE zn)—home of King Pittheus and, therefore, of Theseus as a youth. *(Ch. 34)*

Troy (troi)—famous for its kings, Laomedon and Priam, and for Helen; rich in goods; sacked on more than one occasion. *(Intro.: H.B., Ch. 33)*

Typhon (TY fon)—a monster who tried to overthrow Zeus; was defeated and thrown under Mount Aetna. *(Chs. 5, 32, 33, 34)*

U

Ulysses (u LIS eez)—Roman name for Odysseus; hero of the Trojan War whose father, Laertes, was an earlier hero. *(Chs. 29, 36)*

Urania (u RAY nih uh)—one of the nine Muses; daughter of Mnemosyne and Zeus. *(Ch. 7)*

Uranus (U ruh nus)—ruler of the sky; son and husband of Gaea; father of the Cyclopes, the Hundred-handed giants, the original thirteen Titans, and the goddess Aphrodite. *(Chs. 1, 2, 3, 8)*

V

Venus (VEE nus)—Roman name for Aphrodite, goddess of love and beauty; daughter of Uranus or of Zeus and Dione. *(Chs. 5, 8, 13, 15, 18, 26, 30, 35, 36)*

Vesta (VES tuh)—Roman name for Hestia, goddess of the home; sister of Zeus; daughter of Cronus and Rhea. *(Ch. 2)*

Vulcan (VUL kn)—Roman name for Hephaestus, god of metalwork; the renowned, immortal smith. *(Chs. 9, 11, 17, 18, 25)*

Z

Zephyrus (ZEF uh rus)—the west wind. *(Chs. 19:F.; D.N.E., 35)*

Zetes (ZEE teez)—twin brother of Calaïs; son of Boreas, the north wind; an Argonaut. *(Ch. 36)*

Zeus (ZOOS)—king of the Olympian gods and Lord of the Sky; judged disputes among the gods and maintained order in the universe. *(Intro.: H.B., R.B., Chs. 2–19, 24, 25, 30–36)*

LANGUAGE ARTS BOOKS

Tandem: Language in Action Series
Point/Counterpoint, *Dufour and Strauss*
Action/Interaction, *Dufour and Strauss*

Business Communication
Business Communication Today!,
  Thomas and Fryar
Successful Business Writing, *Sitzmann*
Successful Business Speaking, *Fryar
  and Thomas*
Successful Interviewing, *Sitzmann and
  Garcia*
Successful Problem Solving, *Fryar and
  Thomas*
Working in Groups, *Ratliffe and Stech*
Effective Group Communication,
  Ratliffe and Stech

Reading
Reading by Doing, *Simmons and Palmer*
Literature Alive, *Gamble and Gamble*
Building Real Life English Skills, *Penn
  and Starkey*
Practical Skills in Reading, *Keech and
  Sanford*
Essential Life Skills Series, *Penn and
  Starkey*

Grammar
Grammar Step-By-Step Vol. 1, *Pratt*
Grammar Step-By-Step Vol. 2, *Pratt*

Speech
Getting Started in Public Speaking,
  Prentice and Payne
Listening by Doing, *Galvin*
Person to Person, *Galvin and Book*
Person to Person, Workbook, *Galvin
  and Book*
Speaking by Doing, *Buys, Sill and Beck*
Self-Awareness, *Ratliffe and Herman*
Literature Alive, *Gamble and Gamble*
Contemporary Speech, *Hopkins and
  Whitaker*
Creative Speaking, *Buys et al.*

Journalism
Journalism Today!, *Ferguson and Patten*

Media
Understanding Mass Media, *Schrank*
The Mass Media Workbook, *Hollister*
Media, Messages & Language, *McLuhan,
  Hutchon and McLuhan*
Understanding the Film, *Johnson and
  Bone*
Photography in Focus, *Jacobs and
  Kokrda*
Televising Your Message, *Mitchell and
  Kirkham*

Theatre
Dynamics of Acting, *Snyder and
  Drumstra*
Play Production Today!, *Beck et al.*
Acting and Directing, *Grandstaff*
An Introduction to Theatre and Drama,
  Cassady and Cassady
The Book of Scenes for Acting Practice,
  Cassady

Mythology
Mythology and You, *Rosenberg and
  Baker*
World Mythology: An Anthology of
  Great Myths and Epics, *Rosenberg*

Mystery and Science Fiction
The Detective Story, *Schwartz*
You and Science Fiction, *Hollister*

Writing and Composition
Lively Writing, *Schrank*
Snap, Crackle & Write, *Schrank*
An Anthology for Young Writers,
  Meredith
Writing in Action, *Meredith*
Writing by Doing, *Sohn and Enger*
The Art of Composition, *Meredith*
Look, Think & Write!, *Leavitt and Sohn*
The Book of Forms for Everyday Living,
  Rogers

For further information or a current catalog, write:
National Textbook Company
4255 West Touhy Avenue
Lincolnwood, Illinois 60646-1975 U.S.A.